BLACK&DECKER®

CODES FOR HOMEOWNERS

Your Photo Guide to:

• Electrical Codes • Plumbing Codes • Building Codes • Mechanical Codes

by Bruce A. Barker

Creative Publishing international

MINNEAPOLIS, MINNESOTA
www.creativepub.com

Creative Publishing international

Copyright © 2010
Creative Publishing international, Inc.
400 First Avenue North, Suite 300
Minneapolis, Minnesota 55401
1-800-328-0590
www.creativepub.com
All rights reserved

Printed in the U.S.A.

10 9 8 7 6 5 4 3 2

Library of Congress Cataloging-in-Publication Data

PPresident/CEO: Ken Fund

Home Improvement Group

Publisher: Bryan Trandem
Managing Editor: Tracy Stanley
Senior Editor: Mark Johanson
Editor: Jennifer Gehlhar

Creative Director: Michele Lanci-Altomare
Art Direction/Design: Jon Simpson, Brad Springer, James Kegley
Page Layout Artist: Heather Parlato
Illustrator: Mark Abdella
Additional Illustrations: Bruce A. Barker

Lead Photographer: Joel Schnell
Set Builder: James Parmeter
Shop Help: Charles Boldt, Cesar Fernandez Rodriguez

Author: Bruce A. Barker
Copy Editor: Linnéa Fonnest
Proofreader: Drew Siqveland

Production Managers: Laura Hokkanen, Linda Halls

CODES FOR HOMEOWNERS
Created by: The Editors of Creative Publishing international, Inc., in cooperation with Black & Decker.
Black & Decker® is a trademark of The Black & Decker Corporation and is used under license.

NOTICE TO READERS

For safety, use caution, care, and good judgment when following the procedures described in this book. The publisher and Black & Decker cannot assume responsibility for any damage to property or injury to persons as a result of misuse of the information provided.

The techniques shown in this book are general techniques for various applications. In some instances, additional techniques not shown in this book may be required. Always follow manufacturers' instructions included with products, since deviating from the directions may void warranties. The projects in this book vary widely as to skill levels required: some may not be appropriate for all do-it-yourselfers, and some may require professional help.

Consult your local building department for information on building permits, codes, and other laws as they apply to your project.

Contents

Codes for Homeowners

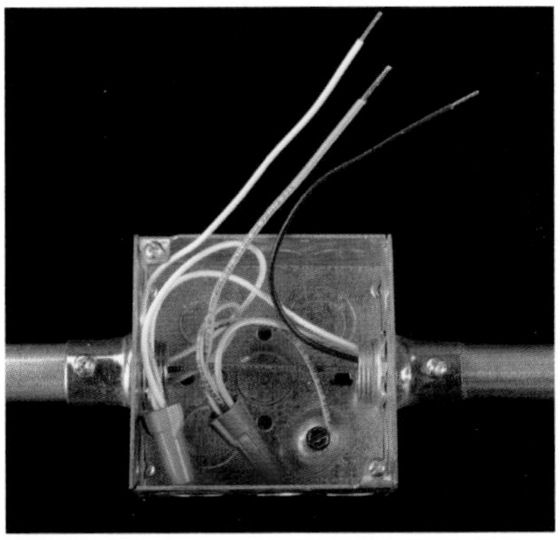

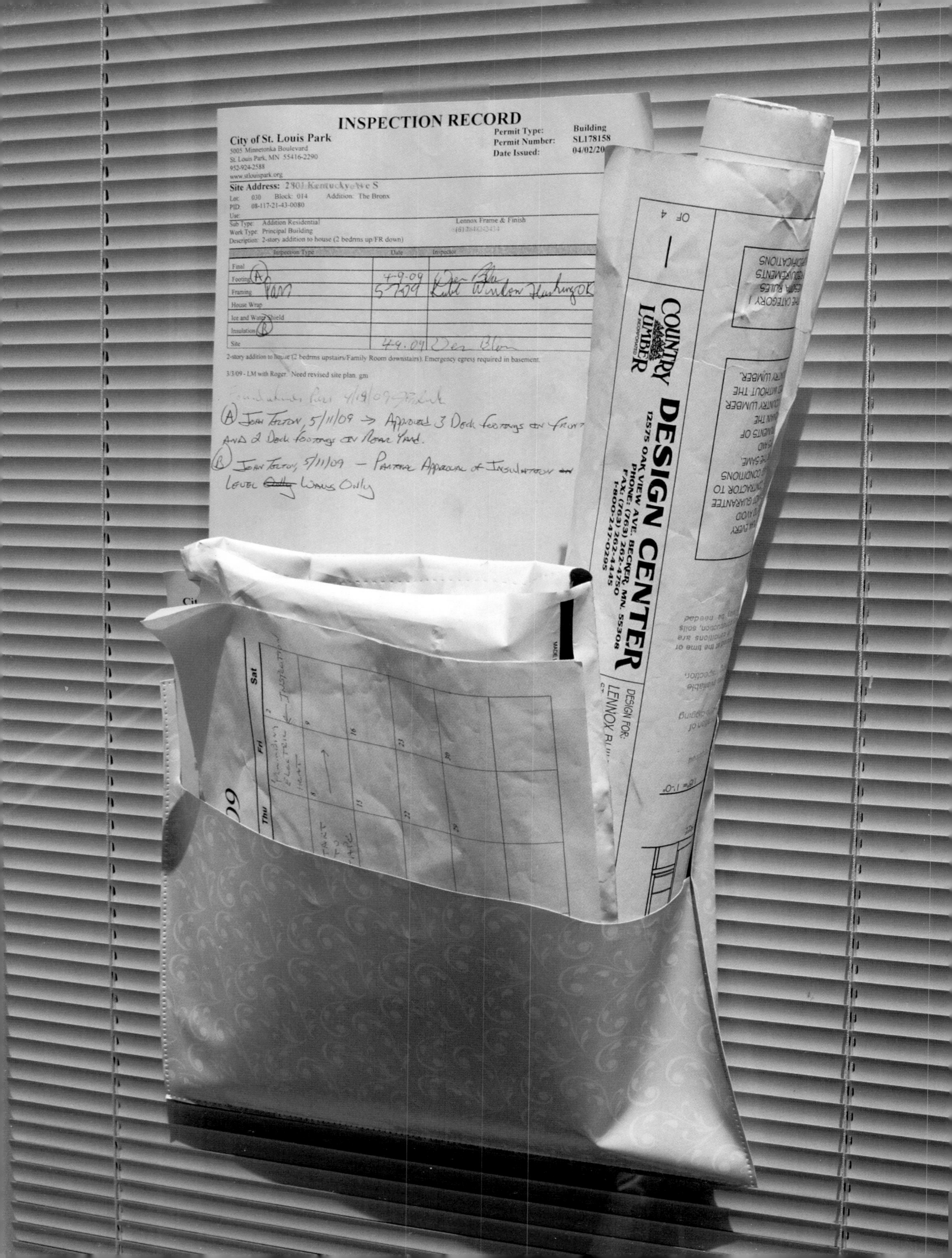
INSPECTION RECORD
City of St. Louis Park
5005 Minnetonka Boulevard
St. Louis Park, MN 55416-2290
952-924-2588
www.stlouispark.org
Permit Type: Building
Permit Number: SL178158
Date Issued:
Site Address:
Lot: 030 Block: 014 Addition: The Bronx
PID: 08-117-21-43-0080
Use:
Sub Type: Addition Residential
Work Type: Principal Building
Description: 2-story addition to house (2 bedrms up/FR down)
Lennox Frame & Finish
Inspection Type
Date
Inspector
Final
Footing
Framing
House Wrap
Ice and Water Shield
Insulation
Site
2-story addition to house (2 bedrms upstairs/Family Room downstairs). Emergency egress required in basement.
3/3/09 - LM with Roger. Need revised site plan. gm
COUNTRY LUMBER
DESIGN CENTER
12575 OAK VIEW AVE. BECKER, MN. 55308
PHONE: (763) 262-4750
FAX: (763) 262-4445
1-800-247-0295
DESIGN FOR:
Sat
Fri
Thu

Introduction

Building codes are adopted by governmental agencies to preserve your family's safety as well as your fiscal well-being. Whether you are someone who likes to do your own home improvement and repair work, a homeowner acting as your own contractor, or anyone else who wants his or her work to conform to applicable building codes, this building code book is for you. Based largely on the 2009 version of the International Residential Code (IRC), it aims to make the most important wiring, plumbing, construction, and HVAC codes more accessible, simpler to navigate, and easier to understand so you can interpret them effectively in your own home.

The key to accomplishing the objective of making codes easier to understand is simple in concept but a little tricky to execute: do it right and take pictures. In this book you'll find hundreds of professional quality images that depict code-compliant practices. No wading through page after page of incomprehensible jargon; no studying jumbles of lines and strange symbols to try and answer your question. Simply see for yourself.

This book does not replace the IRC. It contains IRC provisions that have been selected to help you avoid common code violations, based on largely my years of experience as a professional building inspector. To avoid confusion and keep it simple, this book omits many highly technical IRC provisions and many provisions that you simply are unlikely to encounter. While every effort has been made to accurately present the recommended practices of the IRC with easy to understand language, pictures, and diagrams, this book is not the IRC. In a dispute, the wording in the IRC, as interpreted by the local building official, is the final authority on what IRC provisions mean. And, as we'll discuss, local code provisions and interpretations always overrule code books such as this one.

The intent of *Codes for Homeowners* is to serve as a reference that answers a host of questions that boil down to "What should it look like when I'm done?" You will not find a lot of material that describes the specific steps needed to get there—you'll find many fine step-by-step instruction manuals that perform this part of the job.

By studying this book and understanding its contents you will arrive in the ballpark, metaphorically speaking, of IRC code compliance. But codes do not happen in a vacuum. As we discuss in subsequent sections, each local building department and each local building inspector has his or her own opinions about how building codes apply in their area. **If you have any doubts or questions about how a building code provision applies in your area, you should ask the local building official**. In almost every case, if you approach them as a resource and not as an obstacle you will find your local inspectors to be friendly, knowledgeable, and eager to help.

—Bruce A. Barker
Residential Combination Inspector
International Code Council

Codes & Permits: The Basics

In just the United States you will find hundreds of code books describing thousands upon thousands of building code provisions. On top of this, there are even more books that look and feel like code books but are really only attempting to describe best practices. Almost all of these have their own inherent value. But almost none of them apply to a typical homeowner living in a typical single-family home. As a homeowner and DIYer, perhaps the hardest thing about building codes is learning how to tell which one applies to you and, if there is a disagreement, which takes precedence. As an introduction, here are some brief biographies of the more common codes and enforcement agencies you're likely to encounter.

The International Residential Code

The International Residential Code (IRC) 2009 is one of an extensive collection of model building codes published by the International Code Council (ICC). A model building code is a recommended building code that is developed by a national organization that specializes in writing building codes. When adopted by a government agency, the IRC regulates the construction, renovation, maintenance, and repair of buildings used as homes. The IRC, by itself, has no formal legal status. A government agency must first adopt the IRC before it has any legal status in a local area.

State & Local Building Codes

Almost all areas of the United States have adopted some version of a building code. Some states, such as California, Florida, and New York, have a state building code. Some large cities, such as Chicago and New York City, have a city building code. Many of these state and local building codes are based on model building codes from the ICC.

Smaller cities and counties often use ICC model building codes, such as the IRC. Some rural areas may not have adopted a building code, but this is becoming a rare situation. If you do any work that is regulated by the local building code, you are responsible for knowing, or for hiring someone who knows, the applicable building code where the building is located. Ignorance of the code is no excuse.

The International Residential Code has no jurisdiction of its own but is the basis for many state and local residential building codes.

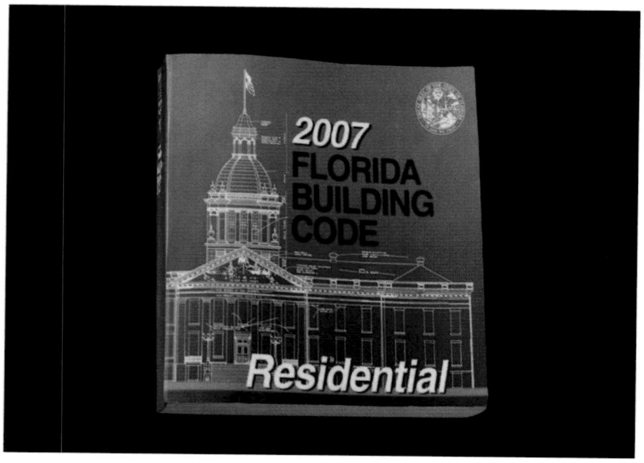

Some states and cities have their own building codes.

Local Code Amendments

Most building departments that use the IRC adopt local changes to the IRC. Many of these changes are minor and help to adapt the IRC to local conditions and needs. Some of these changes can significantly alter IRC provisions. The building department should publish, in writing, any changes adopted by the local government. You are responsible for knowing and complying with all local changes. Ask the building official if there are any local code changes.

Most jurisdictions have their own code amendments. Your city or municipality likely maintains a website with building ordinances posted and updated regularly.

Other Building Codes

The IRC is not the only building code. Other commonly used building codes include: The International Building Code (IBC), The International Mechanical Code (IMC), The International Plumbing Code (IPC), The Uniform Plumbing Code (UPC), The International Fuel Gas Code (IFG), The National Electrical Code (NEC), and The International Energy Conservation Code (IECC). Each of these building codes regulates a different aspect of building construction.

The IBC regulates the structural aspects of all buildings, although it is not commonly applied to residential buildings. The IBC usually applies to commercial, industrial, and multi-family buildings such as apartments. The IRC references the IBC and the IECC when a part of a residential building is not addressed by the IRC.

Each major system in a building has its own code. The IMC regulates heating, ventilation, and air conditioning systems; the IPC regulates plumbing systems; and the IFG regulates gas piping and gas equipment. These codes usually apply to commercial-type buildings. The UPC is a separate code, published by another code writing organization, that also regulates plumbing systems. It may replace the IRC plumbing chapters in areas that adopt the UPC. The NEC regulates electrical systems. The IRC contains an adapted version of the NEC in the IRC electrical chapters. When the IRC does not address an electrical situation in a home, the NEC usually applies.

The IECC regulates energy-related aspects of all buildings. These aspects include: insulation, air infiltration, and window and door energy efficiency. The IRC contains a simplified subset of the IECC in IRC Chapter Eleven.

You should know which codes apply to your construction project. Ask your local building official which codes apply in your area.

Trade-oriented building codes with a more specific focus apply in some situations. Most of these are primarily for nonresidential construction.

Zoning Ordinances

Many areas, particularly the more densely populated ones, have land use and zoning ordinances that control what you can build on your property. You are responsible for knowing and complying with them. In larger jurisdictions, the planning and zoning department may be separate from the building inspection department, and sometimes one does not know what the other is doing. It is possible that the building inspection department might issue a permit that would create a zoning violation. Projects that might run afoul of zoning ordinances include new, free-standing buildings, basement remodels that add a bedroom, bathroom, and kitchen, and any project that adds an additional full kitchen on property zoned for single family use.

Buildings Governed by the IRC

Apply the IRC to buildings containing one or two residential dwelling units in one building. Duplex is a common term for one building containing two dwelling units.

Apply the IRC to townhouses. A townhouse contains three or more dwelling units in one building and the building may have not more than three stories above grade.

Apply the IRC to all single-family homes.

Apply the IRC to two-family homes, including townhomes and duplexes.

Apply the IRC to residential buildings with not more than three stories above grade. Whether a basement is a story above grade depends on a complex set of rules. Basements with walls that are completely or mostly covered by dirt are not a story above grade. Example: a basement with one wall completely covered by dirt and two walls more than 50 percent covered by dirt is not a story above grade. Example: a basement with the rear wall not covered by dirt and two side walls that are less than 50 percent covered by dirt may be a story above grade. Refer to the definitions in IRC Chapter 2 and consult the local building official if there is a question about whether a basement is a story above grade.

Do not apply the IRC to buildings used for business, office, commercial, or industrial purposes. This is true even if the building was once used as a residence. You may apply the IRC to an office in the home if the office is incidental to the residential use of the building. Refer to the IBC for code provisions governing buildings not governed by the IRC.

Building Departments

A local building department enforces the building code in its jurisdiction. The technical term often used to describe this department is the Authority Having Jurisdiction (AHJ). The term used to describe the person responsible for enforcing the code is the Building Official or Chief Building Official. The public name for the local building department varies by jurisdiction. Many building departments will have the terms "building" or "safety" somewhere in the name. In some larger jurisdictions, the building department may be a division of a larger agency that is also responsible for land planning, zoning, and development. Some building department names may not sound like they have anything at all to do with building code enforcement. If you do any work that requires a building permit, you are responsible for finding and contacting the building department. Work done without a permit can have serious legal and financial consequences.

Consider your local building department to be a friendly place with extremely valuable resources to help you get your projects done correctly.

Working with Government Building Inspectors

The building official is the king of his building jurisdiction. Don't mess with the king. He can make your life very difficult. If you must disagree with him, do so respectfully and with facts that support your position. The building official has the right to interpret any code provision. Even if his interpretation seems unreasonable, eventually it will probably prevail. In almost all cases, you should just smile and do what he tells you.

Most building officials and inspectors are honest, hardworking people who want to ensure that your project is safe and complies with local building codes. They can be a valuable resource. Take advantage of that resource. Ask questions and work with them. Most will, in turn, work with you.

A city building inspector is accustomed to making site inspections in person. Make sure you are prepared for the visit at the allotted time and try to be present so you can take notes and answer questions.

Working with Private Building Inspectors ▸

Time is not the friend of government building inspectors. From an eight-hour day, they must subtract doing paperwork, discussing inspections with stakeholders, traveling between inspections, and performing other duties. Divide the remaining time by 20 to 30 inspections per day, or more, and they may have only a few minutes to perform each inspection. It's a credit to government inspectors that they find many major code violations. Most will admit, however, that they cannot find all code violations. They will also admit that they are not even looking for issues that, although they are not code violations, can have a significant negative impact on the cost to operate and maintain the home.

Private building inspectors fill this quality control gap for many people. People building homes and people performing major remodeling projects hire a private inspector who helps the government inspector and the contractor provide quality construction. A private inspector can perform a far more thorough inspection than a government inspector because a private inspector can invest more time on each inspection. In addition, a private inspector usually inspects areas such as attics and roofs, where government inspectors rarely go.

When building a new home or during a major remodeling project, a private inspector is often most useful at two critical points. The most critical point is just before insulation and drywall are installed. This inspection is sometimes called the pre-drywall inspection and is the most important inspection a home will ever have. At this time, an inspector can see many important components that will be covered by finish materials and, in most cases, will never be visible again. The other critical point is at the end of construction. At this time, an inspector can see and test important systems in the home.

Private inspectors are increasingly common on construction sites. While some contractors welcome private inspectors, many do not. Even if you decide not to engage a private inspector, it is wise to discuss the option with the contractor before signing a contract, and it is wise to agree, in writing, to how the contractor will work with the private inspector during construction.

Private building inspectors (such as the author, seen here) may be hired by a client to check the contractor's work at key points.

Manufacturer's Instructions

The IRC requires installing all components, equipment, and appliances according to the manufacturer's instructions. This requirement is so important that it is repeated many times in the IRC. Manufacturer's instructions are an enforceable extension of the IRC. This means that it is a code violation to install something in a manner that does not conform to manufacturer's instructions.

Manufacturer's instructions are an important part of ensuring that components are safe. Independent organizations test many components used to build homes. This includes almost all manufactured components. The tests are conducted under defined conditions that include using the manufacturer's instructions to install the component. The testing organization certifies that the component is safe when installed and used according to manufacturer's instructions. The testing organization places the certified components on a list maintained by the testing organization. This process is called listing, and the components are referred to in the IRC as listed.

The IRC cannot anticipate every possible building component and every possible way the component could be installed. As such, the IRC relies on the manufacturer's instructions to specify how components should be installed.

When a difference between the IRC and the manufacturer's instructions occurs, the IRC assumes that the manufacturer is in a better position to know its product and how it should be installed in a given situation. This is why the IRC usually defers to the manufacturer's instructions. If there is a difference between IRC provisions and the manufacturer's instructions, use the manufacturer's instructions unless the IRC specifies otherwise.

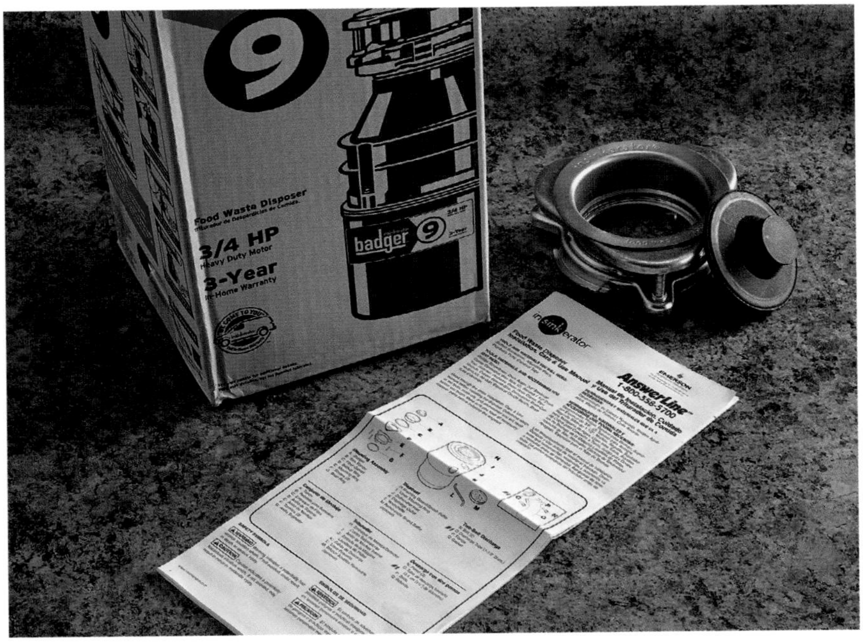

Manufacturer's installation instructions must be followed to the letter, and they are an enforceable extension of the IRC. In just about every case, the manufacturer's specifications overrule local codes.

Grandfathering Existing Work

In almost all situations, you are not required to abandon, remove, or alter existing work that is lawfully in existence and safely functioning. Lawfully in existence means the work was inspected and complied with the code when installed and/or modified.

In almost all situations, when updating, modifying, or repairing existing work, you are required to perform the update, modification, or repair according to the code in force when the work is performed. You are usually not required to make the existing work comply with current code.

Building Permits & Inspections

Contact your local building officials to determine which construction activities require a building permit and to determine the documents and procedures required to obtain a permit. The building official you speak with may not enforce some building permit requirements contained in the IRC, but may add additional building permit requirements not contained in the IRC.

You must wait until the required permit is issued before beginning work. Beginning work before the permit is issued may result in fines, and the building official could require removal of the work.

Comply with the building code applicable to where the building is located. The applicable building code is usually the code in force when the permit is issued. If you do not obtain a building permit, comply with the building code in force when the work is performed. The building code applies whether or not you obtain a building permit. This is important. Lack of a building permit does not relieve the building owner or the contractor of responsibility for code compliance.

When Is a Permit Required?

You typically will need a building permit for:

- Construction of new buildings
- Additions and structural modifications to existing buildings
- Structural repairs to existing buildings
- Replacement of or major repairs to building components, such as roof coverings and exterior wall coverings
- Movement and demolition of existing buildings
- Changes to building occupancy (A change to building occupancy means changing how the building is used. Example: using a single-family home as a place of business is a change in occupancy that may require a building permit and may require a zoning change or zoning waiver)
- Additions to, major changes to, and/or replacement of electrical, plumbing, gas, and HVAC components

You may not need a building permit for:

- Building or installation of one-story detached accessory structures (such as storage sheds and playhouses) with a floor area not more than 200 square feet
- Fences not more than six feet tall
- Retaining walls not more than four feet tall measured from the bottom of the footing to the top of the wall and not supporting a surcharge (a surcharge is a vertical load in addition to and/or above the retained ground)
- Driveways and sidewalks
- Painting, papering, floor covering installation, cabinet and countertop installation, and similar finish work
- Installation of portable plug-and-cord connected decorative lights and similar plug-and-cord connected electrical equipment
- Replacement of fuses and circuit breakers
- Low-voltage lights and other electrical wires and equipment operating at less than 25 volts and not more than 50 watts
- Installation of portable gas heating, cooking, and clothes-drying equipment
- Installation of portable HVAC equipment (such as window air conditioners)
- Clearing of plumbing stoppages and repair of plumbing leaks, and removal and reinstallation of toilets if the repairs do not involve replacement or rearrangement of valves, pipes, or fixtures
- Decks that are not more than 30 inches above ground, are not attached to the building, and do not service the required egress door

You *usually do not need* a building permit for:

- Routine maintenance of existing buildings, fixtures, and equipment, if the building structure is not affected and if the nature and use of the electrical, plumbing, gas, or HVAC system is not changed

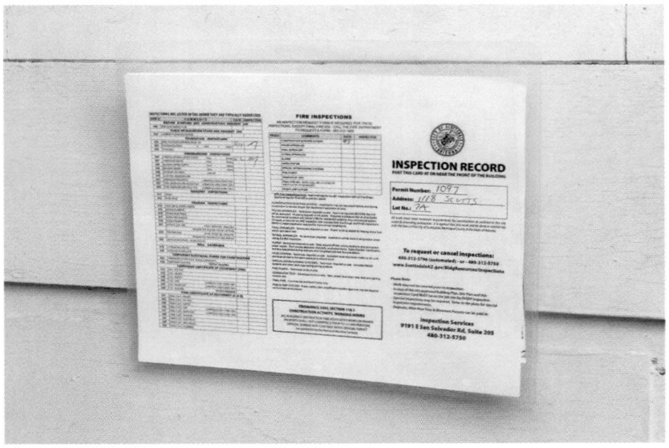

Post the job site inspection card so the inspector can see it.

Certificates of Occupancy ▸

A certificate of occupancy is issued by your building official to affirm that your structure is safe to inhabit. Do not move into or occupy a building until after the building official issues a certificate of occupancy. Do not change the use of a building without a new certificate of occupancy. Example: do not use a building as an office if the building was once a home without receiving a new certificate of occupancy. The new certificate of occupancy may require changes to the building that reflect its new commercial use. You are not required to obtain a certificate of occupancy for accessory structures.

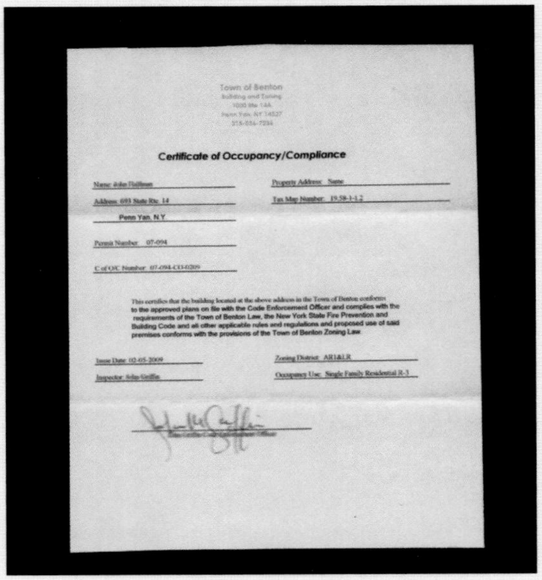

Permit Expiration ▸

Verify building permit expiration rules with your local building official. A building permit may expire if more than 180 days lapse without an inspection or without some other evidence that work is progressing on the project.

Required Inspections

Contact the building official to determine the required inspections for a construction project. Each jurisdiction has its own rules for inspections. These rules include: which inspections it performs, what work must be complete before requesting the inspection, how and when to schedule the inspection, and how it handles inspections of work that fails inspection.

Note that some jurisdictions conduct a separate inspection for each trade, some jurisdictions conduct one inspection when all trade work is complete, and some jurisdictions conduct trade inspections during the framing inspection. Check with the building official to determine if other inspections are required. Further required inspections may include flood plain and elevation, roof coverings, insulation and energy efficiency, interior drywall, and exterior wall coverings such as stucco and masonry.

Final Inspections

Prior to final inspection, you should: Install all plumbing, HVAC, and electrical fixtures, equipment, and appliances; Install all required safety components such as stair handrails and guards, safety glazing, and smoke alarms. Note that jurisdictions have different rules about whether you must install finish components, such as floor coverings, before the final inspection. Jurisdictions also differ on whether tasks such as final grading and landscaping must be installed.

Do not assume that passing an inspection or receiving a certificate of occupancy is a waiver of any code violations. The building owner and contractor are responsible for any code violations regardless of whether the building has passed inspections.

Preparing for Inspections

Concrete footing inspections must be done before concrete is poured. Try to coordinate the inspection for the day before the planned pour, so you leave enough time to make corrections if required.

1. Install, square, and level forms.
2. Dig footing, and pier trenches.
3. Install any required reinforcing bars.

Concrete postholes and holes for column footings must be inspected before the concrete is poured. The holes will be inspected for width (diameter), depth (distance past frostline), and shape—most require a bell shape at the bottom. Some reinforcement may be required as well.

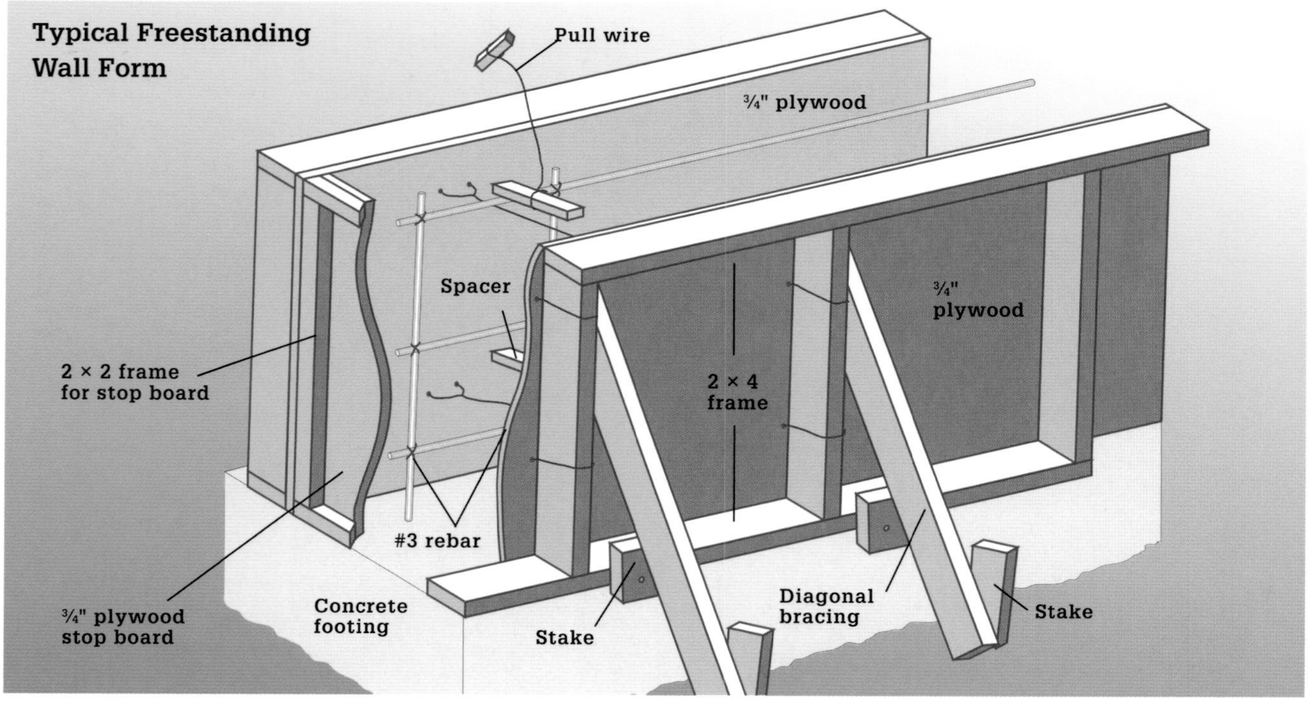
Typical Freestanding Wall Form
Pull wire
¾" plywood
Spacer
¾" plywood
2 × 2 frame for stop board
2 × 4 frame
#3 rebar
¾" plywood stop board
Concrete footing
Stake
Diagonal bracing
Stake

Concrete foundation wall inspections will focus on the wall thickness, base preparation, and reinforcement. All forms must be approved prior to the pour.

1. Install, square, straighten, plumb, and secure wall forms.
2. Install any required reinforcing bars.

Plumbing rough-in inspection.

1. Install plumbing water supply and drain pipes in the building. Note that building sewer and building water supply pipes often require a separate inspection. Install fixtures such as tubs and showers that may be difficult to install after the wall construction is complete.

HVAC inspection.

1. Install HVAC ducts, pipes, and thermostat wires.
2. Install (or have installed) appliances such as furnaces and air handlers that may be difficult to install after the construction is complete.

Electrical rough-in inspection.

1. Have electrical service panel and subpanel cabinets installed.
2. Install boxes for switches, receptacles, and fixtures, and all electrical cables.

Framing inspection.

1. Install all interior and exterior walls, floor joists and subflooring, ceiling joists and rafters, and roof sheathing. Install all required wall bracing, firestops, and draftstops.
2. Note that some jurisdictions may require installation of other components such as moisture barriers and roofing felt before calling for a framing inspection.

Building Design & Safety

One of the most important reasons for building codes is to promote the health and safety of building occupants. Health issues involve topics such as minimum room size, minimum ceiling height, and requirements for removing moisture and fumes that could damage your home and make you sick. **Safety issues involve topics such as the size and location of emergency escape openings, design and construction of stairs (one of the most dangerous areas in a home), and the location and installation of smoke and carbon monoxide alarms.**

This chapter will help you understand building code requirements that you may encounter when doing projects such as adding rooms and remodeling basements and attics. While this chapter will help you avoid the most common health and safety code violations, it does not address all code requirements. You should refer to other sources for more information before tackling complex projects.

In this chapter:

- Habitable Rooms
- Fire Separations
- Stairways
- Emergency Escape Openings
- Egress Doors
- Exterior Doors
- Ventilation & Exhaust
- Smoke & Carbon Monoxide Alarms
- Clearance for Cooking Equipment

Habitable Rooms

Habitable rooms (also called habitable spaces) are living, sleeping, eating, and cooking rooms. Bathrooms, toilet rooms, closets, hallways, storage, and utility rooms are not habitable rooms. Habitable rooms have their own set of requirements for size, ceiling height, heating, lighting, and ventilation. Rooms that are not habitable do not have these requirements.

Habitable Room Area Requirements ▸

- Provide every home with a minimum of one habitable room with a floor surface area of at least 120 square feet.
- To be classified as habitable, a room must have an area of at least 70 sq. ft.
- Provide every habitable room with a horizontal dimension of at least 84". Kitchens may be excepted: In some conditions you may design a kitchen that is smaller than 70 sq. ft. or with a horizontal dimension less than 84".

Measure between finished floor and the lowest part of the ceiling in most rooms and basements to determine if minimum ceiling height standards are met. Ceiling-mounted lights and fans do not factor into the height measurement.

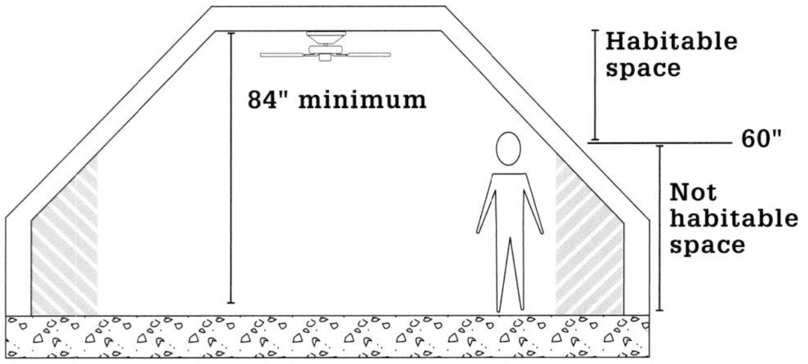

Provide at least 84" of clear ceiling height between the finished floor and the ceiling at the center of the room. If the ceiling slopes, only that floorspace where the ceiling height is at least 60" may be considered habitable. Heights less than 60", such as kneewall areas, may be useful for storage, but they aren't considered living space.

Minimum Ceiling Height

Provide a finished ceiling height of at least 84 inches in all habitable rooms, hallways, bathrooms, toilet rooms, laundry rooms. This applies to all areas in the home, including basements. Measure ceiling height from the finished floor (not the subfloor) to the lowest projection from the ceiling. Projections from the ceiling usually include beams, joists, and HVAC ducts. Projections from the ceiling usually do not include light fixtures and ceiling fans. You must also provide a finished ceiling height of at least 80 inches in the areas of your basement that are without habitable rooms, bathrooms, toilet rooms, or laundry rooms, as well as in the hallways leading to these areas.

You may install beams, girders, and ducts that are at least 76 inches above the finished floor in the parts of basements without habitable rooms, bathrooms, toilet rooms, laundry rooms, and hallways to these areas. Use basements without habitable rooms, bathrooms, toilet rooms, and laundry rooms only for mechanical equipment and for storage.

For rooms with sloped ceilings, such as attic expansions, you need to provide a finished ceiling height of 84 inches or more for at least 50 percent of a habitable room's floor area. This means that every habitable room must have at least 35 square feet of space with a ceiling that is 84 inches tall or higher. Refer to the definition of and to the required dimensions of a habitable room. None of the floor area beneath a ceiling height that's less than 60 inches may be considered habitable.

Bathroom Design Standards

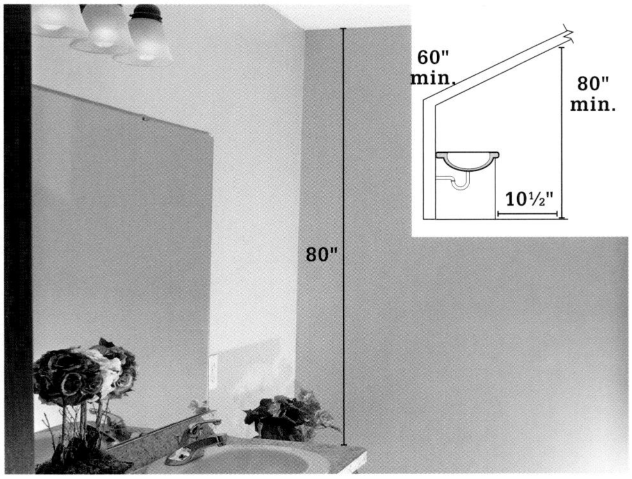

Minimum ceiling height. Provide at least 80" finished ceiling height above sinks, toilets, bidets, and similar fixtures. Provide the required ceiling height at the center of the clearance area in front of the fixture. You may reduce the ceiling height above the center of the fixture to a minimum of 60".

Showers & tubs. Provide at least 80" of finished ceiling height for all of the required floor area in showers and in tubs containing showers.

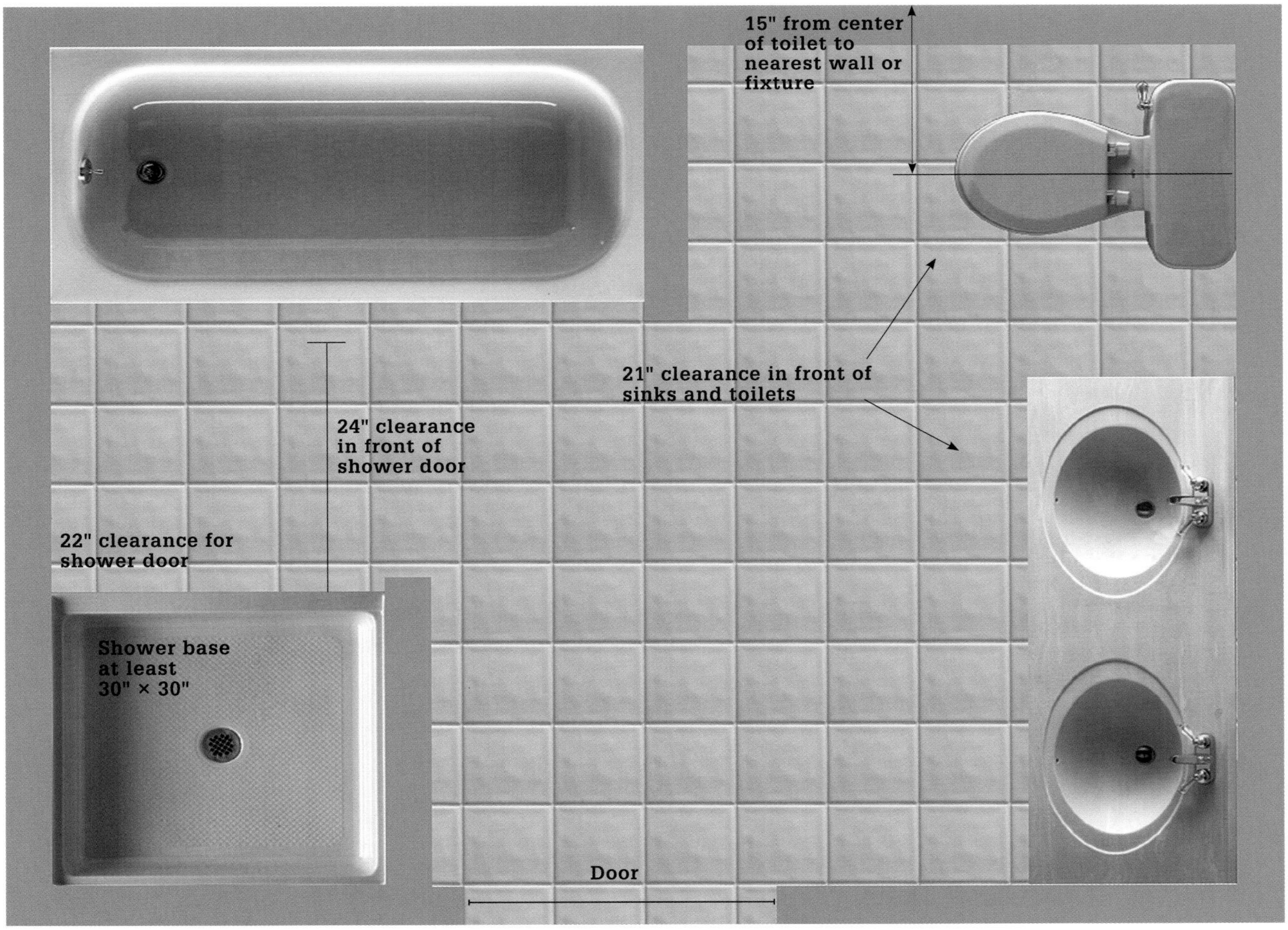

Codes (and good design practices) insist on ample space between bathroom fixtures.

Fire Separations

Fire Separation: Garage & Home

Many fires begin in garages. Unfortunately, garage fires often are more intense than fires that start elsewhere because of the presence of gasoline, cardboard, newspapers, and other flammable materials that are usually stored in the garage. **Fire safety is an important rationale for many IRC provisions. Because of this the IRC has special requirements to help prevent the spreading of garage fires into the home.**

VIOLATION! DO NOT install pet doors in doors that separate the garage from the dwelling.

A fire-rated door with a minimum rating of 20 minutes is required in walls shared between a dwelling and a home.

Fire Separation Doors

In walls that are shared between your dwelling and your garage, use at least a 20-minute fire-rated door. These may be made from solid wood or honeycomb-core steel. Use doors that are at least 1⅞" thick.

Doors in a garage wall cannot open directly into a bedroom. You also may not install pet doors or other openings in doors or walls from a garage into the home unless the pet door or opening is listed to maintain fire separation. Some jurisdictions, particularly in the West, require self-closing hinges on doors between a garage and the home.

Definition of a Garage ▸

A garage is defined as a space for parking motor vehicles that is completely closed to the outdoors on three or more sides. It typically has an overhead door, but a structure that meets the requirement but has no door is still considered a garage. A carport is a space for parking motor vehicles that is open to the outdoors on at least two sides. A space with two solid walls (often the house walls), a partially open wall, and an opening without a vehicle door is considered a carport. Garages and carports may be attached to, or detached from, the dwelling. Garage fire separation requirements do not normally apply to carports.

Fire Separation Walls & Ceilings

Walls and ceilings that separate the home from the garage should be covered on the garage side with gypsum drywall that's at least ½" thick. An attached garage must have a ceiling made of Type X drywall that's a minimum of ⅝" thick if the garage is beneath a habitable room. (Type X has fibrous reinforcement to help the drywall maintain its integrity when exposed to high heat).

Maintain the same fire separation for drywall penetrations, such as attic scuttle holes, pull-down attic stairs, gas vents, and plumbing pipes, as provided by the gypsum drywall. Most pull-down attic stairs interrupt the ceiling fire separation because the panel to which the stairs are attached is thin plywood. Seal penetrations between the garage and the home, such as pipes and ducts, with materials that resist the free flow of fire and smoke. Such materials include fire-resistant caulk.

Type X drywall is required on garage ceilings if the space above is habitable.

VIOLATION! Do not install pull-down stairs in a garage ceiling unless they maintain the required fire separation. The standard plywood covers do not maintain fire separation.

HVAC Ducts & Registers in Garages

Use at least 26-gauge sheet steel or other approved material to construct HVAC ducts that are installed in a garage and ducts that pass through garage walls and ceilings. Do not install HVAC supply or return air openings in the garage. This restriction does not apply to an independent HVAC system that serves only the garage. Do not use flexible HVAC duct or duct board to penetrate garage walls and ceilings. Flexible ducts and duct board may attach to steel ducts after the steel ducts penetrate the garage firewall.

Stairways

Interior and exterior stairways are regulated closely by most codes because they are inherently very dangerous parts of a house. The regulations differ, even on very basic guidelines like the size ratio ranges of stair treads to risers. Many of the regulations deal with lighting issues, including the type and location of fixtures and switches. The size, grippability, and location of handrails and railing balusters also accounts for much of the regulatory wording on stairways.

INTERIOR STAIRWAY LIGHTING & SWITCHING

Codes are specific about the illumination of a stairway as well as the locations of switches that control stairway lights. You should locate a light fixture near each stairway landing, including the top, bottom, and any intermediate landings. You may locate a light fixture near each stairway flight instead of near each landing. The light must be capable of illuminating treads and landings to at least 1 foot-candle. *Note: A foot-candle is a unit of light measurement approximating the amount of light you receive from a birthday cake candle when it is held 12 inches from your eyes. Photographer's light meters may be used to measure foot-candles.*

You must locate a switch for interior stairway lights at the top and bottom of all interior stairs with at least six risers. Only one switch is required for interior stairs with fewer than six risers. Locate all stair switches so they can be used without climbing any steps. You are not required to install switches if lights are designed to be on continuously or are automatically controlled by motion sensors or other devices.

EXTERIOR STAIRWAY LIGHTING & SWITCHING

Codes for outdoor stairways differ somewhat from interior requirements and recommendations. In exterior areas, you must locate a light fixture near the top landing for stairs providing access to doors above grade level. You must also locate a light fixture near the bottom landing for stairs providing access to doors below grade level. Install stairway lights capable of illuminating treads and landings to at least one foot-candle. Locate the switch inside the dwelling for exterior stairs.

Definitions of Stairway Terms ▸

Landing: A landing is a flat surface at the top and bottom of a stairway, or it may also occur at points within a stairway. A landing must be at least as wide as the stairway and at least 36 inches deep.

Nosing: A tread nose (nosing) is the part of a horizontal stair surface that projects outward beyond a solid (closed) riser below.

Riser: A riser is the vertical part of a stair. A closed riser is created with solid material between adjacent treads. An open riser has no material (except for any required guards) between adjacent treads.

Stairway (flight of stairs): A series of risers and treads that is not interrupted by a landing. A flight of stairs includes the landings at the top and bottom of the flight. A stairway with only a top and bottom landing has one flight of stairs. A stairway with a landing in the middle has two flights of stairs.

Tread: A tread is the horizontal part of a stair. A tread is sometimes called the step.

Winder tread: A winder is a tread with one end wider than the other. Winders are often used at intermediate landings to change a stairway's direction.

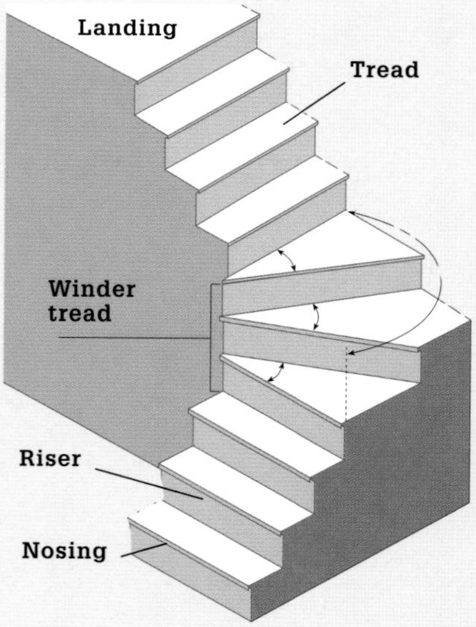

Stairway components include: tread, winder tread, nosing, riser, landing, flight of stairs.

Install a light switch at the top and bottom of stairways with at least six risers.

VIOLATION! Stairway lights. Locate a light near each flight of stairs or near the top, or any intermediate landing. If one landing is illuminated, all landings must be illuminated. The staircase seen here is in violation.

Install a light at the top landing of above-grade exterior stairs.

STAIRWAY WIDTH

1. Provide a finished stairway width of at least 36 inches above handrail to the minimum headroom height.
2. Provide a finished stairway width of at least 31½ inches at and below the handrail for stairs with one handrail, and at least 27 inches at and below both handrails for stairs with two handrails.

Provide a finished width of at least 36" above the handrail and at least 31½" at and below one handrail.

RISER HEIGHT

1. Provide a finished riser height of not more than 7¾ inches. Measure riser height vertically from leading edges of adjacent treads. The IRC does not mandate a minimum riser height.
2. Do not exceed ⅜ inch finished riser height difference between any two risers in a flight of stairs.
3. Do not allow open risers to fit a four-inch-diameter sphere for passthrough. This includes interior stairs and exterior stairs, such as stairs for decks and balconies.
4. Beware of height differences caused by changes in floor covering materials. This often occurs at the top and bottom landings. Stair stringers should be cut so that the finished risers comply with riser height and height difference requirements at treads and landings with different floor covering materials.

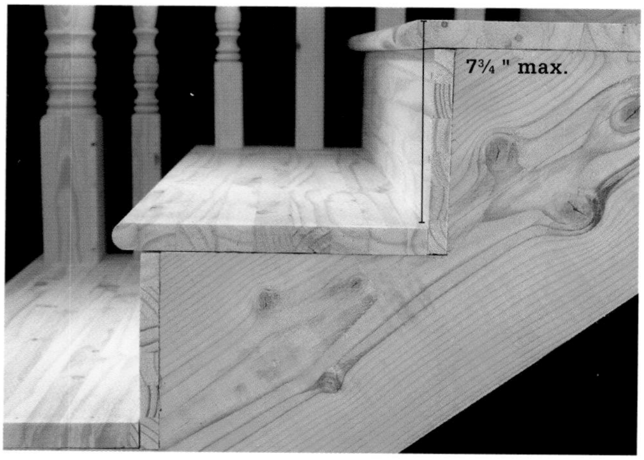

Maximum riser height is 7¾". Maximum difference between two risers in a flight of stairs is ⅜".

Open risers have the potential to trap the head of a small child. Do not allow an open riser to pass a 4" diameter sphere. Install filler strips to reduce riser opening size.

Size your riser height to account for the thickness of floor covering materials to avoid exceeding riser height and riser difference limits.

Tread Depth

1. Provide a finished tread depth of at least 10 inches. Measure tread depth horizontally from the leading edges of adjacent treads.
2. Do not exceed ⅜-inch finished tread depth difference between any two treads in a flight of stairs. This does not apply to consistently shaped winder treads contained within the same flight of stairs.

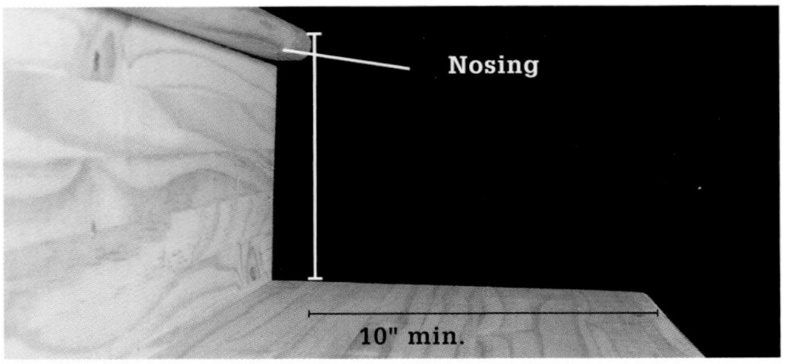

Provide a tread depth of at least 10" if treads have a nosing or at least 11" if treads have no nosing.

Tread Nosing

1. Provide a finished tread nosing depth of at least ¾ inch and not more than 1¼ inches for stairs with solid risers. Add the nosing depth to the 10-inch minimum tread depth. You are not required to provide tread nosing if treads are at least 11 inches deep.
2. Do not exceed ⅜-inch finished tread nosing depth difference between any two treads for all treads between two stories, including at floors and landings. Note that this differs from the tread and riser maximum difference. The tread and riser differences are for a flight of stairs and the nosing depth difference is for all treads between two stories.
3. Do not exceed 9⁄16 inch for the curvature radius of a tread nosing and do not exceed ½ inch for the bevel of a tread nosing.

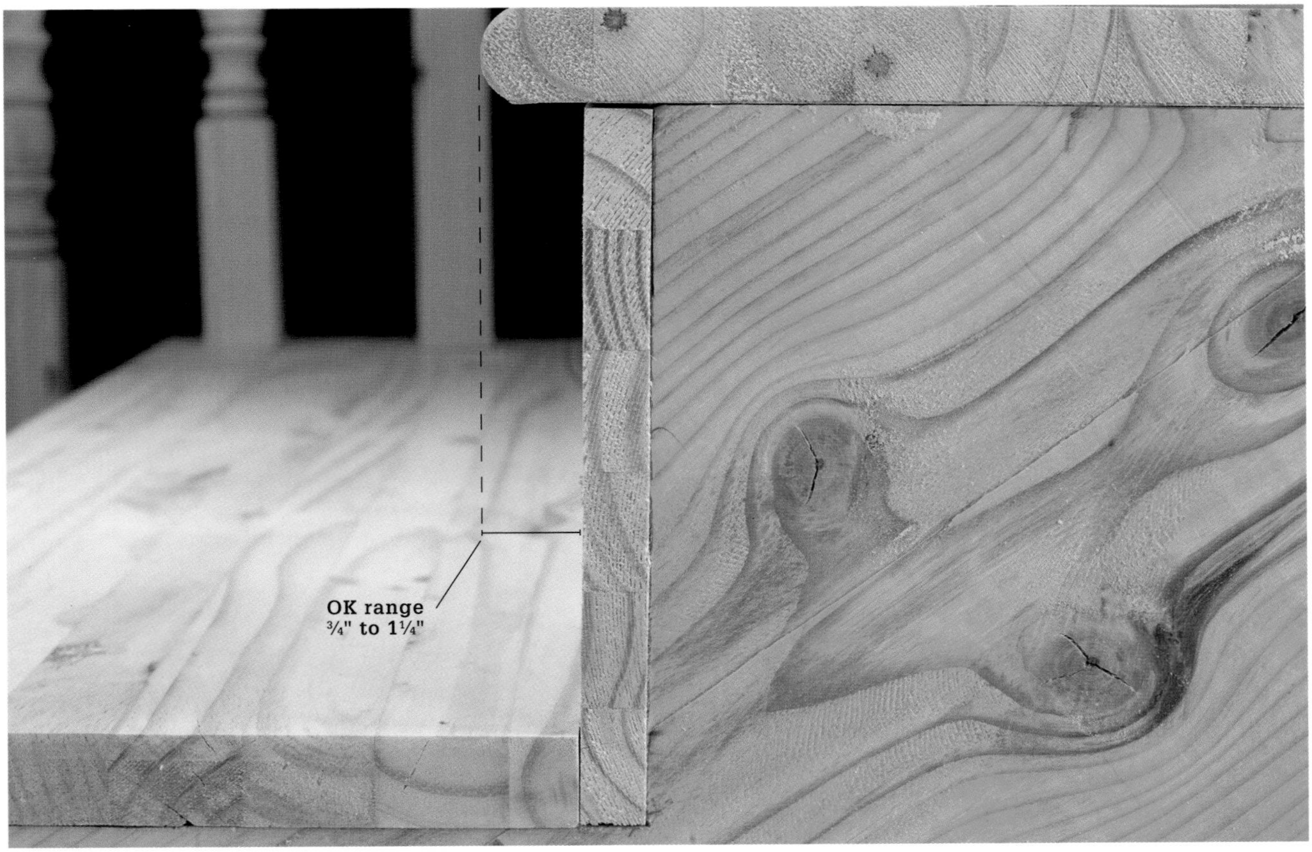

Provide a tread nosing depth of at least ¾" and not more than 1¼". Do not exceed 9⁄16" radius for a curved nosing or ½" depth for a beveled nosing.

TREAD SLOPE

1. Slope treads and landings not more than 2 percent from horizontal in any direction.

WINDER STAIR TREADS

1. Provide a finished winder tread depth of at least 10 inches measured at 12 inches from the tread's narrow side.
2. Provide a finished winder tread depth of at least six inches at any point on a winder tread.

STAIRWAY HEADROOM HEIGHT

1. Provide a finished stairway headroom height of at least 80 inches measured vertically from a sloped plane connecting the tread nosing or from the finished floor of a landing. Projections from the ceiling are permitted above the minimum finished headroom height.

STAIRWAY LANDINGS

1. Provide a landing or floor at the top and bottom of stairs.
2. Make the landing width at least as wide as the stairway. Example: if the stairway is 36 inches wide, build the landing at least 36 inches wide.
3. Make the landing depth at least 36 inches, measured in the direction of travel.
4. You are not required to provide a landing or floor at top of interior stairs, including stairs in an attached garage, unless a door swings over stairs. This means you may terminate a flight of stairs directly into a door if the door swings away from the stairs.

Install a handrail on stairways with at least 4 risers. Provide a continuous handrail beginning above the first riser and ending at or above the last riser.

5. Do not exceed 12 feet vertical rise of a flight of stairs without providing a landing. Example: do not install more than nineteen 7⅝-inch high risers without an intermediate landing.

HANDRAILS & GUARDS: LOCATION

1. Provide a handrail on at least one side of every continuous flight of stairs with four or more risers.

The step up from landings should be not more than 7¾". Measure the step to the top of the threshold. Make landings at least as wide as the stairway and at least 36" deep.

Install handrails at least 34" and not more than 38" above a sloped line connecting the stair treads.

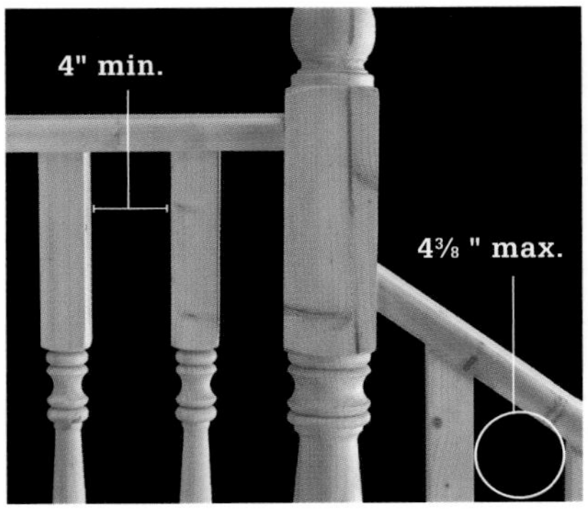

The maximum space between guard vertical members is a 4" diameter sphere. The maximum space for stairway guards is a 4⅜" diameter.

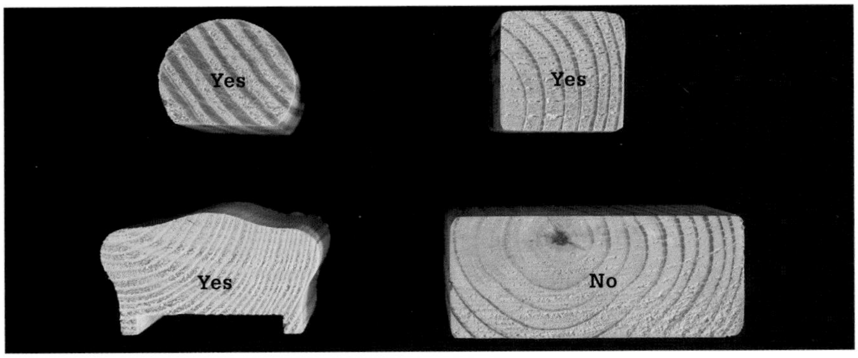

Install handrails that have the required gripping surface dimensions. Any of the above profiles will suffice. Handrails using 2 × 4 and larger lumber are too large to be grippable and thus do not meet the dimensions standard.

HEIGHT

1. Install the handrail at least 34 inches and not more than 38 inches above the treads measured vertically from a sloped plane connecting the tread nosing or from the finished floor of a ramp.
2. You may exceed the 38-inch maximum height where a handrail connects with a guard to provide a continuous structure. Example: a handrail connects to a guard at an intermediate stairway landing. The handrail height at the beginning and ending of the intermediate landing guard may exceed 38 inches high.

CONTINUITY

1. Run the handrail continuously from at least a point directly above the top riser of the flight of stairs to at least a point directly above the lowest riser of the flight.
2. Provide all handrails with a return or terminate them in a newel post, volute, starting easing, or starting newel.
3. Project handrails at least 1½ inches and not more than 4½ inches from any adjacent wall.
4. You may interrupt a handrail by a newel post at a turn.

SHAPE

1. Use material with an outside diameter at least 1¼ inches and not more than two inches for Type 1 circular handrails.
2. Use material with a perimeter dimension of at least four inches and not more than 6¼ inches and a cross-section dimension of not more than 2¼ inches for Type 1 non-circular handrails.
3. Provide Type 2 handrails that have a perimeter dimension greater than 6¼ inches with a graspable finger recess on both sides of the profile.
4. Apply handrail shape requirements to interior and to exterior stairways, including stairways for decks and balconies.

OPENINGS

1. Do not allow openings in guards to pass a 4-inch diameter sphere.
2. Do not allow stair guard openings, such as balusters, to pass a 4⅜-inch diameter sphere.
3. Do not allow openings under stair guards formed by a riser, tread, and the guard's bottom rail to pass a 6-inch diameter sphere.

HANDRAILS & GUARDS LIVE LOADS

1. Install handrails and guards so they will resist a uniform distributed force of at least 200 pounds per square foot applied in any direction at any point along the top.

The maximum space in the triangle formed by a tread, riser, and stair guard bottom rail is a 6" diameter sphere.

Emergency Escape Openings

An emergency escape opening, commonly called an egress opening, is required in all bedrooms and in some basements. Codes are very specific concerning the minimum clearances of the openings and how they can be accessed, as well as how they can be exited from the exterior. Rooms that are not intended for sleeping typically do not need to meet egress requirements. Some codes also excuse from egress standards rooms in houses that are equipped with automatic sprinkler systems.

Egress windows allow emergency exit from a structure and must meet certain minimum size and accessibility codes. They are required primarily in bedrooms and basements.

Escape Opening Locations

1. Provide at least one escape opening in every bedroom including bedrooms above, at, and below ground level.
2. Provide at least one escape opening in basements. You are not required to provide a basement escape opening if: (a) the basement area is not more than 200 square feet, and if (b) the basement is used only to house mechanical equipment. You are not required to provide additional escape openings in basements that have bedroom escape openings.
3. Open all escape openings directly on to an area that leads directly to a public way. This means that escape openings cannot open onto an enclosed courtyard or onto a similar area that does not lead directly and without obstruction to an area that is accessible by the public.
4. You may open an escape opening under a deck or porch if: (a) the escape opening can be opened to the full required dimensions, and if (b) the space under the deck or porch is at least 36 inches high.
5. Note that an escape opening may be required when converting a previously unfinished basement into finished space, especially if the finished space is a bedroom. Verify requirements with the local building official.

Locks & Bars on Openings ▸

Do not cover or obstruct escape openings with locks, bars, screens, or similar devices unless they can be operated from the inside without tools, keys, lock combinations, and special knowledge, and can be operated with the same force required to open the escape opening.

Escape Opening Size

1. Provide escape openings with a clear opening area of at least 5.7 square feet. This includes escape openings above and below grade level. You may reduce an escape opening at grade level to at least 5.0 square feet.
2. Provide each escape opening with a clear opening at least 24 inches high and at least 20 inches wide.
3. Locate the sill of each escape opening not more than 44 inches above the finished floor.
4. Measure escape opening height and width using the clear opening area. Clear opening area does not include obstructions such as window frames.

Window Wells

1. Provide all below-grade escape openings with a window well.
2. Provide each window well with at least 9 square feet clear opening area and a depth and width of at least 36 inches in each direction.
3. Install a permanent ladder if the window well bottom is more than 44 inches below grade. Ladder rung specifications include: a rung width at least 12 inches, a rung projection at least three inches from the window well wall, a rung vertical spacing not more than 18 inches apart, and a ladder may encroach not more than 6 inches into minimum window well width or depth dimension.

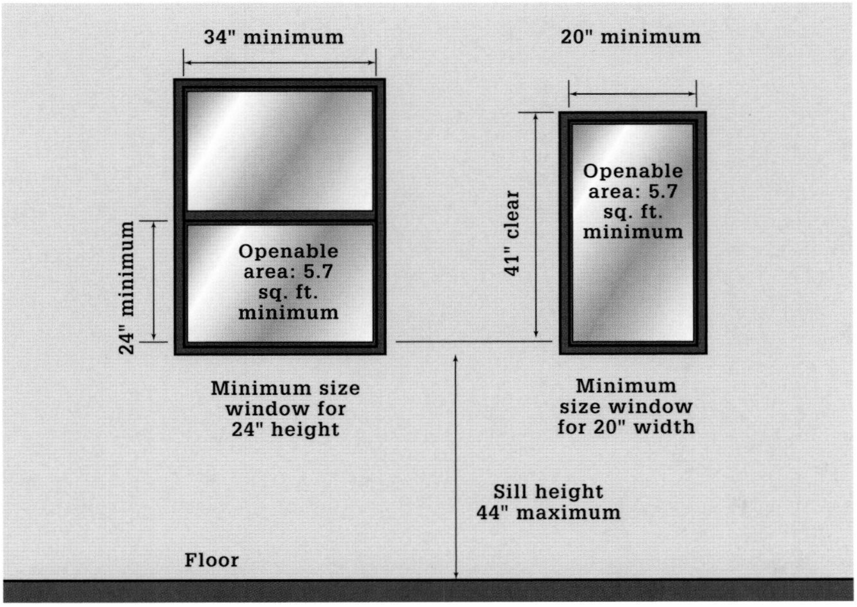

In order to satisfy building codes for egress, a basement window must have a minimum opening of 5.7 sq. ft. through one sash, with at least 20" of clear width and 24" of clear height. Casement, double-hung, and sliding window styles can be used, as long as their dimensions for width and height meet these minimum requirements.

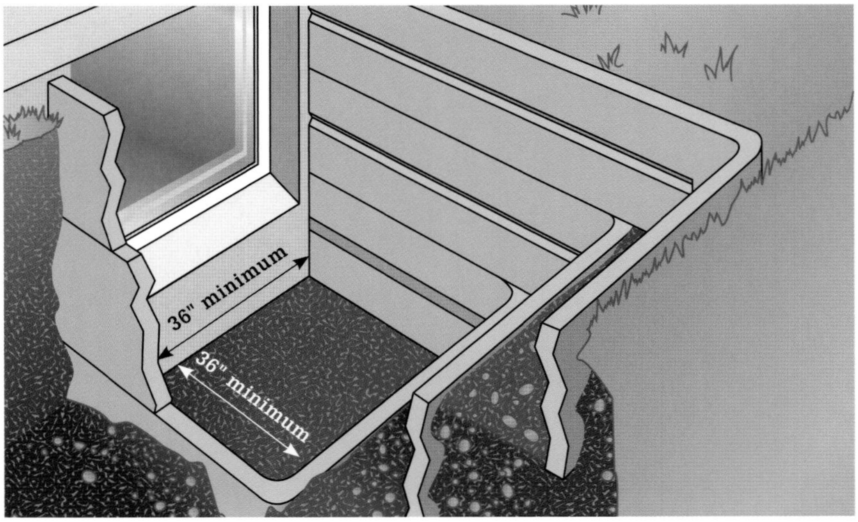

Egress window wells must be at least 36" wide and project 36" from the foundation. Those deeper than 44" must have a means of escape, such as a tiered design that forms steps or an attached ladder. Drainage at the bottom of the well should extend down to the foundation footing drain, with pea gravel used as the drainage material.

Egress Doors

The egress door is a door to the outside that meets all egress door requirements for accessibility and opening size. Every dwelling must have at least one egress door. The egress door is usually the front door. Other exterior doors need not comply with the egress door requirements.

EGRESS DOOR REQUIREMENTS

1. Provide at least one egress door that: (a) is accessible from all areas of the home, and (b) allows people to go directly outside without traveling through the garage.
2. Install a side-hinged door that is at least 36 inches wide and 80 inches high.
3. Provide a landing on the interior and exterior sides of the door. Build each landing at least as wide as the door. Example: if the door is 36 inches wide, then build each landing at least 36 inches wide. Build each landing at least 36 inches deep, measured in the direction of travel.
4. Build the interior and exterior landings not more than 1½ inches below the top of the threshold.
5. You may build the exterior landing not more than 7¾ inches below the top of the threshold, if the egress door does not swing over the landing. You may build the exterior landing with not more than a 2 percent slope away from the door. You may have a storm door or a screen door swing over any landing.
6. Provide a ramp or a stairway to any egress door that is not at grade level.

Egress Door Lock ▸

Do not install a double cylinder dead bolt lock or any other lock or device that requires use of a key, tool, or any special knowledge or effort to open the egress door. This includes screen and security doors.

VIOLATION! Use only thumb-latch deadbolts on egress doors.

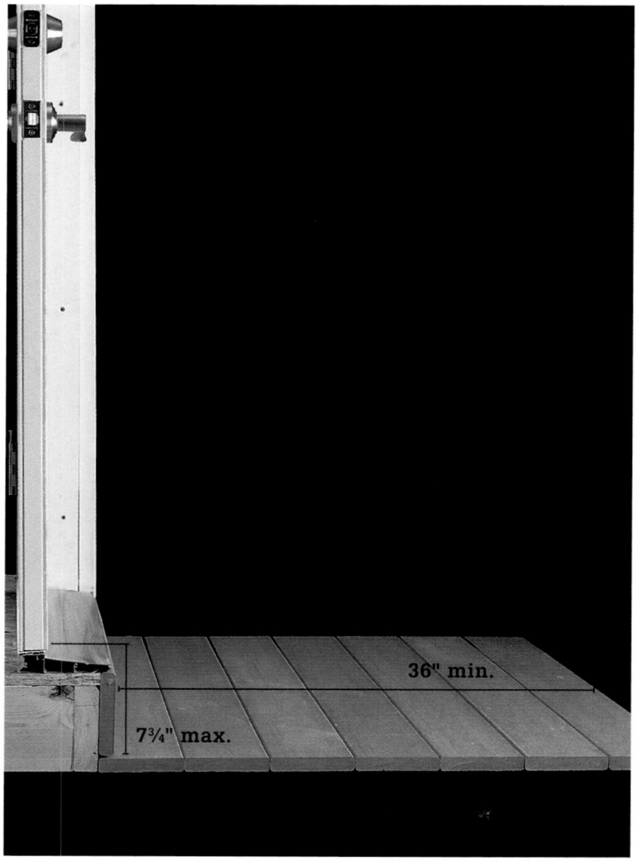

Build a landing at least 36" deep on both sides of the egress door. You may build the exterior landing not more than 7¾" below the top of the threshold.

Exterior Doors

A landing area is required on both sides of exterior doors.

Exterior Door Landing Requirements

1. Provide a landing on the interior and exterior sides of exterior doors.
2. Build each landing at least as wide as the door served. Example: if the door is 36 inches wide, then build each landing at least 36 inches wide.
3. Build each landing at least 36 inches deep, measured in the direction of travel.
4. Build each landing not more than 1½ inches below the top of the threshold.
5. You may build the exterior landing with not more than a 2 percent slope away from the door.
6. You are not required to build a landing on the exterior side of a door if: a stairway of not more than two risers is on the exterior side, and if the exterior door does not swing over the stairway.
7. You may build an exterior landing not more than 7¾ inches below the top of the door threshold if the exterior door does not swing over the landing.
8. Provide a ramp or a stairway to any exterior door that is not at grade level.
9. You may have a storm door or a screen door swing over any stairway and landing.
10. You are not required to build a landing on the exterior side of a door that opens to a narrow above-grade balcony or to a similar structure.

Ventilation & Exhaust

Controlling moisture levels in a home is important for your comfort and health, as well as for the health of your home. Although inadequate moisture levels can cause discomfort for some people and can cause furnishings and some construction materials to become brittle, it is not usually a significant risk to you or to your home, so the IRC has no provisions governing minimum moisture and humidity levels. Too much moisture, however, can be a significant risk to you and your home, so the IRC has several provisions governing the removal of excess moisture. Current indoor air quality best practices also encourage removal of excess moisture and other contaminants from the home.

The greatest threat posed by water vapor is that it provides one of the three things that mold needs to grow. The other two are the correct temperature and food. Mold grows at the same temperatures we humans prefer, so there is little we can do about that. Because mold eats almost any wood-based product and our homes are filled with these products, there is little we can do about the food risk. The one thing we can do something about is moisture.

Water vapor travels in the air. When water vapor condenses on visible surfaces, it provides the moisture that mold needs. We then see what is often called mildew. Mildew is another name for mold. When water vapor travels into attics and wall cavities, it can condense and provide moisture for mold. Mold can grow in these hidden spaces for long periods before it is discovered. Damage to the home can be significant when mold grows for long periods of time.

Water vapor is always present in every home. Some water vapor occurs naturally in the air. We introduce some water vapor into the home with every breath we take. Much of the water vapor in a home results from activities such as bathing, cooking, and clothes drying. The IRC has provisions that help remove the excess water vapor caused by these activities.

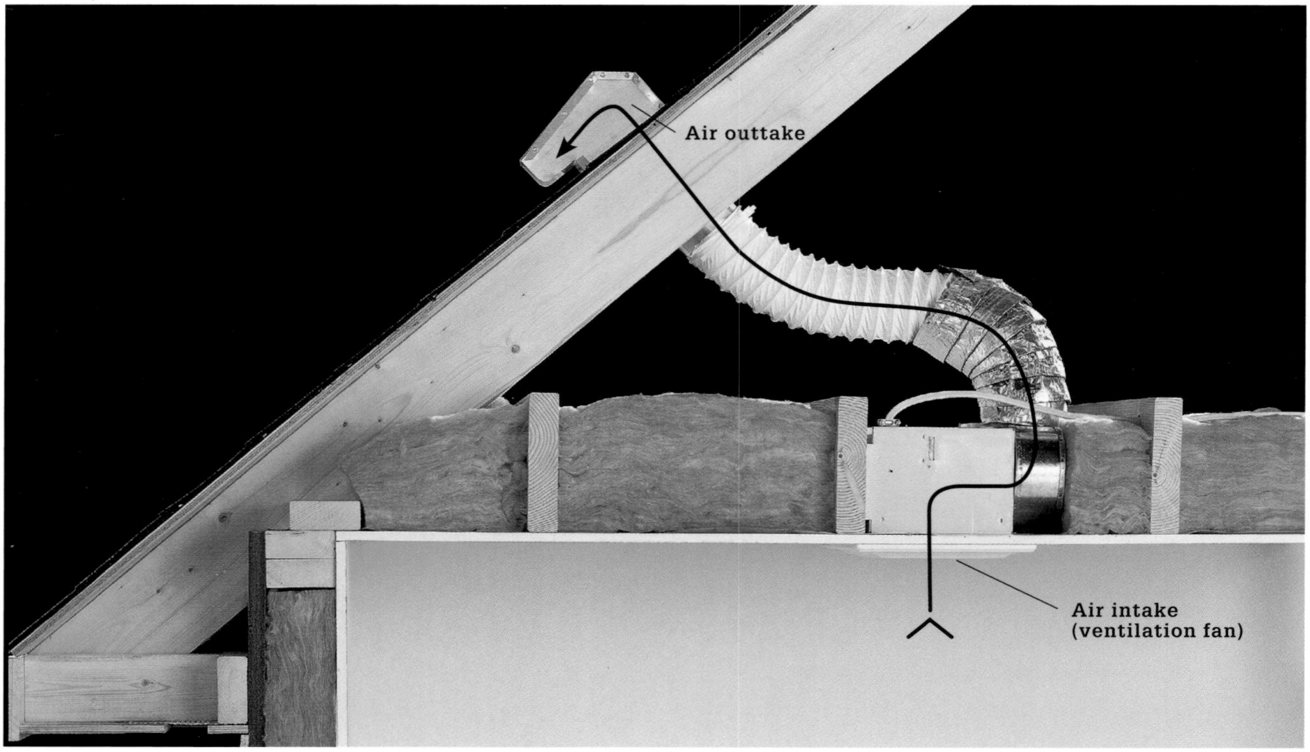

Moisture exhaust requirements generally are met with a combination of natural (windows and doors) and mechanical (ventilation fans) solutions. The bathroom and kitchen are the two rooms where ventilation is most critical.

Air Movement Requirements

1. Provide outdoor light and ventilation to bathrooms, toilet rooms, and similar areas using windows or doors containing glazing. Provide a total glazing area of at least 3 square feet with at least 1½ square feet operable. Open the glazing directly onto a street, public alley, or onto a yard or court located on the same lot.
2. You may replace the glazing with artificial light and exhaust ventilation. Provide exhaust ventilation of at least 20 cubic feet per minute continuous ventilation or at least 50 cubic feet per minute for a switched ventilation fan.
3. Discharge bathroom and toilet room ventilation fan exhaust directly outdoors. Discharging a ventilation fan exhaust duct into or toward an attic, soffit, or crawl space ventilation opening does not comply with this provision.
4. Do not recirculate air from bathrooms within a residence or into another residence.
5. Provide an automatic or gravity-operated damper for exhaust systems that will close the damper when the system is not operating.
6. Do not direct outdoor exhaust openings, such as from bathroom and kitchen exhaust fans, onto a walkway.
7. Protect outdoor air intake and exhaust openings with a corrosion-resistant screen having openings at least ¼ and not more than ½ inch or by louvers, dampers, or similar means. This does not include clothes dryer exhaust openings. Do not cover clothes dryer exhaust openings with a screen.
8. Protect outdoor openings against local weather conditions such as from rain and snow infiltration and from blockage by snow accumulation.

Vent Fan Labels ▸

Check the information label attached to each ventilation fan unit. Bathroom designers recommend a unit with a fan rating at least 5 CFM higher than the square footage of your bathroom. The sone rating refers to the relative quietness of the unit, rated on a scale of 1 to 7. (Quieter fans have lower sone ratings.)

Terminate exhaust ducts directly outdoors with a cover (usually louvered) that protects against weather and pest infiltration.

VIOLATION! Do not terminate exhausts into attic and crawl space areas.

Kitchen Exhaust Requirements

GENERAL INSTALLATION REQUIREMENTS

1. Discharge kitchen exhaust ducts to the outdoors when natural or mechanical ventilation is not provided in the kitchen area. Natural ventilation usually means an operable window in the kitchen area. Mechanical ventilation usually means a central heating system. Most homes have either natural or mechanical ventilation in the kitchen area, so external discharge of range hoods is rarely required.
2. You may install a ductless, recirculating kitchen hood if the kitchen is provided with natural or mechanical ventilation.
3. You need not install a recirculating or an externally ducted kitchen exhaust hood in most homes; however, externally ducted kitchen exhaust hoods are recommended. Verify kitchen exhaust hood requirements with the local building official.

Externally exhausted range hoods are not required by Codes except in very rare situations. Typical cabinet-mounted models like the one seen here are quite popular, however, and are recommended whenever practical.

ABOVE-GROUND EXHAUST DUCT CONSTRUCTION

1. Use smooth, single-wall galvanized steel, stainless steel, or copper to construct kitchen exhaust ducts.
2. Seal the exhaust duct air tight to avoid leaking flammable grease into wall or floor cavities or between the kitchen exhaust hood and the kitchen cabinet.

Use smooth-wall galvanized metal ductwork for range hood ducts, and be sure to seal the joints very well so the airborne grease doesn't escape into walls and cabinets, where it poses a fire hazard.

EXHAUST DUCT TERMINATION

1. Terminate kitchen exhaust hood ducts outside the building. Outside the building does not include attics and crawl spaces.
2. Provide a backdraft damper at the duct termination or other approved location. Many kitchen exhaust hoods and cabinet-mounted microwave ovens have backdraft dampers integrated into the equipment.

KITCHEN EXHAUST FAN RATES

1. Provide an exhaust rate of at least 100 cubic feet per minute for intermittently operated exhaust hoods or at least 20 cubic feet per minute for continuously operating exhaust hoods.
2. Provide makeup air for exhaust fans with a capacity of more than 400 cubic feet per minute. Install a damper or other means to close the makeup air duct that automatically opens and closes with the operation of the exhaust fan.

Downdraft ventilation is a space-saving alternative to exhaust hoods, often used on kitchen islands with built-in cooktops. It is less efficient but will mitigate some of the cooking vapors and airborne particulate matter.

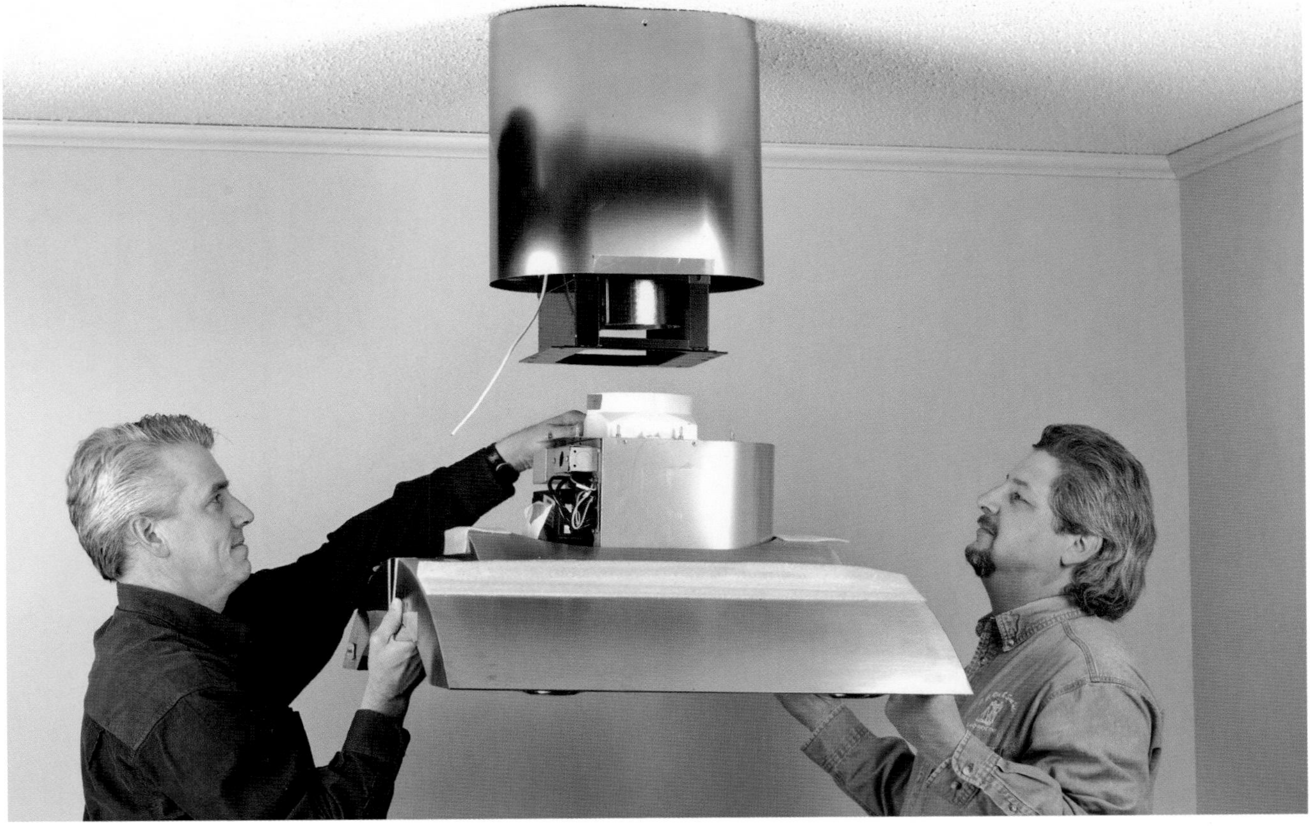

Island exhaust hoods typically are ceiling mounted and exhausted through ductwork running in the ceiling joists. In single-story installations they should be exhausted directly up through the roof or through a gable-end wall.

Clothes Dryer Exhaust Requirements

GENERAL INSTALLATION REQUIREMENTS

1. Construct, install, and terminate clothes dryer exhaust ducts according to the clothes dryer manufacturer's installation instructions. If the clothes dryer manufacturer is not known during construction, use general requirements.
2. Do not connect clothes dryer exhaust ducts to any other system such as bathroom exhaust fan ducts, plumbing vents, and fuel-burning equipment vents and flues.
3. Do not install clothes dryer exhaust ducts in or through any fireblocking, draftstopping, or fire-resistance rated assembly unless the duct is constructed and installed to maintain the code that requires fireblocking or draftstopping.
4. Do not run clothes dryer exhaust ducts into or through other ducts or plenums. Example: do not run a clothes dryer exhaust duct into or through an HVAC supply or return duct or into or through a combustion air duct.
5. Install the clothes dryer exhaust duct during construction if space for a clothes dryer is provided.

DUCT CONSTRUCTION

1. Use a four-inch diameter smooth wall clothes dryer exhaust duct unless another diameter is allowed by the clothes dryer manufacturer's installation instructions.
2. Install duct joints so that the inside part of the joint fits into the outside part of the joint in the direction of the air flow.
3. Do not use screws or other fasteners that penetrate the duct and could trap lint. Pop rivets (¼ inch) are usually considered acceptable fasteners.
4. Support the duct as required. Joints and elbows are vulnerable areas for separation.

DUCT LENGTH

1. Do not exceed 35 feet developed length between the beginning of the clothes dryer duct and the duct termination, unless the clothes dryer manufacturer's installation instructions allow a longer length. Developed length means the straight line length of the duct, reduced by bends in the duct. The clothes dryer manufacturer is rarely known during construction, so the manufacturer's installation instruction exception rarely applies.
2. Reduce developed duct length by 2½ feet for every 45-degree bend and by 5 feet for every 90-degree bend. You may use the manufacturer provided developed length for long radius bends.
3. Do not include the transition duct in the dryer duct developed length.
4. Note that the IRC Fuel Gas Chapter 24 limits the duct developed length to 25 feet for gas-fired clothes dryers.

Use strap hangers to support rigid ducts. Install hangers at joints at intervals not exceeding 4 ft. *Tip:* position the hangers so the ductwork doesn't make contact with floor joists or other structural members.

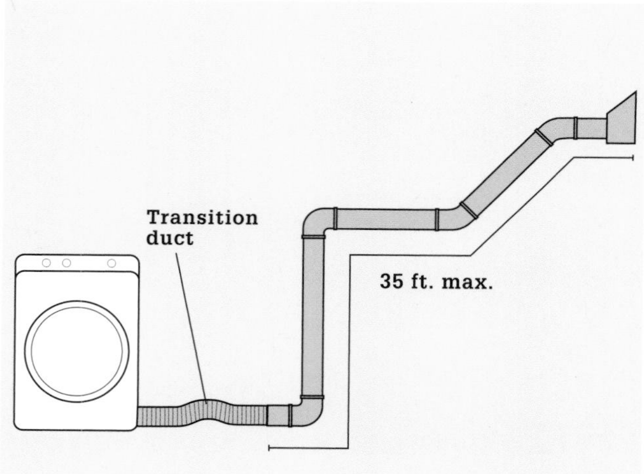

Limit clothes dryer exhaust duct developed length to not more than 35 ft.

DUCT TERMINATION

1. Terminate clothes dryer exhaust ducts outside the building. Outside the building does not include attics and crawl spaces.
2. Locate the clothes dryer exhaust duct termination at least 3 feet from any opening to the building, unless the clothes dryer manufacturer's installation instructions specify another location. The clothes dryer manufacturer is rarely known during construction, so the manufacturer's installation instruction exception rarely applies.
3. Provide a backdraft damper at the duct termination or at another approved location.
4. Do not install a screen at the exhaust duct termination. A screen will trap lint.

Locate the duct termination vent at least 3 ft. away from any opening into the building.

TRANSITION DUCT

1. The transition duct is the duct (usually flexible duct) between the dryer and the start of the smooth wall dryer exhaust duct.
2. Limit the transition duct length to 8 feet.
3. Use only one piece of transition duct. Do not splice together two or more lengths of transition duct material.
4. Do not run the transition duct through walls or in concealed spaces.

Clothes Dryer Makeup Air

1. Provide makeup air for clothes dryers that exhaust more than 200 cubic feet per minute. General codes do not specify how to provide makeup air or specify that the makeup air come from outdoors.
2. Provide a net free opening of at least 100 square inches when clothes dryers are installed in closets or provide makeup air by other approved means.

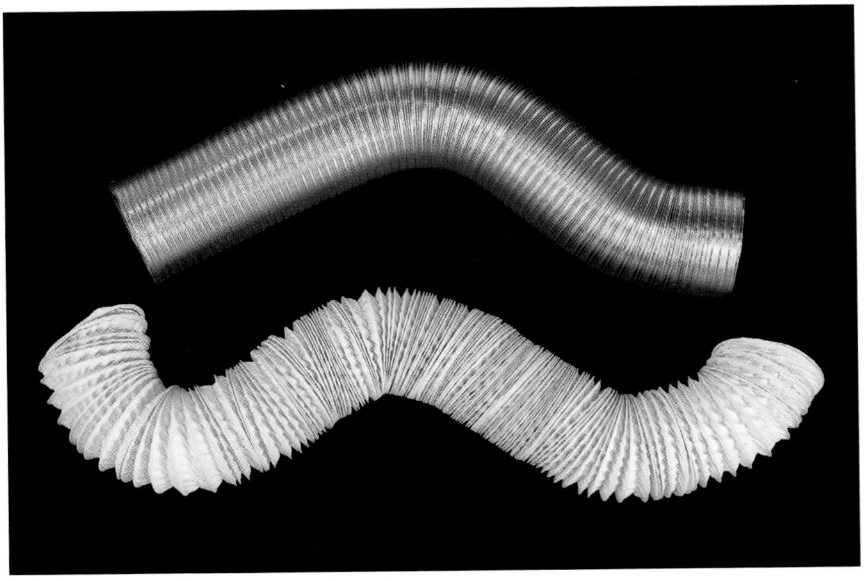

Use and install transition ducts according to the clothes dryer's instructions. Replace plastic transition ducts (bottom in photo) with flexible metal transition ducts (top in photo).

Only plug electric dryers into receptacles that are rated for this usage. Never use adapters. Most household clothes dryers require a 30-amp, 240-volt receptacle.

Smoke & Carbon Monoxide Alarms

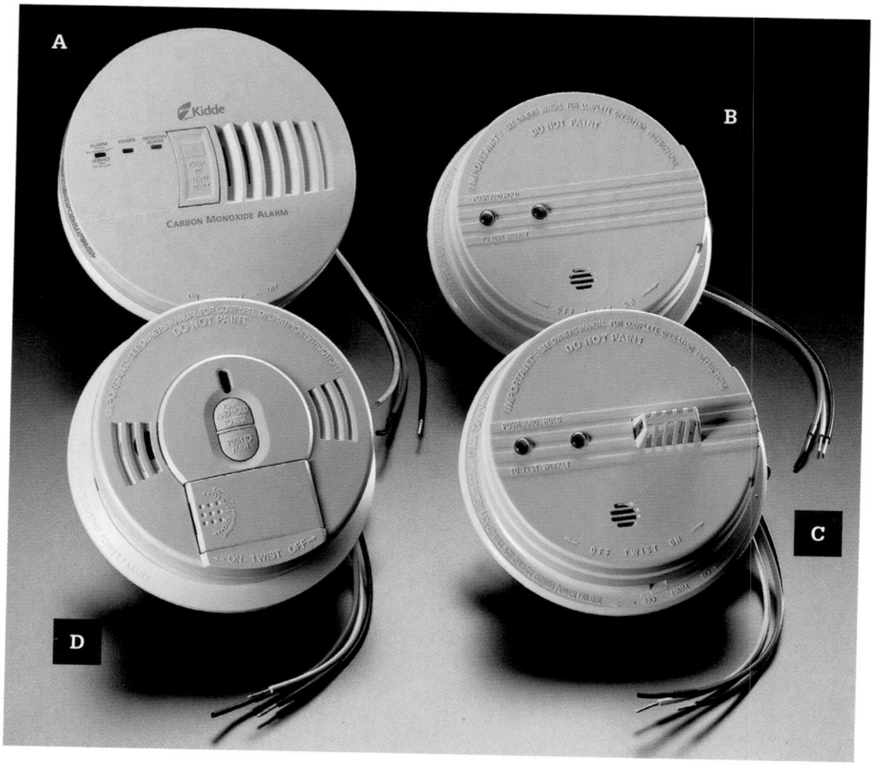

Smoke alarms and carbon monoxide (CO) alarms are required in new construction. Hard-wired carbon monoxide alarms (A) are triggered by the presence of carbon monoxide gas. Smoke alarms are available in photoelectric and ionizing models. In ionizing alarms (B), a small amount of current flows in an ionization chamber. When smoke enters the chamber, it interrupts the current, triggering the alarm. Photoelectric alarms (C) rely on a beam of light, which when interrupted by smoke triggers an alarm. Heat alarms (D) sound an alarm when they detect areas of high heat in the room.

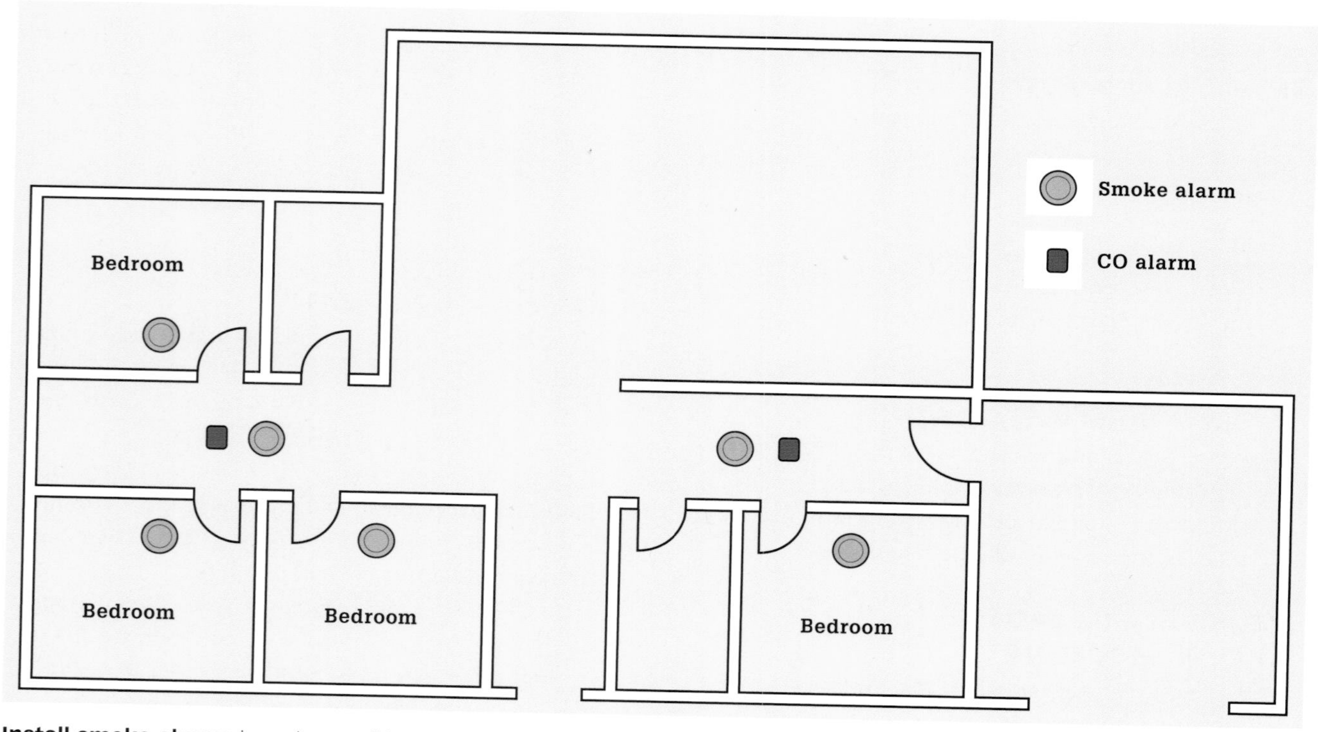

Install smoke alarms in and near all bedrooms and on all levels of a home.

Smoke Alarm Required Locations

1. Locate a smoke alarm: (a) in every bedroom, (b) outside all bedroom areas in the immediate vicinity (usually about 10 feet) of all bedrooms, and (c) on every level in the home, including basements.
2. You may substitute a security system that includes smoke alarms if it provides the same protection as hard-wired smoke alarms. The security system smoke alarms must: (a) comply with the National Fire Protection Association (NFPA) 72 standard, and (b) must be a permanent fixture in the home. Security system smoke alarms installed as a substitute system cannot be leased. They must be a permanent part of the home.

Install a smoke alarm in every bedroom. In new construction, use hard-wired alarms with a battery backup. Alarms should be interconnected so all alarms sound together.

SMOKE ALARM LOCATIONS NOT REQUIRED

1. You are not required to locate smoke alarms: (a) in crawl spaces and in uninhabitable attics, and (b) on the middle level of split-level homes if smoke alarms are installed on the upper level, if the middle level is less than one story below upper level, and if there is no door between levels. Note that some jurisdictions require smoke alarms on all levels of a split-level home.
2. Verify smoke alarm location requirements with your local building official.

SMOKE ALARM POWER SOURCE

1. Install smoke alarms that take primary power from the building electrical wiring and that have a battery backup.
2. Connect all smoke alarms together so one alarm activates all alarms (interconnection).
3. Provide arc-fault circuit-interrupter protection for the smoke alarm primary power.

SMOKE ALARM INSTALLATION

1. Install smoke alarms according to manufacturer's instructions. This often includes locating the smoke alarm on the ceiling or on a wall not more than 12 inches from the ceiling.

SMOKE ALARM UPDATES WHEN REMODELING

1. Update the entire smoke alarm system to current code requirements (including interconnection and hard-wiring) when building alterations or additions require a permit or when bedrooms are added. This update requirement does not apply to: (a) exterior work such as roofing, siding, window, and door repair and replacement, (b) installation of or repairs to plumbing and HVAC systems, and (c) situations where access does not exist to allow installing electrical wires that would provide power and interconnection to the smoke alarms.
2. Verify requirements and exceptions with the local building official. Interpretation and enforcement of this provision varies between jurisdictions.

CARBON MONOXIDE ALARM REQUIREMENTS

1. Install carbon monoxide alarms in homes equipped with fuel-fired equipment, such as gas and oil-fired furnaces, and in homes with an attached garage. The alarms must comply with UL2034.
2. Install an alarm outside of bedroom areas in the immediate vicinity (usually about 10 feet) of all bedrooms. Connection of carbon monoxide alarms to each other is not required.
3. Install carbon monoxide alarms in existing homes when building alterations or additions require a permit or when bedrooms are added.
4. Install carbon monoxide alarms according to manufacturer's instructions.

Clearances for Cooking Equipment

1. Provide at least 30 inches vertical clearance between built-in or freestanding ranges and cooktops and combustible materials, including kitchen cabinets made from wood or metal. This provision applies to gas and other fuel-fired ranges and cooktops. This provision also applies to electric ranges and cooktops when required by manufacturer's installation instructions.
2. You may reduce the clearance to at least 24 inches if: (a) a cooking appliance or microwave oven is installed according to manufacturer's instructions above the range or cooktop, (b) a metal ventilating hood is installed above the range or cooktop with a clearance of at least ¼ inch between the hood and the cabinet, or (c) the underside of the combustible material is covered with at least ¾ inch of sheet metal covered insulating millboard.
3. Do not install and use cooking appliances listed for commercial use in your home.

Provide at least 30" of vertical clearance between cooking appliances and combustible materials such as cabinets.

Universal Design Standards for Kitchens* ▸

*Best practices; not enforcable by codes.

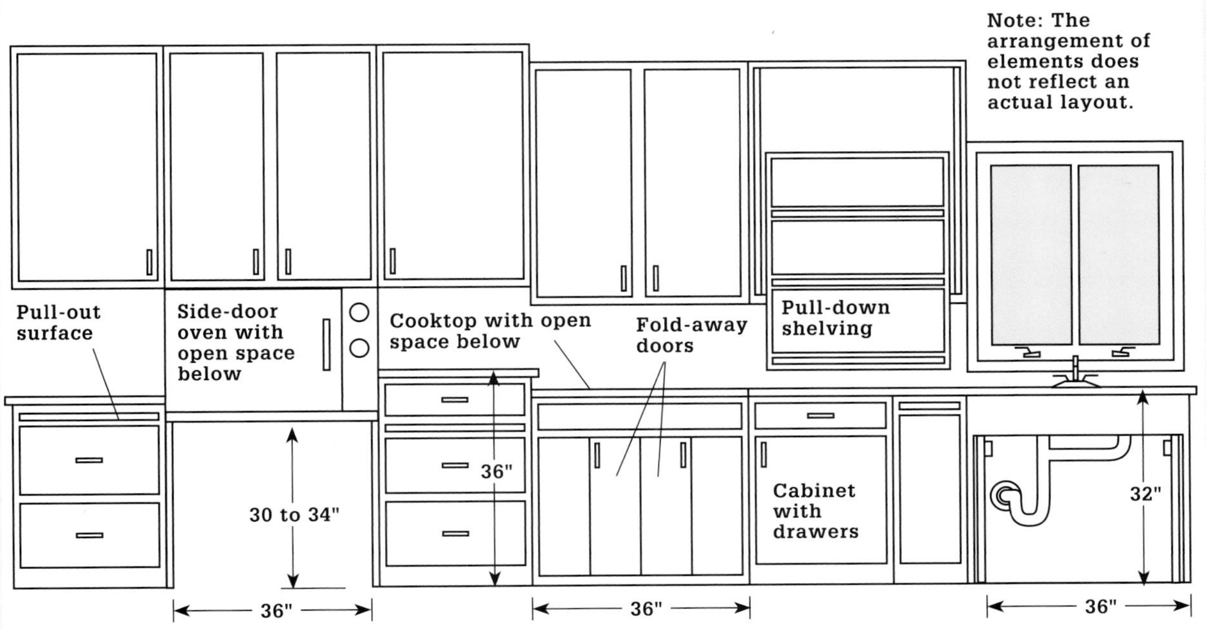

Note: The arrangement of elements does not reflect an actual layout.
Pull-out surface
Side-door oven with open space below
Cooktop with open space below
Fold-away doors
Pull-down shelving
Cabinet with drawers
30 to 34"
36"
36"
32"
36"
36"
36"

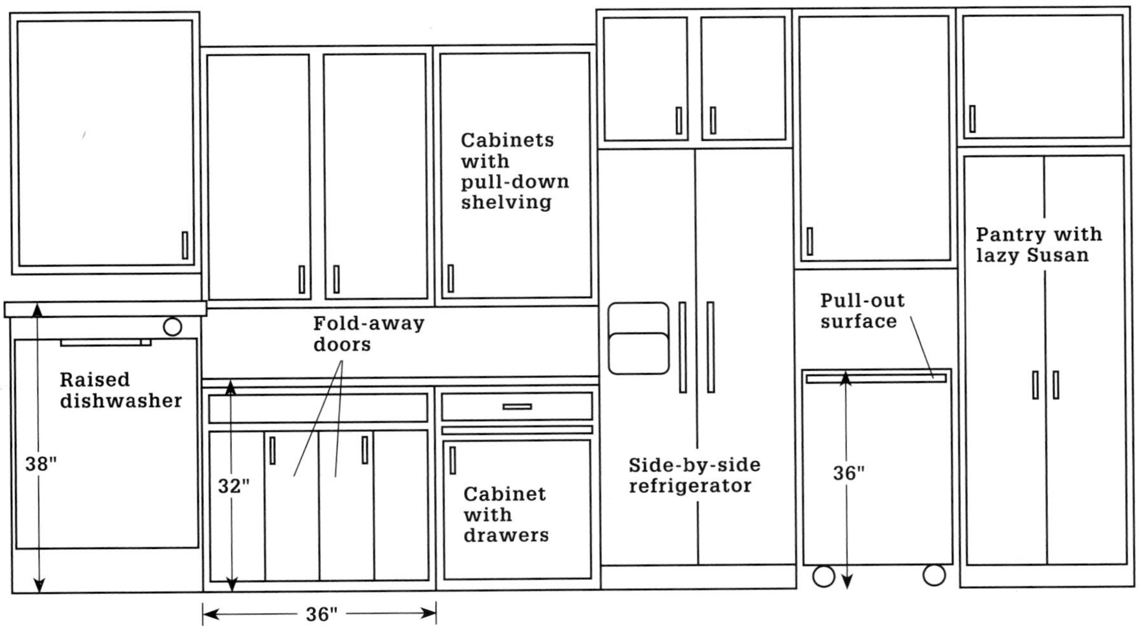

Cabinets with pull-down shelving
Pantry with lazy Susan
Pull-out surface
Fold-away doors
Raised dishwasher
38"
32"
Cabinet with drawers
Side-by-side refrigerator
36"
36"

Design your kitchen around a clear, circular space of at least 5 ft. in diameter to provide room for a wheelchair. If your kitchen doesn't have 60" of clear space, allow 48" for pathways. Plan for 30 to 48" of clear approach space in front of all appliances and workstations.

Structural Components

A safe and healthy building begins with a solidly built structure. The building's foundation should rest on stable, well-drained soil and should be strong enough to support the home during normal conditions as well as during disasters such as hurricanes and earthquakes. The building's floors, walls, and roof should be secured to the foundation and to each other and should be strong enough to support the home during extreme conditions.

This chapter will help you understand basic structural requirements for building as defined by the building codes. The intent is to help you identify work that may violate building codes so that you can bring it to the attention of a contractor or other qualified professional. Except for projects such as simple decks and storage sheds, you should seek guidance from qualified professionals before using the information in this chapter to design you own buildings or to perform structural remodeling on existing buildings.

In this chapter:

- Special Structural Requirements for High Wind & Seismic Risk Areas
- Foundations
- Crawlspaces
- Decks
- Floor Systems
- Wall Systems
- Windows & Doors
- Roof Systems

Special Requirements for High Wind & Seismic Risk Areas

SEISMIC DESIGN AREAS

1. Provide increased strength and structural integrity for foundations, walls, roofs, gas pipes and appliances, and other components in seismic design areas. Refer to the IRC and consult a qualified engineer or other qualified professional when building in seismic design areas.
2. Verify the seismic design category with the local building official. The following areas may be in seismic design areas: large parts of Alaska, California, Hawaii, Nevada, Oregon, and Washington State; small parts of Arizona, Colorado, Idaho, Montana, New Mexico, New York, and Utah; the area near Memphis, Tennessee, and the area near Charleston, South Carolina.

HIGH WIND DESIGN AREAS

1. Provide increased strength and structural integrity for foundations, walls, roofs, windows, and other components in high wind design areas. Refer to general codes and consult a qualified engineer or other qualified professional when building in high wind design areas.
2. Verify the wind design category with the local building official. The following areas may be in high wind design areas: much of Florida and Hawaii; the areas within about 100 miles of the coastlines of Alabama, Alaska, Georgia, Louisiana, Mississippi, North and South Carolina, Texas, and Virginia; the areas within about 50 miles of the coastlines of Connecticut, Delaware, Maine, Maryland, Massachusetts, New Jersey, New Hampshire, and New York. Several "Special Wind Areas" exist in scattered areas of the country. These areas are mostly in mountainous areas and are mostly in the West.

Install rafter ties. If building codes in your area require it, or if you simply want a stronger structure, nail metal rafter connector plates (often called rafter ties) to the wall top plates before installing the rafters.

Deflection of Structural Components

Most readers should not deal with bending of structural components such as floors, walls, ceilings, and roofs. Leave this to qualified engineers and contractors. Because "spongy" floors and rattling walls are common complaints, this section explains some basic concepts involved in deflection and helps you understand when deflection may be excessive.

DEFLECTION & LOADS DEFINITIONS

Deflection is when a component of a building bends under a load. The component can be a single component, such as a floor joist, or it can be a system, such as a floor or a wall. Deflection causes a component to compress on one side (compression) and expand on the other side (tension).

A load is a force (weight) placed on a component of a building. Example: a building's foundation carries the load of the entire building. The dead load is the weight of the construction materials, such as drywall, shingles, siding, and floor coverings, and the weight of fixed equipment, such as a water heater. The live load is the weight of people and furnishings that occupy a building. A point load is a load in a small area. The heel of a high-heel shoe is an example of a point load. Environmental loads include wind, snow, and forces created during earthquakes.

A point load is a type of live load that is concentrated in a small area, such as a footstep. Point loads are temporary and in many cases they can exceed the deflection minimums without causing any particular problems.

Deflection Under Live Load

1. Install structural components, such as joists, studs, and rafters, so that they will not bend more than the amount shown in Table 1 under an evenly distributed live load. L is the unsupported length of the component in inches. H is the unsupported height of the component in inches. Example: for a bedroom floor, the general codes assume that a live load of at least 30 pounds of people, floor coverings, and furnishings will be placed over each square foot of the floor area. Example: the maximum deflection of bedroom floor joists with the length between supports of 180 inches would be 180⁄360, or ½ inch.

Table 1: Deflection Under Live Load

structural component	maximum deflection (inches)
Rafters with greater than 3/12 slope and no attached ceiling finish	L/180
Interior walls	H/180
Floors and plastered ceilings	L/360
Exterior walls with plaster or stucco finish	H/360
Other structural members	L/240
Exterior stucco or plaster walls	H/360

Deflection Discussion

Walking on a floor or slamming a door hard does not generate the live load assumed in deflection tables. In fact, the load created by walking on a floor or slamming a door may be greater than the design live load at the point where the load is applied. Thus, even a floor that feels "spongy" or a wall that shakes often may not exceed the maximum deflection allowed. If a "spongy" floor or a shaky wall is not causing other problems, such as cracking drywall or plaster, then it is probably not exceeding the maximum allowed deflection and should be of little concern.

Note that the maximum deflection allowed by general codes does not apply to some rigid floor coverings, such as tile. Refer to the manufacturer's design and installation instructions when installing stiff finish materials. The manufacturer may stipulate a maximum deflection that's below the amount allowed by codes.

Foundations

SOIL LOAD-BEARING CAPACITIES

1. Place structural footings on undisturbed soil of known bearing capacity or on a bed of fill material approved by an engineer.
2. Have a geotechnical engineer evaluate the soil in areas known to have expansive or other unfavorable soils or if the soil-bearing capacity is unknown. Beware of clay soils. Some clay soils are unstable and can cause serious foundation problems.
3. Use the following table to estimate soil-bearing capacity if the soil type is known and if the local building official approves.

Table 2: Soil Load-bearing Capacities ▸

Soil type	Presumed soil bearing capacity
Bedrock (e.g., granite)	12000 psi
Sedimentary type rock	4000 psi
Gravel & sandy gravel	3000 psi
Sand, silty sand, clayey sand, silty gravel, clayey gravel	2000 psi
Clay, sandy clay, silty clay, clayey silt, silt, sandy silt	1500 psi

Common Soil Types

Gravel and sandy gravel soils have a presumed 3,000 psi load-bearing capacity.

Sandy soils have a presumed 2,000 psi load-bearing capacity.

Clay and silt soils have a presumed 1,500 psi load-bearing capacity.

Footing Width & Depth

FOOTING WIDTH

1. Use Tables 3 and 4 to determine the minimum footing width required to support load-bearing walls. You may also use material found in The American Concrete Institute document ACI 332 (see Resources, page 233).
2. Refer to general codes for special footing and footing reinforcement requirements in seismic design areas.

Leveling footing forms is very important. Measure footing depth and width at the top of the forms. Use Tables 3 and 4 to determine footing width. Here, batterboards and strings are used to level footing forms.

FOOTING THICKNESS & SLOPE

1. Make spread footings at least six inches thick.
2. Extend spread footings at least two inches beyond the framing or foundation wall. Do not project the footing beyond the framing or foundation wall more than the thickness of the footing. Example: if the footing is six inches thick, then the edge of the footing should be not more than six inches beyond the edge of the framing or foundation wall.
3. Locate the bottom of footings at least 12 inches below finish grade or below the local frost line, whichever is deeper. This does not apply to accessory buildings with an area 400 square feet or less and an eave height of 10 feet or less, and this does not apply to decks not supported by the home.
4. Do not place footings on frozen ground unless the frozen condition is permanent (permafrost).
5. Make the top surface of footings level.
6. You may slope the bottom of footings not more than 10 percent, without reducing the minimum thickness.
7. Make step footing thickness at least six inches. Make step footing height not more than the length of the footing above the step.

Table 3: Footing Width (Light Frame Wall Construction) ▸

	1500 psi bearing soil (inches)	2000 psi bearing soil (inches)	3000 psi bearing soil (inches)
1-story home	12	12	12
2-story home	15	12	12
3-story home	23	17	12

Table 4: Wall Footing Width (4" Brick Veneer or 8" Hollow Masonry) ▸

	1500 psi bearing soil (inches)	2000 psi bearing soil (inches)	3000 psi bearing soil (inches)
1-story home	12	12	12
2-story home	21	16	12
3-story home	23	17	12

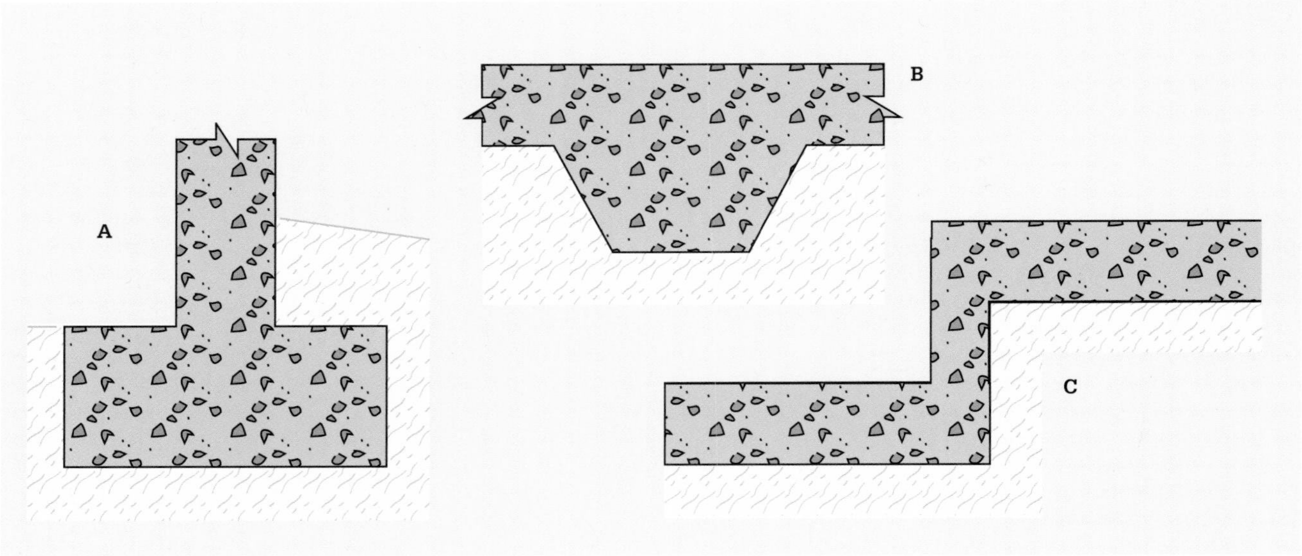

Spread footing for basement or crawlspace (A), interior load-bearing wall footing (B), or step footing (C).

Specifications for Foundation Concrete

CONCRETE IN FOUNDATION WALLS & FOOTINGS NOT EXPOSED TO WEATHER

1. Apply this provision to footings, walls, and other exterior concrete that will be completely buried.
2. Use at least 2,500 psi concrete in all environments with weathering potential.
3. Use air-entrained concrete (between 5 and 7 percent total air content) in environments with severe weathering potential or if the concrete may be subject to freezing and thawing during construction.

CONCRETE IN BASEMENT SLABS & INTERIOR SLABS-ON-GRADE (NOT GARAGE FLOORS)

1. Use at least 2,500 psi concrete in environments with severe weathering potential.
2. Use air-entrained concrete (between 5 and 7 percent total air content) in environments with severe weathering potential or if the concrete may be subject to freezing and thawing during construction.

CONCRETE IN FOUNDATION WALLS, EXTERIOR WALLS & OTHER VERTICAL CONCRETE EXPOSED TO WEATHER

1. Use at least 2,500 psi concrete in environments with negligible weathering potential.
2. Use at least 3,000 psi air-entrained concrete (between 5 and 7 percent total air content) in moderate and severe weathering potential environments.

CONCRETE IN PORCHES, GARAGE & CARPORT FLOORS & OTHER HORIZONTAL CONCRETE EXPOSED TO WEATHER

1. Use at least 2,500 psi concrete in environments with negligible weathering potential.
2. Use at least 3,000 psi air-entrained concrete (between 5 and 7 percent total air content) in moderate weathering potential environments.
3. Use at least 3,500 psi air-entrained concrete (between 5 and 7 percent total air content) in severe weathering potential environments.
4. You may use at least 4,000 psi air-entrained concrete with at least 3 percent total air content in steel-troweled garage floors in moderate and severe weathering potential environments.

FOUNDATION ANCHORS

1. Install at least ½-inch diameter bolts in exterior footings, stem walls, basement walls, monolithic slabs, and other places to which sill or sole plates for loadbearing and braced walls will be attached.
2. Install and tighten a nut and washer on each bolt. Verify washer size with your local building official.
3. Locate the bolts at least seven bolt diameters and not more than 12 inches from the ends of each plate and not more than every six feet on-center in between.
4. Install at least two bolts per plate section. Refer to general codes about exceptions for offset braced walls not more than 24 inches long.
5. Embed the bolts at least seven inches into the foundation.
6. Use approved fasteners to anchor interior load-bearing wall sole plates.
7. You may substitute anchor straps for bolts if they provide equal anchorage. Straps are often installed not more than every three feet.
8. Refer to general codes for special foundation anchor requirements in seismic design and high wind areas.

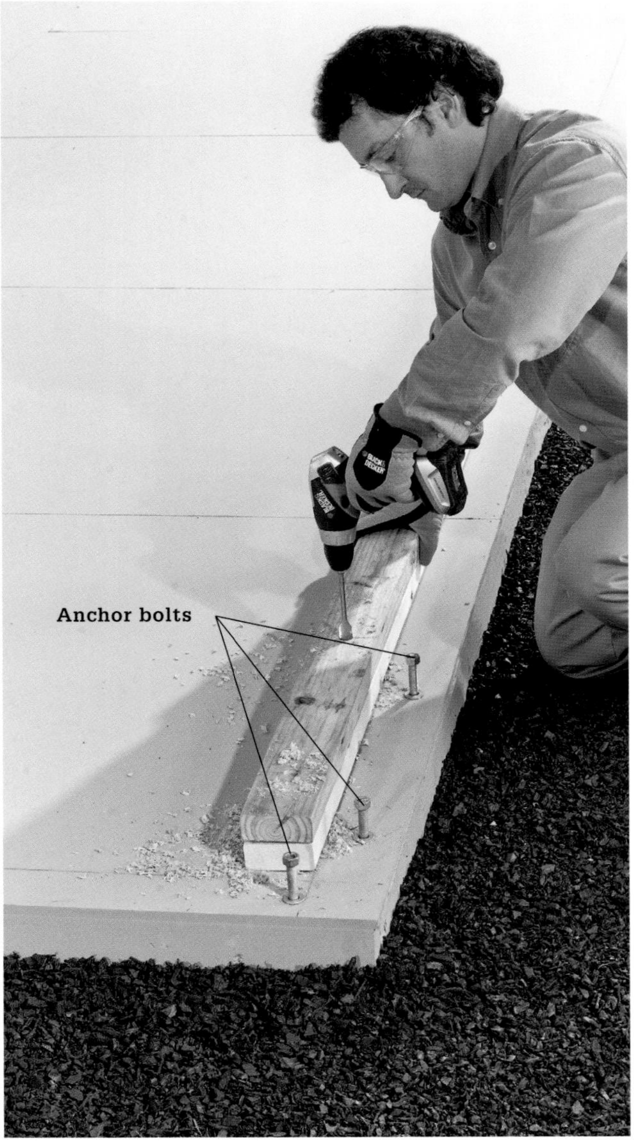

Install ½" diameter anchor bolts every 6 ft. and not more than 12" from the end of each bottom plate.

You may substitute anchor straps for anchor bolts.

Crawlspaces

CRAWLSPACE VENTILATED TO EXTERIOR

1. Provide at least one square foot of net free ventilation area for every 150 square feet of crawlspace floor in a ventilated crawlspace. You may reduce the net free ventilation area to at least one square foot for every 1,500 square feet of crawlspace floor if you cover the floor with a vapor retarder such as six-mil polyethylene sheeting.
2. Install covers such as screens or grates in the ventilation openings. Use screens, grates, grills, or plates with openings at least ⅛ inch and not more than ¼ inch.
3. Subtract the space used by opening covers from the net free ventilation area of a ventilation opening. Example: a one square foot opening may be reduced to an effective ⅔ square foot opening when covered by a cast iron grill or grate. The cover manufacturer's instructions should indicate the cover's opening reduction amount.
4. Locate a ventilation opening not more than three feet from every corner of the crawlspace wall.

UNVENTILATED CRAWLSPACE

1. You may eliminate crawlspace ventilation openings by insulating the crawlspace walls or floor system as required by general codes and by installing the following moisture control and ventilation components:
   (a) cover all exposed dirt in the crawlspace floor with an approved vapor retarder, such as six-mil polyethylene sheeting, and
   (b) lap all vapor retarder seams by at least six inches and seal or tape the seams, and
   (c) extend the vapor retarder at least six inches up the crawlspace wall and attach and seal the vapor retarder to the wall, and
   (d) provide one of the following ventilation methods:
   • continuous mechanical exhaust ventilation, or
   • a conditioned air supply at a rate of at least one cubic foot per minute for every 50 cubic feet of crawlspace floor area and provide a return air opening to the common area of the building interior.

Ventilation Opening Locations

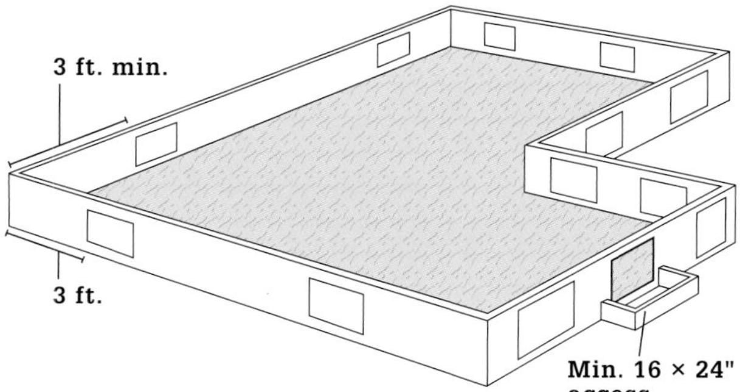

Provide 1 sq. ft. of ventilation for every 150 sq. ft. of crawlspace dirt floor area or 1 square foot for every 1,500 sq. ft. of vapor retarder covered floor area.

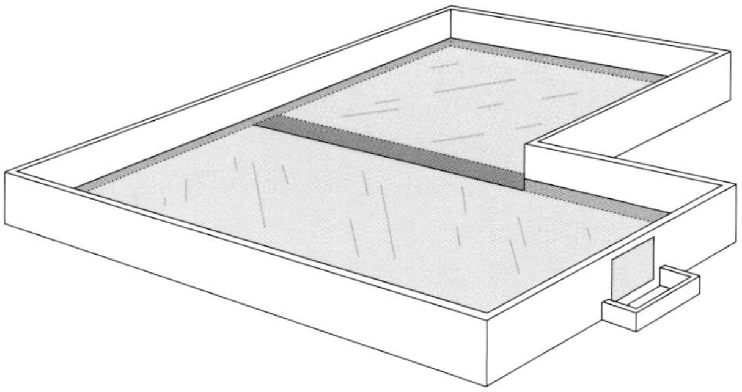

Unventilated and insulated crawlspaces often perform better than ventilated crawlspaces.

What Is a Dry Wall ▸

When building experts warn never to insulate a wall that isn't dry, they have something very specific in mind. A wall that appears dry to the touch may not be classified as dry if it is constantly evaporating small amounts of moisture that will be blocked if you install any kind of vapor retarder (as is likely the case). A dry wall (suitable for interior insulation) is one that is superficially dry to the touch and also meets these criteria:

- The wall has a positive drainage system capable of removing water that accumulates from any source (this is typically in the form of a sump pump).
- The foundation wall and floor are structured to provide drainage of water away from the house, often through the use of drain tiles and footing drains.

Basement Insulation Solution: Exterior Apron Insulation

Insulate foundation walls on the exterior side (and not the interior) whenever you can. The easiest way to accomplish this is by installing insulation in the apron area only, so you do not have to excavate all the way to the bottom of the wall. By adding a layer of horizontal insulation in the bottom of the trench, you can realize at least 70 percent of the energy savings of insulating the whole wall, while limiting your digging to 18 inches down and 24 inches out.

Because you will be adding width to the foundation wall by installing exterior insulation, you will need to install flashing to cover the top of the insulation layer and whatever protective wall surface you cover it with. For the project shown here, the insulation is covered with panelized veneer siding over one-inch-thick rigid foam insulation boards. For extra protection, coat the cleaned walls with a layer of bituminous coating before installing the insulation boards.

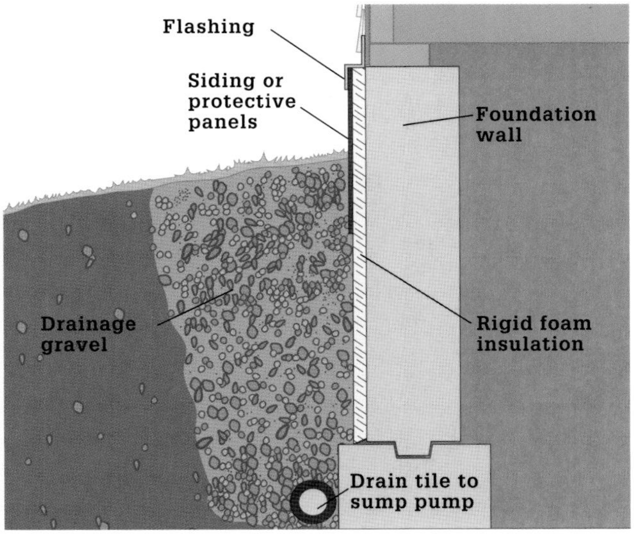

Apron insulation is an easy and effective way to enhance comfort in your basement without causing any major moisture issues.

Insulation Solution for Dry Walls: Interior Wall Insulation

As a general rule, avoid insulating the interior side of your basement walls. It is best to leave breathing space for the concrete or block so moisture that enters through the walls is not trapped. If your exterior basement walls meet the definition of a dry wall however, adding some interior insulation can increase the comfort level in your basement. The exterior walls must be fully insulated for the room to be classified as finished space. If you are building a stud wall for hanging wall covering materials, you can insulate between the studs with rigid foam—do not use fiberglass batts and do not install a vapor barrier. If you are building a stud wall, it's a good idea to keep the wall away from the basement wall so there is an air channel between the two.

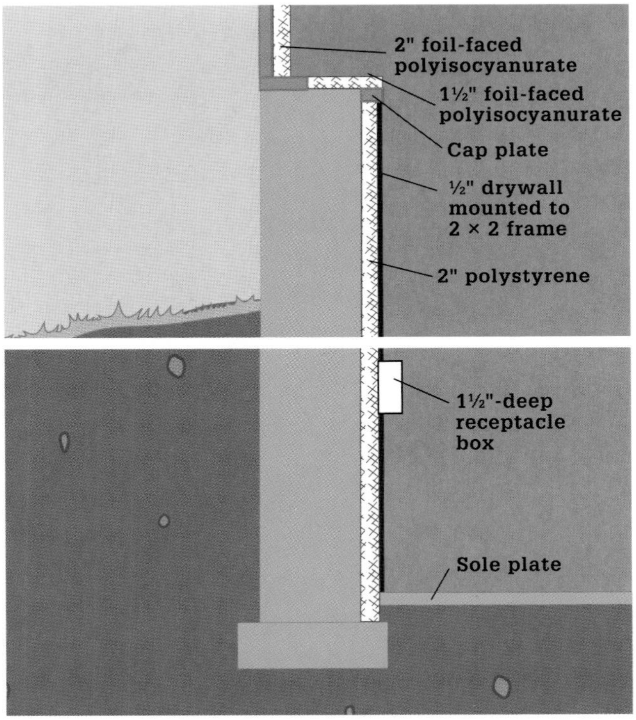

Interior insulation can be installed if your foundation walls meet the conditions for dry walls (see page 50). It is important to keep the framed wall isolated from the basement wall with a seamless layer of rigid insulation board.

Decks

Most decks are relatively simple structures, but even a basic deck project must conform to the requirements of building codes in your area. In fact, virtually every aspect of your new deck—from its location on your property to the design you choose and the materials you buy to build it—must meet stringent guidelines for safety. Codes vary to some degree from state to state, but they are based on general, established regulations. Your local building inspector can provide you with a list of the relevant deck codes and help you interpret them so you can create code-compliant plans for your deck project. You may also want to download a free PDF copy of the "Prescriptive Residential Deck Construction Guide" (see Resources, page 233).

Deck Attachment to Building

GENERAL REQUIREMENTS

1. Design decks to resist both vertical and horizontal (lateral) loads where the deck is attached to the building.
2. Install hold down devices connected to building floor joists to resist horizontal (lateral) loads.
3. Install straps or other devices to resist uplift forces if the deck is attached to the building and if the deck has floor joists that extend beyond a support beam (cantilevered framing). This includes connections at ledgers and at supports such as beams.
4. Leave attachment methods and materials exposed for inspection before applying finish materials.

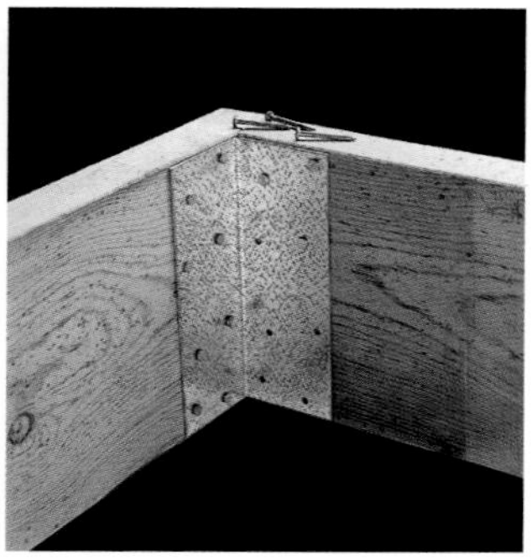

Install metal hardware connectors at the ledger.

Beam rests on shoulder
Shoulder cut
6 × 6"-dia. min.
12"-dia. min.

Meet or exceed all lumber size codes. For example, use lumber that is at least 6 × 6" for all deck posts, regardless of the size of the deck or the length of the post.

DECK LEDGER ATTACHMENT TO THE HOME

1. Install a pressure-treated Southern Pine or Hem Fir deck ledger board that's at least a 2 × 8 in size.
2. Secure the deck ledger board to a two inch SPF band joist (also called rim joist) or a one-inch-thick engineered wood band joist, or a one-inch-thick by 9½-inch wide Douglas Fir laminated veneer lumber rim board. The band joist or rim board must bear on the foundation. Do not attach a deck to the band joist or rim board of a cantilevered floor, such as a chimney or a bay window. Do not attach a deck through wall-covering materials such as siding and brick.
3. You may use alternate attachment methods and materials designed by an engineer to attach the deck ledger board to the band joist or rim board.
4. You may make a deck entirely self-supporting as an alternative to attaching the deck to the building.

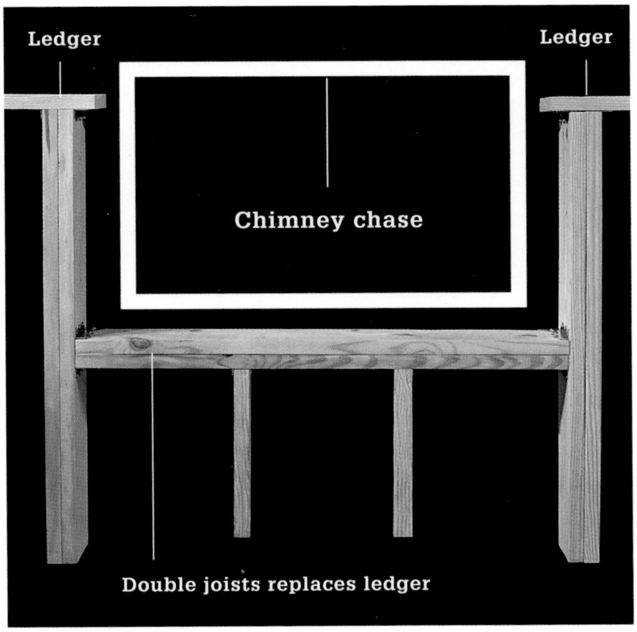

Hang a double joist between joists to support deck in areas where obstructions won't allow a ledger.

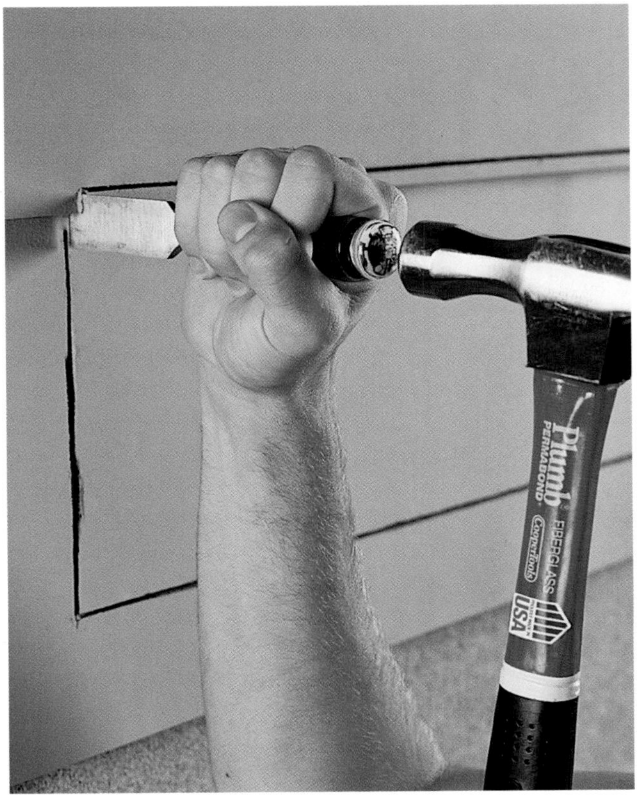

Do not attach the ledger directly to siding. Remove all siding in the installation area so you can attach the ledger to the wall framing members. Cut the siding with a circular saw and finish the corners with a chisel.

Ledger boards should be pressure-treated lumber that's at least 2 x 8 in size.

DECK ATTACHMENT USING SCREWS OR BOLTS

1. Install at least ½ inch hot-dipped galvanized lag screws or bolts as specified in Table 5. Install the screws or bolts at least two inches from the top and bottom of the ledger board and between two inches and five inches from each end. Stagger the screws or bolts vertically along the length of the ledger board.
2. Make the distance between the ledger board and the building sheathing not more than ½ inch.
3. Make the distance between the interior face of the ledger board and the exterior face of the band board (rim joist) not more than one inch.
4. Use lag screws that are long enough to penetrate the band or rim board, but not long enough to penetrate through the interior wall.
5. Flash the ledger board with drip cap molding to direct water away from the ledger and band boards.
6. Design connections to engineered rim boards (such as those commonly used with floor trusses) using accepted engineering practices.

Table 5: Deck Attachment Using Screws or Bolts On Center ▸

Joist span connector	≤ 6 ft.	> 6 ft. & ≤ 8 ft.	> 8 ft. & ≤ 10 ft.	> 10 ft. & ≤ 12 ft.	> 12 ft. & ≤ 14 ft.	> 14 ft. & ≤ 16 ft.	> 14 ft. & ≤ 18 ft.
½-inch lag screw with ≤ 15/35-inch sheathing	30"	23"	18"	15"	13"	11"	10"
½-inch lag bolt with ≤ 15/32-inch sheathing	36"	36"	34"	29"	24"	21"	19"
½-inch lag bolt with ≤ 15/35-inch sheathing and ≤ ½ inch stacked washers	36"	36"	29"	24"	21"	18"	16"

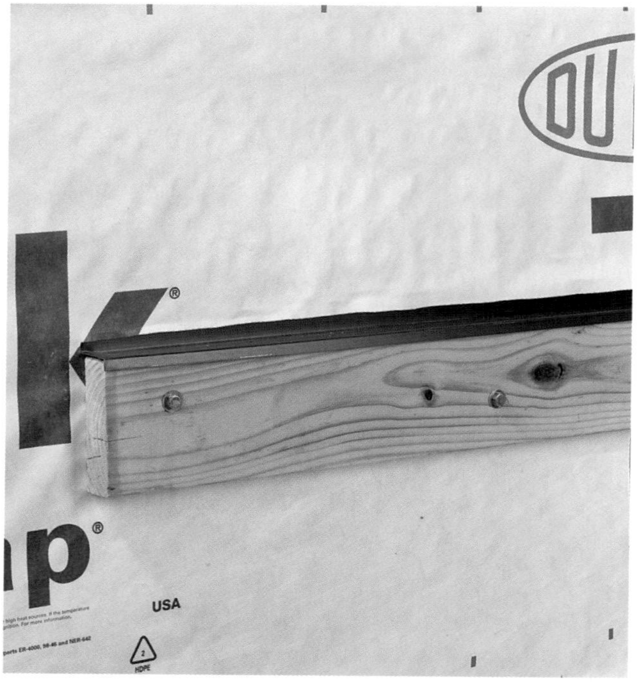

Install staggered fasteners on the ledger board using spacing specified in Table 5.

Proper ledger flashing (normally metal drip cap molding) is critical to keeping deck structural connections dry and safe.

Best Practices for Deck Building

Engineered beams, such as a laminated wood product or steel girder, should be used on decks with very long joist spans, where standard dimension lumber is not adequate for the load. Engineered beams for decks must be rated for exterior use.

VIOLATION! Some codes no longer allow joists to straddle the sides of a post fastened with through bolts, as shown here, and no longer endorse structural posts made of 4 × 4 lumber: 6 × 6 is the minimum size. Railing posts may be 4 × 4.

Post-to-beam attachment. Deck posts, regardless of length or size of deck, should be made of minimum 6 × 6 structural lumber. Notch the posts so that beams can bear fully in the notch, and attach them with pairs of ½-in.-diameter galvanized through bolts and washers. Or, you can mount beams on top of posts with galvanized post cap hardware.

No notched railing posts where they attach to the deck rim joists. Railing posts should be fastened to rim joists with pairs of ½-in.-diameter through bolts and washers. In some cases, hold-down anchor hardware may also be required.

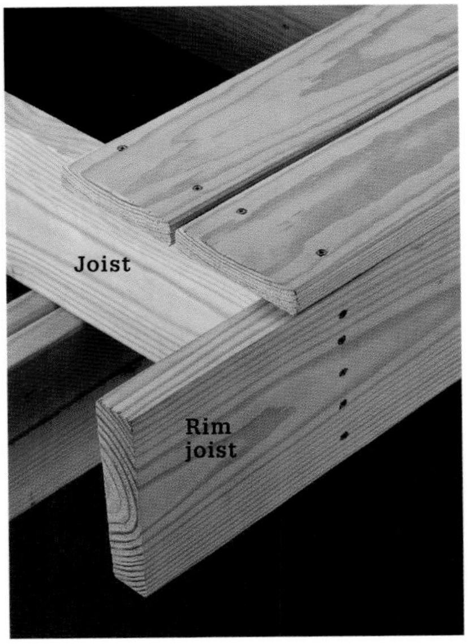

Rim joist connections. Attach rim joists to the end of each joist with three #10 × 3" minimum wood screws. Secure decking to the top of rim joists with #10 × 3". minimum wood screws, spaced every 6".

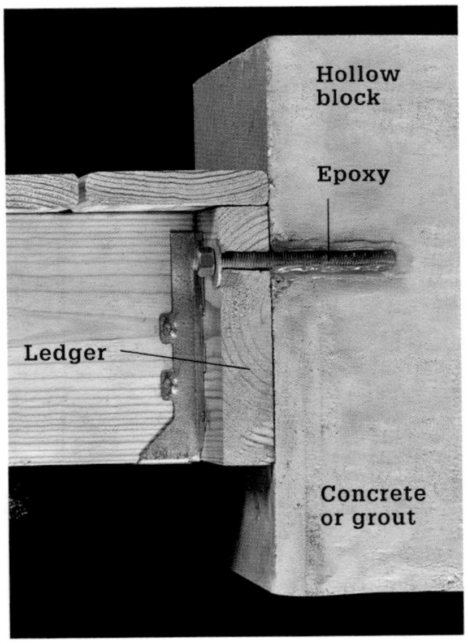

Ledgers and block walls. When fastening ledgers to hollow concrete block walls, the block cells in the ledger attachment areas must be filled with concrete or grout. Secure the attachment bolts to the wall with approved epoxy anchors with washers.

Floor Systems

FLOOR JOIST SPAN TABLES (SELECTED)

1. Use 30 psf live load and 10 psf dead load for joists under bedrooms and in attics with access by permanent stairs, in most cases. Permanent stairs do not include pull-down folding attic ladders.
2. Use 40 psf live load and 10 psf dead load for joists under living areas, other than bedrooms, and under decks, and balconies, in most cases.
3. Use L/360 deflection (length of joist span in inches divided by 360) for all floor joists.
4. Refer to the IRC or to the AF&PA Span Tables for Joists and Rafters to find joist spans not contained in the following tables.
5. Apply the following tables to floor systems framed with nominal two-inch wide dimension lumber such as 2 × 10. **An engineer must design floor truss systems.**

Floor joists and trusses must conform to minimum span rating codes according to how long they are and what type of wood they are made from.

Table 6: Bedroom Floor Joist Spans at 16" On Center

Species	Grade	2 × 8 feet-inches	2 × 10 feet-inches	2 × 12 feet-inches
Douglas fir	2	14-1	17-2	19-11
Douglas fir	3	10-8	13-0	15-1
Hem fir	2	13-2	16-10	19-8
Hem fir	3	10-8	13-0	15-1
Southern pine	2	14-2	18-0	21-1
Southern pine	3	11-6	13-7	16-2
Spruce-pine-fir	2	13-6	17-2	19-11
Spruce-pine-fir	3	10-8	13-0	15-0

Table 7: Bedroom Floor Joist Spans at 24" On Center

Species	Grade	2 × 8 feet-inches	2 × 10 feet-inches	2 × 12 feet-inches
Douglas fir	2	11-6	14-1	16-3
Douglas fir	3	8-8	10-7	12-4
Hem fir	2	11-4	13-10	16-1
Hem fir	3	8-8	10-7	12-4
Southern pine	2	12-4	14-8	17-2
Southern pine	3	9-5	11-1	13-2
Spruce-pine-fir	2	11-6	14-1	16-3
Spruce-pine-fir	3	8-8	10-7	12-4

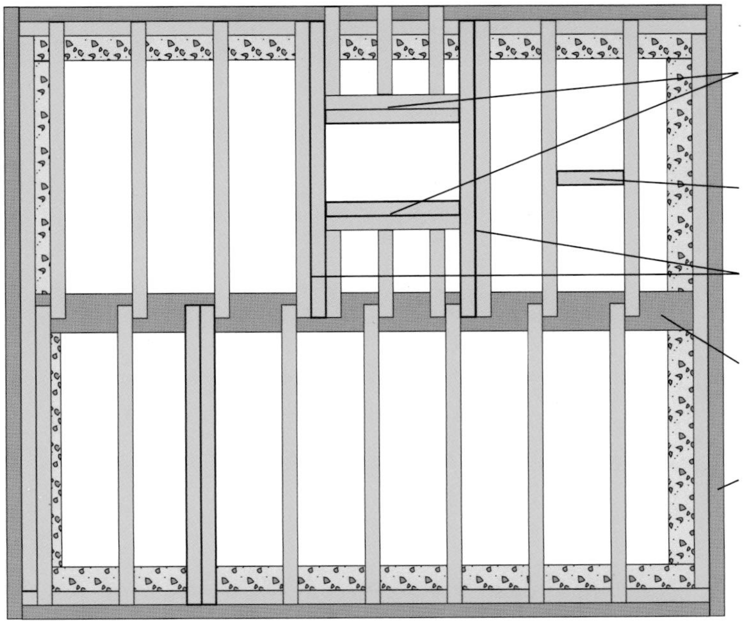
Double headers
Bridging
Double trimmers
Central beam
Rim joist

Install floor system framing members according to this illustration. The provisions in this section refer to floor system framing using nominal 2"-thick dimensional lumber. Follow engineering instructions when using floor truss systems.

Table 8: Living Area Floor Joist Spans at 16" On Center

Species	Grade	2 × 6 feet-inches	2 × 8 feet-inches	2 × 10 feet-inches	2 × 12 feet-inches
Douglas fir	2	9-9	12-7	15-5	17-0
Douglas fir	3	7-6	9-6	11-8	13-6
Hem fir	2	9-1	12-0	15-2	17-7
Hem fir	3	7-6	9-6	11-8	13-6
Southern pine	2	9-9	12-10	16-1	18-10
Southern pine	3	8-1	10-3	12-2	14-6
Spruce-pine-fir	2	9-4	12-3	15-5	17-10
Spruce-pine-fir	3	7-6	9-6	11-8	13-6

Table 9: Living Area Floor Joist Spans at 24" On Center

Species	Grade	2 × 6 feet-inches	2 × 8 feet-inches	2 × 10 feet-inches	2 × 12 feet-inches
Douglas fir	2	8-1	10-3	12-7	14-7
Douglas fir	3	6-10	8-8	10-7	12-4
Hem fir	2	7-11	10-2	12-5	14-4
Hem fir	3	6-2	7-9	9-6	11-0
Southern pine	2	8-6	11-0	13-1	15-5
Southern pine	3	6-7	8-5	9-11	11-10
Spruce-pine-fir	2	8-1	10-3	12-7	14-7
Spruce-pine-fir	3	6-2	7-9	9-6	11-0

FLOOR JOISTS UNDER LOADBEARING WALLS

1. Install additional floor joists under load-bearing walls that run parallel with the floor joists. Ensure that the number of joists is sufficient to support the load imposed by the wall and the loads supported by the wall. Parallel floor joists run the same direction as the wall being supported. Example: install at least two floor joists under a wall supporting a roof and at least three floor joists under a wall supporting a full story and a roof.
2. You may separate the additional joists under a load-bearing wall, if necessary, to fit pipes, vents, or ducts. Install solid two-inch thick blocking at least every four feet along the full depth of the separated joists.
3. Place loadbearing walls that run perpendicular to the floor joists not more than one joist depth from the supporting wall or beam below unless the joists are sized to carry the load. Perpendicular joists run at a 90-degree angle to the wall being supported. Example: place a loadbearing wall that runs perpendicular to 2 × 10 floor joists not more than 10 inches from the supporting wall or beam below.

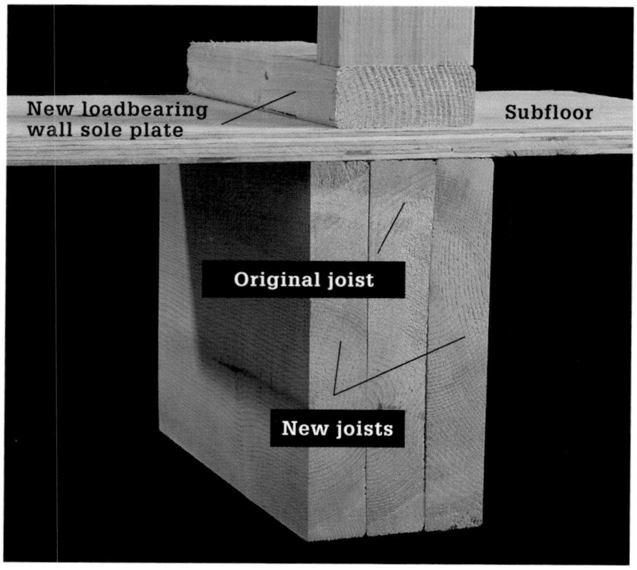

Place additional joists under load-bearing walls running parallel to the joists.

HEADER, GIRDER & FLOOR JOIST BEARING ON SUPPORTS

1. Place at least 1½ inches of a floor joist, header, girder, or beam on the supporting wood or metal wall. Supporting wood includes a sill plate bearing on a masonry or concrete wall.
2. Place at least three inches of a floor joist, header, girder, or beam on the supporting masonry or concrete wall. Comply with this requirement when the member bears directly on the masonry or concrete wall, not on a sill plate that bears on the wall. This requirement usually applies to beams and girders.
3. You may support floor joists on at least a 1 × 4 ledger if the ledger is attached to each stud and if the joist is attached to a stud.

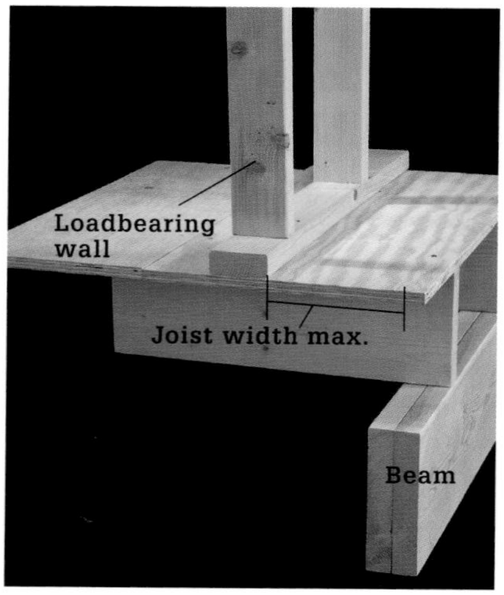

Place load-bearing walls running perpendicular to the joists not more than one joist depth away from the supporting wall or beam.

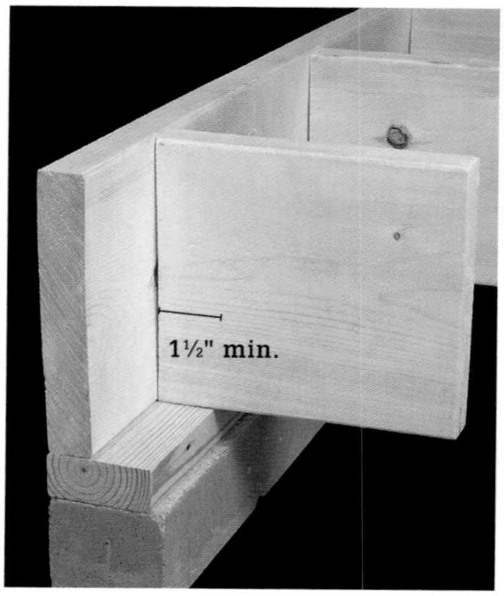

Place at least 1½" of wood on the supporting wood.

Place at least 3" of wood on supporting concrete or masonry.

Lap joists that meet over supports with at least 3" overlap. Reinforce the lap joint with at least three 10d nails.

FLOOR JOIST LAP AT SUPPORTS

1. Lap floor joists from opposite sides that meet over a bearing support at least three inches at the support and nail the joists at the lap using at least three 10d nails. You may substitute a wood or metal splice of equal or greater strength for the nailed lap.

FLOOR JOIST ATTACHMENT TO BEAMS

1. Use an approved joist hanger or at least a 2 × 2 wood ledger to support floor joists that connect to a beam or girder.

FLOOR JOIST BLOCKING

1. Install full-depth solid blocking that's at least two inches thick at both ends of floor joists. Or attach the joists to a header, band, or rim joist, or to an adjoining stud. This helps reduce joist twisting.
2. Install blocking at all intermediate load-bearing supports in seismic design areas.

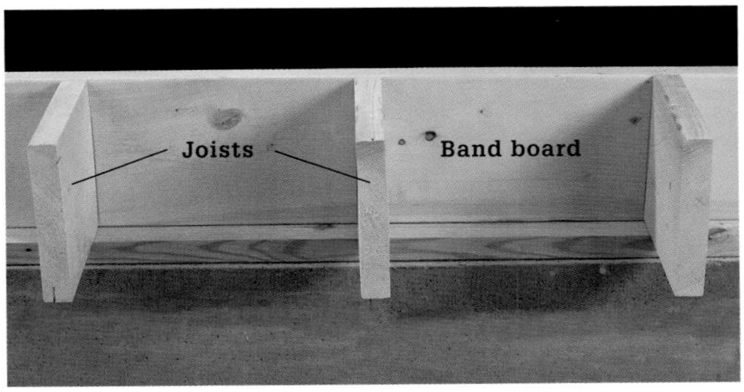

Attaching the ends of the floor joists to a band board is a common method of blocking.

Attach floor joists to beams using metal joist hanger hardware.

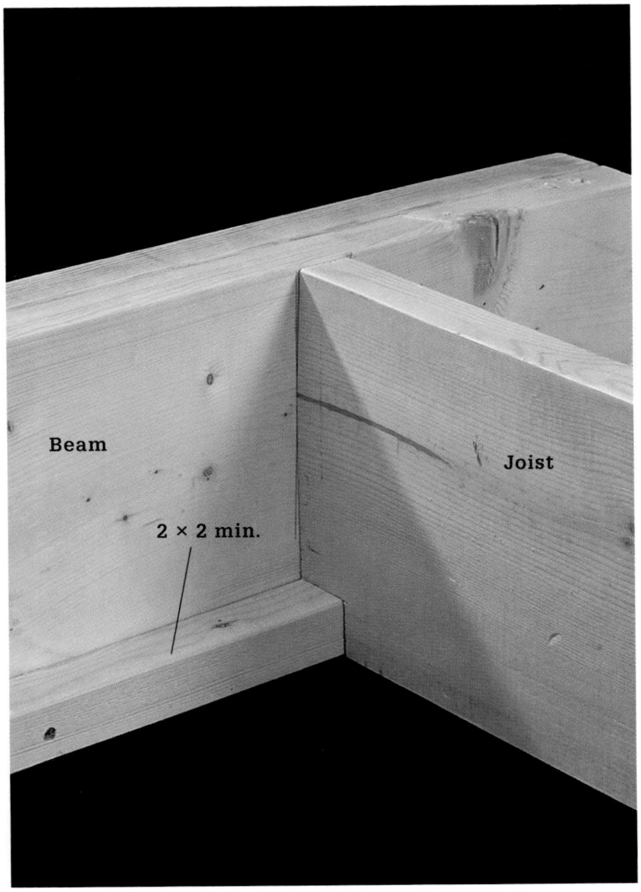

Attach floor joists to beams using a 2 × 2 or larger ledger for support.

FLOOR JOIST BRIDGING

1. Install bridging at intervals not more than every eight feet of floor joist length on floor joists deeper than 2 × 12.
2. You may use solid, full-depth blocking, wood or metal diagonal bridging, or other means to provide required floor joist bridging. Some code officials require bridging on all floor joists regardless of what the code stipulates.

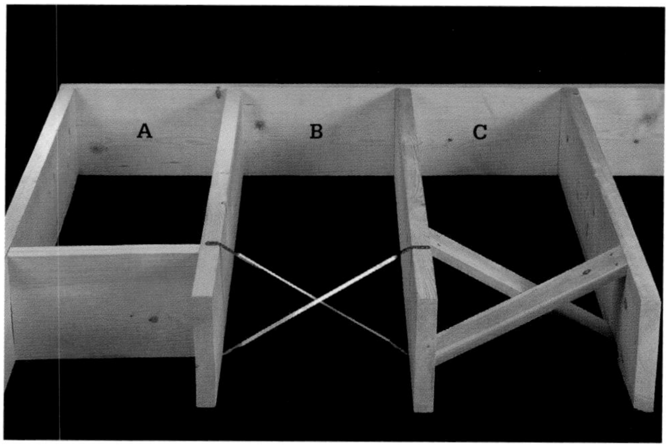

Options for floor bridging include: Full depth lumber bridging (a); metal X bridging (b); wood X bridging (c).

Metal Bridging ▸

Metal bridging (left) can be secured with joist hanger nails. For wood X-bridging, drive 10d common nails to secure the board ends to the floor joists.

Floor Joist Openings ▸

Framed openings in floor joists are used mostly for stairways between floors and for chimneys. The header joists distribute the load of the tail joists to the trimmer joists.

FLOOR JOIST OPENINGS NOT MORE THAN FOUR FEET WIDE

1. Install double trimmer joists on both sides of header joists. You may use a single trimmer joist on both sides of the header joists if the header is not more than three feet from the trimmer bearing point.
2. You may use a single header joist if the header joist span is not more than four feet wide.
3. Install approved joist hangers or a 2 × 2 ledger strip to connect tail joists to header joists if the tail joists are more than 12 feet long.

FLOOR JOIST OPENINGS MORE THAN FOUR FEET WIDE

1. Install double trimmer joists and double header joists if the header joist span is more than four feet wide.
2. Install approved joist hangers to connect header joists to trimmer joists if the header joist span is more than six feet wide.
3. Install approved joist hangers or a 2 × 2 ledger strip to connect tail joists to header joists if the tail joists are more than 12 feet long.

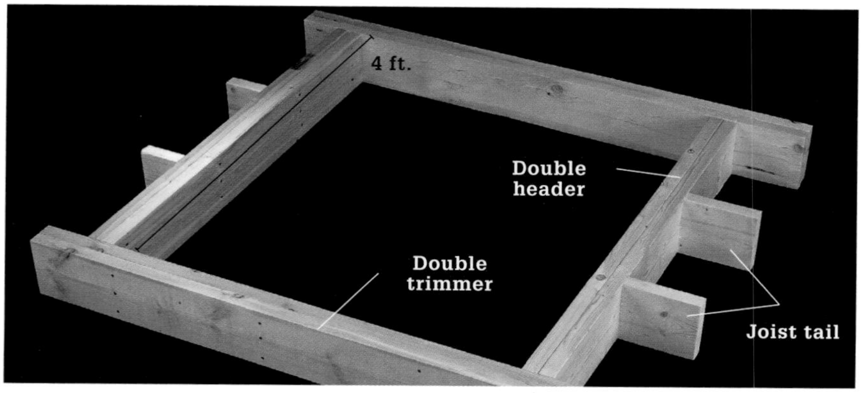

Use double trimmer joists at most openings. Use double header joists if the opening is more than 4 ft. wide.

Floor Sheathing

1. Install wood floor sheathing panels:
   (a) so that they continuously span at least two framing members,
   (b) with the long dimension perpendicular (90-degree angle) to supports, and
   (c) that are at least 24 inches wide. Panels less than 24 inches wide can deflect or fail under load.
2. Support wood floor sheathing panel edges with solid blocking, tongue-and-groove edges, or other approved means. Underlayment or ¾ inch wood flooring can substitute for edge support in some cases.
3. You may use wood floor sheathing panels (such as 23⁄32-inch and ¾-inch nominal thickness plywood or OSB and ¾-inch sanded plywood) as a combination subfloor and underlayment. Do not span these panels more than 24 inches between floor joists. Use tongue-and-groove panels or install blocking at unsupported edges. Be aware that while these panels comply with most codes, they may not comply with manufacturer installation requirements for some floor coverings such as tile.

Support edges of floor sheathing with tongue-and-groove edges.

Support edges of floor sheathing with solid blocking.

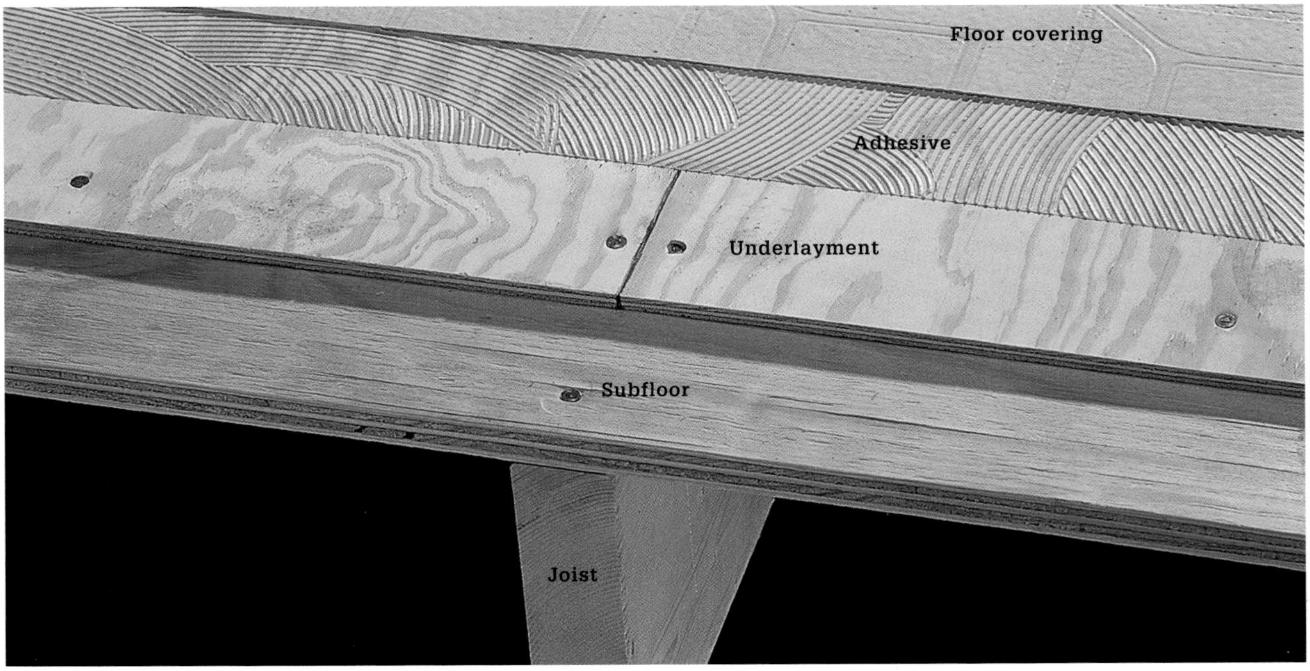

The subfloor is attached directly to floor joists with common nails or ring-shank nails, and many professionals use construction adhesive as well to help ward against squeaks. The flooring underlayment is attached to the subfloor with adhesive (optional) and 1¼" or 1½" ring-shank nails. The underlayment should be positioned so the seams do not align with seams in the subfloor.

Draftstopping

Draftstopping helps limit the spread of fires in floor framing and in floor/ceiling assemblies. It is most often required when using open web floor trusses and when a ceiling is suspended under a floor. Do not confuse draftstopping with fireblocking. Fireblocking occurs in wall assemblies.

INSTALLING DRAFTSTOPPING

1. Install draftstopping when usable space exists both above and below the floor/ceiling assembly and when the open area within the concealed floor/ceiling assembly exceeds 1,000 square feet.
2. Use at least ½-inch drywall, ⅜-inch wood structural panels (plywood or OSB), or other approved material.
3. Divide the space to be draftstopped into areas that are approximately equal.
4. Install the draftstopping material parallel with the framing.
5. Repair draftstopping that is damaged or penetrated by pipes, ducts, or other materials.

Some floor trusses require draftstopping to prevent horizontal air movement that can conduct fire. Solid wood floor joist systems typically do not because they are naturally closed off. Install a draftstop in web floor trusses when there is usable space above and below and when the concealed area is more than 1,000 square feet. Drywall and other structural panels may be used for draft stops.

Notches & Holes in Trusses ▸

Notch, bore, splice, or alter wood I-Beam floor trusses or engineered wood members only according to manufacturer's instructions and with written approval. Altering the top and bottom flange is usually not allowed. Hole boring is usually allowed in the middle third of the span and is restricted near the truss ends. Cutting the ends of engineered wood beams to length is usually permitted.

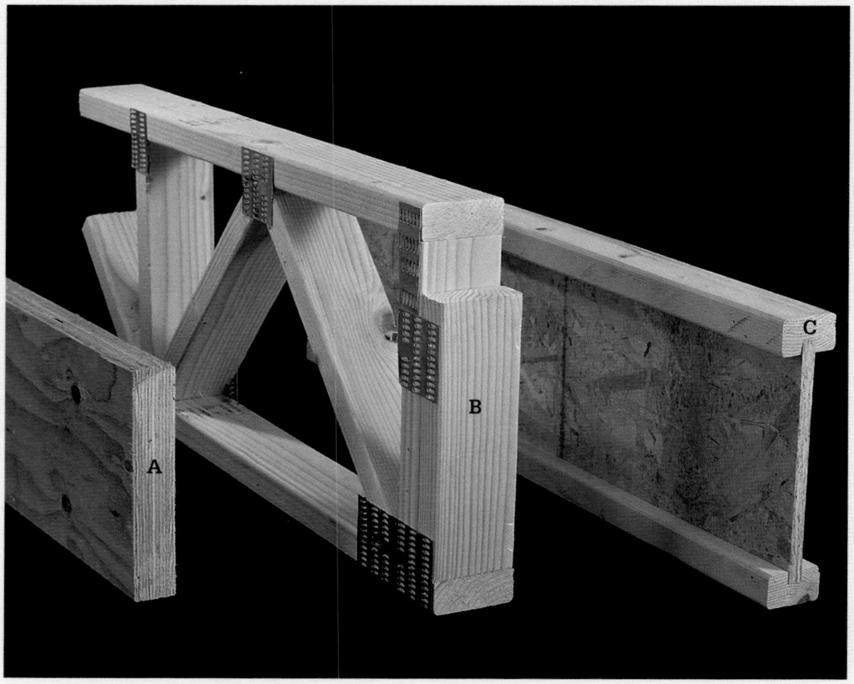

Laminated beam (A), web-type truss (B), I-beam truss (C).

Notches & Holes in Joists & Rafters

BORING & NOTCHING DEFINITIONS

A bore is a hole drilled in a stud or joist. Use the actual dimensions to determine the depth of framing lumber and when calculating the maximum hole diameter.

A notch is a piece cut from the smaller dimension of framing lumber such as a stud or joist. Use the actual dimensions to determine the depth of framing lumber and when calculating the maximum notch depth. Actual dimensions are the dimensions of framing lumber after finishing at the mill. Example: the nominal dimensions of a 2 × 6 are two inches by six inches and the actual dimensions, after finishing, are about 1½ inches by 5½ inches.

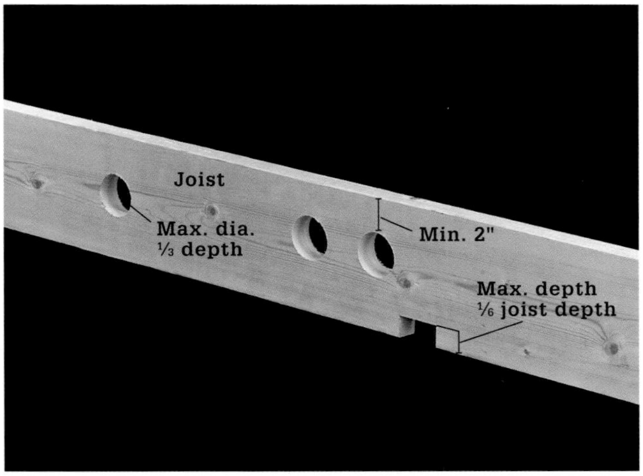

Drill holes not more than ⅓ of the member depth and cut member notches not deeper than ⅙ of the member depth.

WOOD JOIST NOTCHING & BORING

1. You may notch solid lumber rafters, floor and ceiling joists, and beams not deeper than one-sixth the depth of the member. You may notch the ends of the member not deeper than one fourth the depth of the member. Example: notch a 2 × 10 joist not deeper than 1½ inches, except at the ends where you may notch not deeper than 2⁵⁄₁₆ inches.
2. You may notch solid lumber rafters, floor and ceiling joists, and beams not longer than one-third the depth of the member. Example: notch the top or bottom of a 2 × 10 joist not longer than 3¹⁄₁₆ inches.
3. You may notch solid lumber rafters, floor and ceiling joists, and beams only within the outer one-third of the span. Example: notch a 10-foot long joist only within 40 inches from each end.
4. You may notch the tension side (bottom) of solid lumber rafters, floor and ceiling joists, and beams more than four inches thick only at the ends.
5. You may drill holes in solid lumber rafters, floor and ceiling joists, and beams with a diameter not more than one-third of the depth of the member. Example: drill a hole with a diameter not more than 3⅛ inches in a 2 × 10 joist.
6. Locate holes at least two inches from the edge of the member and at least two inches from any other hole or notch.
7. Use actual joist depths, not nominal joist depths. Example: use 9¼ inches for a 2 × 10 joist, not the nominal depth of 10 inches.

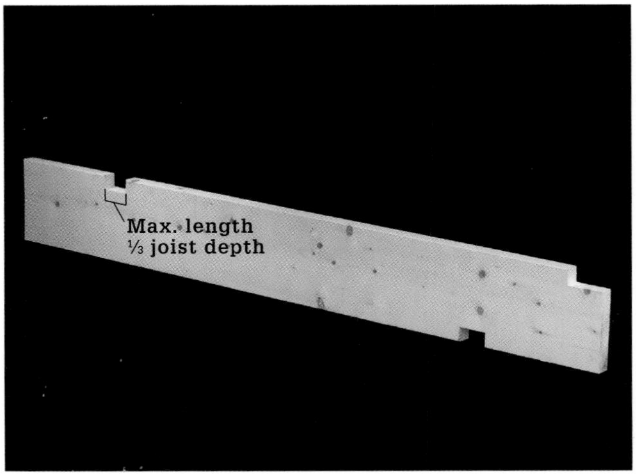

Notch wood joists and rafters not longer than ⅓ of the depth and only in the outer ⅓ of the member.

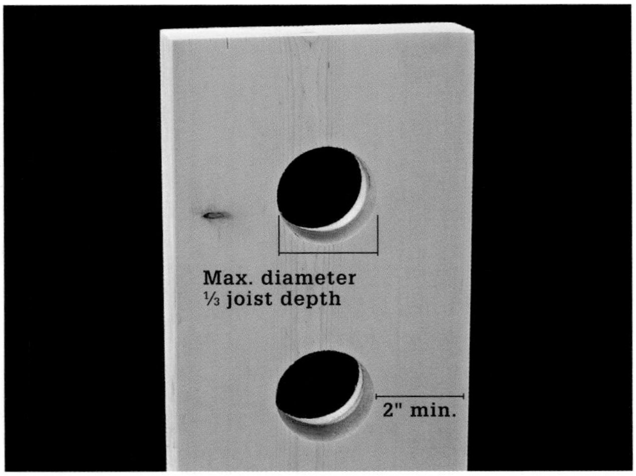

Drill holes in wood joists and rafters not larger than ⅓ the depth and at least 2" from the edge of the member.

Wall Systems

Whether they are interior or exterior, load-bearing or nonload-bearing, made from wood studs or metal, walls must meet very specific construction standards to ensure that they do not impede the structural integrity of a house and do their part to prevent fires from spreading within wall cavities. Nevertheless, be aware that designing and building load-bearing walls is a closely regulated process. **In most cases, you would be well advised to consult a structural engineer to make sure that the lumber sizes and spacing conform to code standards and that any beams are appropriately sized, properly supported, and made from qualifying materials.**

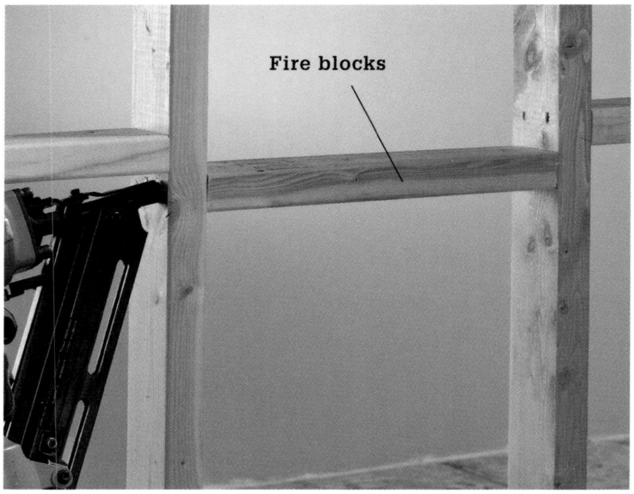

Even nonload-bearing walls must conform to construction codes, including fireblocking.

Wood Nailing Definitions ▸

Using the proper size and type of nail and installing the nail where required is critical to the structural integrity of a building. Analysis of building failures frequently shows that failures result from improper nailing. The following are definitions of nailing methods and installation requirements contained in the IRC.

Edge spacing: Edge spacing means installing a nail every indicated number of inches around the perimeter of a wood structural panel. If blocking is required by the IRC, then edge spacing includes nailing the panel to the blocking.

Endnailing: An endnail is driven straight into the end of the member. An example of endnailing is attaching studs to sill plates through the sill plate before the sill plate is attached to the foundation or subfloor.

Facenailing: A facenail is driven straight into the member, often into the long dimension of the member. Examples of facenailing include ceiling and floor joist laps over supports and attaching wood panels to studs and joists.

Intermediate spacing: Intermediate spacing means installing a nail every indicated number of inches at studs or joists in the interior area of a wood structural panel.

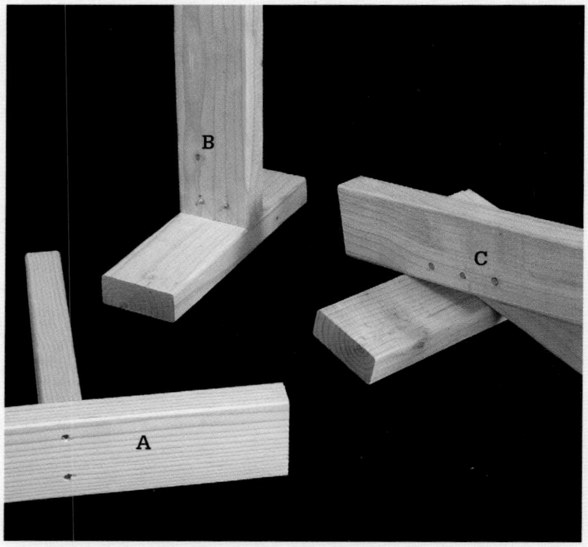

Endnailing (A), toenailing (B) , facenailing (C).

O. C. means "on center." Install nails every indicated number of inches.

Toenailing: A toe nail is driven at an angle through the edge of the member. Toenailing usually occurs when one member is already attached in place, such as when a stud is toenailed to a sill plate that is already attached.

Wood Nailing Requirements

WOOD NAILING GENERAL INSTALLATION REQUIREMENTS

1. Use nails that are at least as thick and long as indicated in the following tables. Common nails and box nails are often thicker and longer than hand-driven sinker nails and pneumatic-driven nails commonly used in residential construction. You cannot directly substitute sinker and gun nails for common, box, and deformed shank nails. Substitution of sinker and gun nails should be based on engineering analysis.

WOOD NAILING TO FRAMING MATERIALS

1. Use Tables 10, 11, and 12 to determine the type of nail and nail spacing for attaching wood framing materials to other wood framing materials in other than high wind and seismic design areas. Refer to the general codes for fastener type, quantity, and spacing in high wind and seismic design areas.

Install nails around the edge of wood panels and at intermediate supports at the required on-center spacing.

Table 10: Nailing OSB and Plywood Sheathing to Framing ▸

Panel thickness	Nail type	Edge spacing	Intermediate spacing
3/8 to 1/2"	6d common (2 × 0.113") subfloor & wall 8d common (2½ × 0.131") roof	6" o.c.	12" o.c.
19/32 to 1"	8d common (2½ × 0.131")	6" o.c.	12" o.c.
1⅛ to 1¼"	10d common (3 × 0.148") or 8d deformed (2½ × 0.120")	6" o.c.	12" o.c.

Table 11: Nailing One-piece Subfloor to Framing ▸

Panel thickness	Nail type	Edge spacing	Intermediate spacing
¾" & less	6d deformed (2 × 0.120") or 8d common (2½ × 0.131")	6" o.c.	12" o.c.
⅞ to 1"	8d common (2½ × 0.131") or 8d deformed (2½ × 0.120")	6" o.c.	12" o.c.
1⅛ to 1¼"	10d common (3 × 0.148") or 8d deformed (2½ × 0.120")	6" o.c.	12" o.c.

Table 12: Nailing Structural Lumber ▸

Lumber description, nailing method	Number/type of fasteners	Fastener spacing
FLOOR NAILING		
Joist to sill, girder, plate, toenail	3-8d (2½ × 0.113")	–
Rim joist to top plate, toenail	8d (2½ × 0.113")	6" o.c.
Ledger supporting joists	3-16d (3-½ × 0.135")	under each joist
Built-up beams, using 2"-thick lumber	3-16d (3-½ × 0.135")	nail each layer: staggered 32" o.c. at top and bottom and 2 nails at ends and at each splice
WALL NAILING		
Sole plate to joist or blocking, facenail	16d (3½ × 0.135")	16" o.c.
Sole plate to joist or blocking at braced wall panels, facenail	3-16d (3½ × 0.135")	16" o.c.
Stud to sole plate, toenail	3-8d (2 ½ × 0.113") or 2-16d (3½ × 0.135")	–
Stud to top or sole plate, endnail	2-16d (3½ × 0.135")	–
Double studs, facenail	10d (3 × 0.128")	24" o.c.
Double top plate, facenail	10d (3 × 0.128")	24" o.c.
Double top plate, minimum 24", offset of end joints, facenail in lap area	8-16d (3½ × 0.135")	–
Built-up corner studs	10d (3 × 0.128")	24" o.c.
Top plates, laps at corners and intersections, facenail	2-10d (3 × 0.128")	–
Headers: 2-piece with ½" spacer, 2-piece	16d (3½ × 0.135")	16" o.c.
Along each edge header to stud, toenail	10d (3 × 0.128")	–
1" let-in brace to each stud and plate, facenail	2-8d (2½ × 0.113")	–
ROOF NAILING		
Blocking between joists or rafters to top plate, toenail	3-8d (2½ × 0.113")	–
Ceiling joist to plate, toenail	3-8d (2½ × 0.113")	–
Ceiling joist, lap over partitions, facenail	3-10d (3 × 0.128")	–
Ceiling joist to parallel rafters, facenail	3-10d (3 × 0.128")	–
Collar tie to rafter and joist, facenail or 1¼" by 20-gauge strap	3-10d (3 × 0.128")	–
Rafter to plate, toenail	2-16d (3½ × 0.135")	–
Rafters to ridge, valley, or hip rafters, toenail	4-16d (3½ × 0.135")	–
Rafters to ridge, valley, or hip rafters, facenail	3-16d (3½ × 0.135")	–

Wall Stud Size & Spacing

WOOD GRADES USED IN WALL CONSTRUCTION

1. Use Number 3, standard, or stud grade wood for most loadbearing walls not more than 10 feet tall. Do not use this wood for load-bearing walls more than 10 feet tall. Use Number 2 grade or better lumber for walls more than 10 feet tall.
2. You may use utility grade wood for nonload-bearing walls.
3. You may use utility grade wood for loadbearing exterior walls that support only a ceiling and a roof if the studs are spaced not more than 16 inches on center and the walls are not more than eight feet tall.
4. Refer to general codes for more information about other wall height and stud spacing combinations.
5. Refer to general codes for wall height and stud spacing requirements in high wind, heavy snow load, and seismic design areas.

Wall studs taller than 10 ft. require No. 2 or better grade construction lumber. Shorter walls may be built with cheaper No. 3 grade in most cases.

STUD SIZE & SPACING FOR LOAD-BEARING WALLS NOT MORE THAN 10 FEET TALL

1. Use Table 13 to determine stud size and spacing when the unsupported vertical height of an exterior load-bearing wall is not more than 10 feet. Measure vertical height between points of horizontal (lateral) support between studs. Vertical wall height is usually measured between the bottom of the sole or sill plate and the bottom of the floor or ceiling. Consult a qualified engineer before measuring unsupported vertical wall height between points other than at floor levels.

Table 13: Stud Size & Spacing for Load-bearing Walls ▸

Stud size (inches)	Column 1 Maximum stud spacing supporting only one floor, <u>or</u> supporting a ceiling and roof with or without a habitable attic	Column 2 Maximum stud spacing supporting one floor and a ceiling and roof with or without a habitable attic	Column 3 Maximum stud spacing supporting two floors and a ceiling and roof with or without a habitable attic
2 × 4	24"	16"	not allowed
2 × 4	24"	24"	16"

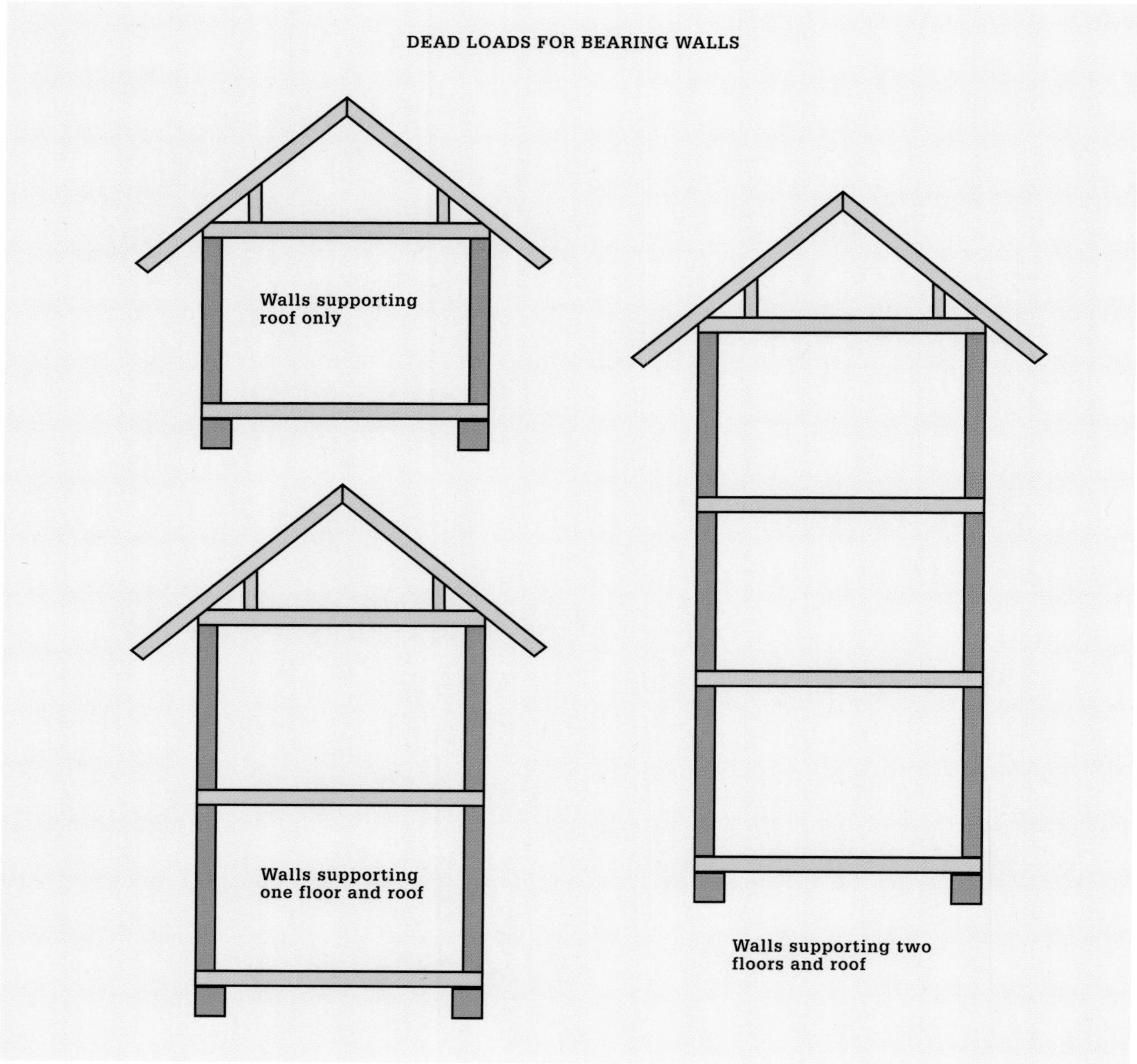
DEAD LOADS FOR BEARING WALLS
Walls supporting roof only
Walls supporting one floor and roof
Walls supporting two floors and roof

Stud size and spacing depends on what the studs are supporting.

STUD SIZE & SPACING FOR NONLOAD-BEARING WALLS

1. Use Table 14 to determine stud size and spacing for nonload-bearing walls. Measure vertical height between points of horizontal (lateral) support between studs. Vertical wall height is usually measured between the bottom of the sole or sill plate and the bottom of the floor or ceiling. Consult a qualified engineer before measuring unsupported vertical wall height between points other than at floor levels.

Table 14: Stud Size & Spacing for Nonload-bearing Walls ▸

Stud size	Maximum stud height	Maximum stud spacing
2 × 4	14 ft.	24"
2 × 4	20 ft.	24"

TOP & BOTTOM PLATE CONSTRUCTION

1. Use at least two 2-inch (nominal) depth top plates that are at least as wide as the studs at the top of load-bearing walls. Example: use two 2 × 4 top plates on top of a 2 × 4 wall and use 2 × 6 top plates on top of 2 × 6 walls.
2. Offset joints where two pieces of top plate meet by at least 24 inches. You do not need to place a stud under a joint in a top plate unless the stud would be placed there for other reasons.
3. Lap one top plate from one wall over the top plate of an intersecting wall at the wall corners and at the intersection with load-bearing walls.
4. You may use a single top plate at the top of nonload-bearing walls.
5. You may use a single top plate on load-bearing walls if wall joints and corners and top plate end joints are secured with at least a three-inch by six-inch by 0.036-inch thick galvanized steel plate secured by at least six 8d nails on each side of the connection; and if the supported framing above (such as joists or rafters) is not more than one inch from the stud below. This exception is not commonly used.
6. Install one galvanized metal strap at least 0.054-inch thick and 1½ inches wide on a top plate if it is cut more than 50 percent of its actual depth. These metal straps are sometimes called FHA straps. It is not necessary to install a strap on both top plates for purposes of this section. You may need to install shield plate to protect plumbing pipes and electrical wires.
7. Extend the strap at least six inches beyond each side of the cut opening. Secure the strap with at least eight 16d nails on each side of the strap.
8. Apply this strap requirement to top plates in exterior and interior load-bearing walls.
9. You do not need to install the strap if wood structural panel sheathing covers the entire side of the wall with the notched or cut top plates.
10. Use at least one 2-inch (nominal) depth bottom plate that is at least as wide as the studs.

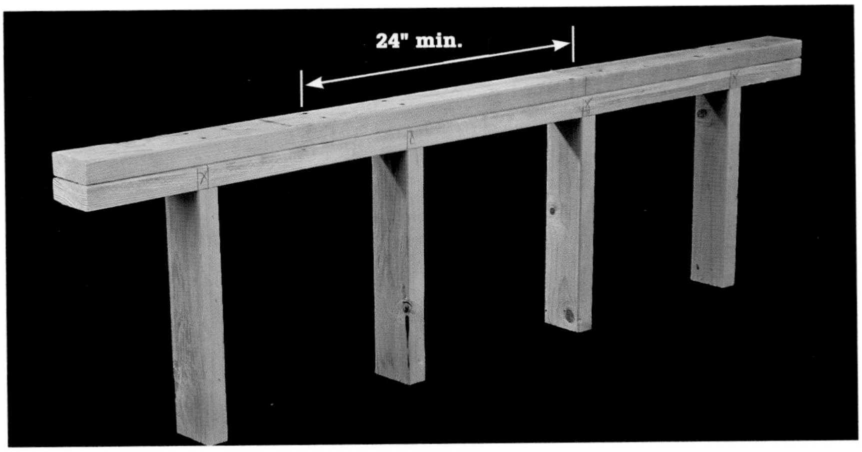

Offset joints where 2 top plates meet by at least 24".

Install a strap across 1 top plate when it is notched more than half its width. Install another strap or a shield plate when required to protect pipes and electrical wires.

Notches & Holes in Wall Studs

BORING & NOTCHING DEFINITIONS

A bore is a hole drilled in a stud or joist. Use the actual dimensions to determine the depth of framing lumber and when calculating the maximum hole diameter.

A notch is a piece cut from the smaller dimension of framing lumber such as a stud or joist. Use the actual dimensions to determine the depth of framing lumber and when calculating the maximum notch depth. Actual dimensions are the dimensions of framing lumber after finishing at the mill. Example: the nominal dimensions of a 2 × 6 are two inches by six inches and the actual dimensions, after finishing, are about 1½ inches by 5½ inches.

WOOD STUD NOTCHING

1. Notch a load-bearing stud not more than 25 percent of its actual depth. Example: notch a 2 × 6 load-bearing stud not more than 1⅜ inches.
2. Notch a nonload-bearing stud not more than 40 percent of its actual depth. Example: notch a 2 × 6 nonload-bearing stud not more than 2¼ inches.

WOOD STUD BORING

1. Bore a hole in a single load-bearing stud not more than 40 percent of its actual depth. Example: bore a 2 × 6 load-bearing stud not more than 2¼ inches in diameter.
2. You may bore holes in load-bearing studs not more than 60 percent of their actual depth if you install a double stud and do not bore more than two successive studs.
3. Bore a hole in a nonload-bearing stud not more than 60 percent of its actual depth. Example: bore a 2 × 6 nonload-bearing stud not more than 3¼ inches in diameter.
4. Leave at least ⅝ inch of undisturbed wood between the hole and the stud edge.
5. Do not place a hole and a notch in the same horizontal section of the stud.

Notch a loadbearing stud not more than 25 percent of its actual depth.

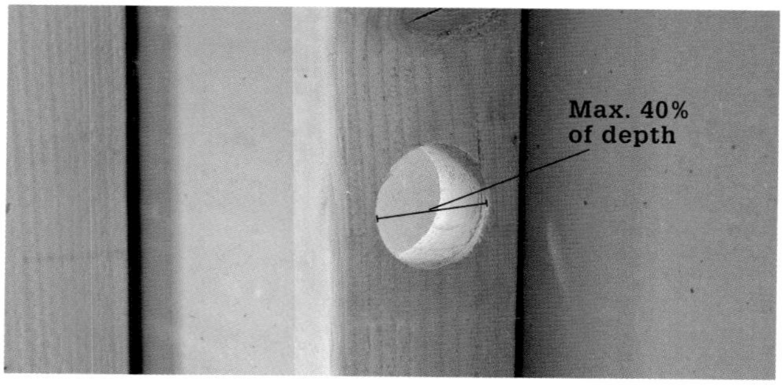

Drill a hole in a loadbearing stud not more than 40 percent of its actual depth.

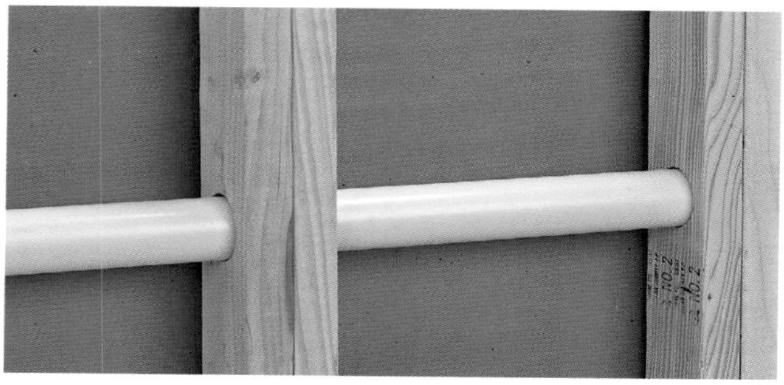

Double two load-bearing studs if the holes are not more than 60 percent of their actual depth.

VIOLATION! Do not locate a notch and a hole in the same part of the stud.

Cripple Wall Framing

Cripple walls are often combined with egress window framing. The cap plate on the block wall supports the floor trusses for this addition. The 2 × 6 construction allows the project to meet minimum wall insulation codes.

CRIPPLE WALL REQUIREMENTS

1. Install cripple walls using studs that are at least the same width as the wall studs above.
2. Frame cripple walls more than four feet tall as though they are full height walls. This means using the stud sizes and framing requirements previously described. Example: if full height wall studs on the same floor level as the cripple wall are 2 × 6, use 2 × 6 studs for the cripple wall.
3. Brace cripple walls as required for the wall above, except: (a) increase the required wall brace length by 1.15, and (b) decrease the distance between wall braces to 18 feet. Example: if the cripple wall is a two-foot tall basement wall and the wall brace length for the first story wall above is 4 feet, brace at least 4.6 feet (3 × 1.15) of the cripple wall.
4. Install sheathing that covers at least one full side of a cripple wall less than 14 inches tall. Fasten the sheathing to both the top and bottom plates.
5. Support cripple walls on a continuous foundation.
6. You may substitute solid blocking for a framed and sheathed cripple wall less than 14 inches tall.
7. Anchor cripple walls to the foundation like other framed walls.
8. Refer to the IRC for additional bracing requirements in seismic design areas.

Cripple Wall Definition ▸

A cripple wall is a framed wall that is less than one story tall. Cripple walls often occur with basement foundations that are stepped down to follow finished grade, and they may occur in split-level homes.

Cripple walls may be load-bearing or nonload-bearing. This bearing version is used to bridge a gap between the foundation wall and the first floor framing members. Anchor cripple walls to the foundation and brace as required.

Wall Bracing

General codes present many methods and rules for framed wall bracing. This section discusses some common wall bracing methods and some general rules about how to install them. Refer to general codes and consult with qualified professionals for more information about wall bracing, particularly when dealing with wall bracing in high wind, seismic design, and heavy snow load areas.

WALL BRACE AND BRACED WALL DEFINITIONS

A braced wall (braced wall line) is an interior or an exterior wall that contains the required length of approved wall braces (braced wall panels). Most exterior walls and some interior walls are braced walls. A wood structural panel (such as OSB) is a common example of an approved wall brace. Be careful not to confuse the similar terms braced wall and wall brace. A braced wall begins and ends where one braced wall intersects perpendicular braced walls.

WALL BRACING METHOD SELECTION CRITERIA

1. Select an appropriate wall bracing method based on factors that include: (a) the mean roof height above grade (less than 30 feet), and (b) the height from the eaves to the roof ridge (less than 10 feet), and (c) the height of each story (less than 10 feet), and (d) the seismic design area, and (e) the wind speed design area (less than 90 mph), (f) and the wind exposure category (B), and (g) not more than less than two parallel braced walls connected to one perpendicular braced wall.
2. Wall bracing requirements may increase or decrease when factors are outside the indicated ranges. The indicated ranges in the factors above will accommodate most homes in most areas of the continental United States.
3. The wall bracing information in this section applies only to one and two-family homes, not to townhomes.
4. The wall bracing information in this section applies only when braced walls are straight and are parallel or perpendicular to each other. Refer to the IRC when bracing angled walls.

WALL BRACING GENERAL INSTALLATION REQUIREMENTS

1. Install a wall brace at each end of a braced wall. Most exterior walls and some interior walls are braced walls.
2. Begin the wall brace not more than 12½ feet from each braced wall end. Begin the wall braces at each braced wall end so that the total distance of both wall braces from the ends of the braced wall is not more than 12½ feet. Example: the wall brace at one end of a braced wall begins 5 feet from the braced wall end and the wall brace at the other end of a braced wall begins 6 feet from the braced wall end. The sum of 5 feet and 6 feet is 11 feet. This is less than 12 feet and is acceptable.
3. Install a wall brace at not less than 25 feet on center along a braced wall when the distance between braces exceeds 25 feet.
4. Install wall bracing material that covers at least the length (in feet) of the braced wall. Refer to the IRC when selection factors are outside the ranges indicated in the previous section.
5. Fasten wall braces to framing and fasten framing (such as roof trusses and rafters) to braced walls according to the brace manufacturer's instructions. Refer to the IRC for additional fastening requirements when selection factors are outside the ranges indicated in the previous section.

Metal strap let-in wall bracing.

Table 15: Minimum Total Length of Braced Wall ▸

Stories above braced wall	Distance between braced walls (feet)	Wood structural panels, hardboard siding panels (feet)	Let-in brace (feet)
0	10	2.0	3.5
0	20	4.0	7.0
0	30	5.5	9.5
1	10	4.0	7.0
1	20	7.5	13.0
1	30	10.5	18.5
2	10	6.0	No
2	20	11.0	No
2	30	15.5	No

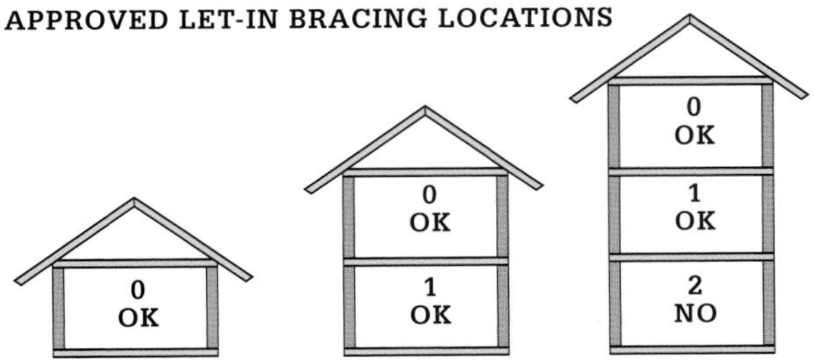

6. Install at least ½" drywall as required in Chapter 7 on the interior of braced walls. You may omit the drywall if you multiply the bracing percentage by 1.5.
7. You may use different wall bracing methods within the same braced wall and you may use different bracing methods on different stories. Example: you may use let-in bracing at one end of a braced wall and structural panel bracing on the other end. Use the highest required bracing length in the table when using different bracing methods in the same braced wall.
8. Install at least 48 inches of wall bracing in every braced wall regardless of the values in codes and any allowed adjustments to those values.
9. Refer to the IRC when braced walls intersect with other braced walls at other than a 90° angle.

LET-IN WALL BRACING

1. Install let-in wall bracing using a continuous wood 1 × 4, or an approved metal strap, cut into the studs diagonally from the top to the bottom plate at an angle at least 45 degrees and not more than 60 degrees from horizontal.
2. Secure wood 1 × 4 bracing to each stud using two 8d nails. Secure metal strap bracing according to the brace manufacturer's instructions.

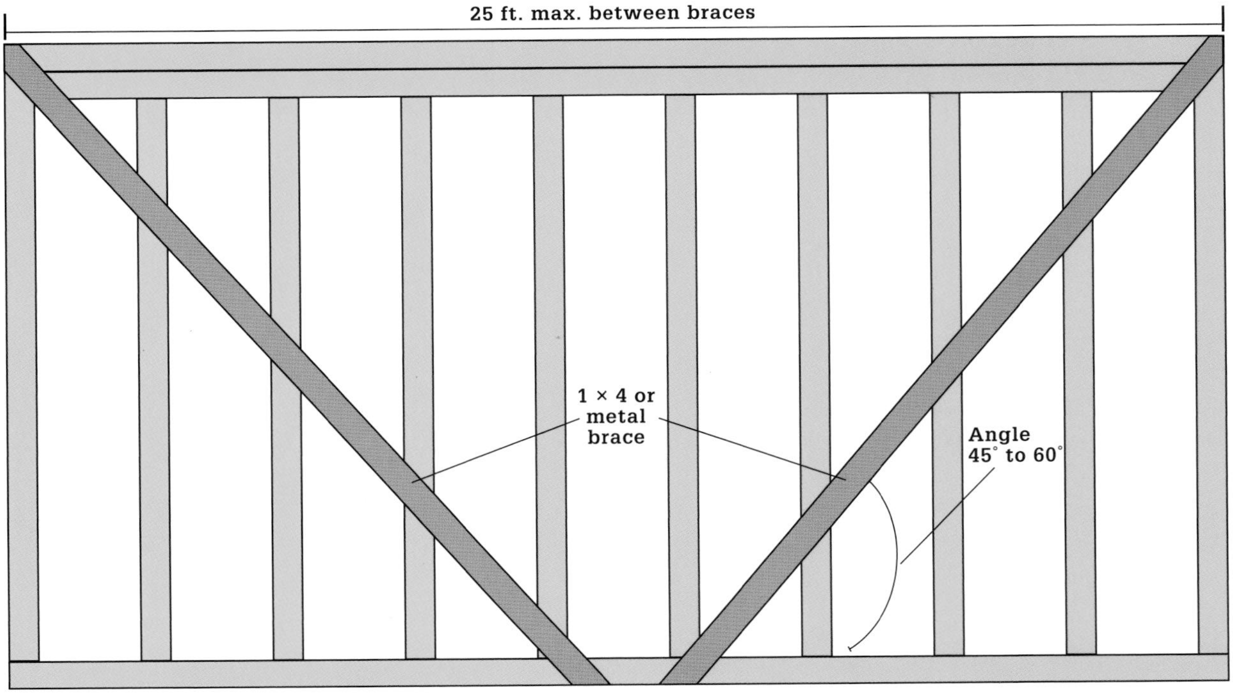

Let-in wall bracing installation and approved locations.

Wood Structural Panel Wall Bracing

1. Install wood structural panel wall bracing using 4 × 8 or 4 × 9 panels at least ⅜-inch thick.
2. Install panels that are at least 48 inches wide and cover at least three stud bays for studs spaced 16 inches on center.
3. Secure ⅜-inch thick wood structural panel bracing to studs using at least 6d common nails spaced not more than 6 inches on center at panel edges and 12 inches on center at intermediate supports. Secure 7⁄16-inch thick panels using 8d common nails spaced as previously described.
4. Install solid blocking where panel joints occur between studs to maintain fastener spacing. Use at least 1½-inch thick wood for blocking. The blocking is usually the same dimensions as the studs.Example: 2 × 6 blocking is normally used with 2 × 6 studs, although 2 × 4 blocking is acceptable.
5. You may use wood structural panel wall bracing on all stories and in all wind speed and seismic design areas.

Wood structural panel wall bracing may be used on all stories and in all seismic and wind design areas.

Fireblocking

Fireblocking (also called firestopping) limits the spread of fires between stories in concealed vertical wood-framed walls. Concealed openings in wood-framed walls can act like a chimney, providing fire an easy and rapid path between stories. Lack of fireblocking increases the chance of property damage and loss of life during a fire. Do not confuse fireblocking with draftstopping (see page 62). Draftstopping limits the horizontal spread of fires in floor/ceiling assemblies. Fireblocking limits the vertical spread of fires between stories.

WHERE FIREBLOCKING IS REQUIRED

1. Install fireblocking in any concealed wall space if an opening exists that allows fire to spread from one story to another or from a lower story into the attic. Examples of such openings include: openings for plumbing pipes, openings for electrical wires and conduit, HVAC duct chases between stories, laundry chutes, and openings at the tops of framed columns, niches, and arches.
2. Install fireblocking in concealed wall spaces at every ceiling and floor level. An intact top and bottom plate usually provides fireblocking in platform framing.
3. Install fireblocking where concealed vertical and horizontal wall spaces intersect. Examples of concealed horizontal spaces include soffits for kitchen cabinets and recessed vanity lights, and drop ceilings.
4. Install fireblocking between stair stringers at the top and bottom of each flight of stairs.
5. Install fireblocking around chimneys and flues where they intersect framing at floor and ceiling levels.
6. Install fireblocking in concealed wall spaces if the concealed space is open for more than 10 feet horizontally. A long concealed horizontal wall space is rare in residential construction. Examples of framing that could produce a concealed horizontal wall space include some methods of framing large arched openings between rooms, and walls built using two rows of staggered studs.

Install fireblocking in framed columns, framed arches, and similar openings between stories.

Install sprayfoam fireblocking at penetrations for wires, pipes, and ducts. Many jurisdictions require listed caulk, not spray foam.

FIREBLOCKING MATERIALS AND INSTALLATION

1. You may use any of the following fireblocking materials:
   (a) two-inch thick lumber (example: a 2 × 4), or
   (b) two pieces of one-inch thick lumber with staggered joints (example: two 1 × 4), or
   (c) at least $^{23}/_{32}$-inch thick wood structural panels, or
   (d) at least ¾-inch thick particleboard, or
   (e) at least ½-inch thick drywall, or
   (f) at least ¼-inch thick cement-based millboard, or
   (g) unfaced batts or blankets of mineral wool or fiberglass insulation if it is secured in place.
2. Install backing at any joints in fireblocking material when using wood structural panels or particleboard. Use the same fireblocking material for the backing. Example: if a joint exists in OSB fireblocking material, place another piece of the same OSB material over the joint. Most general codes do not state how far to extend the backing.
3. Do not use loose fill insulation as a fireblocking material unless it is specifically tested and approved for the intended location and installation method.
4. Repair fireblocking that is damaged or penetrated by pipes, ducts, or other materials.

Windows & Doors

Replacing a window or door with one of the same size and type usually does not require a building permit. However, building codes do specify standards for flashing and sealing around the window or door and these should be followed. If you are adding a new window or door to a new wall, or if you are enlarging or reducing the opening size for the window or door, a permit very likely is required.

Always comply with the manufacturer's instructions for flashing. In general, sill flashing made from formable material (usually self-adhesive) is installed in the opening prior to the window frame.

FLASHING & INSTALLATION GENERAL REQUIREMENTS

1. Install and flash windows according to the manufacturer's written installation instructions. The manufacturer must provide written installation instructions with each window. Manufacturers usually comply with this requirement by attaching a sticker on each window.

Important information about windows, including energy efficiency and installation instructions, is usually affixed to the new unit by the manufacturer. Be sure to remove and save this information and to follow all installation directions exactly.

Housewrap ▸

Housewrap helps protect the house from its worst enemies—water and cold air drafts. Covering exterior walls with housewrap before installing siding can also reduce your energy bills.

WINDOWS SIX FEET ABOVE ADJACENT SURFACE

1. Install operable windows so that the lowest edge of the window opening is at least 24 inches above the finished floor, if the lowest edge of the window opening is more than 72 inches above finished grade or the surface below. This provision applies to all operable windows regardless of where they are located in the home. This provision does not apply to fixed windows and it does not apply if the window opening will not allow a four-inch diameter sphere to pass through the opening.
2. You may install an operable window with an opening less than 24 inches above the finished floor if: (a) you install a device that limits the window opening size so that a four-inch diameter sphere cannot pass through the window, or if (b) you install a fall protection device. Opening size limit and fall protection devices attached to emergency escape windows must be removable as described in the emergency escape opening section (see pages 28 to 29).

In a typical window installation, formable self-adhesive flashing is installed over the side nailing flanges after the window unit is installed. The head flashing is installed last.

Flash and seal the entire rough opening for a door before installing the door unit. Follow manufacturer's instructions for sealing around the door after it is installed and secured to the jambs.

ATTACHING WINDOWS & GLASS DOORS TO THE STRUCTURE

1. Attach windows and glass doors to the structure according to manufacturer's instructions. Use the following if manufacturer's instructions are not available.
2. Attach wood shims or bucks that are at least 1½ inches thick directly to openings for windows and glass doors in masonry and concrete, then attach the window and glass door to the shims or bucks.
3. Attach windows and glass doors directly to masonry and concrete window and glass door openings, when using wood shims or bucks that are less than 1½ inches thick.
4. Attach windows and glass doors directly to wood framing using common small thickness shims, when necessary.
5. You may use frame clips to attach windows and glass doors to concrete, masonry, and wood when allowed by manufacturer's installation instructions.
6. Use and install fasteners that adequately transfer the window and glass door loads to the structure.

Roof Systems

Although the installation of roof coverings and flashings are also covered by most building codes, the primary interest in roof systems falls in the structural area. The number and size of the rafters or trusses is a vital element of home design, as are the methods for fastening these elements to the house structure. If you live in a coastal area or any region that is prone to earthquakes or hurricanes, a separate set of codes exists for your roof system. Be sure to enforce its more rigorous standards when you build.

RIDGE, VALLEY & HIP RAFTER FRAMING

1. Install at least a one-inch (nominal thickness) ridgeboard at roof ridges in houses built with rafters (truss-built roofs do not have ridgeboards). Install a ridgeboard that is at least as deep as the (plumb) cut end of the rafter. Install rafters directly across from each other at the ridgeboard. You may omit the ridgeboard if you secure the rafters to each other with a gusset plate.
2. Install at least a two-inch (nominal thickness) hip rafter and valley rafter at all hips and valleys, including valleys formed when one roof is framed on top of another.
3. Support hip and valley rafters at the ridge with a brace to a load-bearing wall, or design the hip and valley rafters to bear the load at the ridge.
4. Toe nail rafters to the ridge and to valley and hip rafters using at least four 16d nails, or facenail rafters using at least three 16d nails. Toe nail rafters to the top plate using at least two 16d nails.
5. Design and support ridge, hip and valley rafters as beams, when the roof pitch is less than $\frac{3}{12}$.
6. Design and support the ridge as a beam and design the walls supporting the ridge board to bear the ridgeboard load, when framing cathedral and vaulted ceilings without ceiling joists and rafter ties.

A roof system comprises rafters or trusses that support roof sheathing. The sheathing is covered with an underlayment and roofing materials. Soffits, flashing, and ventilation are also important parts of the roof system.

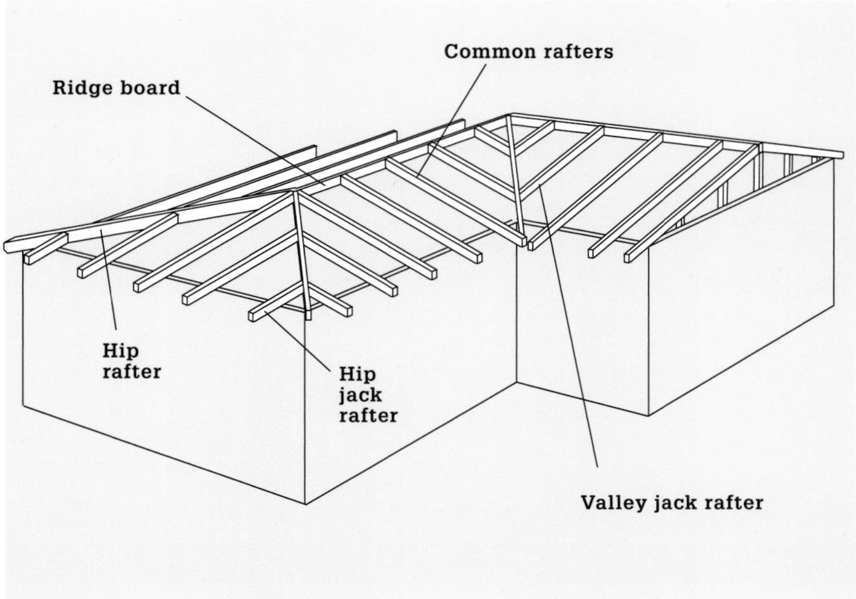

Rafters have specific names that are assigned according to their function in the roof system.

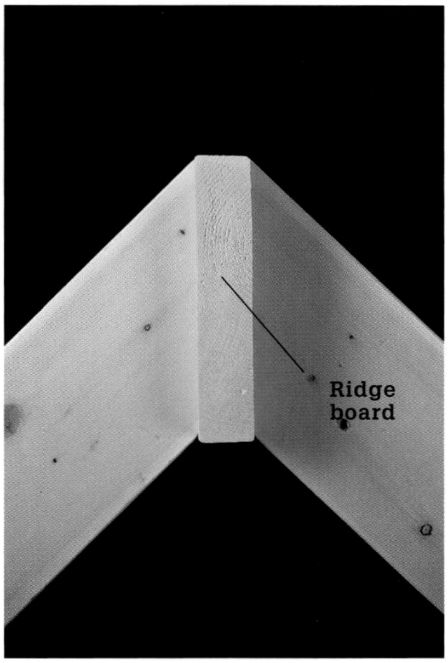

Position rafters across from each other on a ridgeboard or beam that is at least as deep as the rafter plumb cut.

PURLINS

1. You may use purlins to support rafters that would otherwise span a greater distance than allowed. Example: a properly installed purlin at the center of an 18-foot long rafter would allow you to use nine-feet as the rafter span distance.
2. Install purlins that are at least the same depth as the rafters they support. Example: use a 2 × 6 purlin to support a 2 × 6 rafter.
3. Use at least one 2 × 4 brace to carry the purlin load to a load-bearing wall. The purlin brace length should not exceed eight feet without additional bracing (usually an additional 2 × 4 nailed to the brace). Purlin braces should bear on a load-bearing wall and may not slope at less than a 45° angle from horizontal. Space the purlin braces not more than four feet apart.

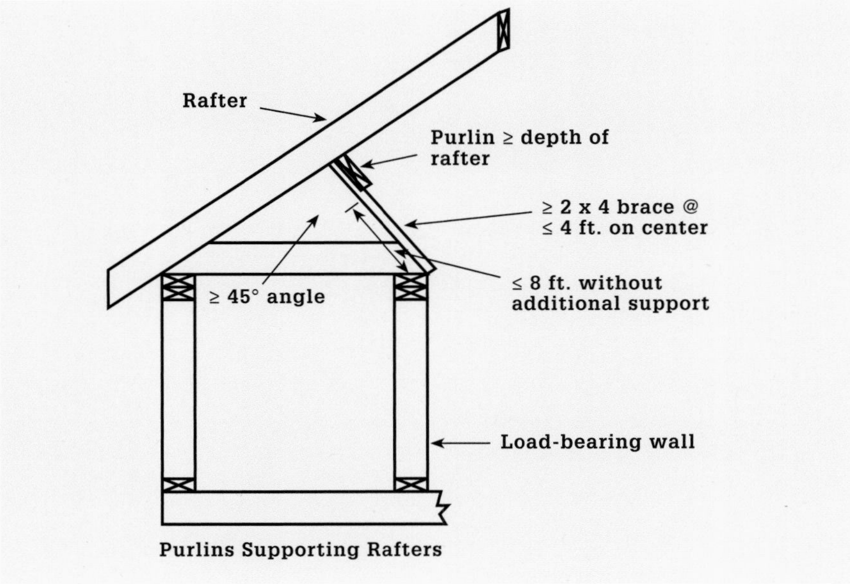

Use purlins to support rafters if the rafter span is longer than allowed.

COLLAR TIES

1. Install 1 × 4 or larger collar ties or use a 1¼ inch × 20-gauge ridge strap between rafters to resist ridge uplift by wind force. You may omit collar ties in vaulted and cathedral ceilings when you design and support the ridge as a beam.
2. Space collar ties not more than four feet on center.
3. Locate collar ties in the upper one-third of the attic space.
4. Connect collar ties and rafters using at least three 10d nails, facenailed.
5. Verify collar tie requirements with the local building official and with the Wood Frame Construction Manual in high wind design areas, when the roof slope is less than 3/12, and when the roof span is greater than 36 feet.

RAFTER & CEILING JOIST BEARING ON SUPPORT

1. Install rafters and ceiling joists with at least 1½ inches of the rafter or joist bearing on supporting wood members (such as a top plate or a valley rafter) and at least three inches of the rafter or joist bearing on masonry or concrete.
2. Toe nail rafters to the top plate using at least two 16d nails.

RAFTER & CEILING JOIST BRIDGING & LATERAL SUPPORT

1. Install bridging on rafters and ceiling joists deeper than 2 × 12 (six to one depth to thickness ratio). Space bridging not more than every eight feet. Bridging should consist of solid full depth blocking, wood or metal diagonal bridging, or by nailing at least a 1 × 3 wood strip to each rafter or ceiling joist. Bridging is required by some building officials on ceiling joists smaller than 2 × 12.
2. Install lateral support at bearing points on rafters and ceiling joists deeper than 2 × 10 (five to one depth to thickness ratio).

CEILING JOIST NAILING TO RAFTER

1. Toe nail all rafters to the top plate using at least two 16d nails regardless of whether the rafter is or is not parallel to the ceiling joist.
2. Connect one rafter to one ceiling joist when the ceiling joists are parallel to the rafters. Face nail these ceiling joists to rafters using 16d common nails or 40d box nails. (See Table 16, page 82.)
3. Connect one rafter to one rafter tie and connect the rafter tie to a ceiling joist when the ceiling joists are not parallel to the rafters. Face nail these rafters to rafter ties and the rafter ties to ceiling joists using 16d common nails or 40d box nails. Use 2 × 4 or larger lumber for rafter ties. Connecting rafters to ceiling joists or to rafter ties helps the walls resist outward thrust pressure from the roof.
4. Lap ceiling joists that meet over interior walls or beams at least 3 inches and face-nail them together. You may butt the ends of ceiling joists together over interior walls or beams and toe nail the ceiling joists to the supporting member using three 10d nails if the ceiling joists are not designed to resist rafter lateral thrust. Ceiling joists are often designed to resist rafter lateral thrust, so this butt end exception may not apply.

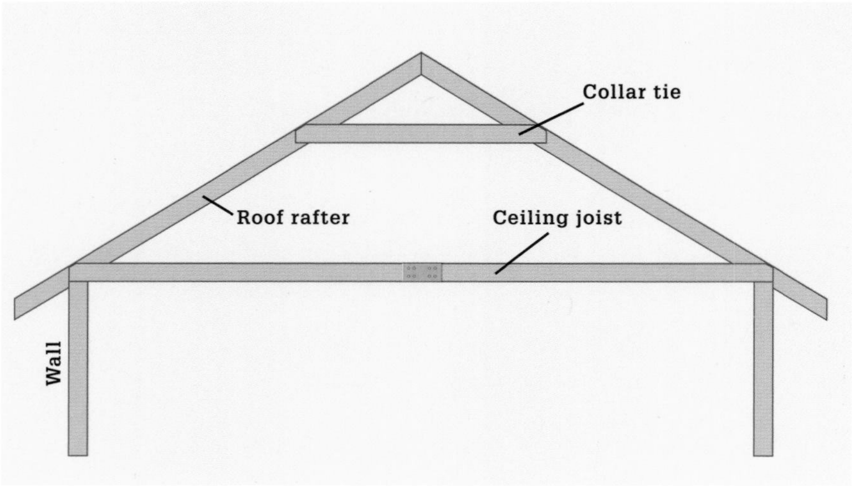

Install collar ties in the upper ⅓ of the attic spaced every 4 ft.

Connect one ceiling joist to one rafter when the ceiling joists and rafters are parallel.

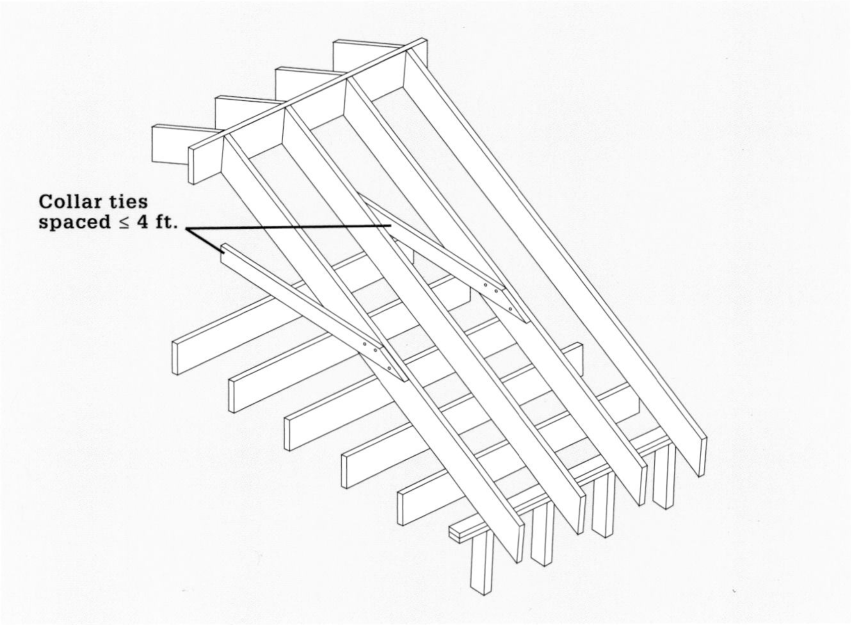

Connect one collar tie to one rafter and to one ceiling joist when the ceiling joists and rafters are perpendicular.

CEILING JOIST NAILING TO RAFTER EXCEPTIONS

1. Note the following exceptions to the quantity of nails required by codes:

(a) you may reduce the required quantity of nails by 25% if the nails are clinched (the pointed ends sticking out from the wood are bent over),

(b) you may use fewer fasteners if you support the ridge board on load-bearing walls or if you design and support the ridge as a beam,

(c) you may use a smaller roof span column if you install purlins to support the rafters, Example: if you install purlins at the center of rafters with a roof span of 24 feet, you may reduce the roof span by 50% and use the 12 feet roof span column,

(d) you may reduce the actual rafter slope by one-third if you substitute rafter ties for ceiling joists, Example: if the actual rafter slope is 9/12, use 6/12 as the adjusted rafter slope, but because there is no 6/12 slope row, use the nearest more conservative 5/12 row,

(e) increase the quantity of nails in the table if the ceiling joists or rafter ties are not located at the bottom of the attic space.

Table 16: Nail Quantities Ceiling Joists & Rafter Ties to Rafters ▸

		ground snow load (psf)															
		20				30				50				70			
	rafter	roof span (feet)															
rafter slope	spacing (inches)	12	20	28	36	12	20	28	36	12	20	28	36	12	20	28	36
3/12	12	4	6	8	10	4	6	8	11	5	8	12	15	6	11	15	20
	16	5	8	10	13	5	8	11	14	6	11	15	20	8	14	20	26
	24	7	11	15	21	7	11	16	21	9	16	23	30	12	21	30	39
4/12	12	3	5	6	8	3	5	6	8	4	6	9	11	5	8	12	15
	16	4	6	8	10	4	6	8	11	5	8	12	15	6	11	15	20
	24	5	8	12	15	5	9	12	16	7	12	17	22	9	16	23	29
5/12	12	3	4	5	6	3	4	5	7	3	5	7	9	4	7	9	12
	16	3	5	6	8	3	5	7	9	4	7	9	12	5	9	12	16
	24	4	7	9	12	4	7	10	13	6	10	14	18	7	13	18	23
7/12	12	3	4	4	5	3	3	3	5	3	4	5	7	3	5	7	9
	16	3	4	5	6	3	4	4	6	3	5	7	9	4	6	9	11
	24	3	5	7	9	3	5	5	9	4	7	10	13	5	9	13	17
9/12	12	3	3	4	4	3	3	3	4	3	3	4	5	3	4	5	7
	16	3	4	4	5	3	3	3	5	3	4	5	7	3	5	7	9
	24	3	4	6	7	3	4	4	7	3	6	8	10	4	7	10	13
12/12	12	3	3	3	3	3	3	3	3	3	3	3	4	3	3	4	5
	16	3	3	4	4	3	3	3	4	3	3	4	5	3	4	5	7
	24	3	4	4	5	3	3	3	6	3	4	6	8	3	6	8	10

RAFTER SPAN MEASUREMENT & SPAN ADJUSTMENT FOR CEILING JOIST LOCATION

1. Measure common rafter spans horizontally beginning at the exterior wall and ending at the ridge board. Measure jack rafter spans horizontally beginning at the hip or valley rafter and ending at the ridgeboard. Do not measure rafter spans along the actual length of the rafter.
2. The rafter span tables assume that ceiling joists or rafter ties are located at or near the wall top plate. If the ceiling joists or rafter ties are located higher on the rafter, reduce the rafter spans in the tables using the following method. Measure the height of the ceiling joists or rafter ties above the top plate. This is the (HCJ). Measure the height of the ridge board above the top plate. This is the (HRR). Divide (HCJ) by (HRR) to calculate the ratio of the vertical height of the ceiling joists or rafter ties (HCJ) to the vertical height of the roof ridge (HRR). Reduce the rafter spans by the factor in Table 17.

Table 17: Rafter Span Reduction for Ceiling Joist Location ▸

HCJ/HRR	Rafter span distance reduction factor
0.33	0.67
0.25	0.76
0.20	0.83
0.167	0.90
0.133 or less	1.00

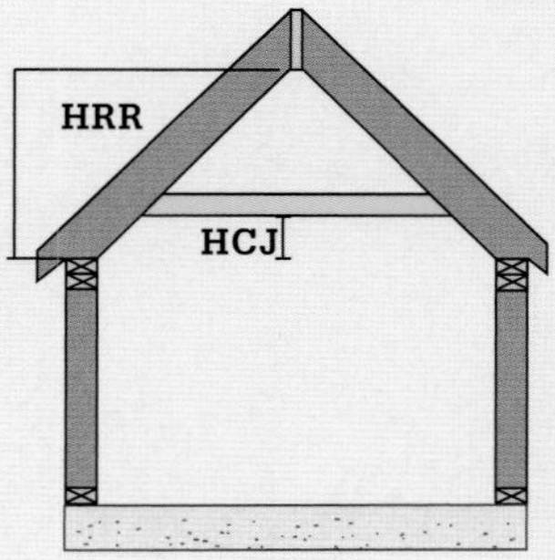

Adjust rafter spans when ceiling joists are not near the top plate.

Ceiling Joist & Rafter Span Definitions ▸

Selecting the correct size and type of ceiling joist requires that you know: (a) whether the attic may be used for limited storage, and (b) the roof loads imposed by the roof covering and by snow accumulation on the roof. These attic storage definitions help you determine which ceiling joist span table you should use. These definitions do not affect requirements for access to attics. Refer to the Attic Access section (page 87) for attic access requirements. Access to attics with limited storage may be through a scuttle-hole or by pull-down stairs. If attic access is by permanent stairs, then you should consider the attic to be habitable space and you should size the joists using the bedroom floor joist span tables rather than the ceiling span joist tables.

An attic without storage, built with joists and rafters, has less than 42" between the top of the ceiling joists and the bottom of the rafters. An attic without storage, built with trusses, has not more than two adjacent trusses with the same web configuration that could contain a cube not more than 42" wide and 24" tall located in the same plane (area) of the truss.

An attic with limited storage, built with joists and rafters, has at least 42" between the top of the ceiling joists and the bottom of the rafters. An attic with limited storage, built with trusses, has at least three adjacent trusses with the same web configuration that could contain a cube more than 42" wide and 24" tall located in the same plane (area) of the truss. An attic with limited storage is designed with an additional 10 pounds per square foot live load compared to an attic without storage. Verify the storage capacity of truss-built attics with the truss engineer before using the attic for storage.

Roof live and snow load. Use the roof live load 20 psf tables in areas where the design ground snow load is less than (<) 30 psf. Use the rafter snow load tables in areas of the country with ground snow loads of 30 psf or more. Verify the design ground snow load with the local building official.

Rafter dead loads. Use the 10 psf rafter dead load columns when using one layer of roof coverings such as fiberglass shingles and wood. Use the 20 psf rafter dead load columns when using roof coverings such as tile and slate.

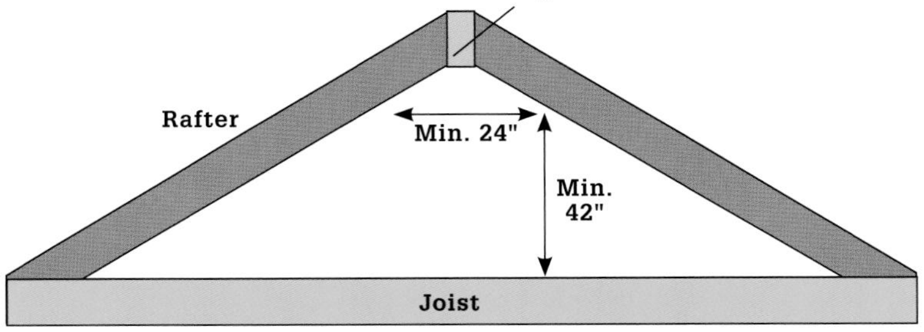

"Limited storage" in attic with rafters

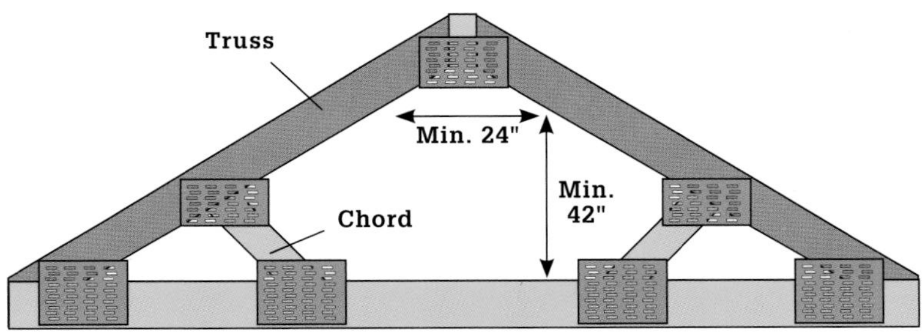

"Limited storage" in attic with trusses

"Limited storage" in an attic with joists and rafters requires a clear span of 42" high and 24" wide. In an attic built with trusses, you must have at least 3 consecutive bays where a 24" high by 42" wide cube can pass through without changing direction.

CEILING JOIST & RAFTER DEFLECTION

1. All ceiling joist spans in the tables use L/240 deflection, where L is the length of the joist or rafter in inches divided by 240.
2. All rafter spans in the tables use L/180 deflection.

CEILING JOIST & RAFTER SPAN TABLES (SELECTED)

1. Use the following tables to determine the maximum unsupported horizontal distance that ceiling joists and rafters can span.
2. Refer to the IRC or to the AF&PA Span Tables for Joists and Rafters to determine spans for lumber widths, species, grades, and snow load factors not in these tables.
3. These tables apply to roof systems framed using standard two-inch (nominal thickness) dimension lumber. An engineer must design roof truss systems.

Table 18: Ceiling Joist Spans 16" on Center Uninhabitable Attics, No Storage ▸

Species	Grade	2 × 6 ft.-in.	2 × 8 ft.-in.	2 × 10 ft.-in.
Douglas fir	2	17-8	23-0	>26-0
Douglas fir	3	13-9	17-5	21-3
Hem fir	2	16-6	21-9	>26-0
Hem fir	3	13-9	17-5	21-3
Southern pine	2	17-8	23-4	>26-0
Southern pine	3	14-9	18-9	22-2
Spruce-pine-fir	2	16-11	22-4	>26-0
Spruce-pine-fir	3	13-9	17-5	21-3

Table 19: Ceiling Joist Spans 24" on Center Uninhabitable Attics, No Storage ▸

Species	Grade	2 × 6 ft.-in.	2 × 8 ft.-in.	2 × 10 ft.-in.
Douglas fir	2	14-10	18-9	22-11
Douglas fir	3	11-2	14-2	17-4
Hem fir	2	14-5	18-6	22-7
Hem fir	3	11-2	14-2	17-4
Southern pine	2	15-6	20-1	23-11
Southern pine	3	12-0	15-4	18-1
Spruce-pine-fir	2	14-9	18-9	22-11
Spruce-pine-fir	3	11-2	14-2	17-4

Table 20: Ceiling Joist Spans 16" on Center Uninhabitable Attics With Limited Storage ▸

Species	Grade	2 × 6 ft.-in.	2 × 8 ft.-in.	2 × 10 ft.-in.
Douglas fir	2	12-10	16-3	22-11
Douglas fir	3	9-8	12-4	17-4
Hem fir	2	12-8	16-0	22-7
Hem fir	3	9-8	12-4	17-4
Southern pine	2	13-6	17-5	23-11
Southern pine	3	10-5	13-3	18-1
Spruce-pine-fir	2	12-10	16-3	22-11
Spruce-pine-fir	3	9-8	12-4	17-4

Table 21: Ceiling Joist Spans 24" on Center Uninhabitable Attics With Limited Storage ▸

Species	Grade	2 × 6 ft.-in.	2 × 8 ft.-in.	2 × 10 ft.-in.
Douglas fir	2	10-6	13-3	16-3
Douglas fir	3	7-11	10-0	12-3
Hem fir	2	10-4	13-1	16-0
Hem fir	3	7-11	10-0	12-3
Southern pine	2	11-0	14-2	16-11
Southern pine	3	8-6	10-10	12-10
Spruce-pine-fir	2	10-6	13-3	16-3
Spruce-pine-fir	3	7-11	10-0	12-3

Table 22: Rafter Spans 16" on Center, Roof Live Load 20 psf, Ceiling Not Attached ▸

Dead load	10 psf	10 psf	10 psf	20 psf	20 psf	20 psf
Species-grade	**2 × 6 ft.-in.**	**2 × 8 ft.-in.**	**2 × 10 ft.-in.**	**2 × 6 ft.-in.**	**2 × 8 ft.-in.**	**2 × 10 ft.-in.**
Douglas fir - 2	14-4	18-2	22-3	12-5	15-9	19-3
Douglas fir - 3	10-10	13-9	16-9	9-5	11-11	14-6
Hem fir - 2	14-2	17-11	21-11	12-3	15-6	18-11
Hem fir - 3	10-10	13-9	16-9	9-5	11-11	14-6
Southern pine - 2	15-1	19-5	23-2	13-0	16-10	20-1
Southern pine - 3	11-8	14-10	17-6	10-1	12-10	15-2
Spruce pine fir - 2	14-4	18-2	22-3	12-5	15-9	19-3
Spruce pine fir - 3	10-10	13-9	16-9	9-5	11-11	14-6

Table 23:Rafter Spans 24" on Center, Roof Live Load 20 psf, Ceiling Not Attached ▸

Dead load	10 psf	10 psf	10 psf	20 psf	20 psf	20 psf
Species-grade	**2 × 6 ft.-in.**	**2 × 8 ft.-in.**	**2 × 10 ft.-in.**	**2 × 6 ft.-in.**	**2 × 8 ft.-in.**	**2 × 10 ft.-in.**
Douglas fir - 2	11-9	14-10	18-2	10-2	12-10	15-8
Douglas fir - 3	8-10	11-3	13-8	7-8	9-9	11-10
Hem fir - 2	11-7	14-8	17-10	10-0	12-8	15-6
Hem fir - 3	8-10	11-3	13-8	7-8	9-9	11-10
Southern pine - 2	12-3	15-10	18-11	10-8	13-9	16-5
Southern pine - 3	9-6	12-1	14-4	8-3	10-6	12-5
Spruce pine fir - 2	11-9	14-10	18-2	10-2	12-10	15-8
Spruce pine fir - 3	8-10	11-3	13-8	7-8	9-9	11-10

Table 24: Rafter Spans 16" on Center, Roof Live Load 30 psf, Ceiling Not Attached ▸

Dead load	10 psf	10 psf	10 psf	20 psf	20 psf	20 psf
Species-grade	**2 × 6 ft.-in.**	**2 × 8 ft.-in.**	**2 × 10 ft.-in.**	**2 × 6 ft.-in.**	**2 × 8 ft.-in.**	**2 × 10 ft.-in.**
Douglas fir - 2	11-11	15-1	18-5	10-8	13-6	16-6
Douglas fir - 3	9-0	11-5	13-11	8-1	10-3	12-6
Hem fir - 2	11-9	14-11	18-2	10-6	13-4	16-3
Hem fir - 3	9-0	11-5	13-11	8-1	10-3	12-6
Southern pine - 2	12-6	16-2	19-3	11-2	14-5	17-3
Southern pine - 3	9-8	12-4	14-7	8-8	11-0	13-0
Spruce pine fir - 2	11-11	15-1	18-5	10-8	13-6	16-6
Spruce pine fir - 3	9-0	11-5	13-11	8-1	10-3	12-6

Table 25: Rafter Spans 24" on Center, Ground Snow Load 30 PSF, Ceiling not Attached ▸

Dead load	10 psf	10 psf	10 psf	20 psf	20 psf	20 psf
Species-grade	**2 × 6 ft.-in.**	**2 × 8 ft.-in.**	**2 × 10 ft.-in.**	**2 × 6 ft.-in.**	**2 × 8 ft.-in.**	**2 × 10 ft.-in.**
Douglas fir - 2	9-9	12-4	15-1	8-8	11-0	13-6
Douglas fir - 3	7-4	9-4	11-5	6-7	8-4	10-2
Hem fir - 2	9-7	12-2	14-10	8-7	10-10	13-3
Hem fir - 3	7-4	9-4	11-5	6-7	8-4	10-2
Southern pine - 2	10-2	13-2	15-9	9-2	11-9	14-1
Southern pine - 3	7-11	10-1	11-1	7-1	9-0	10-8
Spruce pine fir - 2	9-9	12-4	15-1	8-8	11-0	13-6
Spruce pine fir - 3	7-4	9-4	11-5	6-7	8-4	10-2

Roof Truss Installation

TRUSS DESIGN & BRACING WRITTEN SPECIFICATIONS REQUIREMENTS

1. Use a qualified engineer to design all wood trusses such as roof and floor trusses. The engineer and/or truss manufacturer should provide written truss design and installation specifications and deliver them to the job site with the trusses. These specifications should include engineering information, such as chord live and dead loads, and assembly information, such as the size, species, and grade of each truss member, and installation instructions, such as where each truss should be located on the structure and how the trusses should be permanently braced.

TRUSS INSTALLATION TOLERANCE RECOMMENDATIONS

1. Install trusses according to the installation tolerances contained in the written truss specifications. Use the following installation tolerances from the booklet *Guide to Good Practice for Handling, Installation & Bracing of Metal Plate Connected Wood Trusses* only if the engineer and/or truss manufacturer does not provide installation instructions. The IRC does not specifically require installation to these tolerances; however, installation to these tolerances is implied by the general IRC requirement that components be installed according to manufacturer's installation instructions.
2. Install trusses so that a bow in either the top or bottom chord is not more than L/200 or two inches, whichever is less. L is the length of the truss chord in inches.
3. Install trusses that are out-of-plumb (vertical) by not more than D/50 or two inches, whichever is less. D is the depth of the truss in inches at the point of measurement.
4. Install trusses at load-bearing points not more than ¼ inch from the location on the plans.
5. Install trusses that use the top chord as the weight-bearing point with a gap of not more than ½ inch between the inside of the load-bearing support and the first diagonal or vertical truss web.

ALTERATION AND REPAIR OF TRUSSES

1. Do not alter trusses in any way, including cutting, notching, boring, and splicing, without written instructions from a qualified engineer.
2. Do not use trusses to carry the weight of equipment (such as furnaces or water heaters), use the attic area for storage, or hang storage units from trusses unless the trusses have been designed to carry the additional weight.
3. Do not repair damaged trusses without written instructions from a qualified engineer.

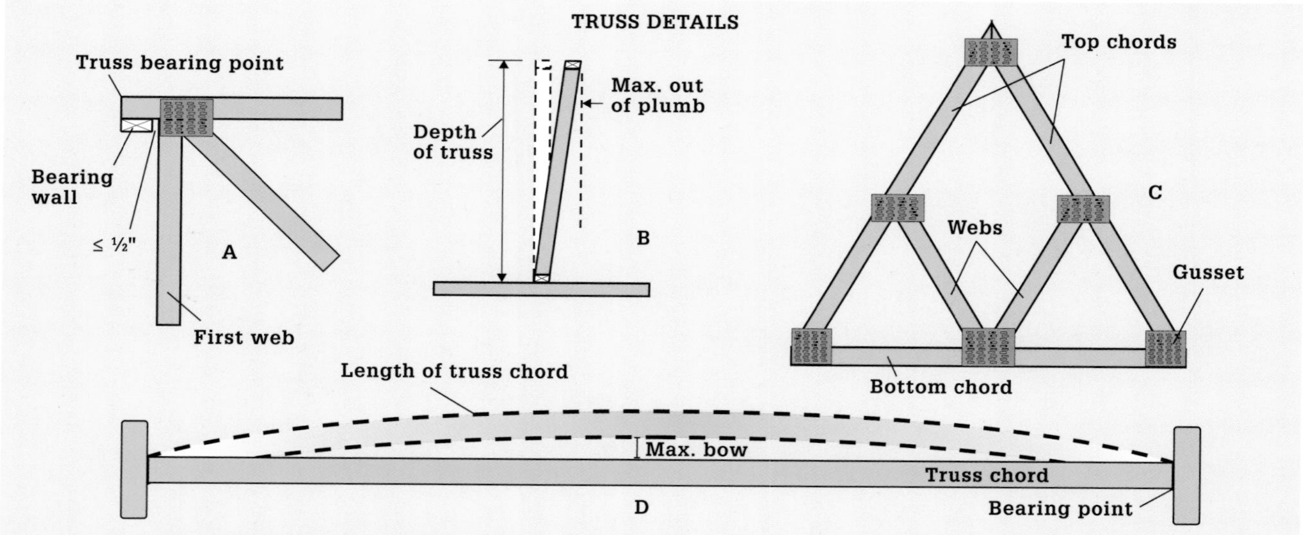

A = Truss bearing on top chord; B = Truss not plumb; C = Truss parts; D = Bowed truss chords

Attic Access

GENERAL ATTIC ACCESS REQUIREMENTS

1. Provide an access opening to every attic with at least 30 square feet of attic area and a vertical height of at least 30 inches at some point in the 30 square feet. Measure the vertical height from the top of the ceiling joists (or truss bottom chord) to the bottom of the rafters (or truss top chord).
2. Provide a rough opening (size before finishing) for a ceiling attic access of at least 22 inches by 30 inches. Locate the opening in a hallway or other readily accessible location. Locate the opening so that at least 30 inches of unobstructed headroom exists at some point above the opening.
3. Provide a rough opening (size before finishing) for a wall attic access of at least 22 inches wide by 30 inches high.
4. You do not need to provide attic access if the ceiling and roof systems are built using non-combustible materials. This is rare in residential construction.

INSULATION CLEARANCE TO HEAT PRODUCING DEVICES

1. Provide at least three inches clearance between combustible insulation and heat-producing devices such as recessed lighting fixtures and fan motors. Most insulation used in modern homes is considered combustible.
2. You may reduce the three-inch clearance requirement if the device is listed for a lesser clearance and is installed according to manufacturer's instructions.
3. Install an insulation shield around any gas or oil vent that passes through an attic or other insulated area (such as a floor/ceiling assembly).
4. Use at least 26-gauge sheet metal for the insulation shield.
5. Extend the shield at least two inches above attic insulation material.
6. Secure the insulation shield to prevent movement of the shield.

Install an insulation shield around equipment vents that pass through insulation.

Exterior Components

The primary function of the exterior components of a building is to keep the elements out. Of these elements, the most destructive is water. Water causes more damage than almost any other natural source, including fire and termites. Water can destroy most building materials, and it is an essential ingredient for mold growth.

In this chapter you will learn about three common water control issues. Shingle roof coverings are the most common type of material for keeping water that falls on the roof out of the home. You will learn about the code requirements for shingle installation and about where to install flashing that keeps water away from vulnerable areas, such as where roofs intersect with walls and chimneys. You will also learn about code requirements for water control around your home so that water stays out of basements and crawl spaces.

This chapter also contains information about fireplaces and chimneys. Water infiltration is common around these components, and fire safety is an additional important consideration.

In this chapter:

- Shingle Roof Covering Installation
- Fireplaces & Chimneys
- Water Control & Drainage Near the Home
- Retaining Walls

Shingle Roof Covering Installation

When it comes to installing roof coverings, it can be a little hard to define where enforceable codes end and where ordinary best practices begin. But it is safe to say that most codes contain guidelines for installing roof coverings that, if followed, will ensure a long-lasting roof that keeps moisture from penetrating your house. The following information applies to all types of asphalt shingles, as well as non-asphalt singles, such as fiberglass and laminated architectural shingles that are installed using similar techniques. It does not include asphalt-based roll roofing.

"Asphalt shingles" is a fairly general description that includes three-tab, two-tab, and architectural shingles containing asphalt, as well as similarly shaped shingles made from fiberglass and other laminated materials.

Roof Slope & Sheathing

ROOF SLOPE RESTRICTION

1. Do not install shingles on roofs with a slope less than $2/12$. Low slope and flat roofs require solid membrane roofs or fully bonded roof coverings.
2. Install a double underlayment layer under shingles on roofs with a slope between $2/12$ and $4/12$.
3. Verify shingle manufacturer's instructions about minimum roof slope.

ROOF DECK TYPE RESTRICTION

1. Install shingle roof covering only on solid sheathed roofs. In residential construction this means roofs covered by OSB or plywood, which includes virtually all houses built in the last generation or two.

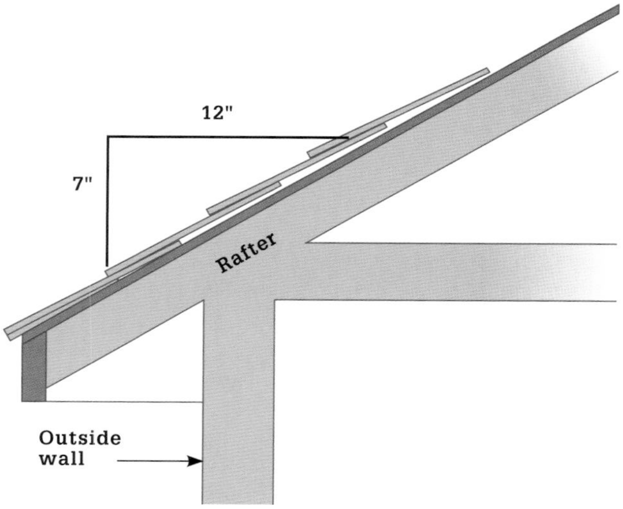

Roof slope is measured by the number of inches the roof increases in height (rise) in 12" horizontally (run).

Endorsed products for roofing underlayment include roofing felt (building paper) in both 15# and 30# thickness as well as self-adhesive ice dam underlayment. Elastomeric roof cement is used for minor patching and sealing as well as for binding underlayment courses together.

UNDERLAYMENT SPECIFICATIONS

1. Use at least 15-pound roofing felt (also called building paper). "Fifteen-pound" refers to the weight of the paper needed to cover 100 square feet of roof (called a square). This is the most common shingle underlayment because 15-pound felt is very inexpensive. Other material, such as modified bitumen sheets, may be acceptable. Refer to general codes for other acceptable underlayment materials.

UNDERLAYMENT APPLICATION FOR ROOF SLOPES 4-IN-12 AND GREATER

1. Begin installing underlayment at the eaves and apply at least a 36-inch wide strip of underlayment parallel to the eaves.
2. Lap horizontal joints by at least two inches with the higher-up strip overlapping the lower strip.
3. Lap end joints by at least six inches.
4. Use sufficient fasteners to hold underlayment in place. Most codes do not specify fastener type and quantity, though staples driven at six-inch intervals is common.
5. Lap underlayment over drip edge at eaves, if using drip edge. Apply drip edge over underlayment at rakes, if using drip edge. General codes do not usually mention drip edge, but shingle manufacturers typically recommend it.

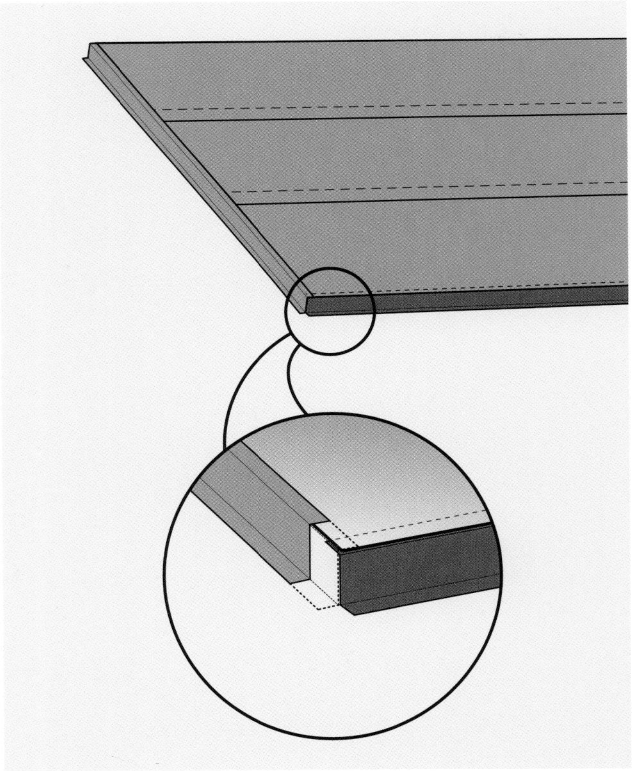

Proper installation of underlayment is important for reducing roof leaks. The underlayment should overlap the top of the drip edge at the eave, with the drip edge along the rake edges installed after the underlayment so it overlaps and directs runoff onto the underlayment.

UNDERLAYMENT APPLICATION FOR ROOF SLOPES BETWEEN 2-IN-12 AND 4-IN-12

1. Begin at the eaves and apply at least a 19-inch-wide strip of underlayment parallel to the eaves.
2. Begin again at the eaves and apply at least a 36-inch-wide strip of underlayment.
3. Lap each successive layer at least 19 inches over the previous layer, with the upper layer lapping over the lower layer.
4. Lap end joints at least six inches.
5. Use sufficient fasteners to hold underlayment in place. Most codes do not specify fastener type and quantity, although staples driven at six-inch intervals are common.
6. Install drip edge as previously described, if using drip edge.

UNDERLAYMENT APPLICATION IN 110-PLUS MPH WIND AREAS

1. Apply underlayment according to the roof slope.
2. Install corrosion-resistant fasteners according to manufacturer's instructions and space them along the overlaps at not more than 36 inches on center.

UNDERLAYMENT APPLICATION IN ICE DAM AREAS

1. Install ice dam underlayment where there is a history of water backup at the eaves caused by ice. Verify ice dam requirements with the local building official. You do not need to install ice dam underlayment on unconditioned detached accessory structures, such as an unheated garage.
2. Install either a sheet of self-adhering, polymer-modified bitumen roofing or at least two layers of roofing felt bonded together with roofing cement. Begin the ice dam underlayment at the lowest edge of all roof surfaces and extend it at least 24 inches beyond the exterior wall of the building.
3. Measure distances horizontally, not up the roof sheathing. Begin the 24-inch measurement from the interior side of the wall. Example: if the eaves extend 12 inches, horizontally, from the exterior wall of the building, extend the ice dam underlayment at least 39 inches, horizontally, from the edge of the eaves (assuming a 2 × 4 wall).

Self-adhesive ice guard (2 courses)

Install one or two courses (depends on local codes) of fully-bonded, self-adhesive ice dam underlayment in cold-weather climates. The ice dam prevents runoff from freezing beneath the shingles when it freezes at the roof eaves.

Roof Flashing

Roof flashing used with asphalt shingles is typically made of metal: primarily galvanized steel, aluminum, or copper. The timing for installing it depends on the type of flashing. Some, such as valley flashing, is installed prior to the finished roof covering (shingles). Other types, such as step-flashing, is interwoven with the shingles during the installation process. In some cases, formable, self-adhesive flashings can be used instead of metal. In some code areas, roll roofing may be used as valley flashing—check with your building inspector.

CLOSED-CUT VALLEY FLASHING

1. Before installing the shingles, install valley flashing material according to the shingle manufacturer's instructions. You may use at least a 36-inch-wide strip of smooth roll roofing material as valley flashing material with at least 18 inches on each side of the valley; or you may use any open valley lining material.
2. Place nails at least six inches away from the valley centerline, unless other spacing is approved by the shingle manufacturer.
3. Apply the shingles across one side of the valley at least 12 inches, or as recommended by the shingle manufacturer.
4. Apply shingles from the other direction to before the valley centerline and trim the edges, as recommended by the shingle manufacturer. Seal the cut shingles in a closed-cut valley, as recommend by the manufacturer. Sealing the cut shingles is frequently omitted.

Open valley flashing leaves an area in the middle of the valley that is not covered by shingles, but only by metal valley flashing. It creates a natural drain pattern for runoff that does not promote wear and tear of shingle surfaces as in a closed valley.

Closed-cut valleys, where shingles are installed across the valley in an interwoven pattern of cut shingles, are the most common shingle valley treatment.

CHIMNEY CRICKETS

1. Install a cricket (also called a saddle) on chimneys that are more than 30 inches wide in the dimension parallel to the roof ridgeline. A cricket is not required if the chimney intersects the roof ridgeline. This also applies to factory-built chimneys that are installed inside a wood chimney chase.
2. Flash the cricket at the chimney wall using step and counter flashing that is compatible with the roof covering material.
3. Install the cricket with a vertical height at the chimney based on Table 26. W is the width of the chimney. Leave at least a one-inch air space between a wood-framed cricket and a masonry chimney wall.

STEP FLASHING

1. Install step flashing at the intersections of a sloped roof and a vertical side wall. Use flashing that is at least four inches wide by four inches high. Install kick-out flashing at the end of the wall to direct water away from the side wall.
2. Flash the intersection of a sloped roof and a chimney according to the shingle manufacturer's instructions. This typically includes step flashing covered with counter flashing.
3. Flash other roof penetrations, such as plumbing and gas vents, according to the shingle manufacturer's instructions.
4. Flash skylights according to the skylight manufacturer's instructions.

Table 26: Chimney Cricket Height ▸

Roof slope	Cricket height
12/12	1/2 W
8/12	1/3 W
6/12	1/4 W
4/12	1/6 W
3/12	1/8 W

A cricket is a raised section of roof custom-bent metal flashing aide that fits on the high side of a chimney to deflect runoff water so it doesn't erode the chimney. Improper installation and flashing of chimney crickets is a common cause of roof leaks.

Flash roof and sidewall intersections using step and counter flashing. Install kick-out flashing at the end of the wall.

Flash all penetrations such as plumbing vents and equipment vents with preformed flashing, often called boots. Make sure the flashing conforms to your roof slope.

Most skylights for residential installation come with a flashing kit. Improper installation and flashing of skylights is a common cause of roof leaks.

Roofing Fasteners

FASTENER TYPE & QUANTITY IN STANDARD SHINGLING CONDITIONS

1. Use the type and quantity of fasteners recommended by the shingle manufacturer. Locate nails on the shingle strip precisely as recommended by the shingle manufacturer. Some manufacturers recommend installing nails below the black adhesive seal strip. Other manufacturers leave a gap in the seal strip for installing nails. Do not install nails above the seal strip unless allowed by the manufacturer. Failure to comply with manufacturer's installation instructions is a code violation and may void the manufacturer's warranty.
2. Use corrosion-resistant roofing nails (usually galvanized steel) with at least a 12-gauge shank and a ⅜-inch-diameter head. Use nails long enough to penetrate into the roof sheathing at least ¾ inch and completely through any sheathing that is less than ¾-inch thick. Install at least four nails per shingle strip, with a nail at one inch from each end and two nails equally spaced in the center of the strip.

Install the starter (first) course according to manufacturer's instructions to reduce damage during high winds.

FASTENER TYPE & QUANTITY IN SPECIAL CONDITIONS

1. Install additional fasteners as recommended by the shingle manufacturer in wind speed areas greater than 110 mph and for very steep roof slopes such as mansard roofs. Install at least six nails per strip in these applications and verify fastening recommendations with the shingle manufacturer.
2. Use shingles labeled on the wrapper as complying with ASTM D3161 in wind speed areas greater than 110 mph.

Staples as Shingle Fasteners ▸

Staples are not endorsed in general codes as an approved shingle fastener. Some shingle manufacturers allow staples, but seldom recommend them. Avoid using staples as shingle fasteners in both new construction and when replacing an existing shingle roof.

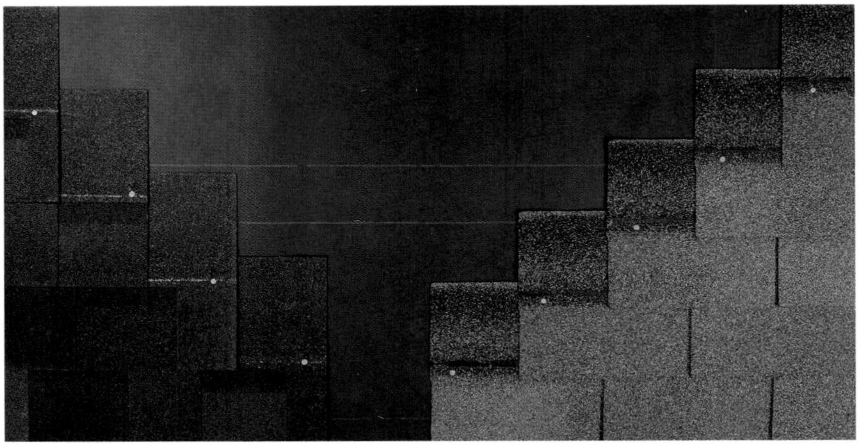

Install fasteners precisely as directed by manufacturer's instruction.

Fireplaces & Chimneys

Installing a factory-built or gas fireplace is a do-it-yourself project because you can design and build the fireplace frame to suit your needs and add your own finish treatments. It all starts with some careful planning. Once you decide on the fireplace model and determine where to place it, order all of the vent pipes and fittings needed to complete the vent run.

Note: Consult the manufacturer's instructions for the specifications regarding placement, clearances, and venting methods for your fireplace.

Start your planning by determining the best location for the fireplace. Placing the unit next to an exterior wall simplifies the venting required. One important specification for a direct-vented gas fireplace located in a basement is that the termination cap (on the outside end of the vent) must be 12 inches above the ground and away from openings such as windows and doors.

For help with any of these planning issues, talk with knowledgeable dealers in your area. They can help you choose the best fireplace model for your situation and help you with venting and other considerations. Remember that all installation specifications are governed by local building codes and that a building permit will be required. Check with the building department to make sure your plans conform to regulations. *Notice: The information on pages 96 to 97 apply specifically to masonry fireplaces, but many are useful guidelines for gas fireplaces as well.*

Masonry Fireplace Clearance to Combustible Materials

MASONRY FIREPLACE HEARTH EXTENSION CLEARANCE TO COMBUSTIBLE MATERIALS

1. The hearth extension is the area in front of the firebox. It must be made of noncombustible material upon which sparks and hot materials from the firebox may land without starting a fire. Tile and masonry units are typical.
2. Build a hearth extension for a masonry fireplace at least 16 inches in front of the firebox opening and at least eight inches to the sides of the firebox opening, if the firebox opening is less than six square feet.
3. Build a hearth extension for a masonry fireplace at least 20 inches in front of the firebox opening and at least 12 inches to the side of the firebox opening, if the firebox opening is six square feet or more.
4. Build a hearth extension for a factory-built fireplace according to the fireplace manufacturer's instructions. The hearth extension size is often the same as for a masonry fireplace.

Provide a hearth extension (the area of the floor adjoining the fireplace) that meets minimum size standards based on the square footage of the fireplace opening.

MASONRY FIREPLACE CLEARANCE TO MANTELS & TRIM

1. Locate all combustible mantels and wood trim at least six inches from a masonry fireplace opening.
2. Provide at least one inch of clearance to the masonry firebox opening for every ⅛ inch that combustible material projects from the fireplace surround. This applies to materials within 12 inches of the fireplace opening. Example: locate one-inch thick fireplace mantel legs at least eight inches from the fireplace opening. Example: locate greater than 12 inches from the fireplace opening any part of a fireplace mantel or mantel leg that is more than 1½ inches thick.
3. Provide clearance to combustible materials for a factory-built fireplace according to the fireplace manufacturer's instructions. The clearance is often the same as for a masonry fireplace.

SPARK ARRESTOR & RAIN CAP

1. You are not required to install a spark arrestor or a rain cap on a masonry chimney, unless the local building official requires one. They are, however, recommended to protect the home and surrounding area from fire and to protect the chimney and home interior from water damage.
2. Comply with all of the following requirements for installed spark arrestors:
   (a) make the unobstructed arrestor area at least four times the area of the flue it serves;
   (b) make the arrestor screen using heat and corrosion-resistant material equal to 19-gauge galvanized steel or 24-gauge stainless steel;
   (c) build the arrestor screen so it does not pass ½-inch-diameter spheres and does not obstruct ⅜-inch-diameter spheres;
   (d) make the arrestor accessible for cleaning and make the cap removable to allow for flue cleaning.

CHIMNEY USED AS APPLIANCE VENT

1. Do not connect an appliance vent to a masonry chimney flue if the area of the appliance connector is larger than the area of the chimney flue.
2. Connect appliances, such as pellet fuel burning and oil fuel burning appliances, to masonry chimney flues only if the flue:
   (a) is built with an approved fire-clay liner, or
   (b) has been relined with a chimney lining system listed for use in a masonry chimney and listed for use with the appliance, or
   (c) is built using approved materials.
3. Install a permanent label in a conspicuous location warning occupants if a chimney has been relined and warning them what types of appliances may be connected to the chimney.
4. Have gas appliance vents connected to masonry chimney flues according to the provisions for gas appliance vents in IRC Chapter 24. Chimneys that are too small may not properly expel all combustion gases. Chimneys that are too large may allow water to condense in the chimney, causing significant damage.

Locate wood trim far enough from the firebox to avoid fires.

A spark arrestor/rain cap is recommended (but not required) for every chimney.

Factory-built Fireplaces

Factory-built fireplaces and chimneys include components tested, listed, and labeled to be installed together as a system. Such fireplaces are usually designed to burn solid fuels, such as wood, though they may be converted to use gas if approved by the fireplace manufacturer. Do not mix components from different manufacturers unless approved by the fireplace manufacturer.

Fireplaces designed to burn only gas are not really fireplaces. They are decorative gas appliances. Vented decorative gas appliances are more like a water heater than like a fireplace. Unvented decorative gas appliances are more like a gas range than like a fireplace. Install and use decorative gas appliances according to manufacturer's instructions and IRC Chapter 24. Note that some jurisdictions do not allow unvented decorative gas appliances. Also note that manufacturers of unvented decorative gas appliances recommend opening a window during use and recommend limits on the duration of use.

Create wall surrounds for fireplaces with cementboard, which has some heat-resistant qualities and also makes a good backer for ceramic tile—a popular choice for finished fireplace surrounds.

Gas Fireplaces ▸

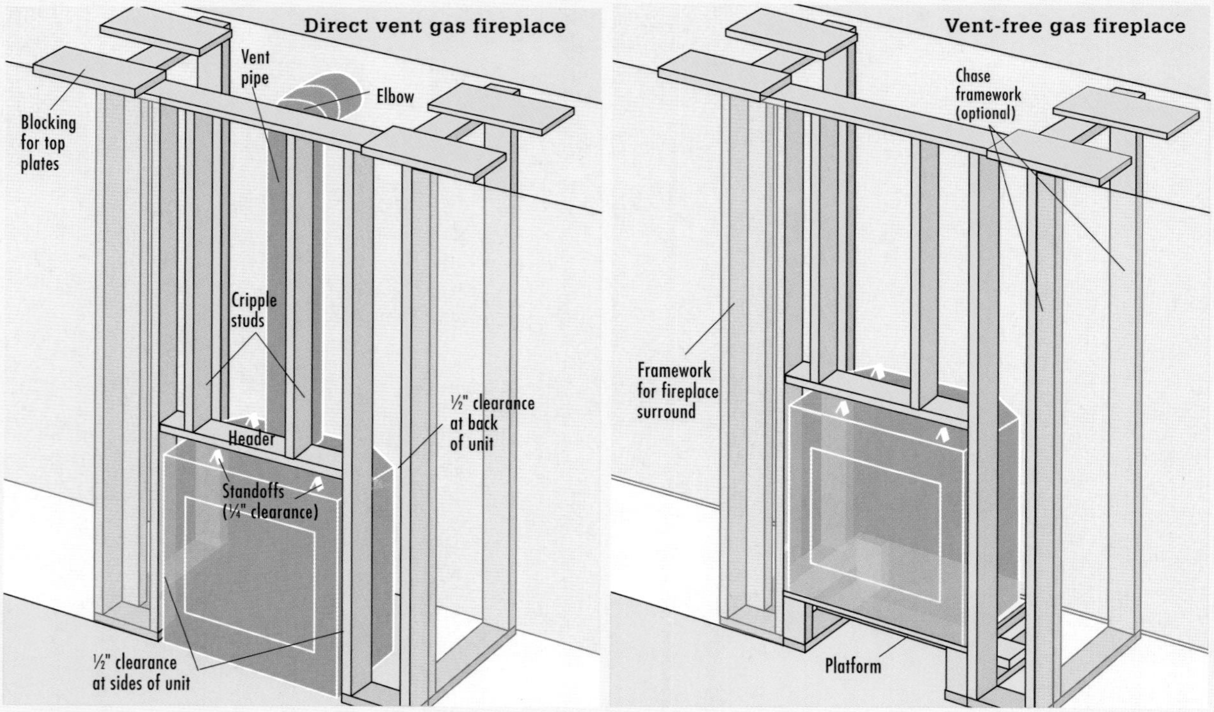

Direct vent gas fireplace
Blocking for top plates
Vent pipe
Elbow
Cripple studs
Header
Standoffs (¼" clearance)
½" clearance at back of unit
½" clearance at sides of unit
Vent-free gas fireplace
Chase framework (optional)
Framework for fireplace surround
Platform

A gas fireplace behaves more like a water heater than like a fireplace, but these appliances do produce dangerous gases and are by their very nature a fire hazard. The two most common types are direct-vent gas fireplaces, which produce heat that can contribute to your home heat plan and are vented to the exterior, and vent-free gas fireplaces (not allowed in some states) that are purely decorative. Because the amount of gas they consume is so small (comparable to a gas range with all burners on), they do not require venting.

FACTORY-BUILT FIREPLACE & CHIMNEY INSTALLATION

Install factory-built chimneys and fireplaces according to the manufacturer's instructions. These instructions include requirements for hearth extensions, clearances to combustible materials, and installation of combustion air ducts.

DECORATIVE CHIMNEY COVERS

Do not install decorative chimney covers, shrouds, or similar components at the chimney termination unless the component is listed and labeled for use with the particular fireplace system.

STRUCTURAL SUPPORT FOR FACTORY-BUILT FIREPLACES

Provide adequate structural support for factory-built fireplaces and chimneys according to manufacturer's recommendations.

Direct-vent gas fireplaces can be vented through an interior wall and the exhaust pipe may run on a horizontal plane (woodburning exhaust chimneys can only be vertical).

Exhaust vents for gas fireplaces must have a protective termination cap.

Factory-built fireplaces (including direct-vent and vent-free gas fireplaces) typically require structural support. If the fireplace is recessed into a wall, structural support is in the form of a mounting platform located on the other side.

Water Control & Drainage Near the Home

Water control at the foundation is one of the most important ways to protect the home. Improper foundation water control can cause wet basements and crawl spaces. Wet foundations provide an environment for fungal growth. Improper foundation water control can cause significant foundation damage in areas with expansive or collapsible soils and in areas subject to frost heaving. Improper foundation water control can leave damp soil around the foundation and provide an attractive environment for termites.

GRADING OF AREA AROUND THE HOME

1. Direct surface water away from the foundation to a storm sewer or other approved collection point.
2. Provide at least six inches of fall away from foundation walls and foundation slabs within the first 10 feet from the foundation (5 percent slope).
3. Provide alternate drainage means, such as swales or underground (French) drains if tight lot lines or physical barriers prevent having six inches of fall within the first 10 feet.
4. Slope impervious surfaces, such as concrete and asphalt, at least 2 percent away from the building.

GUTTERS

1. Provide gutters or other means to control roof runoff in areas with expansive or collapsible soil. Discharge the gutter water at least five feet away from the foundation or into an approved drainage system. Most codes do not require gutters except when unstable soils are present. However, gutters are recommended for all homes.

Slope the ground around the foundation of your house to direct water runoff away. Minimum slopes may vary, but a falloff of 6" over the first 10 ft. is a good standard.

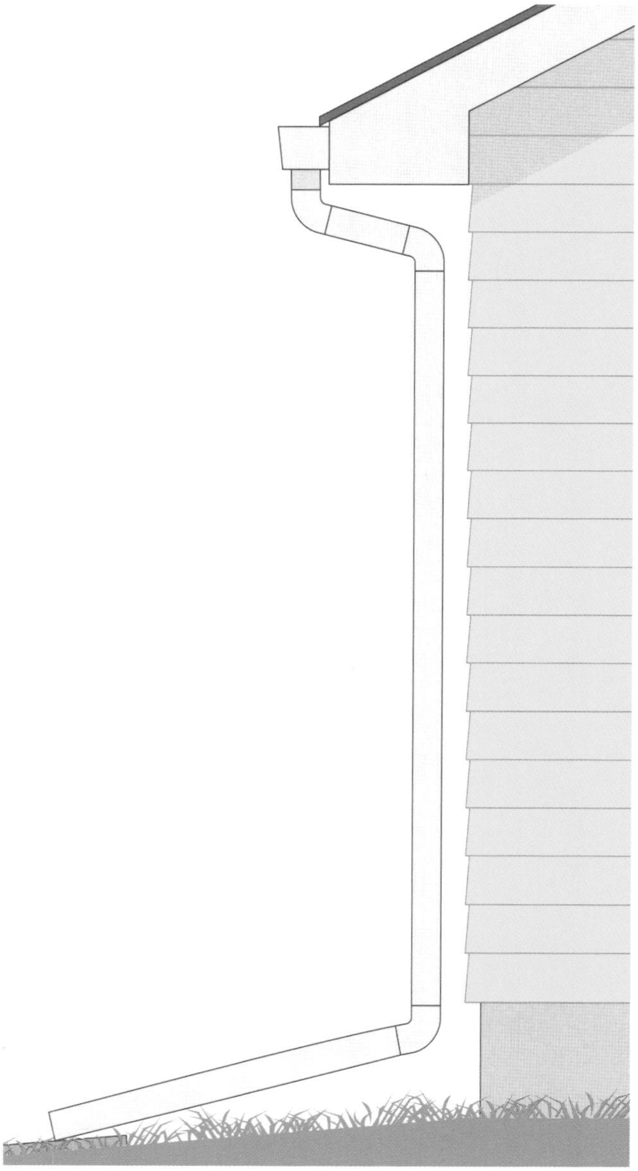

Gutters are recommended but seldom required.

Retaining Walls ▸

Design and build retaining walls to resist problems such as overturning, sliding, and uplift when the wall retains more than 24" of fill and has no horizontal support at the top. Retaining walls more than 48" tall and retaining walls that retain a surcharge may require design by a qualified contractor or engineer. Verify permit requirements for retaining walls with the building official. Provide retaining walls with some means to drain water from behind the wall as part of the required resistance to overturning and sliding. Walls without drainage often fail because of the water pressure that builds behind the wall. Retaining walls made from concrete and concrete blocks should have weep holes near the bottom of the wall. If the soil behind the wall is poorly drained, such as clay soils, separate the weep holes from the soil with gravel covered by a filter fabric. Otherwise, the weep holes may become clogged.

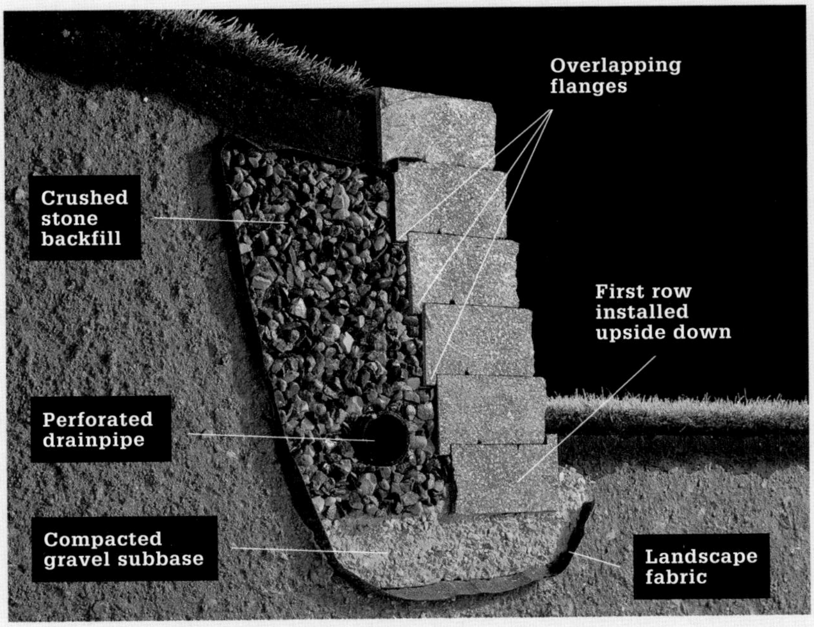

Overlapping flanges
Crushed stone backfill
First row installed upside down
Perforated drainpipe
Compacted gravel subbase
Landscape fabric

Interlocking wall blocks do not need mortar. Some types are held together with a system of overlapping flanges that automatically set the backward pitch (batter) as the blocks are stacked, as shown in this project. Other types of blocks use fiberglass pins.

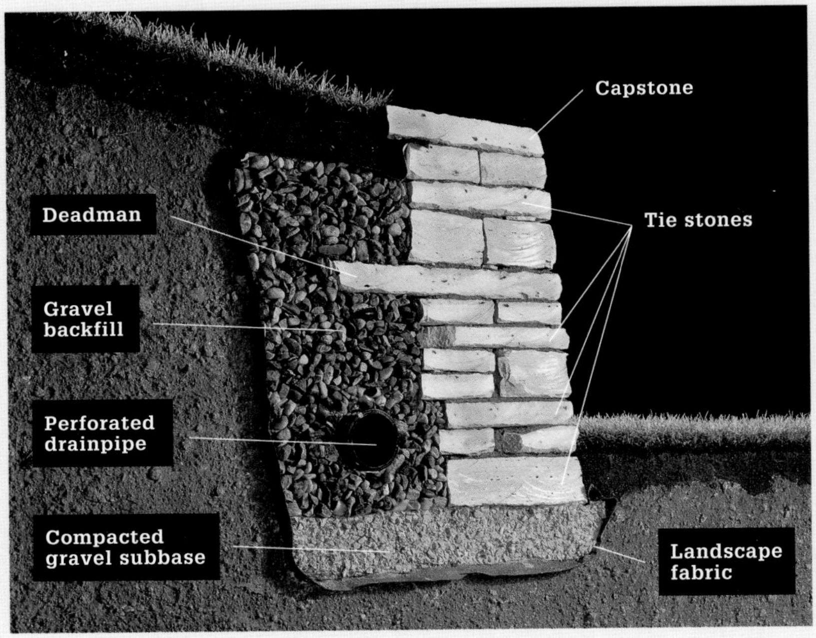

Capstone
Deadman
Tie stones
Gravel backfill
Perforated drainpipe
Compacted gravel subbase
Landscape fabric

Cut stone has flat, smooth surfaces for easy stacking. For a stable retaining wall, alternate rows of "tie stones" that span the entire width of the wall with rows of smaller stones. Install extra-long stones (called deadmen) that extend back into gravel backfill, spaced every 4 to 6 ft.

MASTER FORCE
SELF LOCK
25 ft.
LUXAIRE
Heating • Air Conditioning

Heating & Air Conditioning

Safety is the primary focus of code provisions governing heating and air conditioning systems. Improper appliance installation can cause the appliance to malfunction, creating a fire hazard as well as the potential for carbon monoxide poisoning. Fuel-burning appliances, such as gas and oil furnaces, must be installed in safe locations and must be provided with enough outside air to support fuel combustion. Vents for these appliances must be installed so that they do not ignite combustible materials and so that combustion gases are not circulated back into the building.

In this chapter you will learn about the safe installation of heating and air conditioning appliances and their associated venting equipment. You will also learn about how to identify improperly installed forced-air ducts that can increase your energy costs and decrease your appliance's useful life.

In this chapter:

- HVAC Appliances
- HVAC Duct Installation
- Combustion Air for Fuel-burning Appliances
- Vents for Fuel-burning Appliances

HVAC Appliances

Heating, ventilation, and air conditioning systems are often referred to as a group by the term HVAC. This is because they share a common purpose: to keep the air in your home comfortable. All HVAC systems—even hot-water-based systems—rely on the flow of air to heat, cool, and ventilate your home.

Most homes today include two separate major appliances in the HVAC system: a furnace (usually gas burning) and a central air conditioning unit. In most cases, even when the AC has been retrofitted, the appliances share ductwork.

The information in this chapter is intended mostly for general education purposes and to assist with diagnosing system problems. **Unless you are a very experienced DIYer, installing and servicing HVAC equipment is a job best left to professionals.**

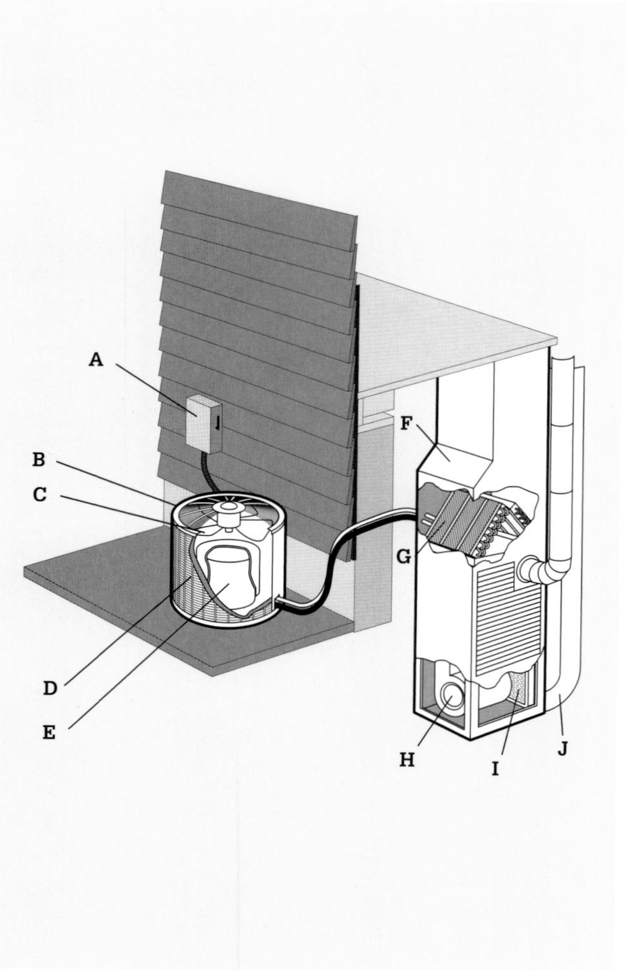

Central air conditioner parts include: (A) Control box with shutoff switch, (B) Condenser unit, (C) Fan, (D) Condenser coil, (E) Compressor, (F) Plenum, (G) Evaporator coil, (H) Blower motor, (I) Filter, (J) Air return.

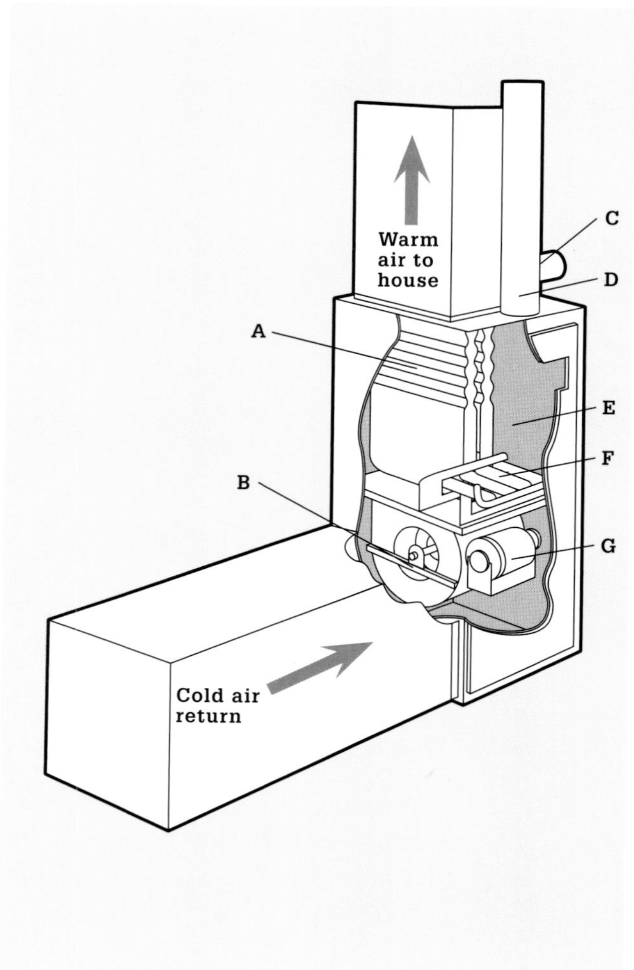

Gas furnace parts include: (A) Heat exchanger, (B) Circulating fan/blower motor, (C) Vent damper, (D) Vent connector/flue, (E) Combustion chamber, (F) Burners, (G) Blower motor.

PROHIBITED LOCATIONS FOR APPLIANCE INSTALLATION

1. Do not locate gas or other fuel-burning appliances in: bedrooms, bathrooms, toilet rooms, or storage closets. Do not draw combustion air for any fuel-burning appliance from these rooms regardless of where the appliance is located.
2. Do not locate appliances anywhere that is not approved by the manufacturer's instructions.
3. Do not apply this provision to appliances powered by electricity.

EXCEPTIONS: PROHIBITED LOCATIONS FOR APPLIANCE INSTALLATION

1. You may install direct-vent appliances in prohibited locations if the appliance draws all combustion air directly from the outdoors.
2. You may install vented room heaters, vented wall furnaces, vented decorative appliances, and decorative appliances listed for installation in vented, solid fuel-burning fireplaces (such as gas logs) in prohibited locations if the room satisfies combustion air volume requirements.
3. You may install one listed, wall-mounted, unvented room heater in a bathroom if the appliance has an oxygen depletion safety shutoff system, if the appliance input rating is not more than 6,000 BTU/hour, and if the bathroom satisfies combustion air volume requirements.
4. You may install one listed, wall-mounted, unvented room heater in a bedroom if the appliance has an oxygen depletion safety shutoff system, if the appliance input rating is not more than 10,000 BTU/hour, and if the bedroom satisfies combustion air volume requirements.
5. You may install appliances in an enclosure accessible from the prohibited locations if all combustion air is drawn directly from the outdoors and if the enclosure is equipped with a self-closing door that is weather-stripped.
6. The standard combustion air volume requirement is at least 50 cubic feet per 1,000 BTU/hour appliance input rating. This standard volume requirement does not apply if the home is tightly sealed with a known air infiltration rate of less than 0.40 air changes per hour. Tightly sealed homes are rare.

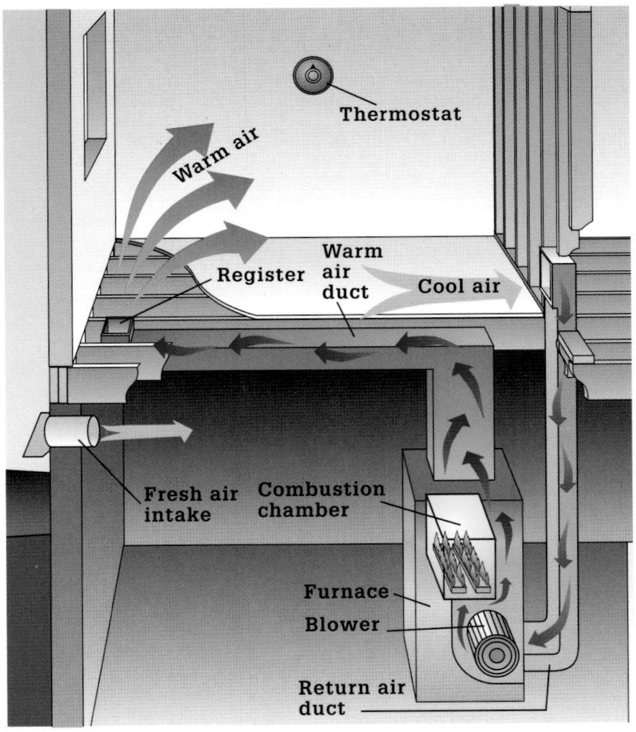

A typical forced air heating system delivers heated air to a room through registers while drawing cool air through return ducts. The cool air is reheated in the furnace and recirculated for maximum efficiency. A fresh air intake provides a constant supply of combustion air.

An air intake vent that draws combustion air into the system allows you to install appliances in areas that lack adequate combustion air.

Electric baseboard heaters often are used to provide supplementary heat. Models (such as the one above) that do not produce external temperatures greater than 125° F may be mounted directly to drywall walls, but a clear space should be maintained between the appliance and the floor.

Electric Radiant (Baseboard) Heating Systems

Electric radiant heating systems provide heat to a single room. They usually have no fan and provide heat by natural movement of the heated air and by thermal radiation. They are common in small, seasonally occupied buildings, some rural homes, and in buildings without ducts for forced-air heating and cooling. These elements become very hot, and proper installation is important to prevent fires and electrical problems.

INSTALLATION REQUIREMENTS

1. Install electric radiant heating panels according to manufacturer's installation instructions and applicable provisions of general and local codes.
2. Install radiant panels parallel to wood framing members and fasten the panels to the surface of the framing members or mount the panels between framing members.
3. Install fasteners only in areas of the appliance's radiant panel designed for fasteners. Install fasteners at least ¼ inch away from a heating element.
4. Install radiant panels as complete units, unless listed and labeled for field modifications.
5. Do not install radiant panels on drywall unless the panel's maximum operating temperature is not more than 125 degrees Fahrenheit.

How Much Heater Do You Need?

1. Measure the area of the room in square feet (length × width): ______
2. Divide the area by 10 to get the baseline minimum wattage: ______
3. Add 5% for each newer window or 10% for each older window: ______
4. Add 10% for each exterior wall in the room: ______
5. Add 10% for each exterior door: ______
6. Add 10% if the space below is not insulated: ______
7. Add 20% if the space above is not well insulated: ______
8. Add 10% if ceiling is more than 8 ft. high: ______
9. Total of the baseline wattage plus all additions: ______
10. Divide this number by 250 (the wattage produced per foot of standard baseboard heater): ______
11. Round up to a whole number. This is the minimum number of feet of heater you need. ______

Appliances Installed in Garages

In warmer areas of the country some major household appliances are routinely located in garages to conserve interior floorspace. Water heaters are code-regulated to be installed in garages. Others, such as central vacuum units, should be installed following the manufacturer's instructions and best practices, but typically are not subject to specific codes beyond applicable wiring, plumbing, and fire safety codes.

ELEVATED APPLIANCES IN GARAGES

1. Elevate the appliance ignition source at least 18 inches above the floor when the appliance is located in a garage or is located in an unconditioned room that opens directly into the garage. Appliances with a potential ignition source include gas and electric water heaters, gas and electric clothes dryers, gas and electric furnaces, and heat pumps with auxiliary resistance-heating elements. Rooms that open directly into the garage include storage and utility rooms that are not part of the conditioned living space. These rooms include rooms separated from the garage by a door opening into the garage.
2. Measure the elevation distance to the ignition source in the equipment, not to the bottom of the equipment (unless the ignition source is at the bottom of the equipment).
3. You may install appliances on the floor in rooms that are adjacent to a garage but do not have an opening into the garage.

PROTECTION OF APPLIANCES FROM VEHICLES

1. Protect HVAC appliances and water heaters from vehicle impact. The appliance or water heater does not need to be located in a garage or carport to qualify for protection from vehicle impact. General codes do not specify how to provide this protection. Common protection methods include steel poles called bollards, vehicle tire stops, and encasing the equipment in substantial framing.

Appliances such as water heaters that are installed in a garage must have the ignition source elevated at least 18" off the floor.

HVAC Appliance & Duct Sizing

APPLIANCE SIZING

1. Size heating and cooling appliances according to *The Air Conditioning Contractors of America* (ACCA) *Manual S* or a similar approved method. *Manual S* and *Manual J* account for conditions such as the direction the structure faces, the size and type of windows and doors, local temperature conditions, and insulation. Contractors should provide a copy of the sizing calculations for all new construction and when replacing existing appliances. Improper appliance sizing may cause inefficient appliance operation or may allow excessive moisture to remain in the home. Excessive moisture can damage the home and provide moisture for mold growth.

DUCT DESIGN

1. Design duct systems according to *ACCA Manual D* or a similar approved method. Contractors should provide a copy of the duct design calculations for all new construction. Improper duct sizing and installation can cause inefficient appliance operation and can cause uneven temperatures in the home.

Air Conditioner Condensate Disposal

The process of removing heat from the air is often called air conditioning. Water is a byproduct of air conditioning because water vapor condenses out from the air when the air temperature is reduced. In areas with high humidity, air conditioning can produce significant amounts of water. The water removed from the air during air conditioning is called condensate.

CONDENSATE DISPOSAL LOCATION REQUIREMENTS

1. Do not discharge condensate on to a street, alley, or any other place that would create a nuisance. Some jurisdictions, particularly in warm moist areas, require that you discharge condensate away from the foundation. Verify discharge location requirements with the local building official.

CONDENSATE DISCHARGE PIPE REQUIREMENTS

1. Use at least ¾-inch internal diameter pipe for primary and auxiliary condensate discharge pipes. Do not decrease pipe size between the collection and discharge point.
2. Install horizontal pipe sections with a uniform slope in the direction of the discharge point of at least ⅛ inch in 12 inches.
3. Use fittings, primers, cements, hangers, and other components that are compatible with the pipe material. Install the pipe according to the provisions in general codes.
4. Use pipe material and use a pipe size that will accommodate the condensate temperature, pressure, and flow rate produced by the air conditioning system.
5. You may use most water supply and drain pipes for condensate discharge pipes. The most common condensate discharge pipes are PVC, CPVC, and ABS.

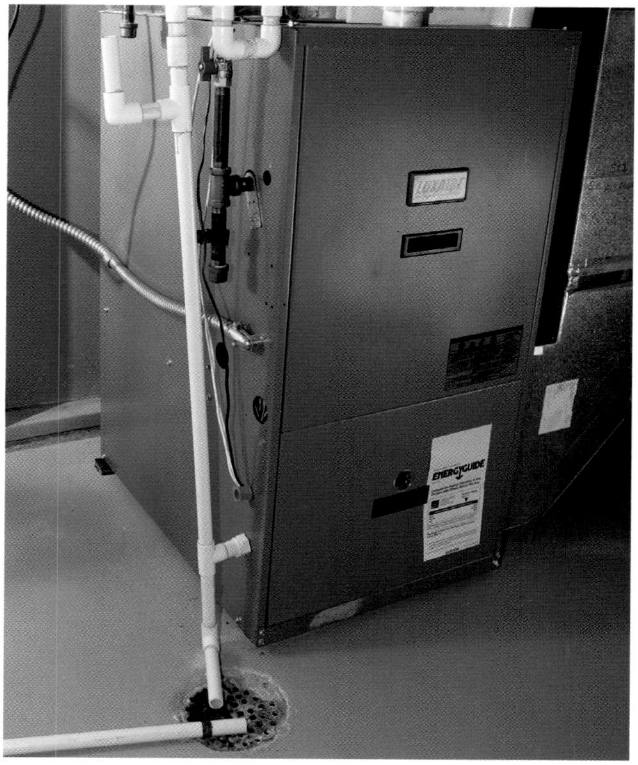

Condensate from air conditioner units should be directed to a drain through discharge pipes.

CONDENSATE AUXILIARY (BACKUP) SYSTEM REQUIREMENTS

1. Install an auxiliary condensate system when the air conditioner evaporator coil is located where building damage may occur if the primary condensate discharge system malfunctions. This usually applies to evaporator coils installed in or above finished space. Many jurisdictions require auxiliary condensate systems for all air conditioning systems, unless all of the equipment is located outside the building.
2. Install one of the following auxiliary condensate systems when an auxiliary condensate system is required.
   (a) Condensate auxiliary drain pan with discharge pipe. Install an auxiliary drain pan under the evaporator coil. Use a pan that is at least 1½ inches deep and at least three inches larger than the evaporator coil in both length and width. Construct the pan using either at least 0.0276-inch galvanized sheet metal or at least a 0.0625-inch, nonmetallic pan. Slope the pan toward the discharge pipe connection. Install the auxiliary discharge pipe using the same materials and methods as the primary discharge pipe. Terminate the auxiliary discharge pipe at a conspicuous point so that the occupants can see that the primary condensate discharge system is not functioning properly (a conspicuous point often means above a window).
   (b) Water level cutoff switch. Install a water level cutoff switch above the primary condensate discharge pipe where it connects to the evaporator coil and below the evaporator coil interior condensate pan overflow rim, or you may install the switch in the primary or secondary discharge pipes. The switch location should allow the switch to shut off the air conditioner before water overflows into the building.

Maintenance Tip: Keep Discharge Tubes Clear ▸

Condensate discharge tubes that run from your air conditioner evaporator have a strong tendency to become clogged with mildew, algae, bacteria, and other unappealing nuisances. To prevent clogging, flush the discharge tube every couple of months with a solution of 2 tablespoons household chlorine bleach dissolved into a cup of hot water.

HVAC Duct Installation

Improper flexible duct installation is a common problem. Ducts that leak, have sharp bends, or sag reduce the volume of air that moves through the duct and increase the friction between the air and the duct walls. This causes the HVAC system to work harder and longer than necessary, wasting energy and money.

Flexible HVAC Duct Installation

REASONS FOR PROPER FLEXIBLE DUCT INSTALLATION

1. Improper flexible duct installation is a common problem. Ducts that leak, have sharp bends, or sag reduce the volume of air that moves through the duct and increase the friction between the air and the duct walls. This causes the HVAC system to work harder and longer than necessary, wasting energy and money.

GENERAL INSTALLATION REQUIREMENTS

1. Install flexible ducts according to manufacturer's installation instructions. The installation instructions that follow are based on material from the Air Diffusion Council. The full, original version may be downloaded from their website (see Resources, page 233).
2. Use flexible ducts that are labeled at least every 36 inches with information such as the manufacturer's name and the R-value of the duct insulation.
3. Do not expose flexible ducts to direct sunlight such as may occur under roof vents. Direct sunlight can damage the duct outer cover.
4. Extend flexible duct to its full length. Do not leave excess duct material in a duct run and do not compress the duct.

DUCT SUPPORT

1. Support flexible ducts using material at least 1½ inches wide. You may support flexible ducts on 1½-inch-wide framing.
2. Support flexible ducts at not more than 5-foot intervals. You may use a fitting or distribution plenum to provide initial flexible duct support.
3. Do not allow flexible duct to sag between supports more than ½ inch per foot.
4. Support bends in long horizontal runs of flexible duct at not more than one duct diameter on both sides of the bend.
5. Support bends in flexible duct that occur near the plenum connection. Allow flexible ducts to run at least several inches beyond a plenum connection before making a bend.
6. Provide independent support for duct fittings and distribution plenums. Support duct fittings at not more than one foot from the fitting.
7. Support vertical runs of flexible duct at more than six-foot intervals.

DUCT BENDS

1. Do not bend flexible ducts at sharp angles across obstructions such as framing lumber and pipes. Such bends reduce the duct area and restrict air flow.
2. Do not bend flexible ducts so that the bend radius at the centerline is less than one duct diameter.
3. Avoid changing the shape of the duct. The area of a round duct is greater than the area of the same duct compressed into an ellipse.

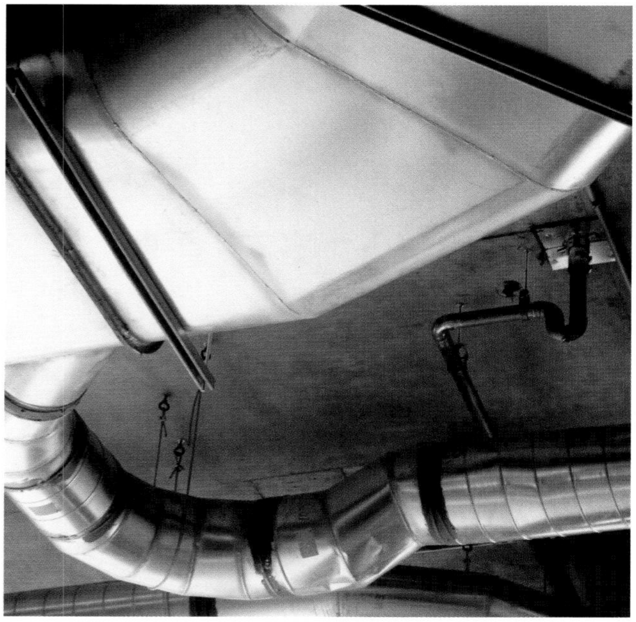

Intervals between supports (hangers) for flexible HVAC ductwork can be no more than 5 ft. apart.

DUCT CONNECTIONS & SPLICES

1. Connect and splice ducts according to manufacturer's instructions.
2. Connect flexible ducts to metal collars that are at least two inches long.
3. Splice two ducts together using a metal sleeve at least four inches long.
4. Use approved clamps and tape to secure nonmetallic flexible ducts to metal collars and sleeves.
5. Use approved tape and mastic to seal duct collars, plenums, and other fittings to ensure minimum air leakage.

Seal plenums, duct collars, and other fittings with mastic or other approved materials.

Prohibited Sources for Return & Outdoor Air

PROHIBITED SOURCES OF RETURN AIR

1. Do not locate a return air register in a closet, bathroom, toilet room, kitchen, garage, mechanical room, furnace room, closet, or alcove.
2. Do not locate a return air register in a room or space if the volume of the room or space is less than 25 percent of the total volume of all space served by the HVAC system. Include spaces connected by permanent openings to other rooms when calculating the volume of a space. You may ignore this minimum volume requirement if the supply air to the room is at least as much as the return air. Example: do not locate the only return air duct in a 240-square-foot bedroom of a 1,000-square-foot house.
3. Use airtight ducts to bring return air directly into the furnace blower housing from outside the furnace room, closet, or alcove.

PROHIBITED SOURCES OF OUTDOOR AIR

1. Locate outdoor air intake openings connected to forced-air heating and cooling systems at least 10 feet horizontally from contaminant sources including gas equipment vents, chimneys, plumbing vents, or the discharge outlet of an exhaust fan.
2. You may locate outdoor air intake openings closer than 10 feet horizontally to a contaminant source if the outdoor air intake opening is at least three feet below the contaminant source.
3. Do not locate outdoor air intake openings where objectionable odors, fumes, or flammable vapors may be present.
4. Locate outdoor air intake openings at least 10 feet above a public walkway or driveway.
5. Do not locate outdoor air intake openings at grade level next to a sidewalk, street, alley, or driveway.
6. Provide an automatic or gravity-operated damper for air intake systems that will close the damper when the system is not operating.

RETURN AIR DRAWN FROM ROOMS WITH FUEL-BURNING APPLIANCES

1. Do not draw return air from a room or space containing a fuel-burning appliance if the room or space is the sole source of return air for the system. Common fuel-burning appliances include furnaces, fireplaces, and water heaters. This restriction does not apply if: (a) the appliance is a direct-vent appliance or does not require a vent, or (b) the volume of the room exceeds one cubic foot for each 10 BTU/hour input rating for all fuel-burning appliances in the room, the volume of supply air approximately equals the volume of return air, and return air inlets are located at least 10 feet from the appliance firebox or draft hood.
2. Do not draw return air for a gas furnace from the room where the furnace is located if the furnace supply air goes to other rooms.

Combustion Air for Fuel-burning Appliances

Fuel-burning appliances, such as gas furnaces, boilers, and water heaters, need air to support the fuel-burning (combustion) process. These appliances also need air for cooling, ventilation of the appliance, and for proper operation of the vent system that expels combustion byproducts outside. The air required to support operation of fuel-burning appliances is called combustion air.

Without adequate combustion air, incomplete fuel combustion may occur. Byproducts of incomplete fuel combustion can include carbon monoxide and soot that can damage the appliance and its vent. This is a health and safety hazard. Appliances operating without adequate combustion air can cost more to operate and maintain.

Do not confuse combustion air with the similar term "makeup air." Makeup air replaces air that is exhausted by clothes dryers, exhaust fans, fireplaces, and similar devices.

APPLIANCES NEEDING COMBUSTION AIR

1. Provide combustion air for Category I gas appliances and for liquid fuel-burning (oil) appliances according to the appliance manufacturer's recommendations and to fuel gas code requirements. Category I gas appliances include the gas furnaces and water heaters found in most homes.
2. Provide combustion air for direct vent and for Category II, III, and IV gas appliances according to the appliance manufacturer's instructions. Do not apply combustion air requirements to these appliances. Category II appliances do not currently exist. Category III and IV appliances include medium and high efficiency gas appliances that operate with positive vent pressure.
3. Do not apply combustion air requirements to fireplaces and fireplace stoves. Refer to other general codes for fireplace combustion air requirements.

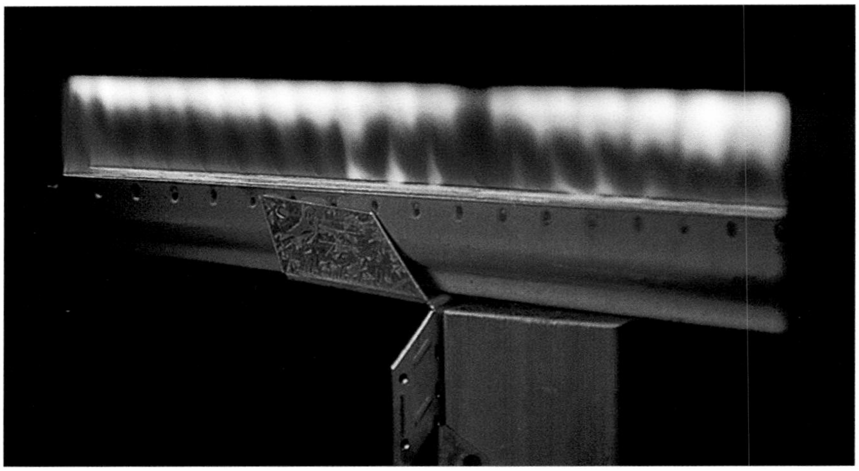

Fuel for appliances (natural gas, propane, fuel oil) requires an adequate supply of fresh combustion air for efficient burning, as well as a means of effective exhaust.

Combustion Air Depletion by Other Systems ▸

Other appliances compete with gas and oil-burning appliances for combustion air. This can create negative pressure that can interfere with operation of the gas and oil-burning appliances and their vents. General codes do not define how to account for air exhausted by other appliances. Gas and oil-burning appliances located in or near rooms containing clothes dryers, exhaust fans, and fireplaces require special attention to ensure that combustion air and venting needs are satisfied.

Account for air exhausted by appliances (such as clothes dryers, bathroom and kitchen exhaust fans, fireplaces) and account for combustion air used by other fuel-burning appliances when determining combustion air requirements. This is important when drawing all combustion air from inside the home

COMBUSTION AIR DUCT MATERIALS & CONSTRUCTION

1. Use galvanized steel to construct combustion air ducts. Refer to other general codes for duct material specifications.
2. You may use unobstructed stud and joist spaces as combustion air ducts if only one required fireblock is removed.
3. Terminate combustion air ducts in unobstructed space that allows free air movement.
4. Do not open combustion air ducts into more than one room or enclosure.
5. Do not use the same combustion air duct for both the upper and lower duct openings.
6. Do not install a screen on any combustion air duct opening in the attic.
7. Do not slope horizontal combustion air ducts downward toward the source of combustion air. Make the duct level or slope it toward the appliance.
8. Do not use the space in a masonry, metal, or factory-built chimney that surrounds a chimney liner, gas vent, plastic piping, or other devices as a combustion air duct.
9. Locate the lowest point of an exterior combustion air opening at least 12 inches above exterior grade.

Use heat-resistant caulk to seal seams between parts of the ductwork system. Seal both hot-air carries and cold air returns.

Airtight Construction ▸

Homes built using airtight construction techniques do not allow enough air infiltration into the home to safely support fuel combustion. The lack of adequate combustion air can cause many problems, including the production of carbon monoxide and soot that can be a health hazard and can damage appliances and vents. Do not draw combustion air from inside the home if it is built using airtight construction techniques. You'll need to bring it in from outdoors.

Although most homes built today use some energy-efficient construction techniques, few are so tight that they are considered "airtight" and therefore require supplementary combustion air. To be considered airtight, a home must have measured air changes that do not exceed 0.4 per hour. You'll need to contact a qualified building energy analyst to determine whether your house meets this standard, but here are some hints:

- If your home is airtight, the thermal envelope walls have a continuous water vapor retarder with a rating of one perm or less and any openings in the vapor retarder are sealed.
- Doors and operable windows meet air leakage requirements of the International Energy Conservation Code.
- Gaps and spaces are sealed—including gaps and spaces between windows and doors and the surrounding framing, between sole plates and floors, between wall and ceiling joints, between wall panels, and at wall penetrations for utilities such as plumbing, electrical, and gas.

Older homes rarely satisfy these requirements. Newer homes may satisfy the first two requirements, but it is still rare for most builders to seal all framing and utility penetration gaps as intended by the third requirement. Many homes may obtain combustion air from inside the home, but you should verify with the builder if the home was built using airtight construction techniques.

Combustion Air from Within a Room

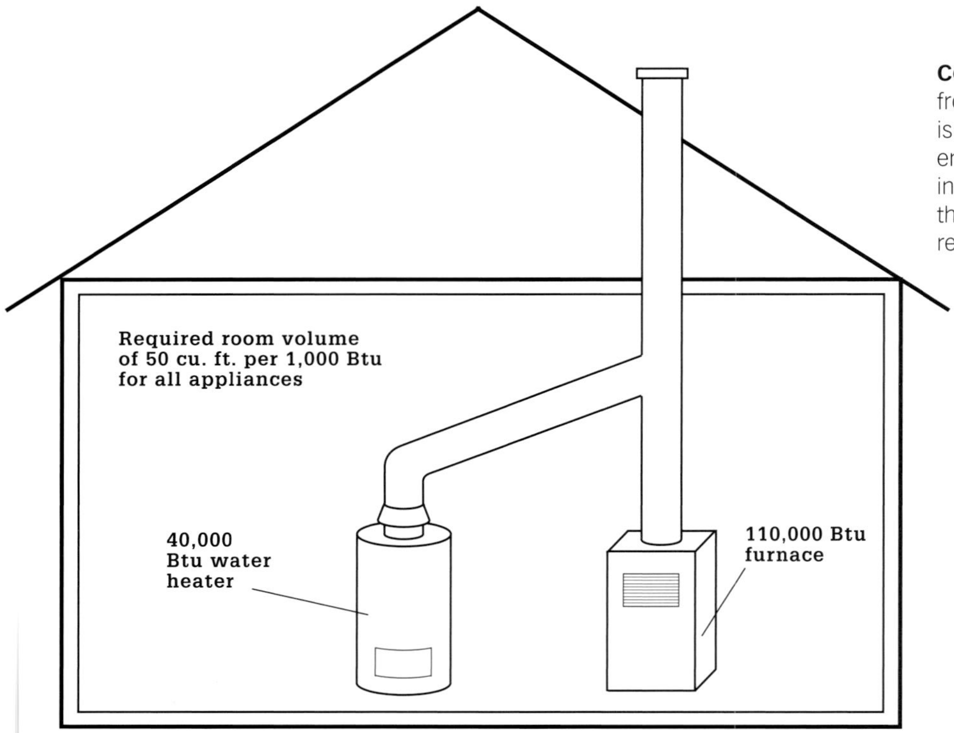

Required room volume of 50 cu. ft. per 1,000 Btu for all appliances
40,000 Btu water heater
110,000 Btu furnace

Combustion air may be drawn from the room where the appliance is located if the room is large enough. Consult with an engineer or inspector to help you determine if the room meets the minimum size requirement for your appliance.

Combustion Air Using One Permanent Opening to Outdoors

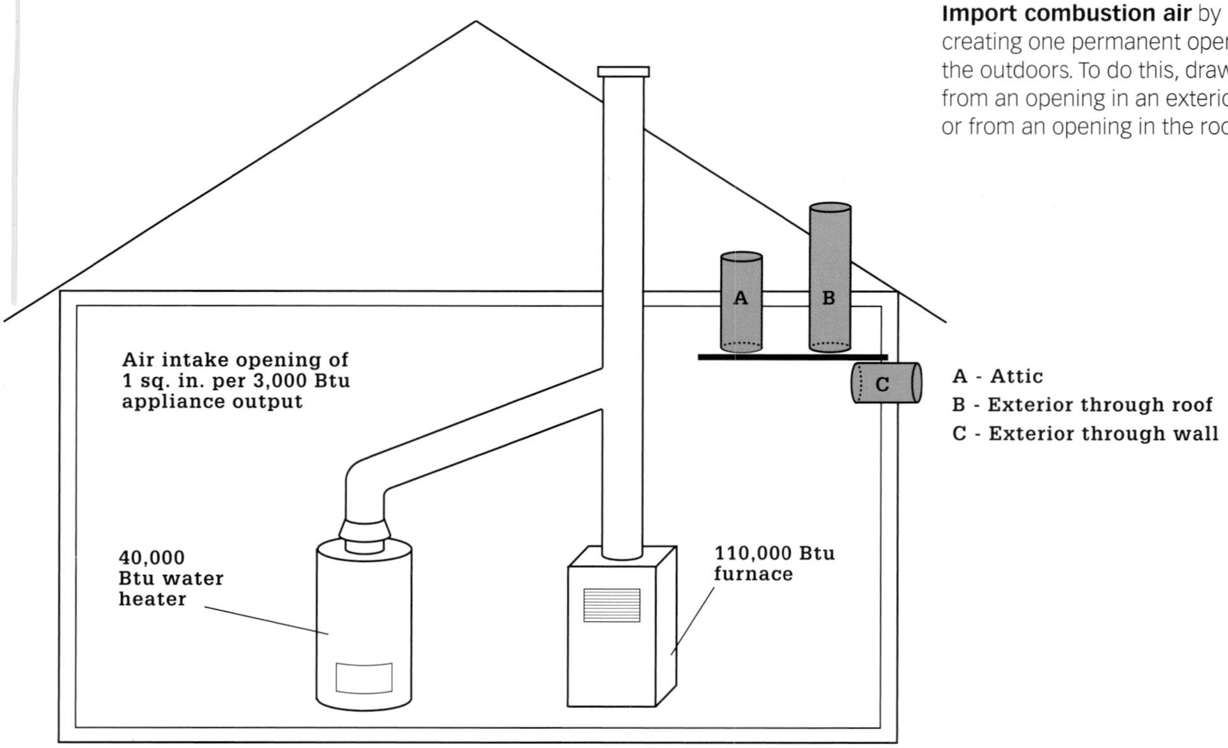

Air intake opening of 1 sq. in. per 3,000 Btu appliance output
40,000 Btu water heater
110,000 Btu furnace
A
B
C
A - Attic
B - Exterior through roof
C - Exterior through wall

Import combustion air by creating one permanent opening to the outdoors. To do this, draw air in from an opening in an exterior wall or from an opening in the roof.

Vents for Fuel-burning Appliances

A vent is generally a vertical component, such as a metal pipe, that conducts combustion products from a gas or oil-burning appliance to the outdoors. A vent for a single appliance begins at the fitting where the vent connector, if any, connects to the vent. A common vent for multiple appliances begins at the highest connector fitting. If a vent is located directly over the appliance draft hood or flue collar, or if the vent connects directly to the appliance, then the vent begins at the appliance and there is no vent connector.

A vent connector is a pipe that connects an appliance to its vent or flue. A vent connector is required if the appliance is not located directly under its vent. A vent connector for a Category I gas appliance may be a listed vent material, such as a Type B vent, a listed flexible vent connector, or a field constructed single-wall metal pipe made of at least 26-gauge galvanized steel. While a vent connector is part of the venting system, it is not the vent itself.

Common types of vents and vent connectors include the Type B vent used with most gas appliances, Type L vents used with oil-burning appliances, flexible connectors used with gas appliances, and single-wall connectors that may be used with either gas or oil-burning appliances.

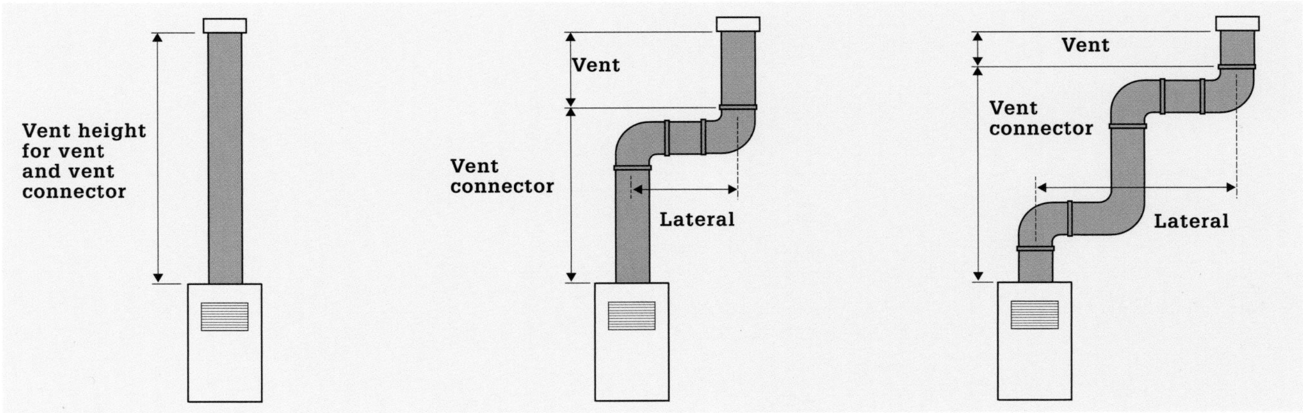

Vents and vent connectors often look the same, but they have different installation requirements.

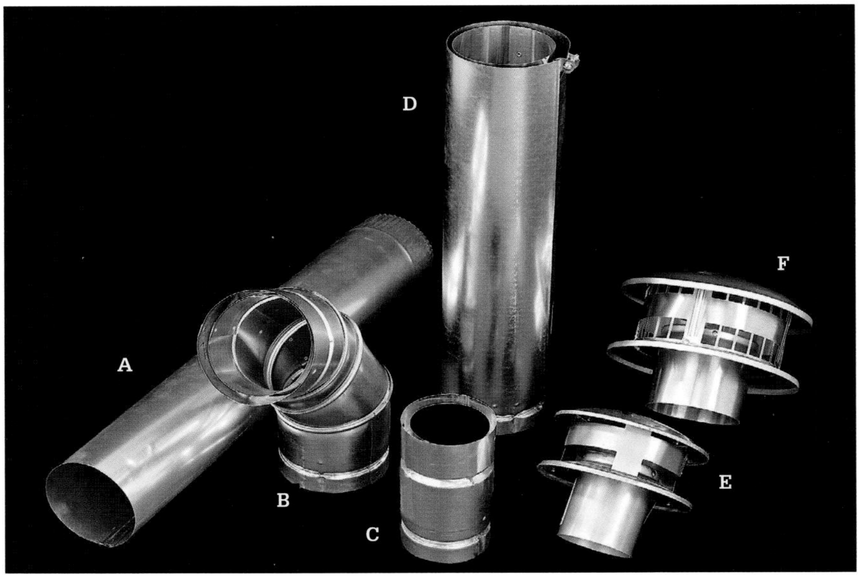

Vent connectors and fittings include: (a) Single wall-vent connector; (b) Type B elbow; (c) Type B vent; (d) Type L vent; (e, f) vent caps.

VENT CLEARANCE TO COMBUSTIBLE MATERIALS

1. Provide the distance between a vent or a vent connector and combustible materials based on the vent or vent connector manufacturer's installation instructions and based on the appliance manufacturer's installation instructions. Table 27 contains typical clearance distances for common types of vents and vent connectors. Confirm the distances in Table 27 with the appliance manufacturer's instructions and with the vent manufacturer's instructions.

VENT CLEARANCE TO ROOF & OBSTRUCTIONS

1. Terminate a Type L vent at least two feet above the roof and at least two feet above any part of the home within 10 feet of the vent. Measure termination height above the roof from the highest point where the vent penetrates the roof to the bottom of the vent cap.
2. Terminate a masonry chimney at least three feet above the roof and at least two feet above any part of the building within 10 feet of the chimney. Measure termination height above the roof from the highest point where the chimney penetrates the roof to where the flue exits the chimney. This provision also applies to many factory-built chimneys. Confirm factory-built chimney termination height using the manufacturer's installation instructions.
3. Use Table 28 to determine the minimum height above the roof of a Type B gas vent not more than 12 inches in diameter. Measure termination height above the roof from the highest point where the vent penetrates the roof to the bottom of the listed cap. For thick roof-covering materials such as tile, measure from the tile to the bottom of the listed cap.

Avoid fires by maintaining distance between vents and combustible materials.

4. Do not use Table 28 if a Type B vent is closer than eight feet to a vertical side wall, gable end, or similar vertical obstruction. Terminate these vents at least two feet higher than the highest point where the vent penetrates the roof and at least two feet higher than any part of the roof or building within 10 feet horizontally.
5. Terminate all vents and chimneys at least 10 feet horizontally from operable windows unless the vent is at least two feet above the window.
6. Do not install a decorative shroud or surround at a vent termination unless the shroud or surround is listed for use with the specific venting system and unless the shroud or surround is installed according to manufacturer's instructions. This prevents an unlisted shroud from interfering with the drafting characteristics of the vent system.

Table 27: Typical Clearance Distances to Combustible Materials for Common Types of Vents & Vent Connectors ▸

vent or connector type	application	typical clearance distance
Type B vent and vent connector	Category I gas appliance	1"
Type L vent and vent connector	Oil-burning and Category I gas appliance	3″
Single-wall vent and vent connector	Category I gas appliance	6″
Single-wall vent and vent connector	Oil-burning appliance listed for Type L vent	9″

JOINTS BETWEEN VENTS & VENT CONNECTOR SECTIONS

1. Secure joints between the vent or vent connector and the flue collar or draft hood, vent or vent connector sections, and vent connector and the vent using (a) sheet metal screws (usually three); (b) listed, interlocking vent material (such as Type B vent) connected according to the vent manufacturer's instructions; or (c) other approved means.

SLOPE OF VENTS & VENT CONNECTORS

1. Slope vents and vent connectors up toward the roof termination at least ¼ inch per foot. Do not allow any dips or sags in the vent or vent connector.

APPLIANCES NOT REQUIRING A VENT

1. You are not required to vent the following gas appliances:
   (a) ranges and other domestic cooking appliances listed and labeled for optional venting,
   (b) domestic (Type 1) clothes dryers,
   (c) portable, countertop, and similar small kitchen and laundry appliances,
   (d) gas-fueled refrigerators,
   (e) listed, unvented room heaters, and
   (f) listed, unvented decorative gas appliances (unvented gas fireplaces).

Table 28: Type B Gas Vent Height Above Roof ▸

Roof pitch	Min. vent height
Flat to 6/12	12"
Over 6/12 to 7/12	15"
Over 7/12 to 8/12	18"
Over 8/12 to 9/12	24"
Over 9/12 to 10/12	30"
Over 10/12 to 11/12	39"
Over 11/12 to 12/12	48"
Over 12/12 to 14/12	60"
Over 14/12 to 16/12	72"
Over 16/12 to 18/12	84"
Over 18/12 to 20/12	90"

2. Verify venting requirements using manufacturer's instructions. Some manufacturers of appliances such as unvented gas fireplaces recommend limiting the duration of use and/or opening a window while the appliance is operating.

Safety Tip ▸

Always have combustion ventilation installations diagnosed and inspected by a qualified professional.

A gas vent roof terminator cap protects the exhaust line from moisture and pests. These fittings are designed so they do not impede or restrict airflow.

Plumbing System

Plumbing projects are popular among do-it-yourselfers, so naturally there's a strong demand for information on home plumbing subjects to make sure home projects are accomplished correctly. Water supply pipes must be properly sized, supported, and connected to avoid water leaks and to avoid low water flow at fixtures.

Wastewater drain pipes must be properly installed to avoid water leaks and sewage backups. Traps and vents must be correctly hooked up in drain lines.

Finally, in this chapter you'll learn basic requirements for installing water supply pipes, water drain and vent pipes, as well as installing common plumbing fixtures such as water heaters, faucets, tubs and showers.

In this chapter:

- The Home Plumbing System
- Water Supply Piping
- Drain, Waste & Vent Piping (DWV)
- Plumbing Vents
- Plumbing Traps
- Plumbing Appliances & Fixtures
- Water Heaters
- Toilets
- Dishwashing Machines
- Food Disposers
- Clothes Washing Machines
- Whirlpool Bathtubs
- Showers
- Irrigation Systems

Definitions of Plumbing Terms ▸

Air admittance valve: An air admittance valve is a one-way valve attached to a plumbing vent pipe. It is used when extending a vent to the roof or to another vent is impractical or not desirable. The valve allows air into the vent system when there is negative pressure in the vent pipe and closes to limit the flow of sewer gas into the home.

Branch drain: A branch drain is a drainage pipe that takes soil and waste from fixture drains to a stack or to the building drain.

Branch vent: A branch vent connects other vents, usually individual and common vents, to a vent stack or stack vent.

Braze (Brazing): A method of joining metal pipe (such as copper and brass) at temperatures exceeding 1,000 degrees Fahrenheit. Brazing is sometimes called "silver soldering," because it uses a silver alloy as the brazing material. Brazed joints are stronger than soldered joints.

Building drain: The building drain is usually the lowest horizontal drainpipe in the building and collects material from branches and stacks. It extends to 30" beyond the foundation, where it connects with the building sewer. A building with fixtures below the building drain (such as in a basement) has a building sub-drain. Material in a sub-drain must be pumped up to the building drain.

Building sewer: Building sewer usually refers to the pipes beginning at the building drain and ending at the public sewer or septic tank.

Drainpipe: Drainpipe usually refers to the pipes inside the building that take soil and waste to the building sewer pipe.

Fittings: Devices that connect parts of the plumbing system together and allow pipes to change direction. Drainage fittings include wyes, sweeps, bends, tees, and couplings. Water supply fittings include elbows, tees, couplings, and valves.

Fixture: A device that connects to water supply pipes and connects to plumbing waste pipes. Fixtures include toilets (water closets), bathroom sinks (lavatories), kitchen and laundry sinks, bathtubs, and showers.

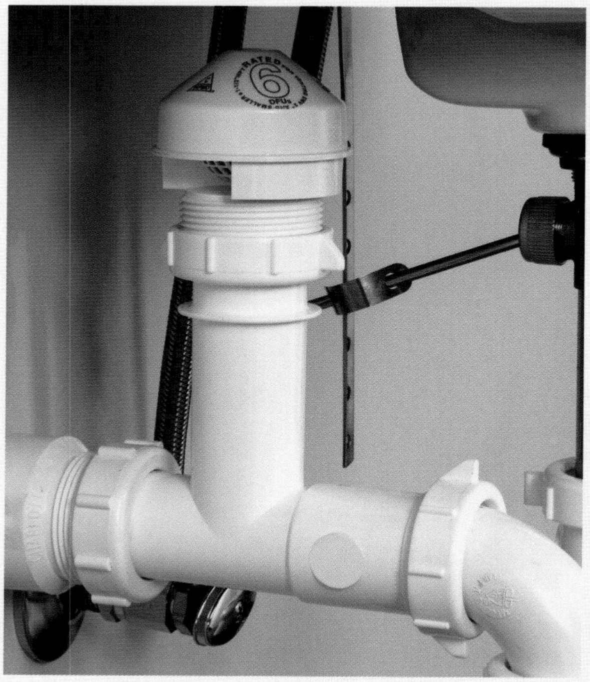

A relatively new device, the air admittance valve (AAV) has been endorsed as a substitute for individual exterior vent termination by most codes.

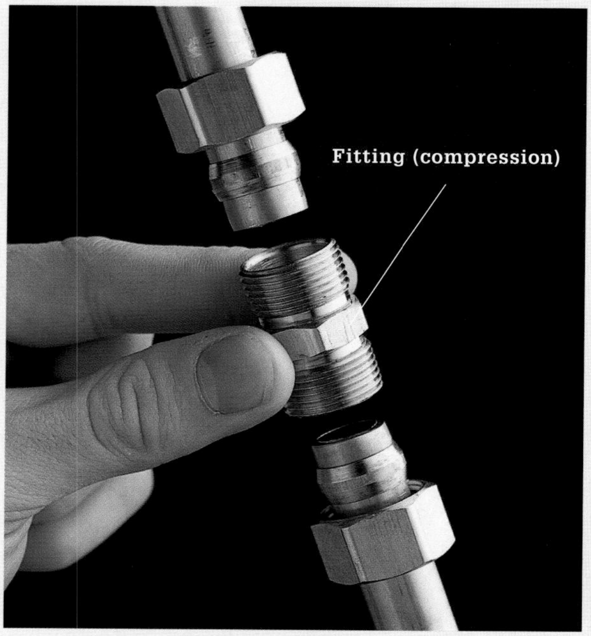

The general term "fitting" is for any device from any material that is used to connect plumbing pipes. A brass compression fitting for copper supply pipe is shown here.

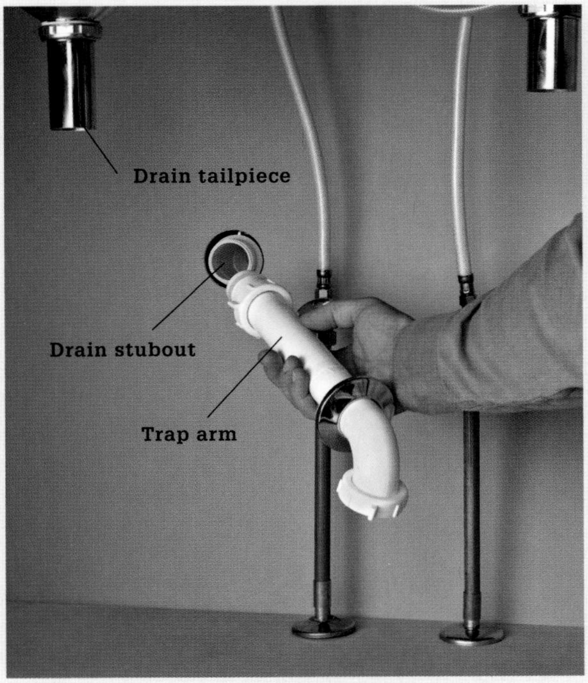
Drain tailpiece
Drain stubout
Trap arm

The fixture drain, or trap arm, is a piece of drain tubing that connects a fixture and its drain line to the drain stubout in the wall or floor.

An indirect waste receptor collects drain water from a source and introduces it to the drain system, but it is not connected directly to the wastewater source. Floor drains (above) are common indirect receptors.

The hub is the enlarged fitting, usually in cast-iron drain pipe. The spigot is the end of the pipe that fits into the hub.

Fixture drain: The horizontal pipe between a trap outlet and the fitting, connecting it to another drain pipe. A fixture drain is sometimes called a "trap arm." Any pipe after the fixture drain fitting is not part of the fixture drain.

Hub: An enlarged opening molded on the end of a pipe or a fitting into which a section of pipe (the spigot) is inserted. In older plumbing, cast-iron hubs and spigots were sealed with oakum or hemp and lead. In modern plumbing, you may seal cast-iron hubs and spigots with an elastomeric O-ring gasket, or you may remove the hub and convert the pipe into a hubless pipe. Hubless pipe joints are often sealed by an elastomeric sleeve held in place by stainless steel rings (also called a banded coupling).

Laundry tray: A sink, usually located in a laundry area, used for various laundry-related and other purposes. It is also known as a laundry sink or a deep sink. You may discharge a clothes washing machine into a laundry tray instead of a standpipe.

An offset in a vertical drainpipe (drain stack) is any change in direction in the pipe from vertical to an angle other than vertical, then back to vertical. Offsets are most often used to run a stack around an obstruction (such as a wall or beam) that cannot be drilled or notched. An offset that is not more than 45° from vertical is defined to be vertical.

Receptor (indirect waste): The term receptor refers to a device such as a floor sink or a floor drain. Indirect waste receptors have a source of water that is not directly and permanently connected to the receptor. Example: a floor drain could receive condensate water from an air conditioning system. The condensate drain is not directly and permanently connected to the floor drain.

Definitions of Plumbing Terms ▸

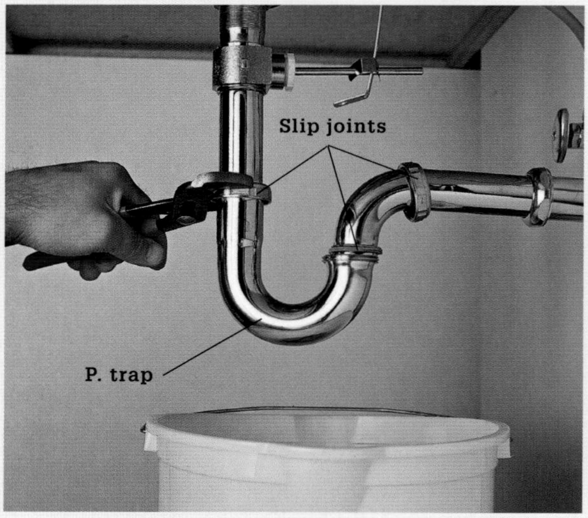

Install slip joints only on accessible traps.

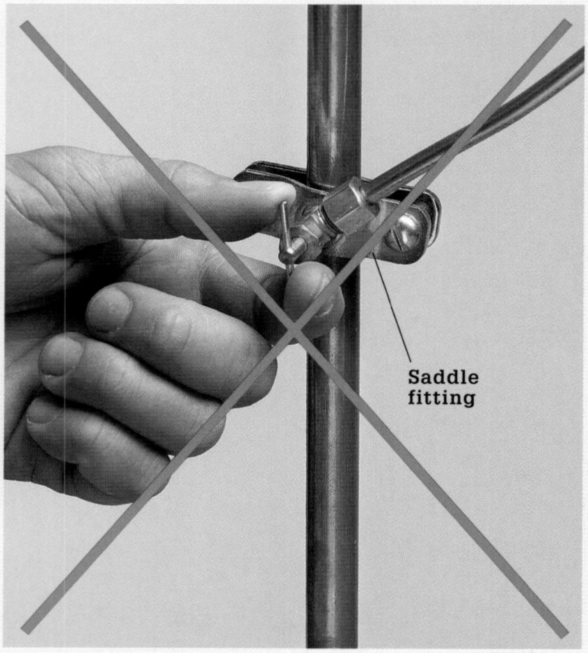

VIOLATION! Saddle fittings that tap into water supply lines by piercing have been outlawed by most codes.

Saddle fitting: A prohibited connection between pipes where a new pipe is attached to an existing pipe by puncturing the existing pipe and clamping the new pipe to the existing pipe. Saddle fittings were used to tap existing water supply pipes for low volume applications such as refrigerator icemakers and reverse osmosis water-treatment systems.

Slip joint: A hand-tightened fitting at the inlet and outlet side of traps. Slip joints allow easy removal of the trap for cleaning. Slip joints must be accessible.

Soil: Material in the plumbing drainage system that contains urine or fecal material.

Solder (Soldering): A method of joining metal pipe (such as copper and brass) at temperatures that do not exceed 800° F. Soldering usually uses a tin alloy as the joining material. Soldered joints are weaker than brazed joints.

Stack: A stack is a vertical plumbing drain or waste pipe that extends one or more stories. A stack collects waste material from horizontal drainage pipes and conducts it to the building drain or other horizontal drain.

Stack vent: A dry vent that connects to a soil or waste stack above the highest horizontal drainage connection and may extend through the roof to the outdoors or may terminate with a stack-type air admittance valve.

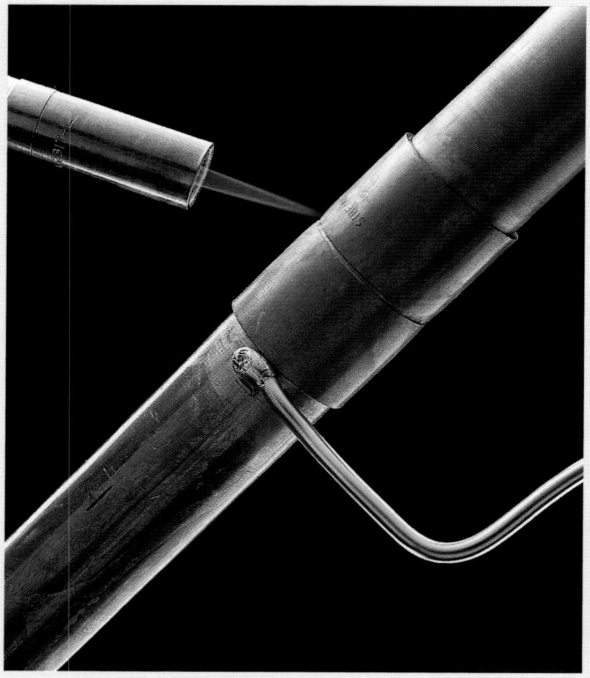

Soldering is a technique, often called "sweating," that's used to join copper and brass tubing and fittings. It is less strong than brazing, but code approved for virtually all residential plumbing joints.

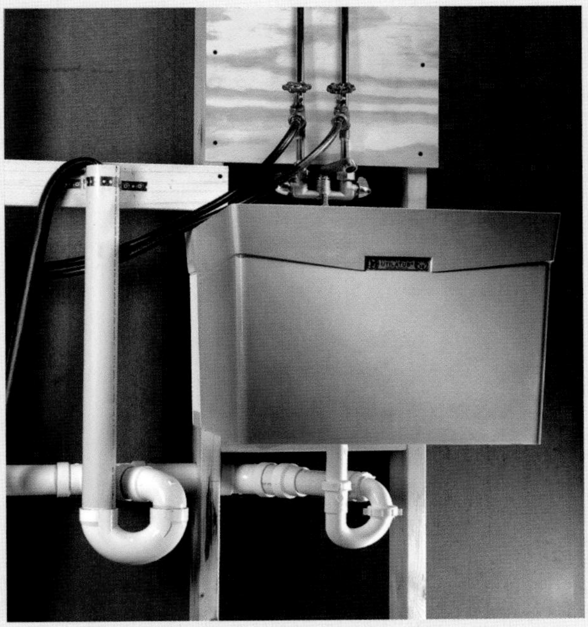

A standpipe is an open pipe mounted vertically and leading into a branch drain system. Standpipes often are installed as receptors for washing machine discharge tubes.

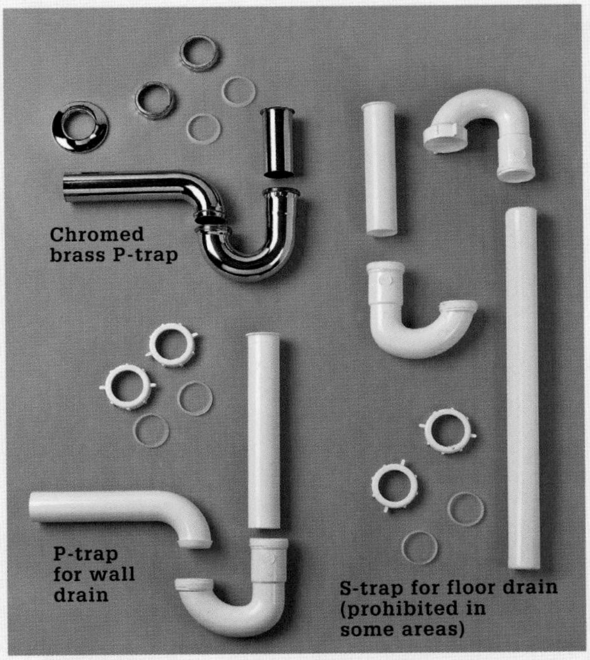
Chromed brass P-trap
P-trap for wall drain
S-trap for floor drain (prohibited in some areas)

Traps are the S- or P-shaped pipes in a fixture drain. Their purpose is to prevent sewer gas from coming up through the drain opening.

Standpipe: A vertical pipe used as an indirect waste receptor. Standpipes are most often used as the receptor for a clothes washing machine.

Stop-and-waste valve: A water supply valve with an opening that allows draining of the non-pressure side. These valves are most common in cold climates and are used to protect exterior water fixtures from freeze damage.

Tailpiece: A tailpiece is a short piece of vertical pipe that runs from the plumbing fixture waste outlet (drain) to the inlet side of the fixture's trap.

Trap: A trap is a fitting, usually located either inside or under fixtures, that prevents sewer gases from escaping from the plumbing waste pipes. Traps maintain a water seal (trap seal) extending from the trap's crown weir to its dip. Vents help protect the water seal from siphoning.

Vent: Pipe or mechanical device that allows air into the plumbing drainpipes to equalize air pressure in the pipes. Plumbing vents help avoid draining (siphoning) traps and help wastewater flow freely through the system. Plumbing vents usually terminate on the roof, although mechanical vents (called air admittance valves) are allowed in some circumstances.

Vent stack: Dry vent that connects at or near the connection of a soil or waste stack and a horizontal drain. A vent stack runs vertically and often runs parallel to the soil or waste stack that it vents.

Yard hydrant (freeze proof): A freeze proof yard hydrant is an outdoor water supply outlet that has a valve and outlet above ground and a drain opening below the frost level. When the valve is opened, water flows. When the valve is closed, the water supply to the hydrant is shut off below the frost level and a drain hole is opened that allows the water in the yard hydrant pipe to drain into a gravel bed. This drains the yard hydrant and its riser so that the hydrant will not freeze.

Waste: Liquid material in the plumbing drainage system that does not contain urine or fecal material. Waste is sometimes referred to as gray water. Waste comes from all plumbing fixtures except toilets and urinals.

The Home Plumbing System

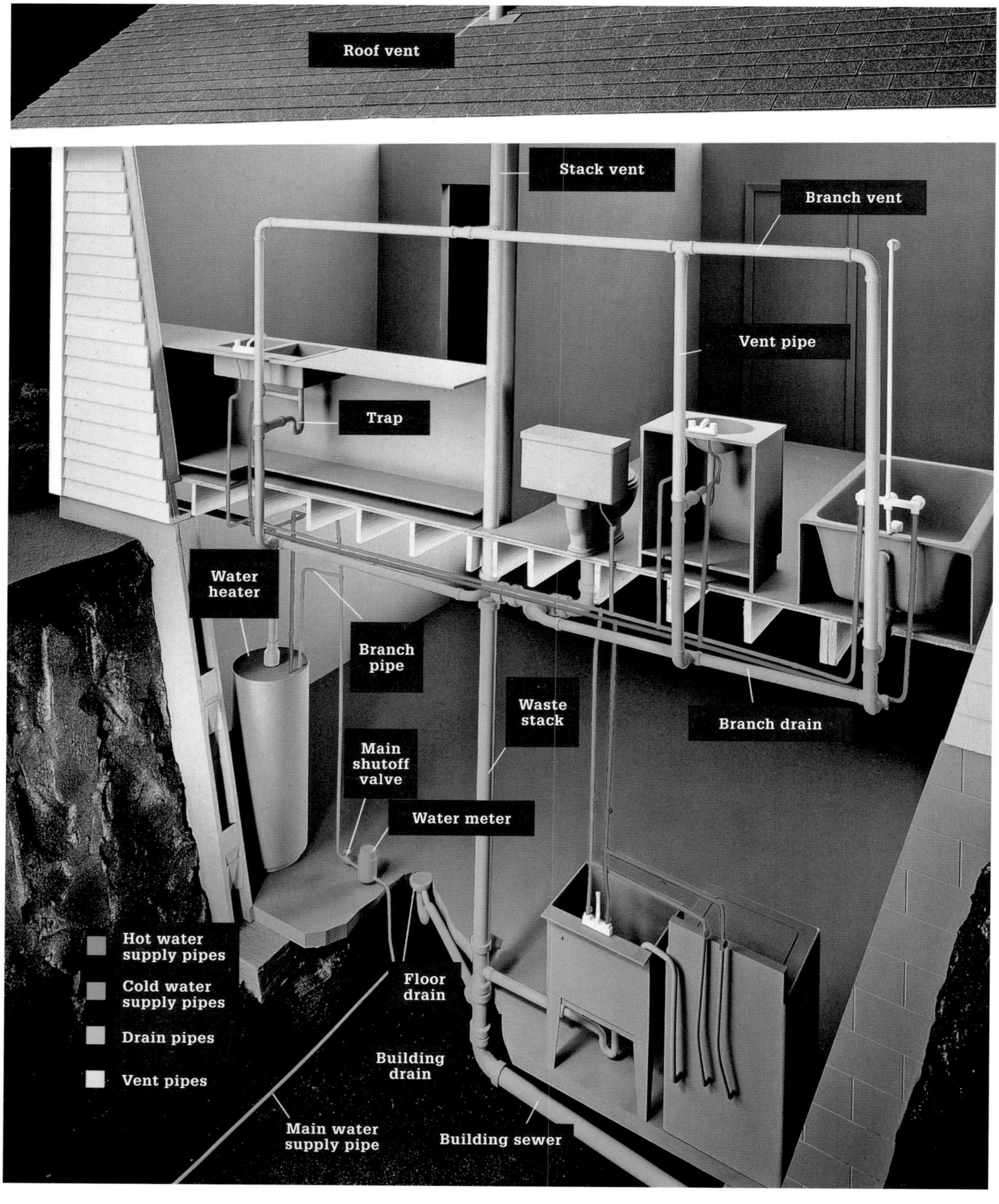

Roof vent
Stack vent
Branch vent
Vent pipe
Trap
Water heater
Branch pipe
Waste stack
Branch drain
Main shutoff valve
Water meter
Hot water supply pipes
Cold water supply pipes
Drain pipes
Vent pipes
Floor drain
Building drain
Main water supply pipe
Building sewer

Water Supply Piping

Water supply pipes carry hot and cold water throughout a house. In homes built before 1960, the original supply pipes were usually made of galvanized iron. Newer homes have supply pipes made of copper. In most areas of the country, supply pipes made of rigid plastic or PEX are accepted by local plumbing codes.

Water supply pipes are made to withstand the high pressures of the water supply system. They have small diameters, usually ½ inch to one inch, and are joined with strong, watertight fittings. The hot and cold pipes run in tandem to most parts of the house. Usually, the supply pipes run inside wall cavities or are strapped to the undersides of floor joists. They are sometimes run in the attic in warm climates.

Hot and cold water supply pipes are connected to most fixtures and appliances. Fixtures include sinks, tubs, and showers. Some fixtures, such as toilets and hose bibbs, are supplied only by cold water. Appliances include dishwashers and clothes washers. A refrigerator icemaker uses only cold water. Tradition and codes say that hot water supply pipes and faucet handles are found on the left-hand side of a fixture, with cold water on the right.

Because it is pressurized, the water supply system is prone to leaks. This is especially true of galvanized iron pipe, which has limited resistance to corrosion.

HOT WATER SUPPLY SYSTEM
Hot water supply lines
In from municipal water supply

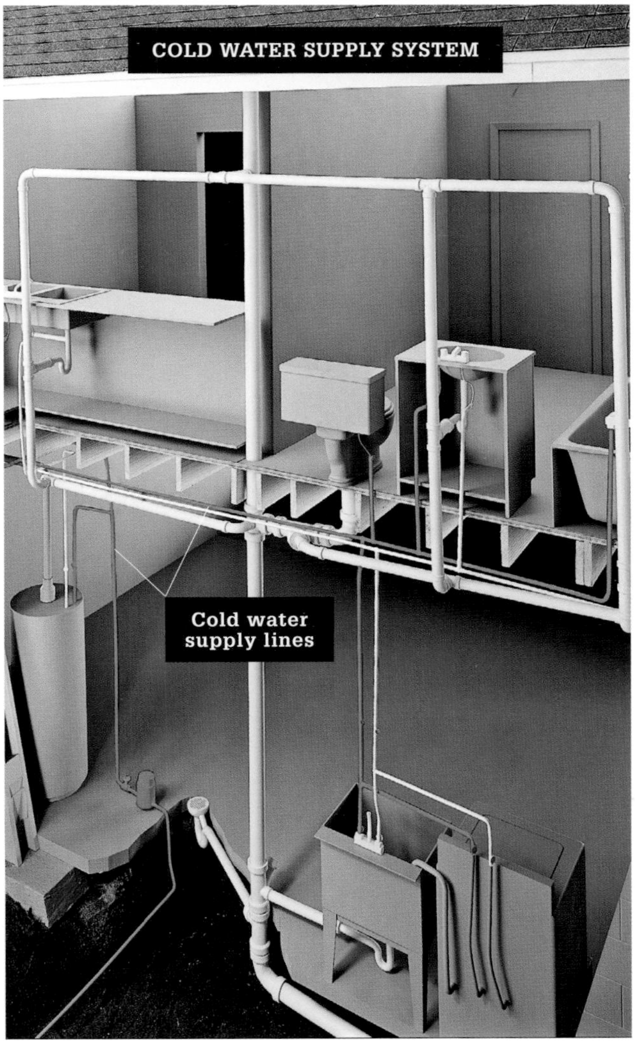
COLD WATER SUPPLY SYSTEM
Cold water supply lines

Water Pressure vs. Water Flow

Water flow and water pressure are often confused. Water flow is the amount of water you can get from a full water pipe. Water pressure is the amount of force that the water exerts on the walls of a full water pipe. Once a pipe is full of water, a water pressure increase will not increase the water flow in the pipe. In fact, a water pressure increase beyond a certain amount will cause the pipe to burst. The ideal water pressure is between 40 and 60 pounds per square inch (psi).

Water flow is primarily a function of the size, type, and installation of water supply pipes and supply fixtures. You can achieve more flow in a larger pipe than you can in a smaller pipe. Different pipe materials, such as PEX and copper, have different flow rates for the same size pipe. Many current water supply fixtures have flow restriction devices that limit the water flow rate to conserve water.

Water pressure is primarily a function of the force behind the water as it enters the piping system. A system with too little water pressure may not provide sufficient water flow when multiple supply fixtures are being used. Too much water pressure, exceeding 80 psi, can cause premature failure of water supply pipes and fixtures. A pressure regulator is recommended to reduce excessive water pressure.

Install a pressure-reducing valve when the water pressure exceeds 80 psi.

Table 29: Min. Water Flow Rate at Fixture Supply Pipe ▸

Fixture	Minimum flow rate (gpm)
Bathtub	4
Bidet	2
Dishwasher	2.75
Laundry tub	4
Lavatory	2
Shower	3
Hose bibb	5
Sink	2.5

MINIMUM & MAXIMUM WATER PRESSURE

1. Provide each dwelling with at least 40 psi of static water pressure. The minimum pressure applies to both public and private (well supplied) water supplies. Measure the water pressure as close as possible to where the water supply enters the building.
2. Do not exceed 80 psi static water pressure.
3. Install an approved pressure-reducing valve at the main water supply connection to the dwelling if the static pressure exceeds the maximum. Measure the water pressure to the point where the water supply enters the building as closely as possible.

MINIMUM FLOW RATE AT FIXTURES

1. Provide at least the water flow rate in Table 29 for the indicated fixtures. Water flow rate is measured in gallons per minute. Water flow rate means the water flow from the pipe without the fixture attached. The water flow rate in the table does not mean that the water flow from the fixture must be at least the amount in the table. Some fixtures contain required flow restrictors that will limit the actual water flow from the fixture to less than the water flow rate in the table. Example: the minimum water flow rate for a shower is three gallons per minute but the maximum flow-restricted rate from the showerhead is 2.5 gallons per minute.

MAXIMUM FLOW RATE AT FIXTURES

1. Use fixtures that allow a water flow rate that is not more than the flow rate in Table 30. Water flow rate is measured in gallons per minute. If either the water supply pressure to the building or the water pressure loss in the pipes reduces the water pressure at the fixture to less than the design pressure, the flow rate at a flow-restricted fixture may be less than the maximum.

Table 30: Max. Water Flow Rate at Fixture ▸

Fixture	Maximum water flow rate at design pressure
Lavatory	2.2 gpm at 60 psi
Shower head	2.5 gpm at 80 psi
Sink	2.2 gpm at 60 psi

COMMON WATER DISTRIBUTION PIPES

1. Install water service pipe that has a working pressure rating of at least 160 psi at 73 degrees Farenheit, or the highest available pressure, whichever is greater.
2. Common water distribution pipe materials used in modern residential construction include those in Table 31.
3. You may use other approved materials if allowed by local codes. Copper, CPVC, and PEX are the most common water distribution pipes.

Table 31: Common Water Distribution Pipe Materials ▸

Common water distribution pipe materials	Approved for use under concrete slabs
CPVC plastic pipe	yes
Copper and copper alloy pipe and tubing	Copper tubing, minimum Type M
PEX-AL-PEX pipe	yes
PEX tubing	yes
PE-AL-PE pipe	yes

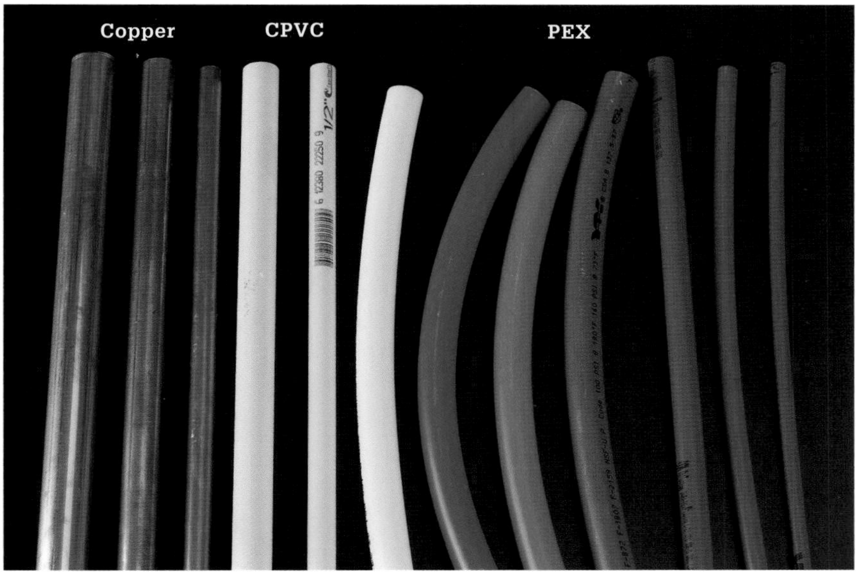

Water supply pipes include: copper, CPVC, and PEX (blue for cold, red for hot).

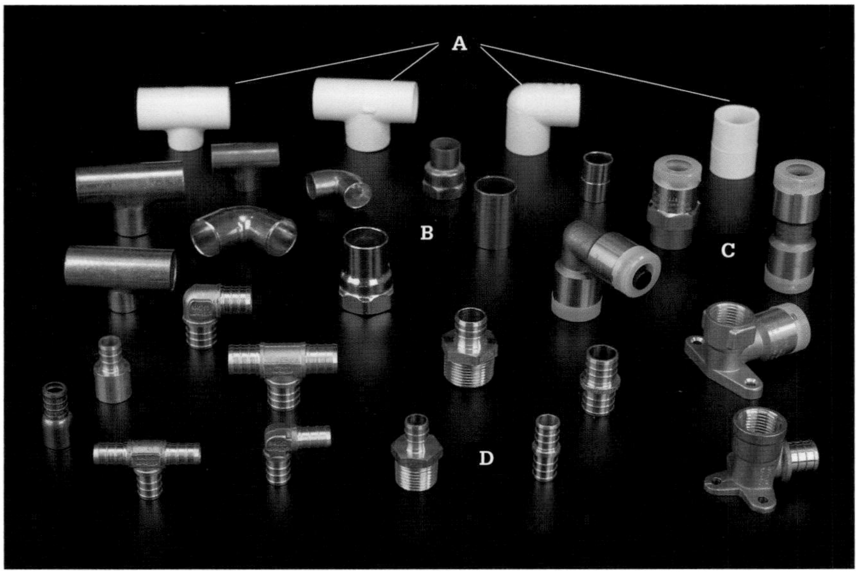

Fittings for water supply lines include: (A) PVC and CPVC tee, elbow and coupling; (B) copper tees and elbows; (C) brass compression fittings; (d) brass fittings, with barbs.

Table 32: Plumbing Pipe Support, Water Supply & DWV Pipes ▸

Pipe material	Maximum horizontal spacing	Maximum vertical spacing	Mid story guide req'd for pipe dia. ≤ 2"
ABS pipe	48"	120"	yes
Cast-iron pipe	60"*	180"	no
Copper tubing (≤ 1¼" dia.)	72"	120"	no
Copper tubing (≥ 1½" dia.)	120"	120"	no
CPVC pipe or tubing (≤ 1" dia.)	36"	120"	yes
CPVC pipe or tubing (≥ 1¼" dia.)	48"	120"	yes
Polybutylene (PB) pipe or tubing	32"	48"	no
PEX	32"	120"	yes
PEX-AL-PEX and PE-AL-PE	32"	48"	yes
PVC pipe	48"	120"	yes
Steel pipe	144"	180"	no

* You may increase cast-iron pipe horizontal spacing to 120" when using 10 ft. pipe lengths.

PIPE SUPPORT

1. Support pipes so they will maintain alignment and will not sag.
2. Support and install pipes so they can move with the normal expansion and contraction of the piping system without scraping or rubbing against supports or framing materials.
3. Use pipe supports that will carry the weight of the pipe and that are sufficiently wide to prevent crimping and distortion of the pipe.
4. Use pipe supports that will not cause corrosion or galvanic reaction between the pipe and the support. Example: do not use steel supports with copper pipe or copper supports with cast-iron pipe.
5. Provide rigid sway bracing at changes in pipe direction more than 45 degrees for pipe sizes at least 4 inches in diameter.
6. Provide horizontal and vertical support for pipes according to Table 33 (see page 131).

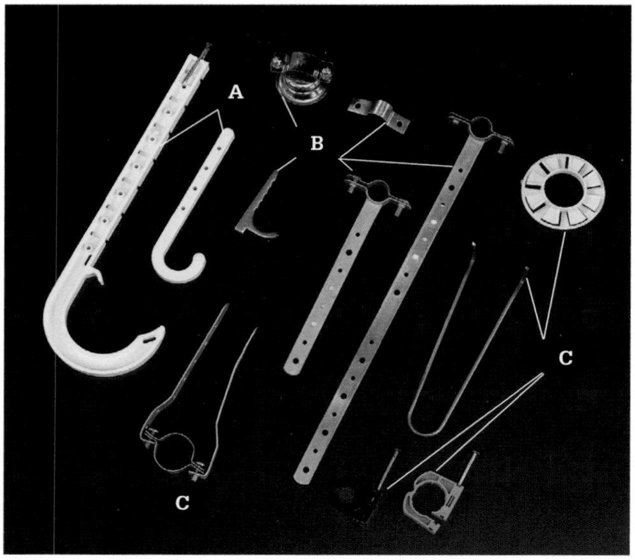

Support hangers and clamps for: CPVC and PVC (A), Copper (B), PEX (C).

Support copper tubing with compatible hangers.

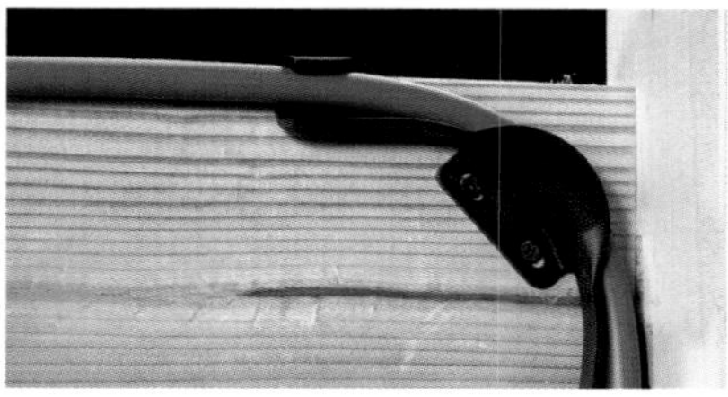

Support for PEX tubing is particularly important near manifolds and fittings.

Provide vertical support for pipes running parallel to wall studs. Install supports according to Table 32.

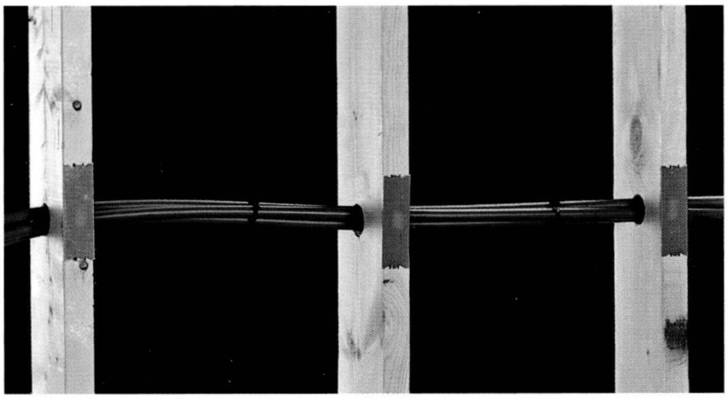

Protect pipes 1½" from the edges of studs and joists.

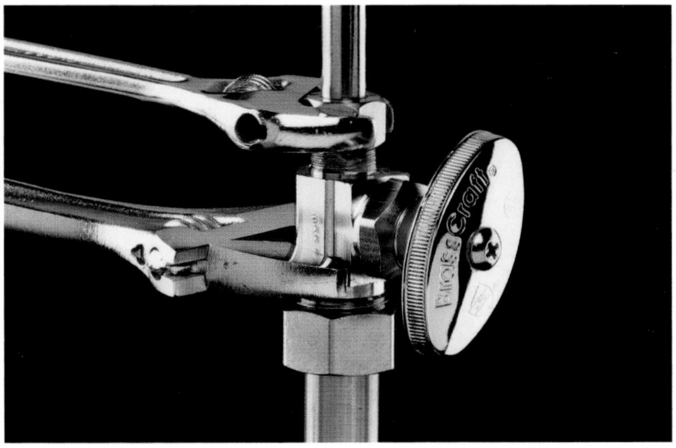

Install fixture cutoff valves on hot and cold water supply pipes to most fixtures.

PROTECTING PIPES FROM PUNCTURES

1. Protect plumbing pipes (other than cast iron or galvanized steel) with shield plates, if the pipe is closer than 1½ inches from the edge of studs, joists, rafters, or similar framing members. Extend the shield plate at least two inches below top plates and at least two inches above bottom plates.
2. Use shield plates at least 0.062 (1/16)-inch thick.
3. Apply these rules to pipes running through holes and notches in framing materials. While not required by most general codes, it is a best practice to protect pipes (other than cast iron or galvanized steel) that are closer than 1½ inches from the edge of framing materials. The most common example of such pipes is a pipe installed parallel to the edge of a stud or joist.

PROTECTING PIPES FROM FREEZING

1. Do not install water supply and waste pipes: outside of a building, in exterior building walls, in attics and crawl spaces, or in any other place subject to freezing temperatures unless the pipes are protected by insulation or heat or both.
2. Install water service pipe at least 12 inches deep or at least six inches below the frost line.
3. Verify minimum water service and building sewer pipe depth with the local building official.
4. Apply these requirements only to areas with a winter design temperature of 32 degrees Farenheit or less.

FIXTURE CUTOFF VALVE (ANGLE STOP)

1. Provide each plumbing fixture, except for bathtubs and showers, with an accessible cutoff valve on the hot and cold water supply pipes. These valves are sometimes called "angle stop valves." You may install cutoff valves at bathtubs and shower, but these valves are not required.

VALVES & OUTLETS INSTALLED BELOW GROUND

1. Do not install water supply outlets and stop-and-waste valves below ground. Example: do not install a hose bibb below ground.
2. You may install a freeze-proof yard hydrant below ground if the water supply to the hydrant is protected with a backflow preventer and the yard hydrant is permanently labeled as a "non-potable water source."

HOSE BIBB CUTOFF VALVE

1. Provide hose bibbs that are subject to freezing with a stop-and-waste valve inside the building. This includes frost-proof hose bibbs.
2. You need not install a stop-and-waste valve on a frost-proof hose bibb if the stem extends into an open heated or semi-conditioned area of the building.

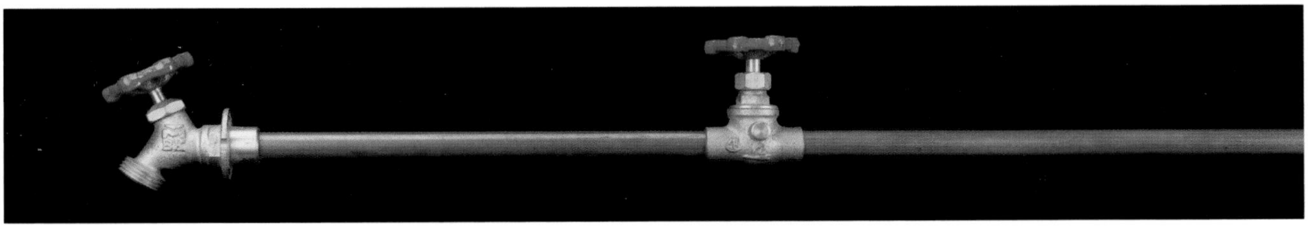

Hose bibbs that are subject to freezing require a stop-and-waste valve inside the building.

Drain, Waste & Vent Piping (DWV)

Drainpipes use gravity to carry wastewater away from fixtures, appliances, and other drains. This waste water is carried out of the house to a municipal sewer system or septic tank.

Drainpipes are usually plastic or cast iron. In some older homes, drainpipes may be made of copper or lead. Because they are not part of the supply system, lead drainpipes pose no health hazard. However, lead pipes are no longer manufactured for home plumbing systems.

Drainpipes have diameters ranging from 1¼ inches to four inches. These large diameters allow waste to pass through easily.

Traps are an important part of the drain system. These curved sections of drainpipe hold standing water, and they are usually found near any drain opening. The standing water of a trap prevents sewer gases from backing up into the home. Each time a drain is used, the standing trap water is flushed away and is replaced by new water.

In order to work properly, the drain system requires air. Air protects trap from being drained. To allow air into the drain system, drainpipes are connected to vent pipes. All drain systems must include vents, and the entire system is called the drain-waste-vent (DWV) system. One or more vents, located on the roof, provide the air needed for the DWV system to work.

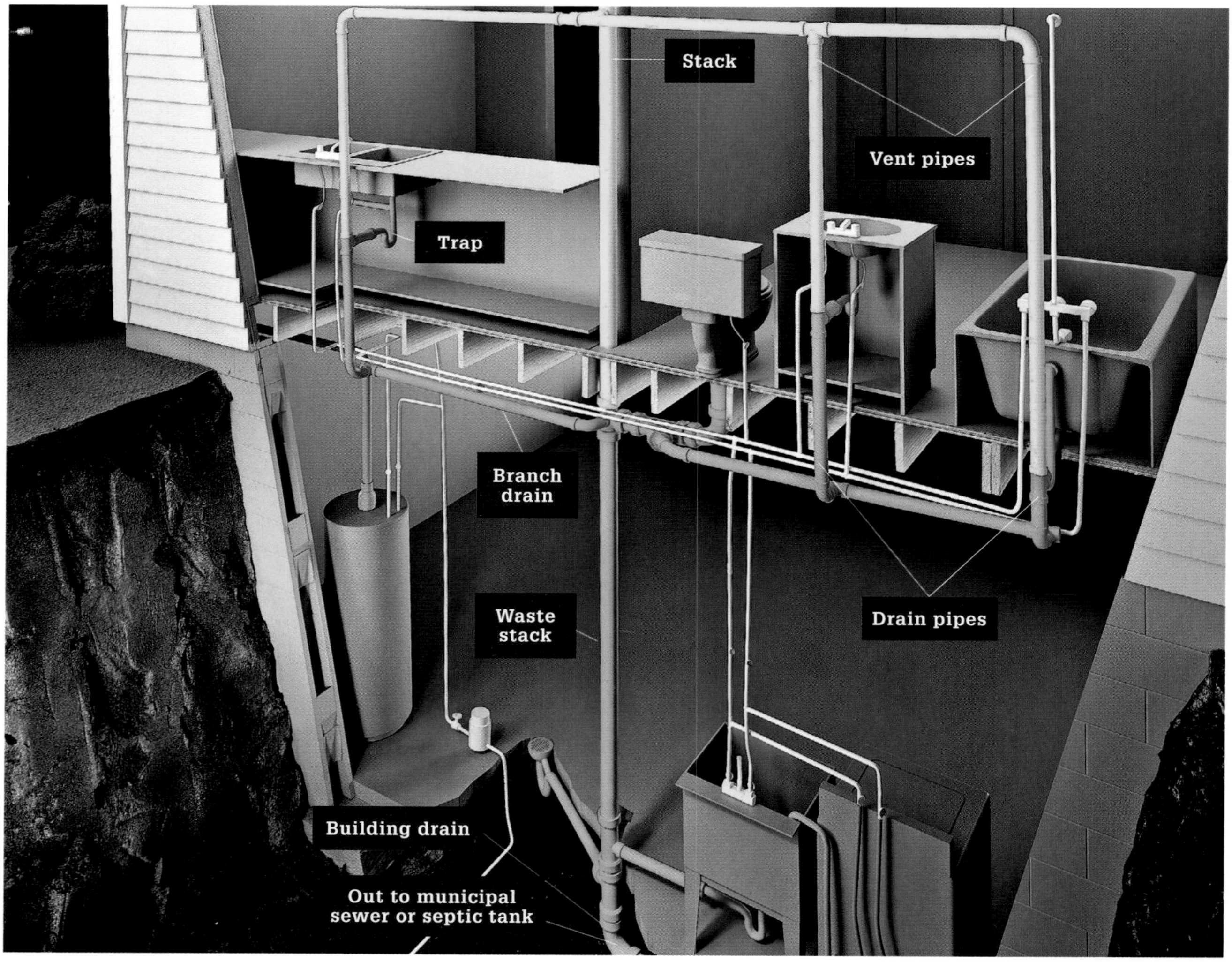
Stack
Vent pipes
Trap
Branch drain
Waste stack
Drain pipes
Building drain
Out to municipal sewer or septic tank

Use vent tee fittings only in vent pipes, not in drain pipes that carry wastewater. Drain pipes must maintain a minimum 2% slope that is not supported by a tee with perpendicular pipe outlets.

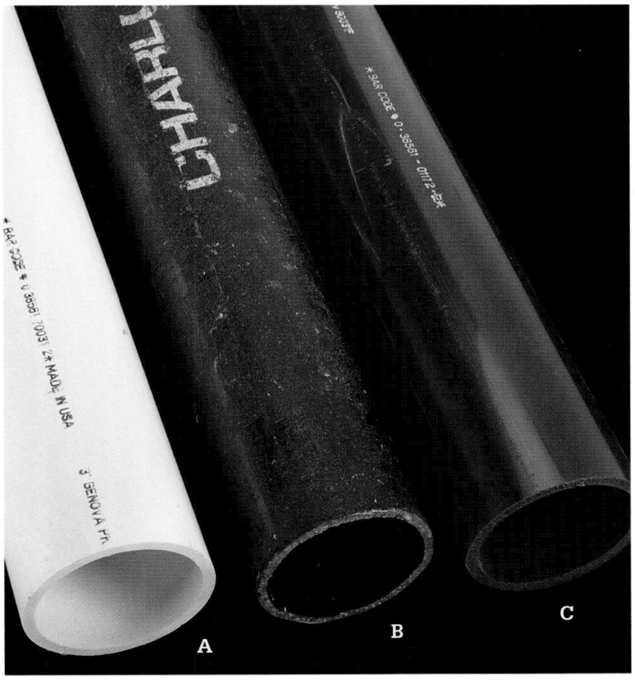

Common sewer pipe materials: PVC (A) cast iron (B), and ABS (C) are allowed for use in DWV systems.

DRAIN & SEWER PIPE GENERAL REQUIREMENTS

1. Install fittings that have a smooth interior surface and are compatible with the pipe to which they are attached. Example: do not use ABS fittings with PVC pipe.
2. Do not use fittings that contain ledges, shoulders, or reductions that may retard or obstruct drainage flow.
3. Install fittings that maintain a two percent slope and are approved for use where installed. Example: do not use a vent tee in a drainage pipe where water flows.
4. Do not use threaded connections in pipes where the threads run on the inside of the pipe and could retard or obstruct drainage flow.
5. Do not drill, tap, burn, or weld drainage, sewer, and vent pipes. Example: do not drill into a vent pipe to insert the discharge hose from a water softener.
6. Do not use the following types of joints and connections: cement or concrete, mastic or hot-pour bituminous, fittings not approved for the specific type of pipe or installation, joints between different pipe diameters made with elastomeric rolling O-rings, solvent-cement joints between different types of plastic pipe, and saddle fittings.

COMMON DWV PIPE MATERIAL

1. You may use any of the common drainage and sewer pipe materials listed in Table 33. You may use other materials listed if approved by your local codes.
2. Install galvanized steel drainage pipe at least six inches above the ground.

Table 33: Common Drainage and Sewer Pipe Materials ▸

Common drainage & sewer pipe materials	Used for drainage	Used for sewer
Cast iron soil pipe	yes	yes
ABS-DWV pipe	yes	yes
PVC plastic pipe	yes	yes
Steel pipe (black or galvanized)	yes	no

DWV Fitting Descriptions ▸

Bend: A fitting used to change the direction of waste flow. It is similar to an elbow used in water pressure pipes. Some people refer to a DWV bend as an "elbow." A single bend has two openings; a double bend has three openings, two of which are directly across from each other. Some bends have side inlets. Use vent bends only in the dry vent sections of vent pipes.

Closet bend: A fitting used to connect a closet flange (a part of your toilet drain system) to other plumbing pipes. Closet bends often reduce the pipe size from the four inches of the closet flange to three inches.

Closet flange: The fitting upon which a toilet (water closet) sits. Many different closet flanges are available to accommodate different fitting and pipe configurations. One type of closet flange allows you to offset the closet flange around a floor joist.

Coupling: A fitting used to join two lengths of pipe in a straight line. It has two female openings, one on each end.

Inlet: An additional opening in a fitting. A low-heel-inlet is located in a straight line with one opening of the fitting. A high-heel-inlet is located above the curved portion of the fitting. A side-inlet occurs on one side of the fitting.

Table 34: Bend Direction Change ▸

Bend name	Direction change
¼ bend	90°
⅙ bend	60°
⅛ bend	45°
1⁄16 bend	22½°

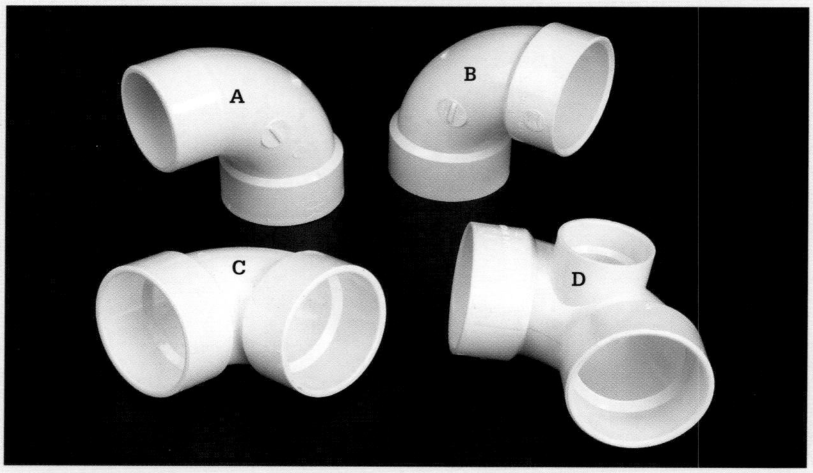

Bend pipes for DWV systems include: (A) ¼ street bend, (B) ¼ bend, (C) ¼ vent bend, (D) ¼ bend with side inlet.

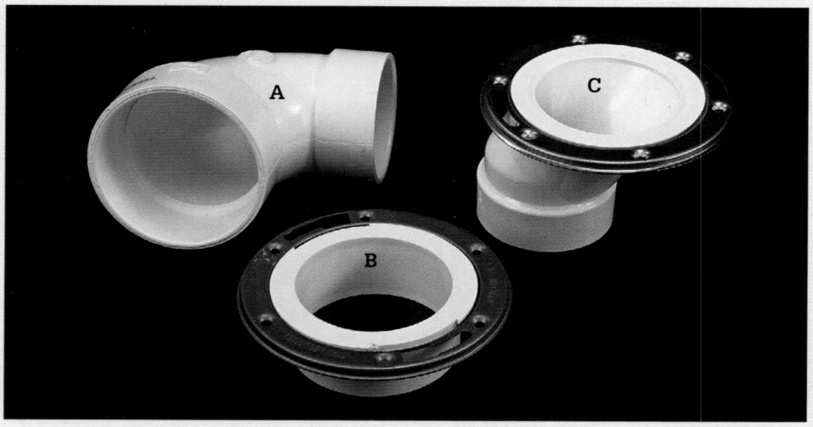

Parts of a toilet drain system include: closet bend (A), closet flange (B), offset closet flange (C).

Sanitary tee. A sanitary tee is a tee fitting combined with a ¼-bend fitting.

Street fitting: A street fitting has a female opening (hub) on one end and a male opening (spigot) on the other end. Most drainage fittings have female openings on both ends.

Sweep: A fitting used to change the direction of waste flow. Sweeps have a large curvature radius. Short sweeps have a smaller radius than large sweeps.

Tee: A fitting with three openings. Two openings are in a straight line, and one opening is at an approximate 90-degree angle to the others. Double tees, with four openings, are also available. Use vent tees only in the dry vent sections of vent pipes.

Wye: A fitting with three openings. Two openings are in a straight line and one opening is at an approximate 45-degree angle to the others. Wye fittings can be made with other fittings to make combination fittings such as a tee-wye and a combination wye and ⅛ bend. Double wye and double tee-wye fittings are also available.

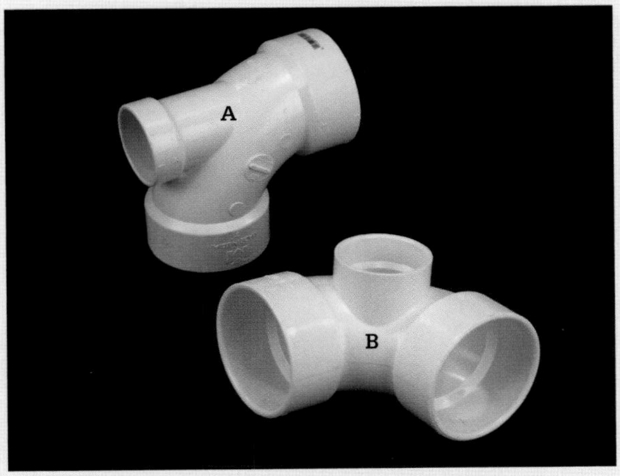

Inlet fittings include: bend with low-heel inlet (A), bend with side inlet (B).

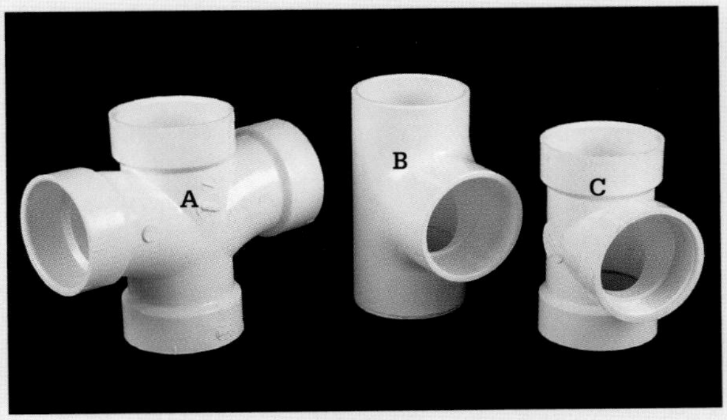

Tees for use in DWV systems include: Double fixture tee (A), vent tee (B), test tee (C).

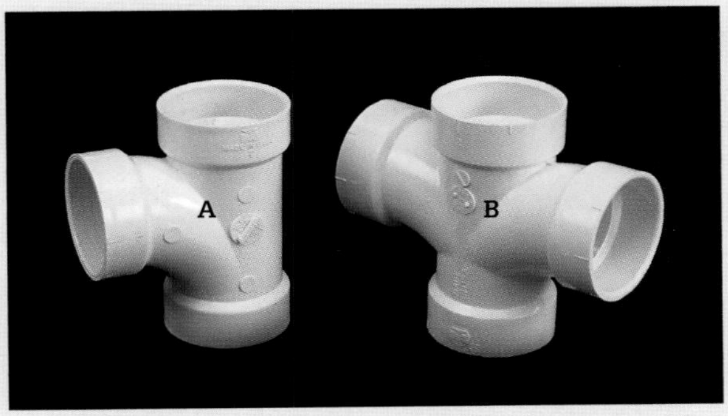

Two types of sanitary tees include: Single sanitary tee (A), double sanitary tee (B).

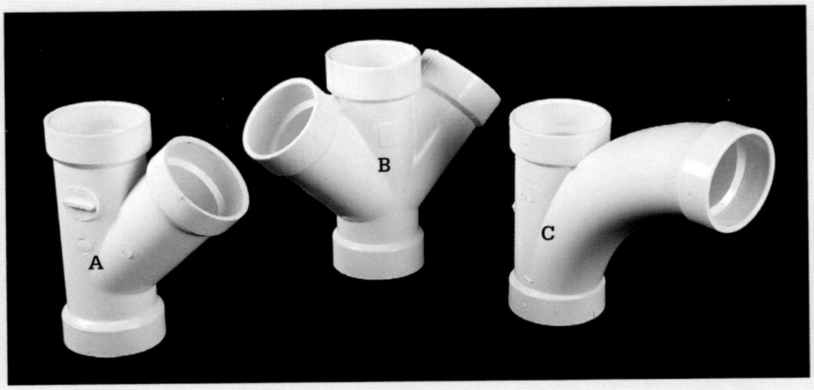

Wye fittings for DWV use include: Wye (A), double wye (B), tee-wye (C).

DRAINAGE & SEWER PIPE FITTINGS FOR CHANGING FLOW DIRECTION

1. Use the fittings in Table 35 to change the direction of flow in drainage and sewer pipes.

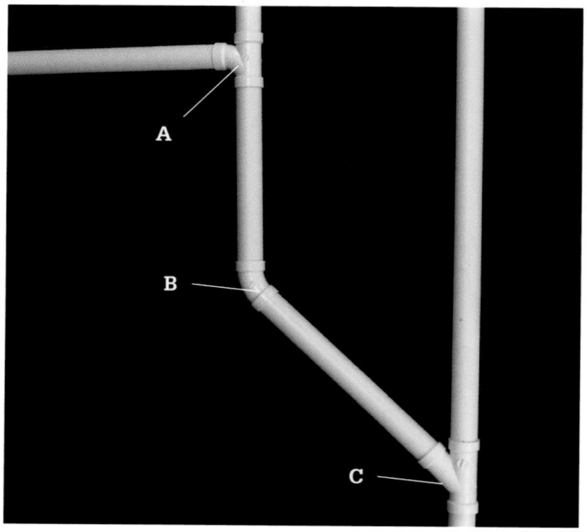

Changing flow direction from horizontal to vertical using: sanitary tee (A), ⅛ bend (B), wye (C).

Table 35: Approved Drainage Fittings for Changing Flow Direction ▸

Type of fitting	Horiz. to vert.	Vert. to horiz.	Horiz. to horiz.
1/16 bend	yes	yes	yes
⅛ bend	yes	yes	yes
⅙ bend	yes	yes	yes
¼ bend	yes	yes, for fixture drains ≤ 2"	yes, for fixture drains ≤ 2"
Short sweep	yes	yes, for fixture drains ≤ 2" and for drains ≥ 3"	yes, for fixture drains ≤ 2"
Long sweep	yes	yes	yes
Sanitary tee	yes, with limits	no	no
Wye	yes	yes	yes
Long radius tee-wye	yes	yes	yes

Drain & Sewer Pipe Connections & Joints

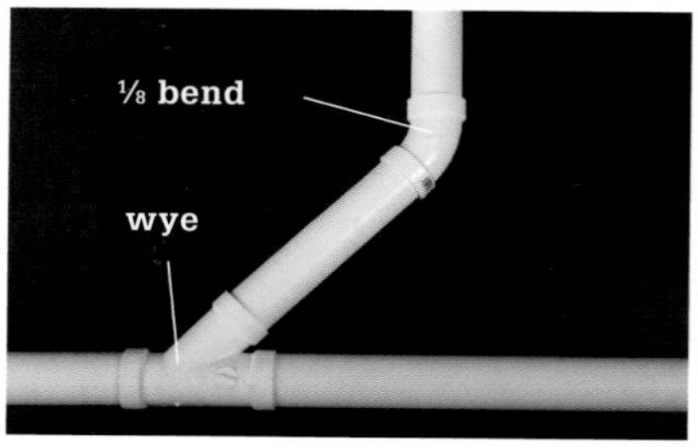

Changing flow direction from vertical to horizontal using a wye fitting and ⅛ bend.

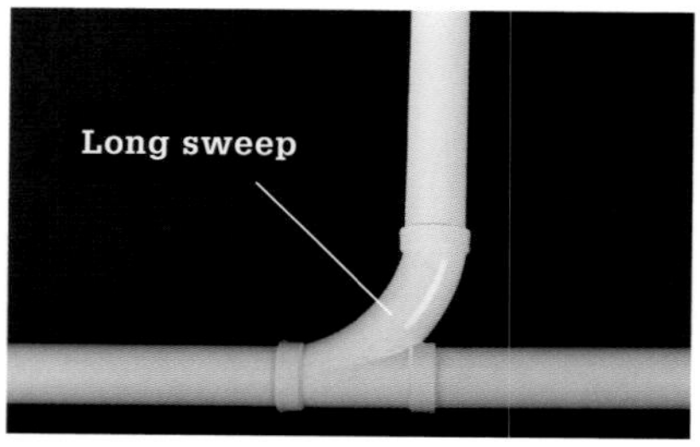

Changing flow direction from vertical to horizontal using a long sweep.

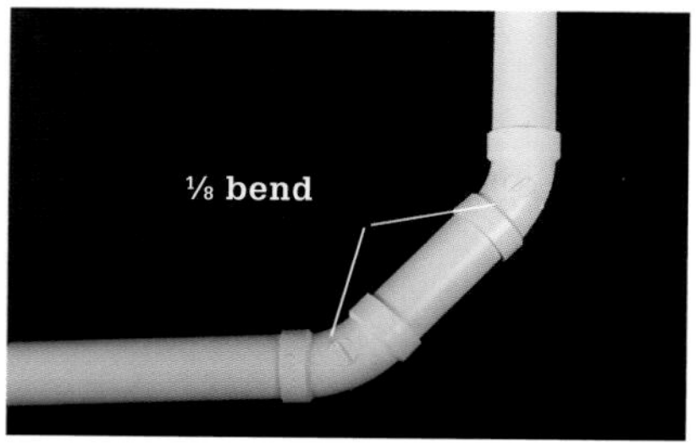

Changing flow direction from vertical to horizontal using two ⅛ bends.

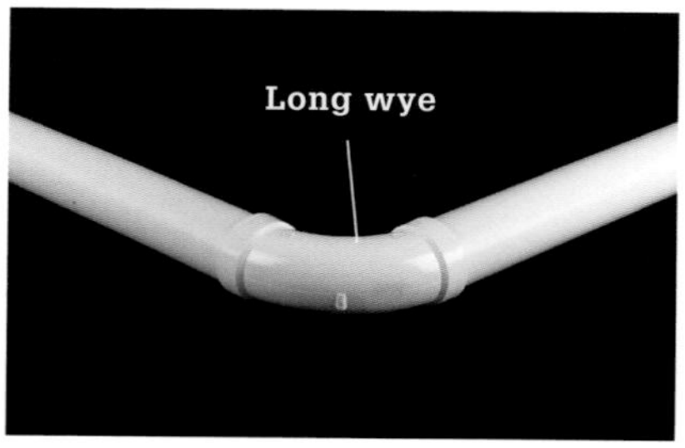

Changing flow direction from horizontal to horizontal using a long sweep fitting.

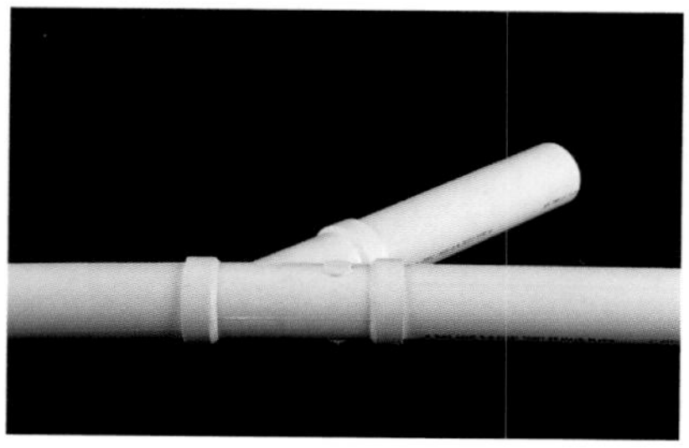

Changing flow direction from horizontal to horizontal using a wye fitting.

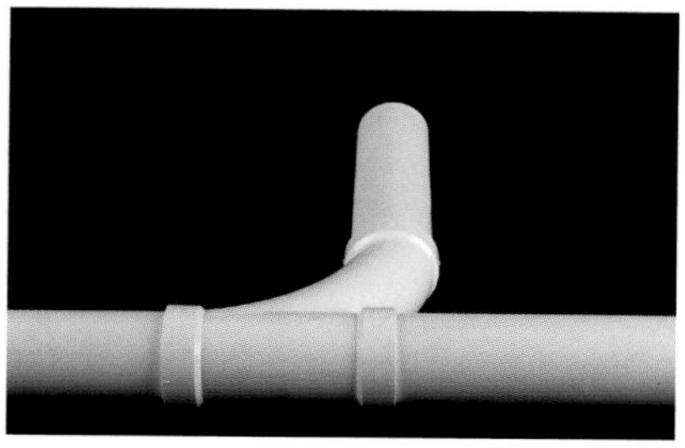

Changing flow direction from horizontal to horizontal using a long-radius tee-wye fitting.

DRAINAGE & SEWER PIPE FITTINGS: CHANGING FROM HORIZONTAL TO VERTICAL USING MULTIPLE FITTINGS

1. You may use multiple fittings and double fittings (such as double sanitary tees) to connect back-to-back fixtures and two or more branch drains on the same level if directly opposite fitting connections are from the same size pipe, and if directly opposite fitting connections are from similar fixture types or fixture groups.
2. Do not use a double sanitary tee to receive discharge from back-to-back toilets and from fixtures or appliances with pumping action (such as washing machines and dishwashers). You may use a double sanitary tee if the distance between the center of the closet flange and the inlet of the sanitary tee is at least 18 inches.

QUARTER BENDS WITH HEEL OR SIDE-INLET

1. You may use a heel-inlet quarter bend to change drainage flow direction, except:
   (a) you may not discharge a toilet into any opening of a heel-inlet quarter bend unless the heel-inlet is used as a dry vent and the heel-inlet is installed vertically (facing up), and
   (b) you may not discharge flow from a wet-vented fixture into the low-heel inlet of a quarter bend.
2. You may use a side-inlet quarter bend to change the flow direction in any drainage configuration. The side-inlet may accept drainage flow from any fixture.
3. You may connect a dry vent to a heel or side-inlet quarter bend only when the inlet is vertical (facing up). You may connect a dry vent to a quarter bend with a horizontal (side facing) inlet only if the entire quarter bend fitting is used as part of a dry vent.

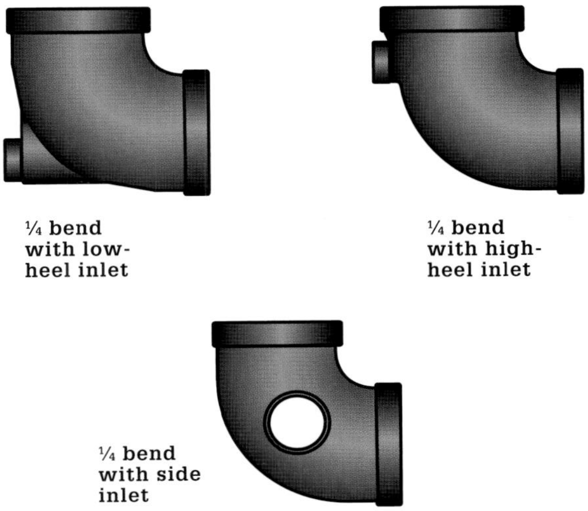

¼ bend with low-heel inlet
¼ bend with high-heel inlet
¼ bend with side inlet

Common bend configurations.

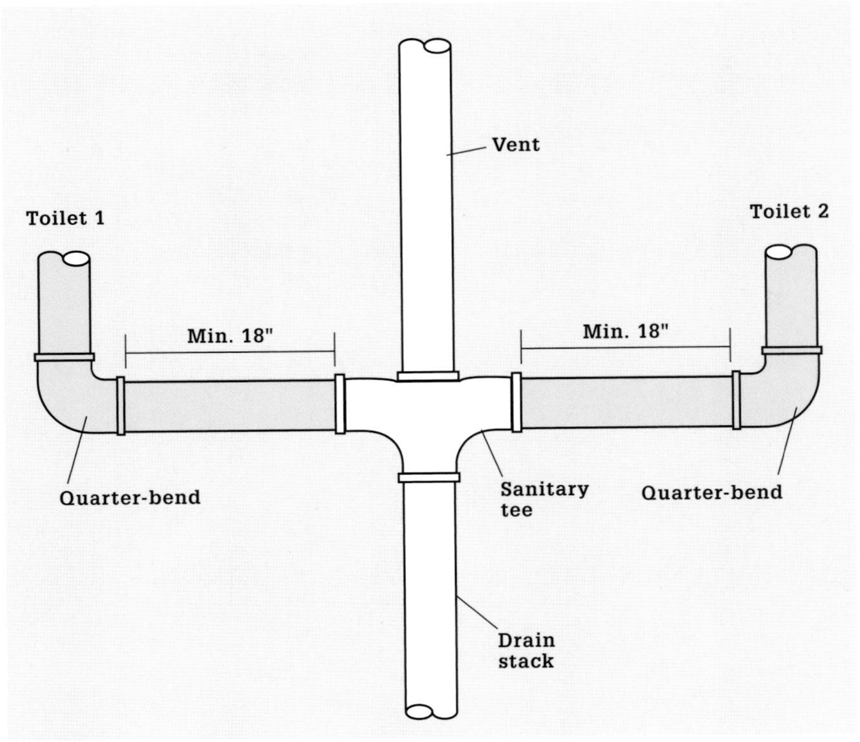

Vent
Toilet 1
Toilet 2
Min. 18"
Min. 18"
Quarter-bend
Sanitary tee
Quarter-bend
Drain stack

Separate two toilets discharging into the same sanitary tee by at least 18" between the sanitary tee and each toilet.

WATER CLOSET CONNECTION BETWEEN CLOSET FLANGE & PIPE

1. You may use a three-inch quarter bend to connect to a closet flange if you install a four-inch-by-three-inch flange to receive the closet fixture horn.
2. You may use a four-inch-by-three-inch reducing closet bend to connect to the closet flange.

TAILPIECES

1. Provide sinks, dishwashers, laundry tubs, and similar fixtures with tailpieces and traps at least 1½ inches in diameter.
2. Provide vanity sinks, bidets, and similar fixtures with tailpieces and traps at least 1¼ inches.

SLIP JOINTS

1. Use slip joints only on a trap inlet, outlet, and within the trap seal.
2. Provide access to slip joints with access of at least 12 by 12 inches.

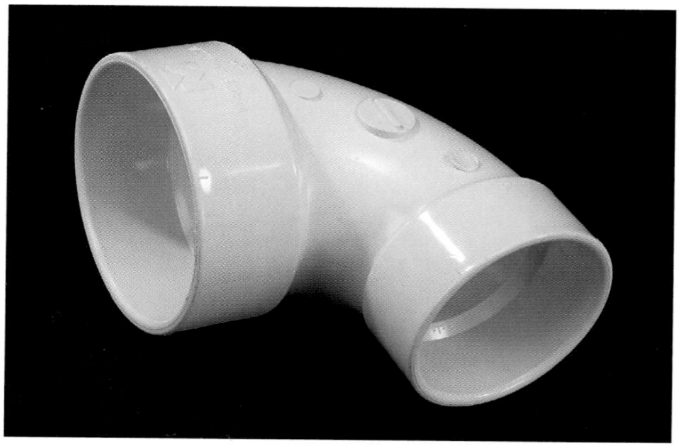

4 × 3 reducing closet bend (horn).

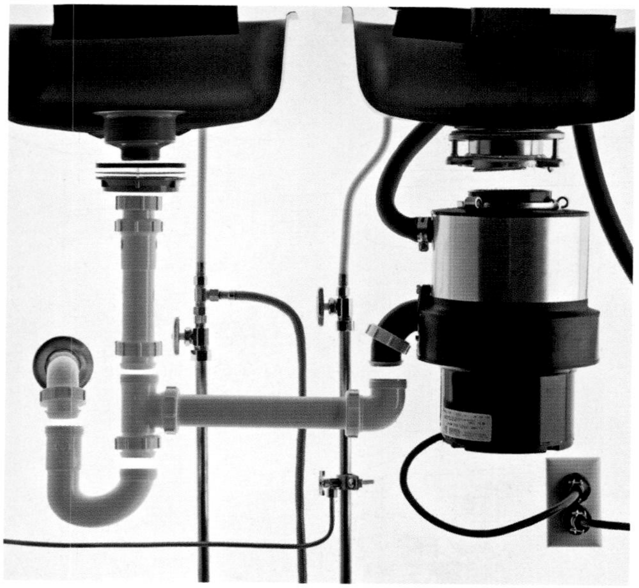

Drain tailpieces must match the diameter of the other pipes in the drain kit: 1¼ or 1½" depending on the type of fixture being drained.

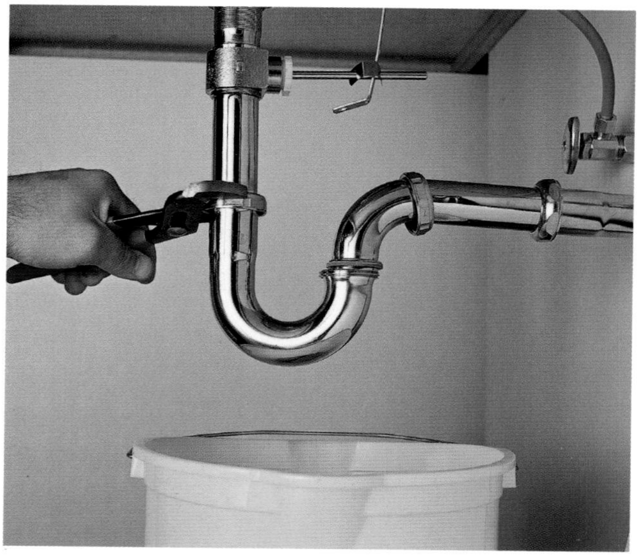

Chromed P-trap with slip joints on lavatory sink.

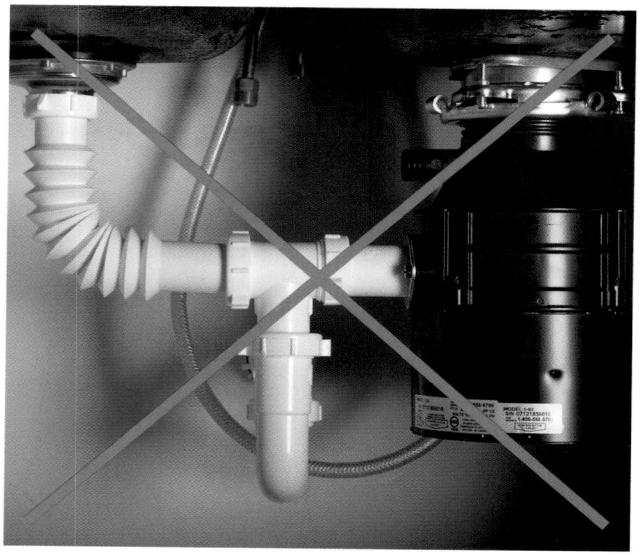

VIOLATION! Flexible, ribbed material is not approved anywhere in a DWV system.

Drain & Sewer Pipe Connections & Joints

ABS PLASTIC PIPE JOINTS

1. You may use approved elastomeric gaskets to join buried ABS pipes. You may use elastomeric gaskets above ground when other joints are not practical and when approved by the building official.
2. You may use solvent cement to join ABS pipes above and below ground. Clean and dry pipes and fittings before applying solvent cement to all joint surfaces. Make the joint while the solvent cement is wet. Use solvent cement that complies with ASTM D 2235. Do not use PVC cement with ABS pipe.
3. You may use threaded joints for Schedule 80 and heavier ABS pipe. The threads should be NPT type.

STEEL PIPE JOINTS

1. You may use threaded joints for galvanized steel pipes. The threads should be NPT type.
2. You may use approved mechanical joints to join galvanized steel pipes. Install the mechanical joints according to manufacturer's instructions.

PVC PLASTIC PIPE JOINTS

1. You may use approved elastomeric gaskets to join buried PVC pipes. You may use elastomeric gaskets above ground and when approved by the building official.
2. You may use solvent cement to join PVC pipes above and below ground. Clean and dry pipes and fittings before applying primer to all joint surfaces. Apply purple-colored primer that complies with ASTM F 656. Apply solvent cement that complies with ASTM D 2564. Make the joint while the solvent cement is wet. Do not use ABS cement with PVC pipe.
3. You may use threaded joints for Schedule 80 and heavier PVC pipe. The threads should be NPT type.

JOINTS BETWEEN DIFFERENT TYPES OF PIPE

1. Use compression or mechanical-sealing elastomeric fittings approved for joining the different types of pipe. Install all fittings according to manufacturer's instructions.
2. Use an approved brass ferrule with a caulked joint or a mechanical compression joint when joining copper tubing to cast-iron pipe.
3. Use a brass converter fitting or a dielectric fitting when joining copper tubing to galvanized steel pipe.

Use the correct solvent for the type of pipe you're using: PVC and CPVC should be welded with PVC solvent; AB requires AB solvent.

Cast-iron drain pipe joints originally were made with hubbed fittings. Since new cast iron is seldom installed, joinery with cast iron is normally accomplished by connecting the original cast iron to another material, such as PVC, with a banded coupling.

DRAIN & SEWER PIPE SLOPE

1. Install horizontal drainage and sewer pipe with a uniform slope and alignment.
2. Install pipe not more than 2½ inches in diameter with at least a ¼ unit in 12 units (2 percent) slope.
3. Install pipe at least three inches diameter with at least a ⅛ unit in 12 units (one percent) slope.

DRAIN & SEWER PIPE DEAD ENDS

1. You may not extend a drainage or sewer pipe more than two feet beyond the waste flow unless the extension is necessary to install a required cleanout or unless the extension is part of an approved rough-in for future fixtures.

DRAIN & SEWER PIPE SIZE REDUCTION

1. Do not reduce drainage and sewer pipe size in the direction of the waste flow. (*Note: A four-inch by three-inch closet bend fitting is not classified as a reduction in size.*) Example: do not drain a two-inch trap into a 1½-inch drainpipe.

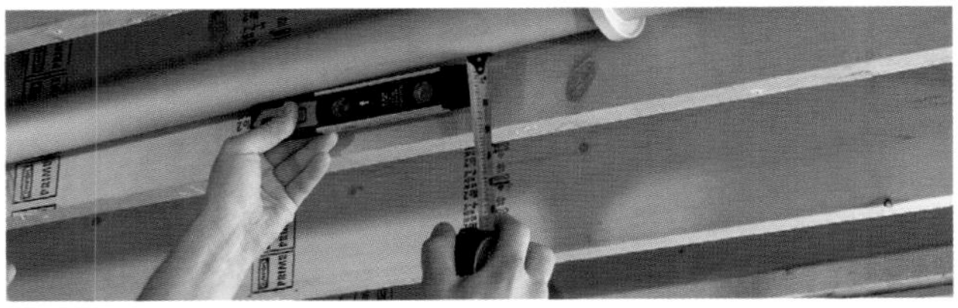

Install and support DVW pipe to maintain the required uniform slope.

Drain & Sewer Cleanout Openings

CLEANOUT LOCATIONS & SPACING

1. Install a cleanout in every horizontal drainpipe so that the distance between cleanouts is not more than 100 feet, measured along the pipe length. Install at least one cleanout for every horizontal drainpipe regardless of drainpipe length. This provision applies to the building drain, building sewer, and horizontal branch drains.
2. Install a cleanout near the building drain and building sewer junction. You may install this cleanout inside or outside the building. Make this cleanout accessible at the lowest floor level inside or at grade level outside. You may install this cleanout in at least a three-inch diameter soil stack if the cleanout fitting is not more than 10 feet from the building drain connection to the building sewer. Measure the 10 feet along the developed length of the pipe from the cleanout fitting to the building drain and sewer junction.
3. Install a cleanout near the base of every vertical waste or soil stack. You may install this cleanout in the vertical stack or horizontal drainpipe.
4. Install a cleanout at every change of pipe direction more than 45 degrees when the direction change uses one fitting. You do not need to install a cleanout if the change in pipe direction uses two or more fittings. When multiple direction changes occur in one pipe run, only one cleanout is required, spaced not more than 40 feet apart. This provision applies to the building drain, building sewer, and horizontal branch drains. Example: a direction change using one quarter-bend fitting requires a cleanout, but a change in direction using two eighth-bend fittings does not require a cleanout.

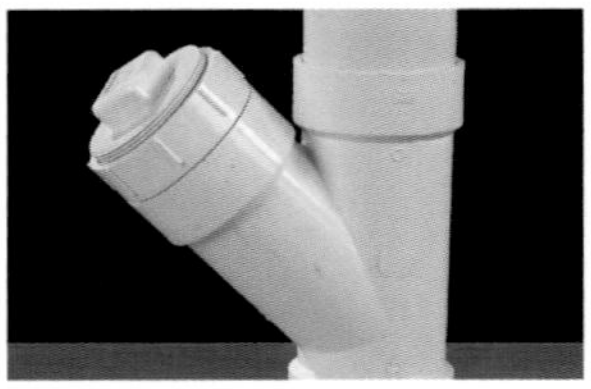

Install a cleanout near the foundation where the interior building drain pipe connects with the exterior building sewer pipe.

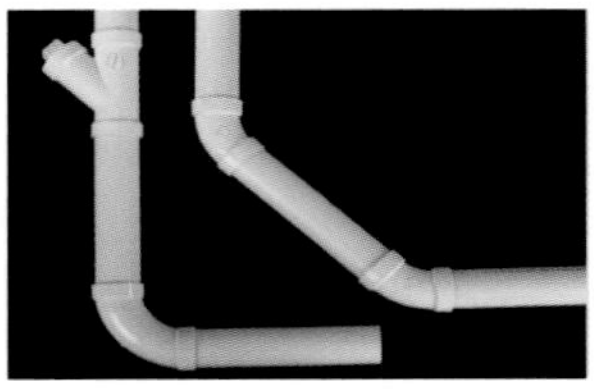

A cleanout is required when one fitting changes flow direction by more than 45°. A cleanout is not required when you use two or more fittings to change flow direction.

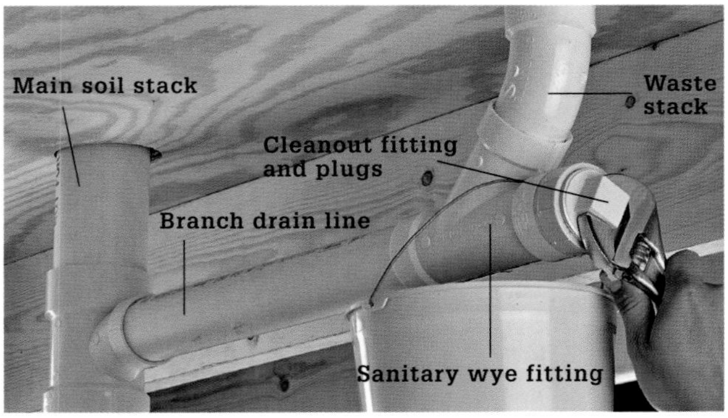

Install a cleanout near the base of a vertical soil or waste stack.

CLEANOUT SUBSTITUTES

1. You may use a fixture trap (such as a sink) or a fixture with an integral trap (such as a toilet) as a cleanout if the:
   (a) trap or fixture is readily removable without disturbing concealed piping;
   (b) cleanout is accessible; and
   (c) fixture trap or fixture provides the required cleanout size for all pipes that will be cleaned from the cleanout substitute.
2. Note that drainage pipes three inches and larger require a cleanout size that is larger than most fixture drains. You cannot use a 1½ or two-inch fixture drain as a cleanout for pipes three inches and larger.

CLEANOUT SIZE

1. Install cleanouts at least as large as in Table 36. You may install different size cleanouts in cast-iron drainage pipes because these pipes have different cap sizes.

CLEANOUT ACCESSIBILITY

1. Provide at least 18 inches in front of cleanouts three inches and larger and at least 12 inches in front of cleanouts smaller than three inches.
2. Provide enough access around concealed cleanouts to remove the cleanout plug and use the drain cleaning equipment.
3. Do not conceal cleanouts with permanent finishing materials.
4. Extend underground cleanouts to or above finished grade. Do not extend cleanouts above surfaces where they may become trip hazards or where they may be damaged by traffic.

CLEANOUT PLUGS

1. Install brass or plastic plugs in cleanout fittings.
2. Make cleanouts gas and liquid tight.

Table 36: Cleanout Size ▸

Pipe size	Min. cleanout size
1½"	1½"
2"	1½"
3"	2½"
≥ 4"	3½"

CLEANOUT DIRECTION

1. Install cleanouts so that they open toward the direction of the waste flow.

CLEANOUT FIXTURE CONNECTIONS

1. Do not connect other pipes or fixtures to an existing cleanout unless the connection is approved by the local building official and you install an alternate cleanout. Example: do not remove a cleanout plug and use the cleanout opening as the drain for a laundry sink.

Install cleanouts to branch drain lines in areas so there is enough access for you to reach into the drainline with clog-clearing equipment.

Seal cleanout plugs before capping cleanout fittings.

Plumbing Vents

To understand the purpose of plumbing vents, you must first understand the purpose of plumbing traps. A trap is required for all fixture drains connected to the DWV pipes. A trap can be a separate fitting, such as a P-trap for a sink or a shower or it can be part of the fixture, such as the trap in a toilet. A trap maintains a water seal that keeps noxious and potentially explosive sewer gas in the DWV pipes and away from the air in the home. Water flows into a fixture and through a trap when you use a fixture. When you stop using the fixture, some of the water remains in the trap and recharges the trap's water seal.

When water flows in a pipe near a trap, the suction caused by the flowing water can create enough negative pressure at the trap to pull the water out of the trap. This is sometimes called siphoning the trap because it is similar to what happens when you use a hose to siphon fuel out of fuel tank. If the trap looses its water seal, the home is open to the flow of sewer gas.

A plumbing vent protects the trap's water seal by allowing air into the DWV pipes. The air provided by the vent replaces the air that is drawn along with the flowing water. This replacement air reduces the suction and protects the trap. Without properly sized and installed vents, the DWV system will not function as intended.

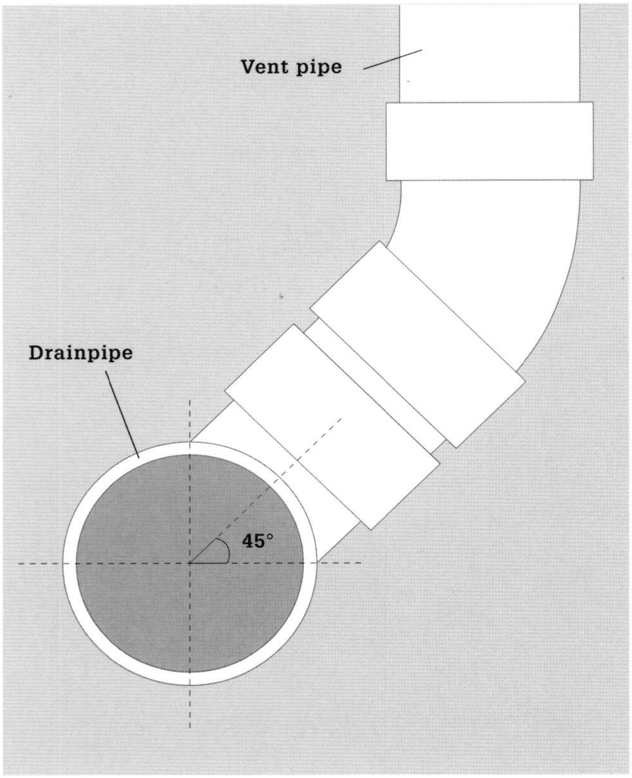

Vent pipes should extend in an upward direction from drains. This ensures that waste water cannot flow into the vent pipe and block it. At the opposite end, a vent pipe should connect to an existing vent stack or stack vent at a point at least 6" above the flood rim of the highest fixture draining into the system.

Vent Slope & Connection to Pipes

PLUMBING VENTS REQUIRED

1. Install an approved vent for every trap and trapped fixture. This means that every plumbing fixture (such as a sink or a shower) and every plumbing fixture with an integrated trap (such as a toilet) must be protected by an individual vent or an approved vent system in which one vent protects multiple fixtures.
2. Terminate at least one vent outdoors. Connect the outdoor vent to the building drain or to a branch or extension of the building drain. The branch or extension cannot be an island fixture vent.

Support vent pipes so they slope toward drain pipes.

VENT PIPE SLOPE & SUPPORT

1. Install all vent pipes using adequate supports so that the vent pipes slope toward the soil or waste pipe. Moisture in any form should flow toward the soil or waste pipe by gravity. General codes do not specify support intervals for vent pipes. Supporting vent pipes at the same interval required for drain pipes is recommended, but not required.

VENT PIPE CONNECTION TO HORIZONTAL DRAINAGE PIPES

1. Connect vent pipes to horizontal drainage pipes above the centerline of the horizontal drainage pipe. This protects the vent pipe from filling with solid material.

VENT CONNECTION HEIGHT MINIMUMS

1. Connect dry vent pipes to vent stacks, stack vents, and to stack-type air admittance valves so that the connection point is at least six inches above the flood rim level of the highest fixture served by the vent. A common violation of this provision is when a dry vent runs parallel to the drainage pipes under the fixture. This provision helps protect the vent pipe from filling with solid material.
2. Install horizontal branch vent pipes at least six inches above the flood rim level of the highest fixture served by the vent.

VENT ROUGH-IN FOR FUTURE FIXTURES

1. Install a vent for roughed-in (future) fixtures that is at least one-half the diameter of the drainpipe, rough-in.
2. Connect the roughed-in vent to the vent system or provide another approved means to terminate the roughed-in vent.
3. Label the roughed-in vent pipe to indicate that it is a vent.

CROWN VENTING

1. Connect the vent fitting at least two pipe diameters from the trap weir.

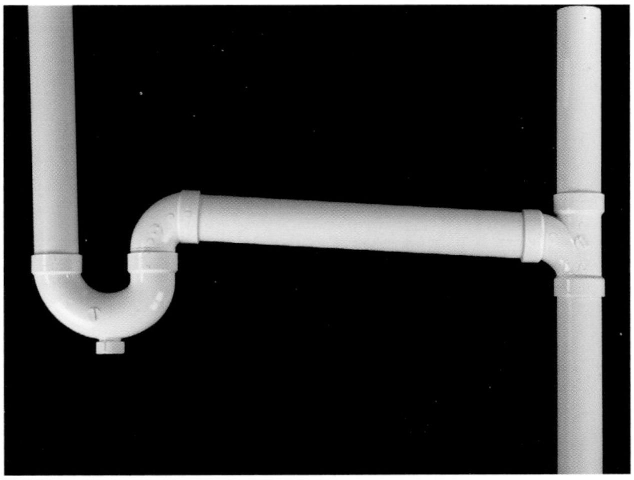

Connect vent pipes above the centerline of the drain pipe so that the vent pipe will not become clogged with solid materials.

Connect vent pipes to other vents at least 6" above the highest fixture so that the vent pipe will not become clogged with solid materials.

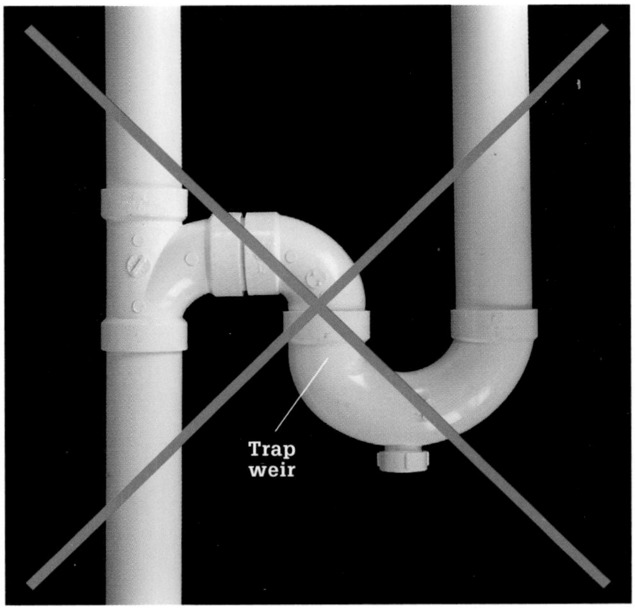

VIOLATION! Do not connect the vent pipe within 2 pipe diameters of the trap weir.

Vent Termination

VENT HEIGHT ABOVE ROOF

1. Extend vent pipes above the roof at least six inches, or the number of inches required by local snow accumulation and temperature conditions, whichever is higher. Measure height from the low side of the vent. Obtain the snow accumulation height from the local building official.
2. Extend vent pipes at least seven feet above any roof used as a balcony, observation deck, or similar accessible walking surface.

VENT FREEZING & FROST CLOSURE PROTECTION

1. Protect exterior vent terminals from freezing by using heat or insulation, or both.
2. Increase the diameter of exterior vent terminal pipes to at least three inches, beginning at least one foot below the roof or inside the wall.
3. These provisions apply only where the 97.5 percent winter design temperature is less than 0 degrees Farenheit. Obtain this information from IRC Chapter 3 and from your local building official.

Make sure vent termination covers in side walls are protected from entry by birds or rodents.

Use approved vent flashing boots to seal around the vent projections in a roof. Make sure boot angle is compatible with your roof slope.

VENT FLASHING

1. Use approved flashing to make vent pipes extending through a roof watertight.
2. Use caulk to make vent pipes extending through a wall watertight.

VENT EXTERIOR TERMINATION LOCATIONS

1. Locate plumbing vent terminations at least four feet below, at least two feet above, or at least 10 feet horizontally from any:
   (a) door or operable window,
   (b) other air intake opening of the building, and
   (c) air intake opening of any adjacent building.
2. Locate plumbing vent terminations running through a side wall at least 10 feet from the lot line and at least 10 feet above the highest grade within 10 feet horizontally from the vent termination.
3. Protect side-wall vent terminations from entry by birds or rodents.
4. Do not locate vent terminations directly under the building's overhang if the overhang contains soffit vents.

VENT CONNECTION DISTANCE FROM TRAP

1. Use Table 37 to determine the maximum length of a fixture drain between a trap weir and a vent fitting. The vent fitting may be at a vent pipe, such as an individual vent, or at a vented pipe, such as a wet vent.
2. The table does not apply to self-siphoning fixtures, such as toilets. No fixture drain length limitations apply to these fixtures.

FIXTURE DRAIN SLOPE

1. Connect the fixture drain pipe with not more than one pipe diameter of fall between the bottom of the trap outlet and the bottom of the vent fitting inlet. This parallels the distance requirements in Table 37 and reduces the chance that the trap will drain because the fitting is below the trap. Example: five feet by ¼ inch per foot equals 1¼ inches. See the first row of Table 37.
2. Connect the top of the fixture drainpipe to the vent fitting above the trap weir. This provision does not apply to toilet fixture drains.

Table 37: Vent Distance from Trap ▸

Trap size	Slope	Distance from trap to vent fitting
1¼	¼" per ft.	5 ft.
1½	¼" per ft.	6 ft.
2	¼" per ft.	8 ft.
3	⅛" per ft.	12 ft.
4	⅛" per ft.	16 ft.

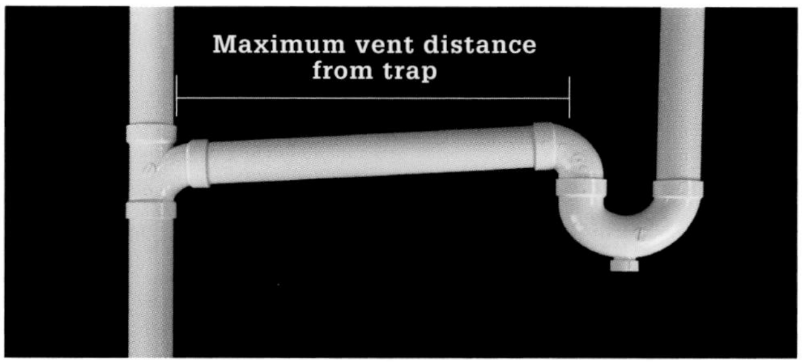

Maximum vent distance from trap

The distance from the trap to the vent fitting is limited. Note that the vent fitting may connect to a vent pipe or to a pipe that is vented, such as a wet vented pipe.

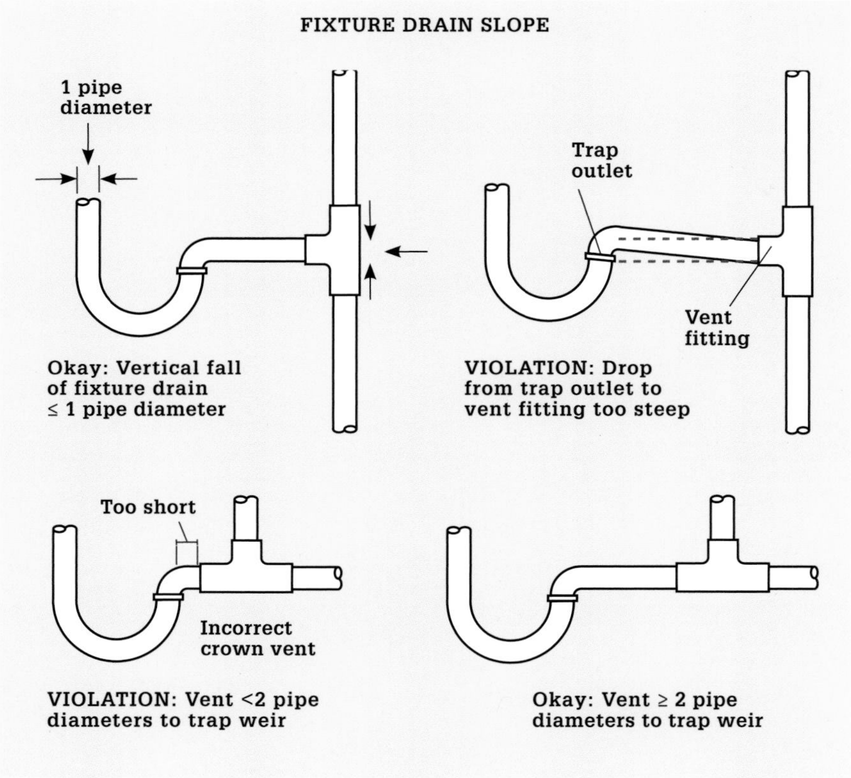

FIXTURE DRAIN SLOPE
1 pipe diameter
Okay: Vertical fall of fixture drain ≤ 1 pipe diameter
Trap outlet
Vent fitting
VIOLATION: Drop from trap outlet to vent fitting too steep
Too short
Incorrect crown vent
VIOLATION: Vent <2 pipe diameters to trap weir
Okay: Vent ≥ 2 pipe diameters to trap weir

The slope of a fixture drain is limited to avoid siphoning the trap seal.

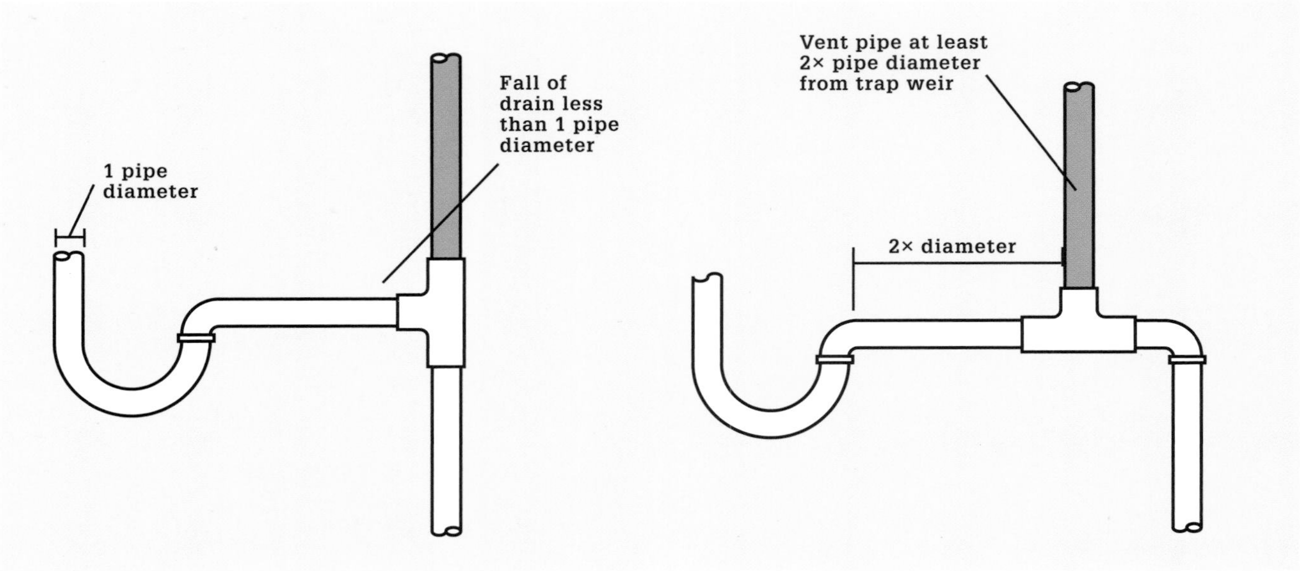

Examples of correct individual vent configurations.

VENT PIPE SIZE

1. Use at least a 1¼-inch-diameter vent pipe or a vent pipe at least one-half the diameter of the drainpipe being vented, whichever is larger, as the dry vent.
2. Increase the vent pipe diameter by at least one pipe size over the entire length of the vent pipe when the vent's developed length is greater than 40 feet.

VENT PIPE DEVELOPED LENGTH

1. Measure the developed length of individual, branch, and circuit vents beginning where the vent connects to the drainage system and ending where the vent connects to a vent stack, stack vent, air admittance valve, or the vent's termination point outside the building.

INDIVIDUAL VENTS

1. Fixture types: Use an individual vent to protect any fixture.
2. Number of fixtures: Use an individual vent to protect only one fixture.
3. Fixture location: Use an individual vent to protect one fixture located anywhere in the structure.
4. Individual vent connection location: Connect the individual vent on the fixture drain of the fixture being vented or at the fixture drain connection to the drainage system.
5. Fixture drain length to vent connection: Use Table 37 to determine the maximum distance between the fixture trap weir and the individual vent fitting.
6. Individual vent pipe size: Use at least a 1¼-inch pipe or a pipe at least one-half the size of the drainpipe being vented, whichever is larger.

Individual vents are the easiest to install. They protect one fixture.

COMMON VENTS

1. Fixture types: Use a common vent to protect any two fixtures. You may common vent different types of fixtures, such as a sink and a shower or a shower and a toilet.
2. Number of fixtures: Use a common vent to protect only two fixtures.
3. Fixture location: Use a common vent only for fixtures located on the same floor level. You may connect the fixture drains at different vertical levels if the fixtures are on the same floor level.
4. Common vent connection location: You may connect the common vent where the fixture drains intersect. You may connect the common vent downstream from where the fixture drains intersect only when the fixture drains connect to the branch drainpipe at the same horizontal level.
5. Fixture drain length to vent connection: Use Table 37 to determine the maximum distance between each fixture trap weir and the common vent fitting.
6. Common vent pipe size: Use at least 1¼ inches of pipe or a pipe at least one-half the size of the drainpipe being vented, whichever is larger, for the common vent.

Common vent with vent connecting at fixture drain intersection.

1½" dia. pipe
2" dia. pipe

Fixtures with different drain sizes should be vented individually where possible. The 1½" dia. tub/shower drain vent and 2" dia. toilet vent seen here are connected to the main drain stack in the attic.

WET VENTS

1. Fixture types: Use a wet vent to protect any combination of fixtures from not more than two bathroom groups.
2. Number of fixtures: Use a wet vent to protect not more than two toilets, two bathtubs or showers, two lavatory sinks, and two bidets.
3. Fixture location: Use a wet vent only for approved bathroom fixtures located on the same floor level.
4. Wet vent connection location:
   (a) Begin the wet vent with an individual or common vent for a lavatory, bidet, shower, or bathtub. This vent does not need to be at the first wet vented fixture in a horizontal wet vent. This vent must be at the first wet vented fixture in a vertical wet vent. End the wet vent at the last wet vented fixture connection to the wet vented pipe.
   (b) Do not connect more than one fixture upstream from the beginning individual or common vent in a horizontal wet vent.
   (c) Connect each fixture individually to the wet vented pipe. Do not connect two or more fixtures together and connect that branch drain to the wet vented pipe.
5. Horizontal wet vent fixture drain connection location:
   (a) Connect each individual fixture drain horizontally to a horizontal wet-vented pipe. Example: you may not install a sanitary tee fitting vertically and connect a fixture drain to the vertical opening of the sanitary tee in a horizontal wet vent. You may install the sanitary tee horizontally and connect the horizontal fixture drain to the horizontal opening of the sanitary tee.
   (b) You may connect a fixture drain vertically to a horizontal wet-vented pipe if you install a dry vent on the vertically connected fixture. Example: you may install a sanitary tee fitting vertically if you connect an individual vent to the fixture.
   (c) Do not connect any fixtures to the horizontal wet-vented pipe other than those fixtures being wet-vented. You may connect other fixtures to the horizontal pipe downstream after the wet vent ends. Example: do not connect a bedroom bar sink to a wet-vented pipe.
6. Vertical wet vent fixture drain connection location:
   (a) Connect all toilet fixture drains at the same vertical level.
   (b) Connect fixture drains from bathtubs, showers, lavatory sinks, and bidets at or above where the toilet fixture drains connect to the vertical wet vent.
7. Fixture drain length to wet-vented pipe: Use Table 37 (see page 143) to determine the maximum distance between each fixture trap weir and the fixture drain fitting at the wet-vented drain pipe. You may use individual and common vents to protect any fixture where the fixture drain length limit is a problem.
8. Wet vent pipe size:
   (a) Use a dry vent that is at least a $1\frac{1}{4}$-inch pipe or a pipe at least one-half the size of the wet-vented pipe, whichever is larger, for the individual or common vent that begins the wet vent.
   (b) Use Table 38 to size the horizontal and vertical wet-vented drainage pipe. You may not connect a toilet to a drainage pipe smaller than three inches regardless of what is allowed in the table.

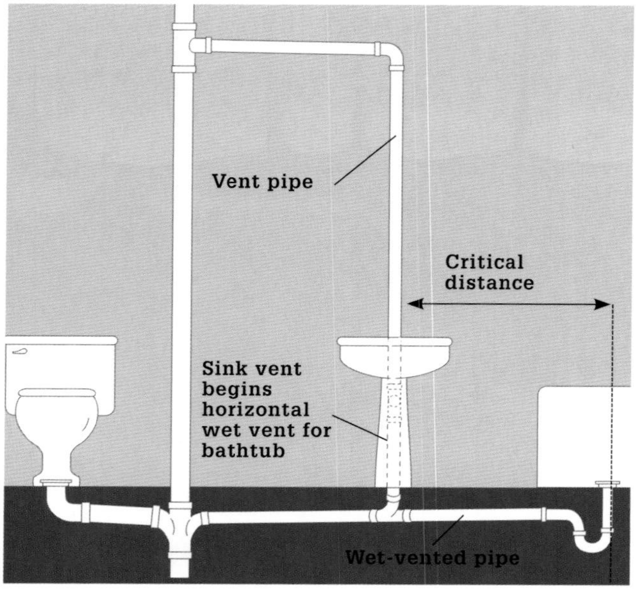

Using a wet vent eliminates the need for an individual vent for each fixture.

Table 38: Horiz. and Vert. Wet-Vented Drainage Pipe Size ▸

Wet-vented pipe size	Max. dfu load
$1\frac{1}{2}$"	1
2"	4
$2\frac{1}{2}$"	6
3"	12
4"	32

KITCHEN ISLAND FIXTURE VENT

1. Fixture types: Use an island fixture vent to protect only sinks such as those in kitchens and bathrooms. You may connect a dishwasher and disposal to a kitchen sink.
2. Use an island fixture vent to protect any number of approved fixture types.
3. Use an island fixture vent only for fixtures located in the same island and on the same floor level.
4. Pipe configuration:
   (a) Extend the loop portion of the island fixture vent vertically to above the drain outlet of the fixture being vented before extending the horizontal and/or vertical downward portion.
   (b) Use drainage fittings and pipe slopes for any portion of the vent below the fixture flood rim level. Do not use vent fittings or slope the vent pipe as a vent below the fixture flood rim level.
   (c) Connect the downward portion of the vent loop downstream from where the fixture drain connects with the horizontal drainage pipe. Make the connection using a full size fitting.
   (d) Provide cleanouts at the downward portion of the loop vent and in the vertical portion of the vent pipe before it connects to the exterior vent pipe.

AIR ADMITTANCE VALVES

1. Install air admittance valves according to manufacturer's installation instructions and general code provisions.
2. You may use air admittance valves to vent individual vents, branch vents, circuit vents, and stack vents. Use individual and branch type air admittance valves to vent fixtures that are on the same floor level and that are connected to a horizontal branch drain.
3. Use air admittance valves that are rated for the vent size to which the valve is connected.
4. Locate individual and branch type air admittance valves at least four inches above the horizontal branch drain or fixture drain being vented.
5. Locate stack type air admittance valves at least six inches above the flood rim level of the highest fixture being vented.
6. Locate the air admittance valve within the vent's developed length limits.
7. Locate air admittance valves in attics at least six inches above insulation.
8. Provide air admittance valves with access and adequate ventilation.

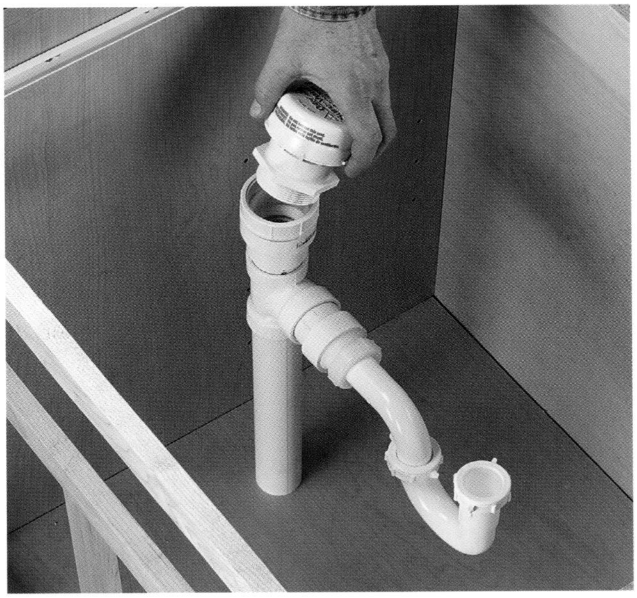

Air admittance valves can be installed in an island cabinet to vent a sink drain line.

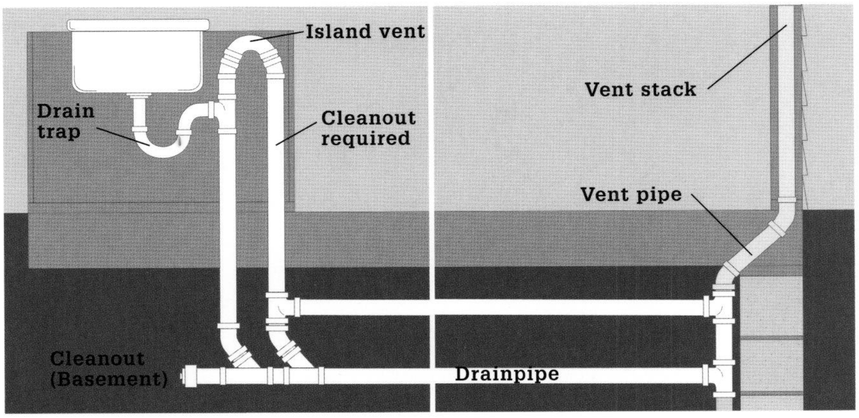

An island fixture vent is a fairly complicated venting configuration used to vent fixtures installed in a kitchen island.

Plumbing Traps

TRAP SIZE

1. Use Table 39 to determine the minimum trap size for most plumbing fixtures.
2. Do not install separate traps on toilets, urinals, and other fixtures that have traps in the fixture itself.
3. Do not install a trap that is larger than the drainage pipe into which the trap discharges. Example: do not connect a two-inch trap to a 1½-inch pipe on the discharge side of the trap.

TRAP SEAL

1. Install traps with a water seal of at least two inches and not more than four inches.
2. Install floor drain traps that have a deep seal (near four inches) design or a trap primer. Connect trap primer valves above the trap seal level.

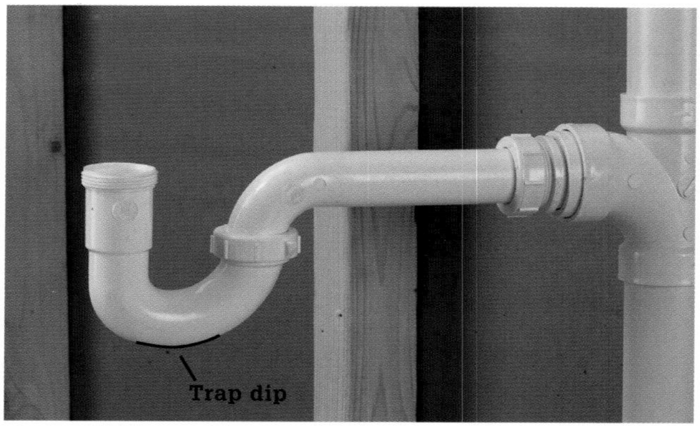

Measure the water seal from the trap dip to the crown weir.

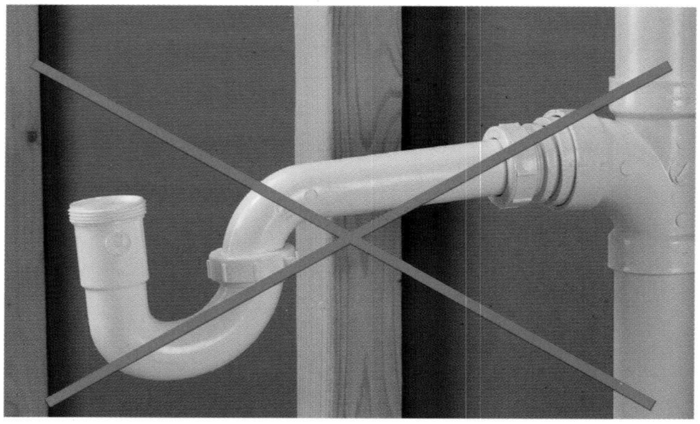

VIOLATION! Install traps so that the water seal is level. Traps set out of level may lose their water seal and will not drain properly.

Table 39: Minimum Trap Size for Plumbing Fixtures ▸

Plumbing fixture	Minimum trap size
Bathtub (equipped or not equipped with shower head or whirlpool)	1½"
Bidet	1¼"
Clothes washing machine standpipe	2"
Dishwasher (separately trapped)	1½"
Floor drain	2"
Kitchen sink (equipped or not equipped with dishwasher or disposal and trapped using one or two traps)	1½"
Laundry tubs (≥ 1 compartments)	1½"
Lavatory	1¼"
Shower (total flow rate of all showerheads and body sprays)	
≤ 5.7 gallons per minute (gpm)	1½"
> 5.7 gpm and ≤ 12.3 gpm	2"
> 12.3 gpm and ≤ 25.8 gpm	3"
> 25.8 gpm and ≤ 55.6 gpm	4"

TRAP INSTALLATION

1. Set traps level with respect to their water seal.
2. Protect traps from freezing.
3. Provide access to traps with slip joints at the trap inlet or outlet.
4. Do not install more than one trap per fixture.
5. Limit the vertical distance between the fixture drain outlet and the trap weir to not more than 24 inches.
6. Limit the horizontal distance between the fixture drain outlet and the center of the trap inlet to not more than 30 inches. Note that this 30 inches horizontal distance may be eliminated or not enforced in some jurisdictions. Verify if this provision applies in your jurisdiction.

PROHIBITED TRAPS

1. Do not install the following types of traps: bell traps, drum traps, S-traps, traps with moving parts, and building traps.

Plumbing Appliances & Fixtures

The installation and hookup of appliances that are part of your home plumbing system is the part of the plumbing process that DIYers are most likely to attempt. The information in this section provides a good general backdrop for making plumbing hookups, but be sure to read the manufacturer's installation recommendations carefully. As always, manufacturer specifications take precedence over codes.

Water Heaters

Replacing a water heater is a relatively easy DIY plumbing task as long as it is a like-for-like replacement. In an ideal situation, you'd replace the old unit with one of the exact same size and make, and thereby avoid having to move any gas, water, or electrical lines. But if you choose to upgrade or downgrade in size, or perhaps replace an old electric water heater with a gas water heater that costs less to run, you'll find that relocating the necessary lines isn't that difficult.

Water heaters for primary duty in residences range in size from 30 gallons to 65 gallons. For a family of four, a 40- or 50-gallon model should be adequate. While you don't want to run out of hot water every morning, you also don't want to pay to heat more water than you use. Base your choice on how well your current water heater is meeting your demand.

PROHIBITED LOCATIONS FOR WATER HEATERS

1. Do not install fuel-fired water heaters in rooms used as storage closets. You may install water heaters in closets used solely to store the water heater if you provide adequate combustion air in the closet. You may install electric water heaters in any closet when allowed by the manufacturer.
2. Do not install fuel-fired water heaters in bedrooms or bathrooms unless the water heater is installed in a sealed enclosure where combustion air does not come from the living space. This restriction does not apply to direct vent water heaters.
3. You may provide access to water heaters located in attics or crawl spaces through bedrooms, bathrooms, or their closets if ventilation of the bedroom, bathroom, or closet complies with codes.

Safety Tip ▸

You can save money by installing the new appliance yourself, and by making the plumbing hookups. Hire a professional to make gas hookups.

Water heaters typically last for at least 10 years, but once they start to show signs of aging, it's a good idea to replace them with a new, more efficient appliance.

WATER HEATER RELIEF VALVES

1. Install either a separate temperature relief valve and a separate pressure relief valve or a combination temperature and pressure relief valve on all appliances used to heat or store hot water. Combination temperature and pressure relief valves (T&P valves) are used almost exclusively in modern water heaters. This provision applies to tank-type, tankless, and swimming pool water heaters.
2. Install the temperature relief or T&P valve on the top of the water heater or on the side of the water heater within six inches of the top. Do not install an extension pipe between the water heater and the T&P valve.
3. Do not install a check valve or shutoff valve anywhere that might interfere with the operation of the relief valve or the flow of water or steam from the discharge pipe.

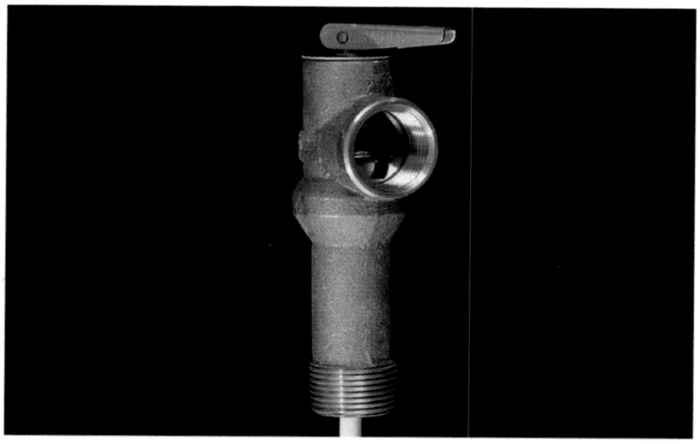

The T&P valve is a critical safety device that is required on all water heaters.

T&P valves should be installed on your water heater prior to placing the appliance in position. Many water heaters today come with the T&P valve preinstalled.

WATER HEATER RELIEF VALVE DISCHARGE PIPE

1. Use water distribution pipe listed in Table 31 (see page 127) as the relief valve discharge pipe. Copper and CPVC are the most commonly used discharge pipes. It is difficult to maintain uniform slope and fall on flexible pipes such as PEX.
2. Install the discharge pipe so hot water and steam will not cause personal injury or property damage if the relief valve discharges.
3. Install the discharge pipe so that any leaking from the pipe outlet is readily observable by the building occupants.
4. Use a discharge pipe that is at least as large as the relief valve opening. This size is usually ¾ inch in diameter.
5. Run the discharge pipe full size to the floor, to an indirect waste receptor (such as a floor drain) inside the building, to the water heater drip pan, or outside the building. If the area is subject to freezing, terminate the discharge pipe through an air gap into an indirect waste receptor located inside the building. You may use other discharge points in areas subject to freezing, if approved by the local building official.
6. Slope the discharge pipe so that it drains by gravity from the relief valve to the discharge point.
7. Do not connect the discharge pipe directly to the building's drain, waste, and vent system. Leave an air gap between the discharge pipe and the floor, ground, or other termination point.
8. Do not install a trap or a valve or a threaded outlet in the discharge pipe.

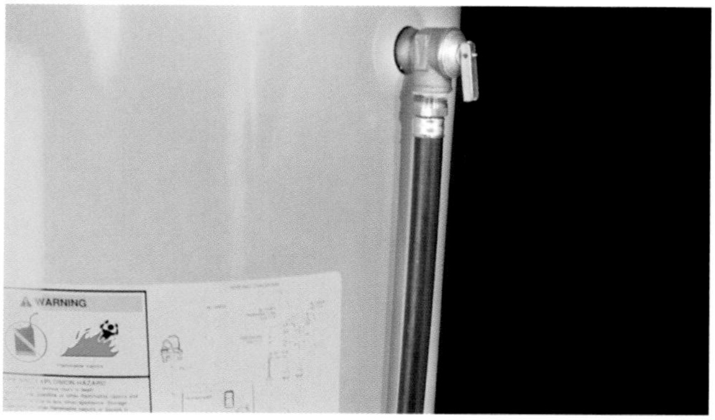

A discharge tube should run downward from the T&P valve and terminate near a receptor or drain pan. Terminate the discharge tube not more than 6" from the floor so that any spray is less likely to injure or damage.

WATER HEATER DRIP PANS

1. Install a drip pan under water heaters located where leakage could cause damage. These locations often include attics and all areas within the conditioned area of the home, including finished basements.
2. Use a drip pan at least 1½-inches deep and made with at least 24-gauge galvanized steel or other approved materials. Use a pan with a size and shape to catch all leaks and condensation from the water heater.
3. Run the discharge pipe to an indirect waste receptor (such as a floor drain) or to the outside of the building.

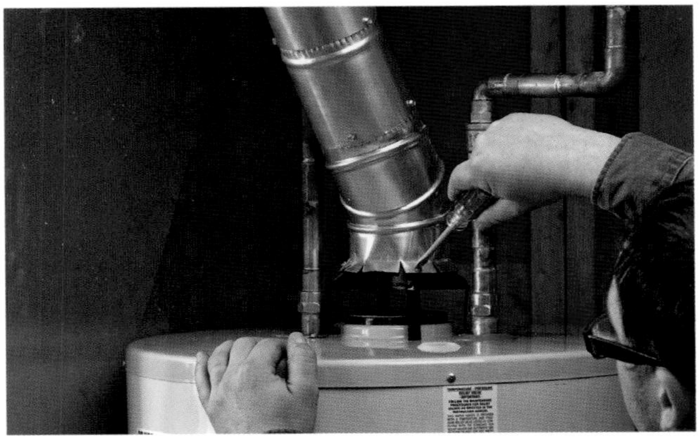

The exhaust vent for a gas water heater should be connected securely to the draft hood at the top of the appliance.

Install a drip pan under a water heater when water leaks might damage surrounding areas. Use at least a ¾" diameter discharge pipe to drain the drip pan. Use a larger discharge pipe if the connection to the drip pan is more than ¾" diameter.

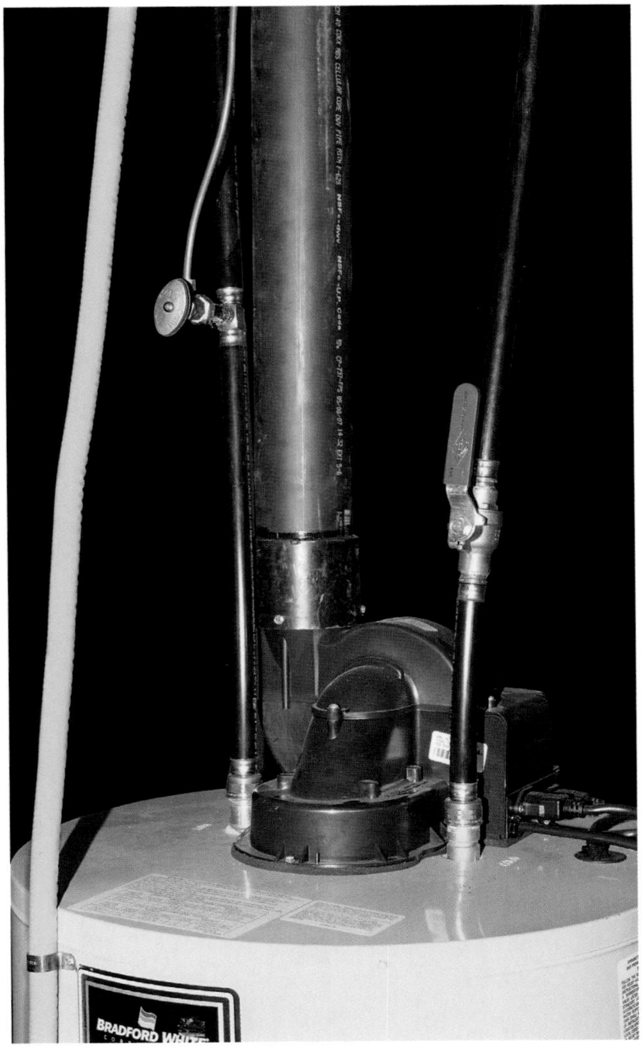

Codes vary on whether nonmetallic supply pipes may be attached directly to a water heater. Because it has better heat resistance, PEX is less likely to require a copper transition pipe than CPVC plastic pipe.

Toilets

You can replace a poorly functioning or inefficient toilet with a high-efficiency, high-quality new toilet in just a single afternoon. All toilets made since 1996 have been required to use 1.6 gallons or less per flush, which has been a huge challenge for the industry. Today, the most evolved 1.6-gallon toilets have wide passages behind the bowl and wide (three-inch) flush valve openings—features that facilitate short, powerful flushes. This means fewer second flushes and fewer clogged toilets. These problems were common complaints of the first generation of 1.6-gallon toilets and continue to beleaguer inferior models today. See what toilets are available at your local home center in your price range, then go online and see what other consumers' experiences with those models have been. New toilets often go through a "debugging" stage when problems with leaks and malfunctioning parts are more common. Your criteria should include ease of installation, good flush performance, and reliability. With a little research, you should be able to purchase and install a high-functioning economical gravity-flush toilet that will serve you well for years to come.

GENERAL REQUIREMENTS

1. Install toilets with an approved flushing mechanism that provides enough water to clear and refill the toilet bowl and refill the toilet's internal trap. Approved flushing mechanisms are the common gravity feed flush tanks (one and two piece tanks) and power-assisted tanks or valves.
2. Install toilets that use an average of not more than 1.6 gallons per flush.
3. Provide the toilet with an adequate supply of water. Control the water supply with an automatic device (such as a float valve) that will refill the toilet tank after each flush and completely stop the flow of water to the tank when the tank is full. The device should also supply enough water to refill the toilet.
4. Install toilets with a flush valve seat in the toilet tank that is at least one inch above the flood level of the toilet bowl. An alternate design (used by low-profile one piece toilets) is acceptable. This design closes the flush valve when the toilet is clogged and prevents water from flowing back into the tank.
5. Provide toilet tanks with an overflow pipe or mechanism that is sufficient to prevent the tank from flooding if the fill valve malfunctions.
6. Provide access to all parts in the toilet tank for repair and replacement.
7. Use toilet seats made of smooth, nonabsorbent material properly sized for the toilet bowl.
8. Use corrosion-resistant screws, nuts, bolts, and washers to secure toilets to the closet flange.

Approved flushing mechanisms for toilets may require power assistance if simple gravity-fed flushing is inadequate.

BACKFLOW PROTECTION OF TOILET FILL VALVES

1. Protect toilets with an approved antisiphon fill valve.
2. Locate the backflow preventer at least one inch above the opening of the overflow pipe. Fill valves with all parts below the tank water line usually violate this provision.

TOILET (CLOSET) FLANGE

1. Install a closet flange that is firmly attached to a structural support (floor) to connect a toilet to drainage piping. Use a closet flange that is compatible with the connected drainage pipe. Example: do not use a PVC closet flange with ABS pipe. Do not use the closet flange to provide structural support to the toilet.
2. Use non-corrosive bolts and an approved gasket (O-ring) or other approved setting compound to secure the toilet and closet flange and to make the seal watertight.

An overflow tube must be provided inside the toilet tank to keep water from rising out of the tank if the fill valve is malfunctioning.

The water inlet of a fill valve should usually be above the tank's water line to reduce backflow of waste water into the drinking water system.

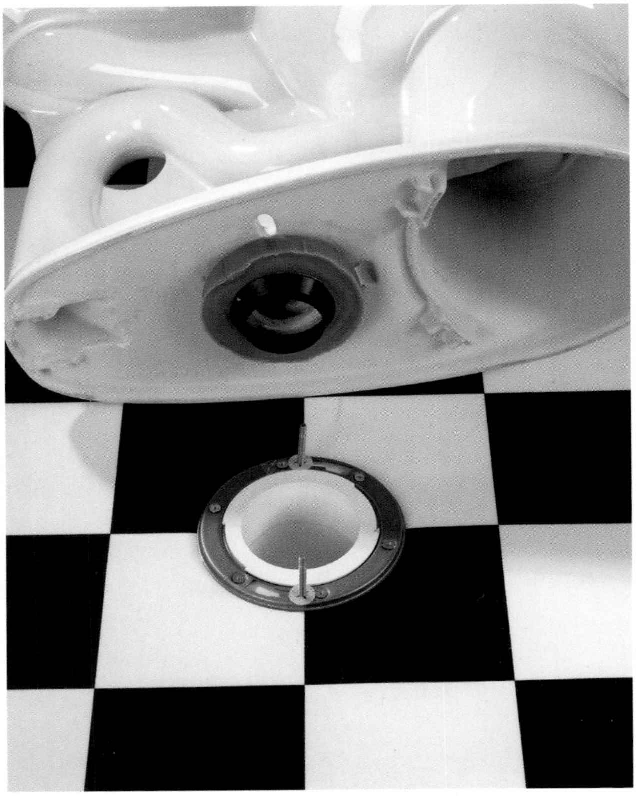

The closet flange and O-ring hold the toilet in place and seal the plumbing connection. The closet flange does not support the toilet.

Dishwashing Machines

GENERAL REQUIREMENTS

1. You may discharge a dishwashing machine, a disposal, and a kitchen sink into one 1½-inch-diameter drain (trap). Use a ¾-inch-diameter dishwashing machine drain tube when discharging the dishwashing machine into either a sink drain (trap) or a disposal. Connect the dishwashing machine drain tube to a wye fitting in the sink tailpiece when connecting the drain line directly to the sink tailpiece. Loop the dishwashing machine drain line as high as possible in the sink cabinet and securely fasten or install an air gap device. An air gap device is not required in the dishwashing machine drain tube.

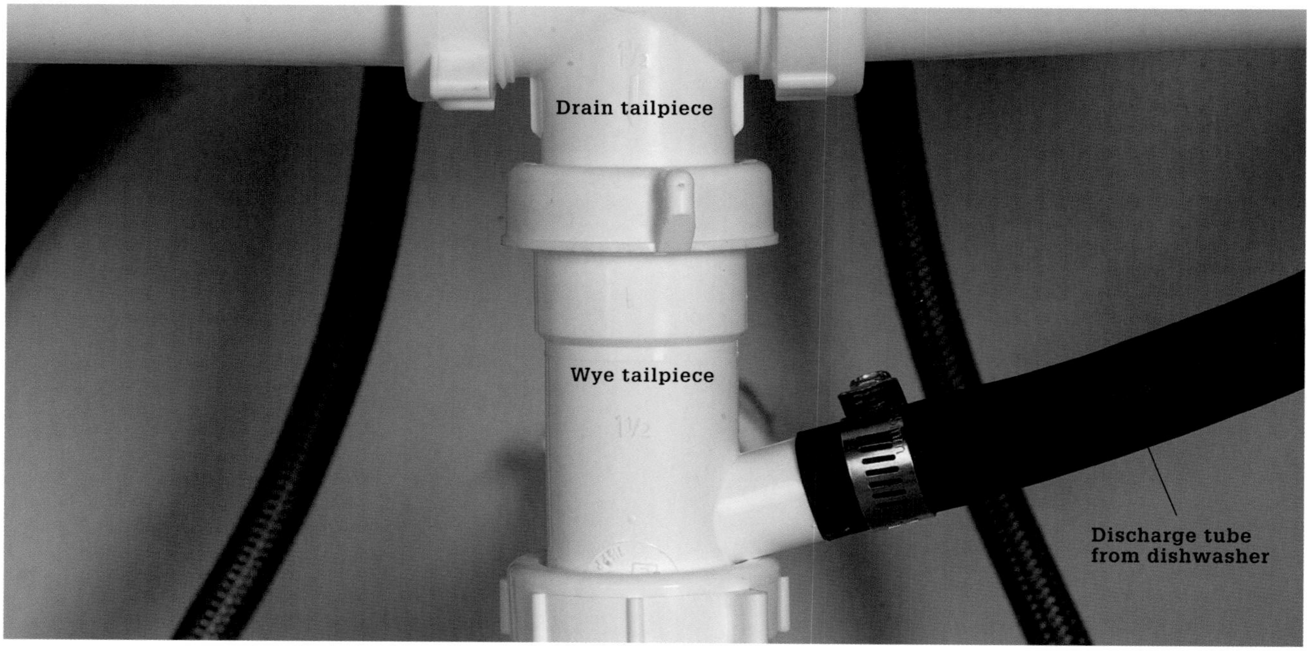
Drain tailpiece
Wye tailpiece
Discharge tube from dishwasher

Use a wye tailpiece fitting when connecting a dishwashing machine drain tube directly to a sink.

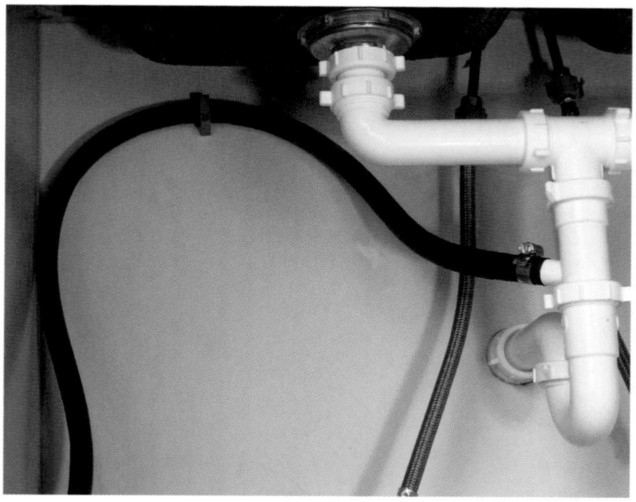

A dishwashing machine drain tube high loop is one method of backflow prevention. Secure the tube as high as possible in the sink base cabinet.

A dishwashing machine drain air gap device is one method of backflow prevention. Install the device according to manufacturer's instructions.

Food Disposers

FITTINGS

1. Use an approved directional fitting on the tailpiece when connecting a disposal or dishwashing machine. This helps direct the waste down into the plumbing drain system and avoids blockage and blow back up the tailpiece when these appliances discharge under pressure. Examples of directional fittings include the waste tee with a baffle and a sanitary tee.

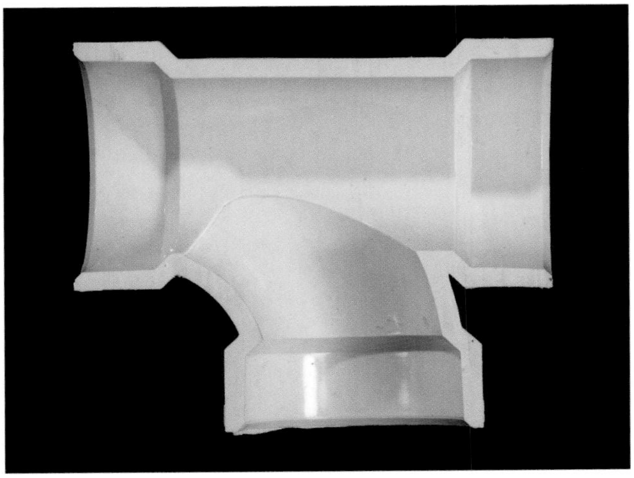

A sanitary tee fitting is one possible directional fitting when draining a dishwashing machine or food disposer into a kitchen sink.

A waste tee with a baffle is one possible directional fitting when draining a dishwashing machine or food disposer into a kitchen sink.

Clothes Washing Machines

FITTINGS

1. Discharge the wastewater from a clothes washing machine through an air gap. Do not connect the clothes washing machine drain line directly to the plumbing waste pipes. Inserting the clothes washing machine drain hose into the standpipe is the most common acceptable method of providing the required air gap.
2. Install a water-hammer arrestor where required to control water flow and reduce the possibility of water hammer. A water-hammer arrestor may be used near a quick-closing valve such as in a clothes washing machine.

Water-hammer arrestors may be required in some jurisdictions at clothes washing machine hose connections.

Whirlpool Bathtubs (Jetted Baths)

GENERAL REQUIREMENTS

1. Install whirlpool tubs according to manufacturer's instructions. This includes: testing the tub for leaks and pump operation, usually prior to installation, and providing adequate support for the tub, water, and occupants. Some whirlpool tub manufacturers allow plaster as a tub support method. Plaster is not the same as drywall joint compound. Do not use drywall joint compound to support bathtubs unless it is specifically approved by the tub manufacturer.
2. Provide a door or access panel large enough to allow service personnel to repair and replace the pump. The door size will depend on where the pump is located relative to the door. The door may have to be larger than the specified minimum size if the pump is located far away from the door.
3. Make the access opening at least 12 inches by 12 inches if the manufacturer does not specify an opening size. Make the access opening at least 18 inches by 18 inches if the pump is located more than two feet away from the opening. Do not place obstructions, such as tub support framing and pipes, between the access opening and the pump.
4. Locate the circulation pump above the crown weir of the trap.
5. Install circulation pipes and pump drain line so that they are self-draining and retain minimum possible water after using the tub.
6. Install whirlpool bathtub motors on a GFCI-protected circuit. Do not use the bathroom receptacle circuit for this purpose.
7. Install a copper bonding wire at least #8 AWG connecting all metal pipes, pump motors, and other electrical equipment associated with the whirlpool bathtub. Do not bond grounded double insulated whirlpool bathtub pump motors.

Whirlpool tub motors need access for maintenance and replacement. The access opening must be large enough to allow effective access to the motor. Connect a bonding wire between the tub motor and metal water pipes for electrical safety.

A bathtub can crack and drain connections can loosen and leak unless it is properly supported. Here, the tub is installed on a bed of hardened mortar.

Showers

SHOWER SIZE

1. Provide showers with a finished area of at least 900 square inches and a finished minimum dimension of at least 30 inches. Maintain the minimum dimensions from the top of the threshold to at least 70 inches above the shower drain outlet. Measure the shower from the centerline of the threshold (curb). You may install valves, showerheads, soap dishes, and grab bars that encroach into the minimum dimensions. You may install a fold-down seat in the shower if the minimum dimensions are maintained when the seat is up.
2. You may provide a shower with a finished minimum dimension of at least 25 inches if the finished area is at least 1,300 square inches.
3. Provide shower compartment access of at least 22-inch finished width.

WATER SUPPLY RISER

1. Secure the pipe between the shower valve and the showerhead to the permanent structure. This provision applies whether the riser is visible or concealed. Securing the riser helps avoid leaks if the riser twists and becomes loose at joints.

SHOWER RECEPTOR CONSTRUCTION

1. Install shower thresholds (curbs) at least one inch below the sides and back of the receptor.
2. Install shower thresholds (curbs) at least two inches and not more than nine inches above the top of the drain.
3. Slope the shower floor at least ¼ unit in 12 units (two percent slope) and not more than ½ unit in 12 units.
4. Use a flanged shower floor drain that provides a watertight seal at the floor.
5. Use hot-mopped felt, approved sheet lead, copper, or approved plastic lining material when installing a site-built shower receptor. Plastic liners (such as chlorinated polyethylene) are the most common modern, site-built liner material.
6. Extend the lining material at least three inches beyond and around the rough jambs of the shower receptor. Extend the lining material at least three inches above the finished thresholds (curbs).
7. Attach the lining material to an approved backing. Nail or perforate the lining at least one inch above the finished threshold. Seal joints in plastic lining material according to manufacturer's instructions.

A sufficiently large shower stall is more than a convenience—it is a safety issue.

Attaching the shower riser pipe to framing helps avoid water leaks caused when adjusting the showerhead loosens the pipe fittings.

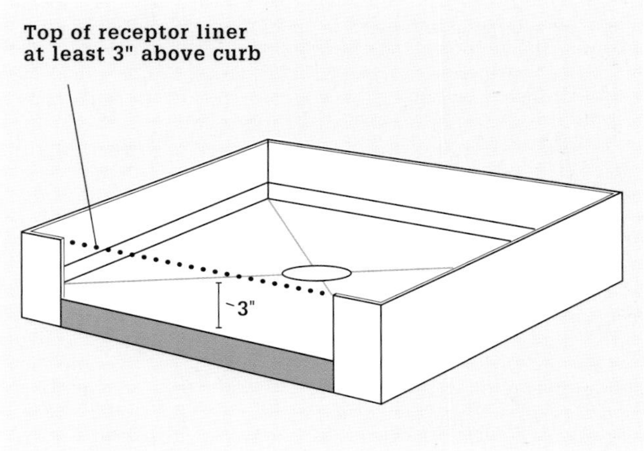

Proper installation of a site-built shower receptor is critical to avoiding costly water leaks.

8. Install an approved flanged shower drain that is equipped with weep holes into the drain and is equipped with a flange that makes a watertight seal between the lining material and the drain.

Water Supply Backflow Prevention ▸

An important part of the design and use of the drinking (potable) water supply system is preventing contamination of the potable water. Contamination can occur when the potable water supply is intentionally or unintentionally connected to a contaminate source. Connection between the potable water supply and a contaminate source is called a cross-connection. Contamination occurs when contaminated material backflows into the potable water system through a cross-connection. A backflow is when material (usually liquid) travels in the reverse of the intended direction.

Some cross-connections are intended. Examples of intended cross-connections include toilet tank fill valves, automatic fill systems for swimming pools, and lawn irrigation systems. In all of these examples, the potable water supply is directly connected to a source of contaminated material that could backflow into the system under certain conditions.

Some cross-connections are unintended. Examples of unintended cross-connections include spray hoses connected to a laundry tub faucet, handheld showerheads with a hose long enough for the head to hang inside a tub or shower pan, and garden hoses. In all of these examples, a sudden loss of water pressure in the potable water supply system could allow any liquid at the end of these hoses to be drawn back into the potable water system. If the liquid was weed killer in a spray bottle at the end of a garden hose, the weed killer could be drawn into the potable water system.

Backflow into the potable water system can occur by backpressure or by "backsiphonage." Backpressure occurs when the pressure in the cross-connection source exceeds the pressure in the potable water supply system. Contaminated material is forced under pressure into the potable water system. Sources of backpressure include pumps, liquid storage tanks at a higher elevation than the cross-connection point, and thermal expansion from a heat source such as a water heater. Backsiphonage occurs when the pressure in the potable water supply system falls below atmospheric pressure. Air pressure can force contaminated material into the potable water supply system, or negative pressure in the potable water supply system can draw contaminated material into the potable water supply system.

General codes require protections of all potable water supply outlets and all intentional cross-connections by an air gap or by an approved backflow prevention device.

Air Gap Terms ▸

Air gap: An air gap is the unobstructed distance between a water supply fixture outlet opening and the flood rim level of a receptor. Example: the vertical distance between a sink spout and the highest level that the water in the sink could reach without overflowing is the air gap.

Air gap distance measurement: Measure the air gap distance between the plumbing fixture outlet opening and the flood rim of the fixture or receptor. Measure the fixture outlet opening diameter without the aerator attached. Measure the vertical air gap distance with the aerator attached.

Air gap minimum distances: Provide an air gap distance based on the effective size of the fixture outlet opening. In most cases this distance is twice the fixture outlet opening diameter. Example: if a bathroom sink faucet outlet opening is ½", then the minimum vertical air gap between the faucet outlet opening and the flood rim of the sink is 1".

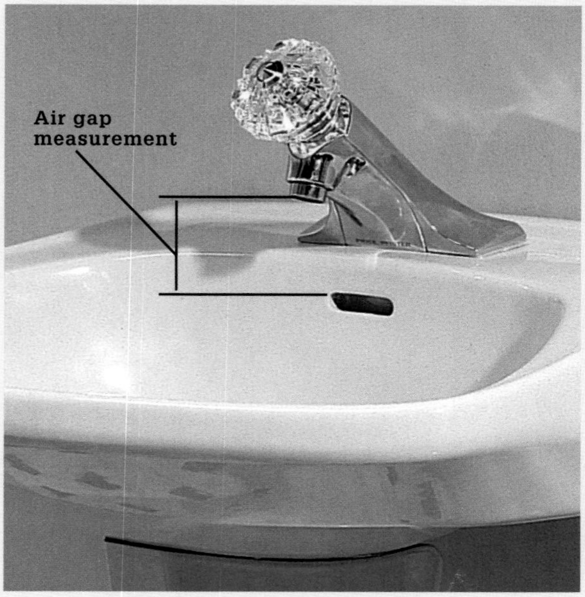

Most commercially available faucets are designed to provide the required minimum air gap distance.

Irrigation Systems

1. Protect lawn irrigation system water connections by installing an atmospheric vacuum breaker, a pressure vacuum breaker, or a reduced pressure backflow preventer.
2. Do not install a valve downstream from an atmospheric vacuum breaker.
3. Install a reduced pressure backflow preventer if chemicals are introduced into the irrigation system.

VIOLATION: Pressure vacuum breakers are a common way to protect lawn irrigation systems. This manifold is missing a backflow preventer and is a code violation.

TIP: Irrigation systems typically employ outdoor flexible plastic pipe. Pipe connections are made by inserting barbed connectors into the mating sections of pipe and then securing the connectors with pipe clamps.

Drawing Plumbing Maps & Plans

Start planning by drawing maps. Mapping your home's plumbing system is a good way to familiarize yourself with the plumbing layout and can help you when planning plumbing renovation projects. With a good map, you can envision the best spots for new fixtures and plan new pipe routes more efficiently. Maps also help in emergencies, when you need to locate burst or leaking pipes quickly.

Draw a plumbing map for each floor on tracing paper, so you can overlay floors and still read the information below. Make your drawings to scale and have all plumbing fixtures marked. Fixture templates and tracing paper are available at drafting supply stores.

Snoop around your basement for clues about the locations of supply, drain, vent, and gas pipes in your walls.

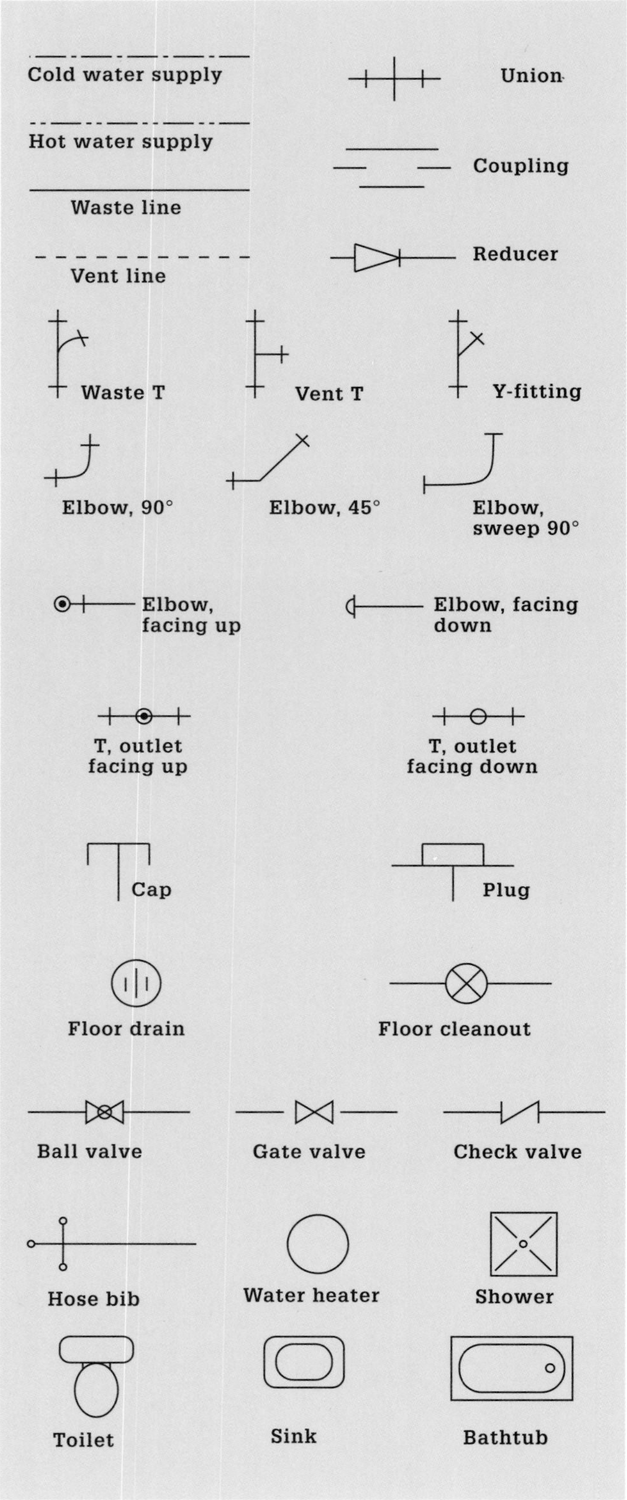

Use standard plumbing symbols on your map to identify the components of your plumbing system. These symbols will help you and your building inspector follow connections and transitions more easily.

How to Map Your Plumbing System

Draw a floorplan for the basement. The drawing should be scaled, legible, and accurate. Note the plumbing features using the symbols on the previous page.

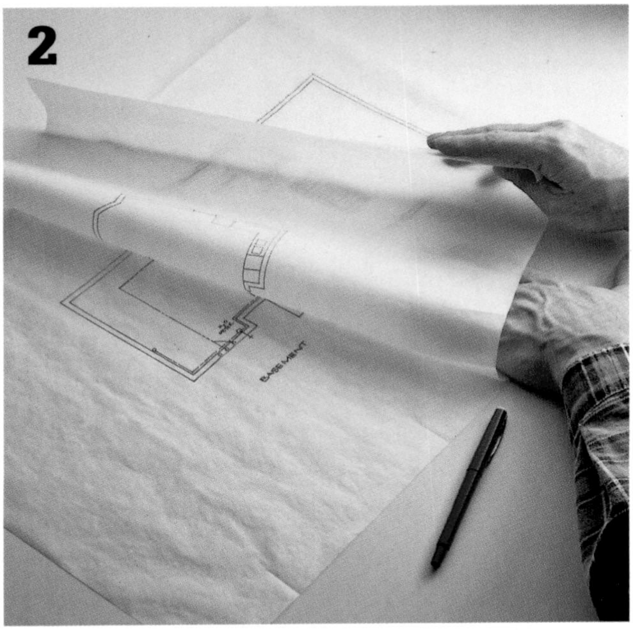

Draw the first floor on a separate piece of transparent drafting paper, using the same scale that you used for the basement. Draw separate floorplans for any additional floors.

Overlay upper-floor diagrams onto the first-floor map, and mark the location of pipes—generally they will extend directly up from fixtures below. If first-story and second-story fixtures are not closely aligned, the supply pipes follow an offset route in wall or floor cavities. By overlaying the maps, you can see the relation and distance between fixtures and accurately estimate pipe routes.

Option: Use floor plans of your house to create your plumbing map. Convert the general outlines for each story to tracing paper. The walls can be drawn larger than scale to fit all the plumbing symbols you will map, but keep overall room dimensions and plumbing fixtures to scale. Be sure to make diagrams for basements and attic spaces as well.

Testing New Plumbing Pipes ▸

When the building inspector comes to review your new plumbing, he or she may require that you perform a pressure test on the DWV and water supply lines as he or she watches. The inspection and test should be performed after the system is completed but before the new pipes are covered with wallboard. To ensure that the inspection goes smoothly, it is a good idea to perform your own pretest, so you can locate and repair any problems before the inspector visits.

The DWV system is tested by blocking off the new drain and vent pipes, then pressuring the system with air to see if it leaks. At the fixture stub-outs, the DWV pipes can be capped off or plugged with test balloons designed for this purpose. The air pump, pressure gauge, and test balloons required to test the DWV system can be obtained at tool rental centers. Testing the water supply lines is a simple matter of turning on the water and examining the joints for leaks. If you find a leak, you will have to drain the pipes, then remake the faulty joints.

A pressure gauge and air pump are used to test DWV lines. The system is first blocked off at each fixture and at points near where the new drain and vent pipes connect to the main stack. Air is then pumped into the system to a pressure of 5 pounds per square inch (psi). To pass inspection, the system must hold this pressure for 15 minutes.

How to Test New DWV Pipes

Insert a test balloon into the test T-fittings at the top and bottom of the new DWV line, blocking the pipes entirely. *Note: Ordinary T-fittings installed near the bottom of the drain line and near the top of the vent line are generally used for test fittings.*

Block toilet drains with a test balloon designed for a closet bend. Large test balloons may have to be inflated with an air pump.

Cap off the remaining fixture drains by solvent-gluing test caps onto the stub-outs. After the system is tested, these caps are simply knocked loose with a hammer.

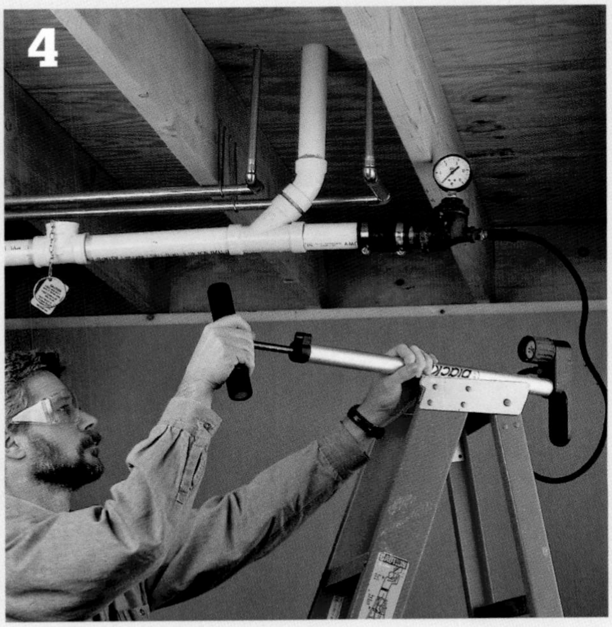

At a cleanout fitting, insert a weenie—a special test balloon with an air gauge and inflation valve. Attach an air pump to the valve on the weenie and pressurize the pipes to 5 psi. Watch the pressure gauge for 15 minutes to ensure that the system does not lose pressure.

If the DWV system loses air when pressurized, check each joint for leaks by rubbing soapy water over the fittings and looking for active bubbles. When you identify a problem joint, cut away the existing fitting and solvent-glue a new fitting in place, using couplings and short lengths of pipe.

After the DWV system has been inspected and approved by a building official, remove the test balloons and close the test T-fittings by solvent-gluing caps onto the open inlets.

Electrical System

Home wiring is a very popular do-it-yourself subject that is fundamentally hazardous. When it comes to electricity, mistakes and accidents do pose threats including fire, injury, and death. Therefore, safety is the primary focus of the electrical code provisions.

In this chapter you will find many of the rules governing safe installation of electrical wires, electrical equipment—including conduit, electrical receptacles, switches, lights, and other fixtures. Use this information to inspect your wiring and make sure it all conforms to code. If it does not, or if you are unsure about it, have a professional electrician upgrade your electrical system.

In this chapter:

- Understanding Electrical Circuits
- Electrical Grounding & Bonding
- Electrical Branch Circuit Requirements
- Electrical Receptacle Installation
- Ground-fault (GFCI) & Arc-fault (AFCI) Protection
- Junction Boxes & Device Boxes
- Switch Installation
- Light Fixture Installation
- Satellite Dishes, Television & Radio Antennas
- Broadband Cable Wiring

Definitions of Electrical Terms ▸

Accessible (wires): Wires are accessible if they can be exposed without removing or damaging permanent parts of the building and if a person can reach them for inspection, repair, or maintenance. Examples: wires are accessible if they are behind suspended ceiling panels, or if access requires opening a door, removing an access panel, or climbing a ladder. Wires are not accessible if you must cut drywall to expose the wires or if they are located in an area that cannot be reached for repair, inspection, or maintenance.

Accessible (readily): Electrical components are readily accessible if they can be reached quickly without using keys, lock combinations, ladders, tools, or devices. Panelboards and service disconnect equipment must be readily accessible in case circuits need to be shut off during an emergency.

Bonding: Metallic components are bonded if they are physically and electrically connected. Components are bonded when a bonding wire connects them together. Example: a bonding wire should connect a swimming pool motor and nearby metal parts of the electrical supply system. Bonded metallic components are part of an electrically conductive path that will safely conduct current imposed by a ground fault. A proper bonding connection will conduct the fault current on the conduit safely to ground and allow proper operation of the circuit breaker or fuse.

Branch circuit: A branch circuit begins at a circuit breaker or fuse in a panelboard and conducts electricity to where it is used. A branch circuit can serve one device, such as an oven, or it can serve multiple devices such as receptacles and light fixtures.

Cable: Any two or more wires contained in an insulating sheath or jacket. Most wire used in residential construction is actually a cable called nonmetallic cable and abbreviated NM. "Romex" is a common brand name belonging to one manufacturer of NM cable.

Ground: A ground in an electrical system is the return path through which alternating current electricity flows to complete a circuit. A grounded conductor is connected to the earth or to some body that serves as the earth. A grounded connection may be intentional (as in a circuit's grounded conductor) or it may be unintentional (as in a ground fault).

Grounded wire: A grounded conductor, broadly defined, is any conductor that is intentionally grounded. The common term for the grounded conductor in residential electrical systems is the "neutral" wire. The grounded conductor is a current-carrying conductor. You should treat it as such when working with electrical circuits. Grounded conductors are usually insulated with white or light gray colored insulation.

Grounding wire: A grounding conductor, also called an equipment grounding conductor, connects electrical equipment directly to a grounding electrode. This connection usually occurs at a grounding bus or terminal bar at the service equipment that is in turn connected to a grounding electrode. Grounding conductors are bare wires or may be insulated with green colored insulation.

Grounding electrode: A component in contact with the earth that provides the grounding connection for the electrical system. Common residential grounding electrodes include a copper rod driven at least eight feet into the ground, or a copper water service pipe, or a piece of reinforcing steel embedded in the footing.

Grounding electrode wire: The grounding electrode conductor is a wire that connects the grounding electrode to the grounded conductors. In most residential electrical systems, the only connection between the grounding electrode conductor and the grounded conductors should occur at the service equipment.

Ground fault: A ground fault occurs when metal that is not normally energized becomes energized. Examples of a ground fault: (a) the hot (ungrounded) wire in a motor is damaged or disconnected and touches the motor's case energizing the case; (b) a screw penetrates the insulation of a hot (ungrounded) wire in an electrical panelboard and energizes the cabinet; (c) damaged insulation on a hot (ungrounded) wire allows the conductor to touch copper water pipe energizing the pipe.

Location (damp): Damp locations are subject to moderate levels of moisture but are not subject to direct saturation by liquids. Examples of damp locations include covered porches and some basements. Many inspectors consider ceilings over showers and bathtubs as damp locations but general codes do not specifically cite these as damp locations.

Location (wet): Wet locations are subject to direct contact with liquids or the elements. Examples of wet locations include exterior house walls not protected by a roof, concrete and masonry in contact with the earth, and any components buried or in contact with the earth.

Multiwire branch circuit: A multiwire branch circuit is a three-wire branch circuit with two hot (ungrounded) wires and one neutral (grounded) wire. In residential electrical systems, the voltage between the two hot (ungrounded) wires is 240 volts, and the voltage between the hot (ungrounded) wires and the neutral (grounded) wire is 120 volts. When a multiwire branch circuit is operating as intended, the voltage on the shared neutral (grounded) wire is zero. Split-wired receptacles that provide the required two 20-amp kitchen countertop receptacle circuits are one example of a multiwire branch circuit. Clothes dryer and range circuits are another example. Water heater and air conditioning condenser circuits are usually not multiwire branch circuits because there is no neutral (ungrounded) wire in the circuit.

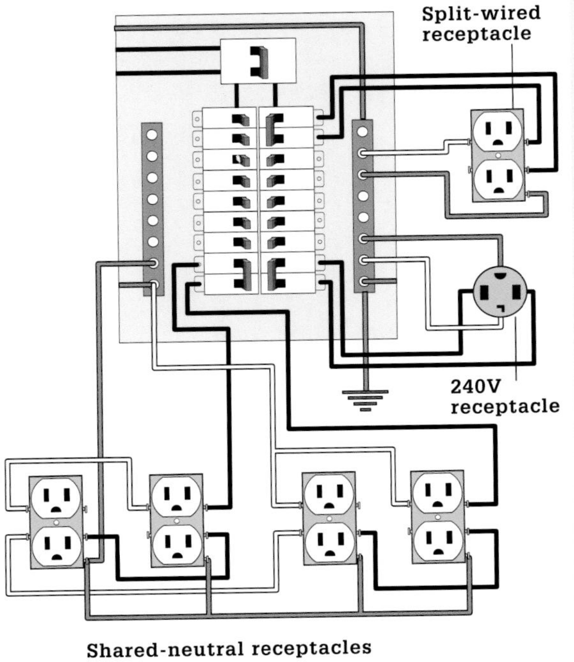
Split-wired receptacle
240V receptacle
Shared-neutral receptacles

Multiwire branch circuits.

Outlet: An outlet is a connection point where electricity is taken for use. An outlet could be a receptacle, a light fixture box, a junction box connected to an oven, or an air conditioning condenser disconnect box. Switch boxes, junction boxes, and panelboards are not outlets.

Overcurrent protection device: An overcurrent protection device automatically interrupts the flow of electricity if the current flowing through the device exceeds a design maximum amount. Common examples in residential electrical systems are fuses and circuit breakers.

Receptacle: A device into which a plug is inserted and through which electricity flows to equipment that uses electricity. Receptacles include the familiar single (one plug) and duplex (two plug) 120-volt devices and the 240-volt devices most often seen in laundry rooms to serve electric clothes dryers.

Service drop: The service drop describes overhead electrical wires beginning at the power pole and ending where the service drop wires connect to the service entrance wires. This is usually at the service point near the mast on the roof.

Service entrance wires: Service entrance wires run from the service point to the service equipment. Typically, the service entrance wires mark the point in your home wiring system where the equipment is the responsibility of the homeowner and not the utility company.

Ungrounded conductor: An ungrounded conductor is one that intentionally carries electricity. The common term for an ungrounded conductor in residential electrical systems is the "hot" or "live" wire or conductor. Ungrounded conductors are usually insulated with red or black colored insulation.

Typical Home Wiring System

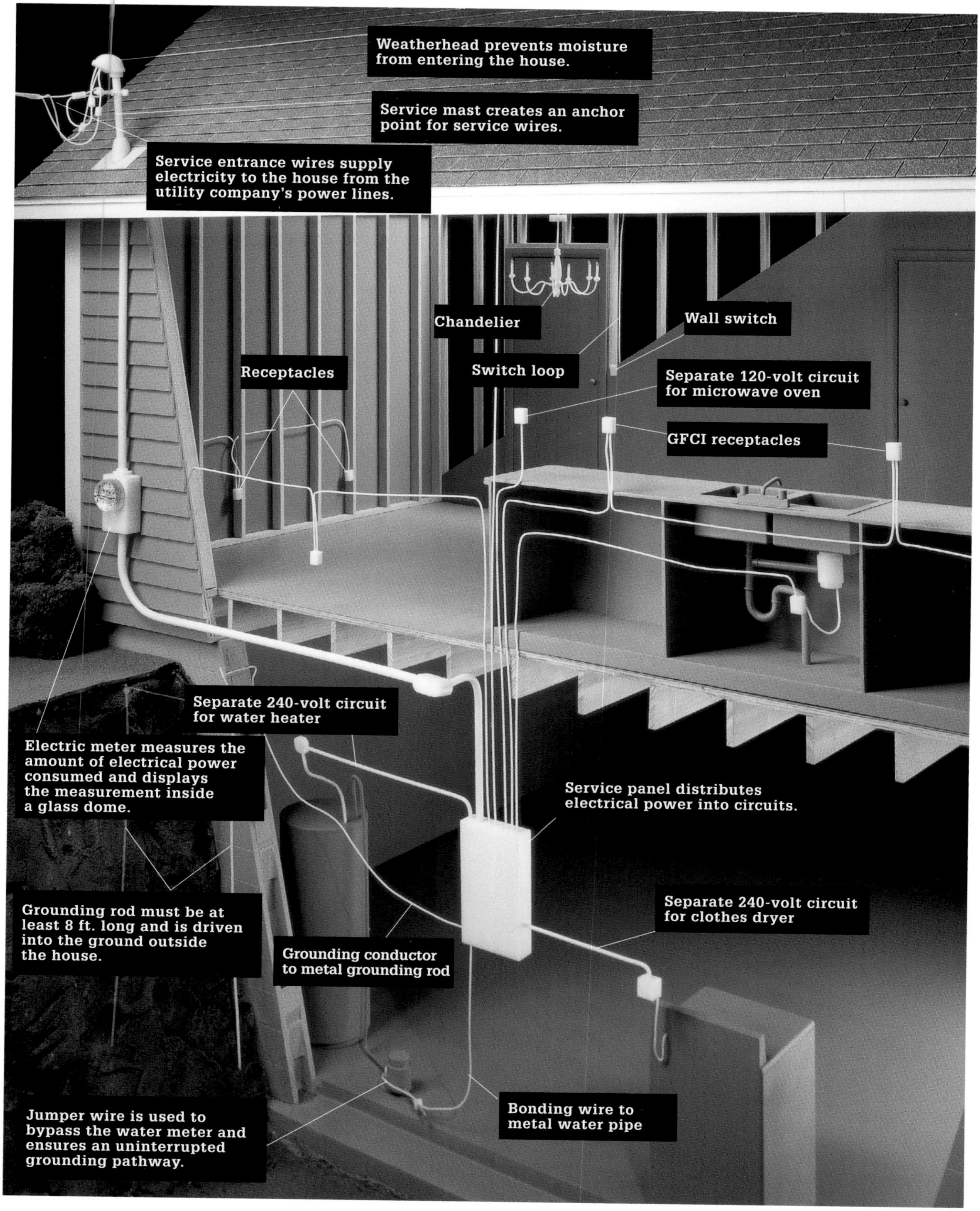
Weatherhead prevents moisture from entering the house.
Service mast creates an anchor point for service wires.
Service entrance wires supply electricity to the house from the utility company's power lines.
Chandelier
Wall switch
Switch loop
Receptacles
Separate 120-volt circuit for microwave oven
GFCI receptacles
Separate 240-volt circuit for water heater
Electric meter measures the amount of electrical power consumed and displays the measurement inside a glass dome.
Service panel distributes electrical power into circuits.
Separate 240-volt circuit for clothes dryer
Grounding rod must be at least 8 ft. long and is driven into the ground outside the house.
Grounding conductor to metal grounding rod
Jumper wire is used to bypass the water meter and ensures an uninterrupted grounding pathway.
Bonding wire to metal water pipe

Understanding Electrical Circuits

An electrical circuit is a continuous loop. Household circuits carry power from the main service panel, throughout the house, and back to the main service panel. Several switches, receptacles, light fixtures, or appliances may be connected to a single circuit.

Current enters a circuit loop on hot wires and returns along neutral wires. These wires are color coded for easy identification. Hot wires are black or red, and neutral wires are white or light gray. For safety, most circuits include a bare copper or green insulated grounding wire. The grounding wire conducts current when wires or equipment are malfunctioning and helps reduce the chance of severe electrical shock. The service panel also has a bonding wire connected to metal water pipes and metal grounding rod buried underground.

If a circuit carries too much power, it can overload. A fuse or a circuit breaker protects each circuit in case of overloads.

Current returns to the service panel along a neutral circuit wire. Current then leaves the house on a large neutral service wire that returns it to the utility pole transformer.

Wiring Safety ▸

Safety should be the primary concern of anyone working with electricity. Although most household electrical repairs are simple and straightforward, always use caution and good judgment when working with electrical wiring or devices. Common sense can prevent accidents.

The basic rule of electrical safety is: Always turn off power to the area or device you are working on. At the main service panel, remove the fuse or shut off the circuit breaker that controls the circuit you are servicing. Then check to make sure the power is off by testing for power with a current tester. Restore power only when the repair or replacement project is complete.

Follow the safety tips shown on these pages. Never attempt an electrical project beyond your skill or confidence level. Never attempt to repair or replace your main service panel or service entrance head. These are jobs for a qualified electrician and require that the power company shuts off power to your house.

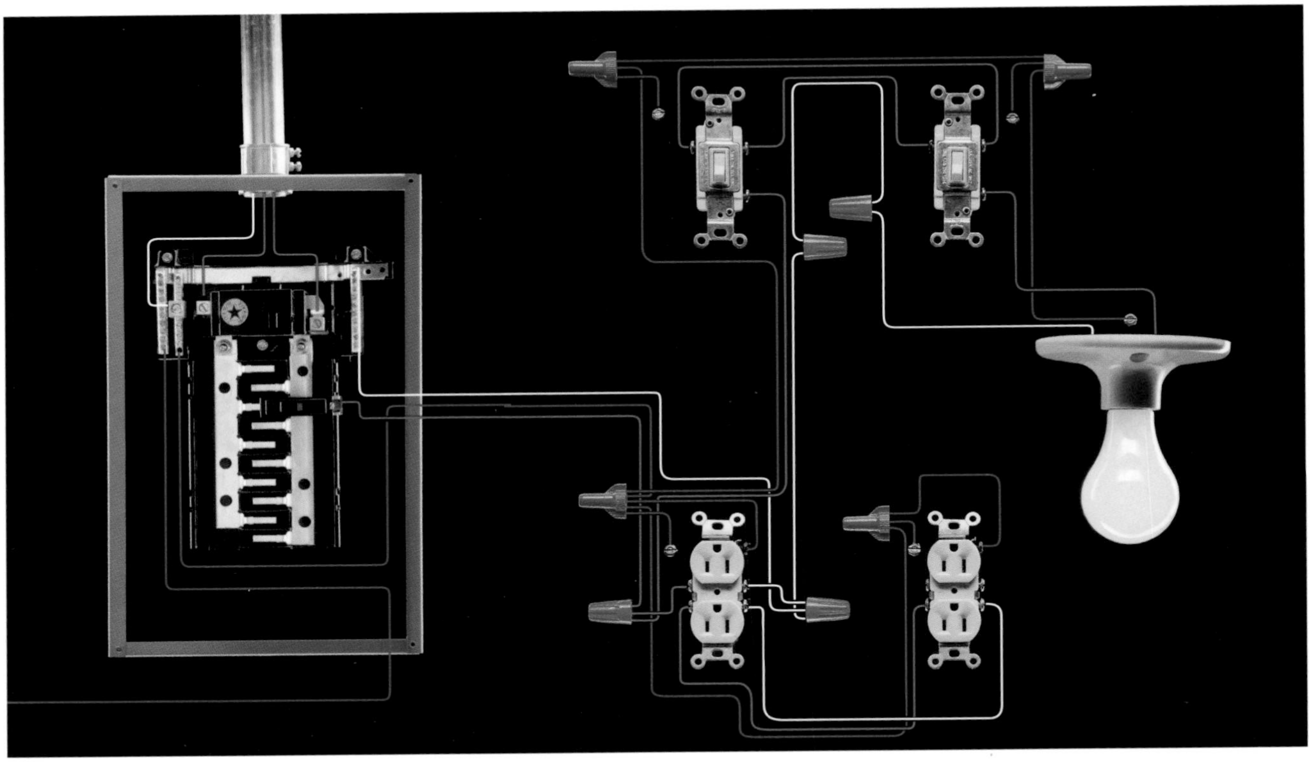

General Requirements

CLOSURE OF UNUSED OPENINGS

1. Close all openings in boxes, conduit bodies, and cabinets with material that provides protection equal to the original opening cover. This means using plastic or metal knockout covers. Tape and cardboard do not provide equal protection.
2. Recess metal knockout covers in nonmetallic boxes and conduit bodies at least ¼ inch from the surface of the box or conduit body.
3. Cover open outlet boxes with a blank cover, a blank plate, or fixture canopy. Switch plates and receptacle plates do not provide complete closure for electrical boxes.
4. Ground metal covers and plates.

IDENTIFICATION OF CIRCUITS IN ELECTRICAL PANELS

1. Provide a legible and permanent marking or label that identifies the purpose of circuit breakers, fuses, and other equipment used to disconnect power from a circuit. Identify the circuit in enough detail so that it can be distinguished from all other circuits. Example: do not identify a circuit as general lighting. Identify the specific rooms or outlets served by the circuit. A marking or label is not required if the purpose of the disconnecting equipment is self-evident. Use marking or labeling materials that will withstand the environment where the disconnecting equipment is located.
2. Locate the circuit identification on the face of the panelboard enclosure or on the inside panelboard door.

Cover open circuit breaker knockouts with an approved plastic or metal cover.

PROHIBITED LOCATIONS FOR EXISTING ELECTRICAL PANELS

1. Do not locate electrical panels and circuit breakers or fuses in clothes closets, bathrooms, or spaces designated for storage.

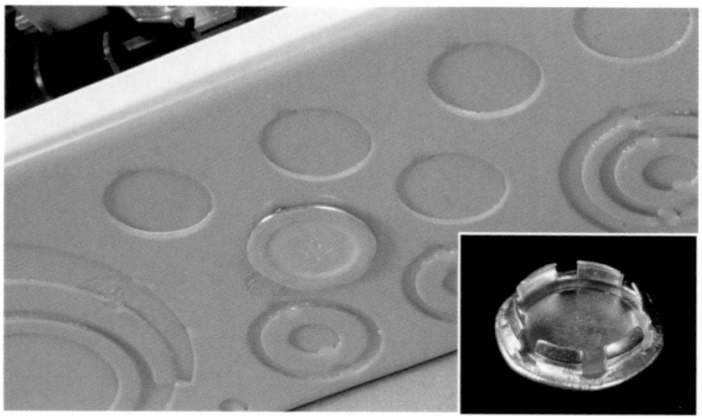

Cover open conduit knockouts in electrical boxes with an approved plastic or metal cap (inset).

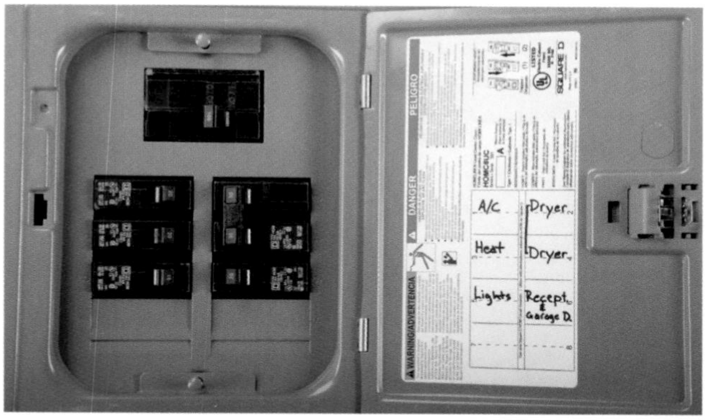

Label each circuit in all electrical panels so that the purpose of each circuit is clear.

WORKING CLEARANCES AROUND ELECTRICAL PANELS

1. Inspect your electrical service panel to make sure it conforms to Code. If not, hire a professional electrician to relocate it. Panel should have a clear working space in front of electrical panel enclosures and other equipment and enclosures that require access while interior parts are energized. Examples of other enclosures and equipment include air conditioner and furnace service-disconnect boxes.
2. Clear working space should be at least 36 inches deep, and at least 30 inches wide (or as wide as the enclosure, if it is wider than 30 inches), and at least 78 inches high. Measure the clear working space in front of the enclosure beginning at the front of the enclosure. Measure the clear working space from the energized parts, if the parts requiring access are not in an enclosure.
3. Panel should have enough clearance so that the enclosure door can be opened at least 90 degrees.
4. Do not allow any objects located above or below the electrical enclosures to extend into the clear working space more than six inches beyond the front of the electrical enclosure.
5. Panel should provide access to the clear working space. Do not block access with shelves, workbenches, or other difficult to move objects.

CLEAR SPACE ABOVE & BELOW ELECTRICAL PANEL ENCLOSURES

1. Maintain a clear space directly above and below electrical panel enclosures, free from any components not associated with the electrical system. This space is intended for wires entering and leaving the electrical panel. Do not install plumbing pipes, HVAC ducts, and similar components in this space.
2. Maintain a clear space that is at least the width and depth of the electrical panel enclosure.

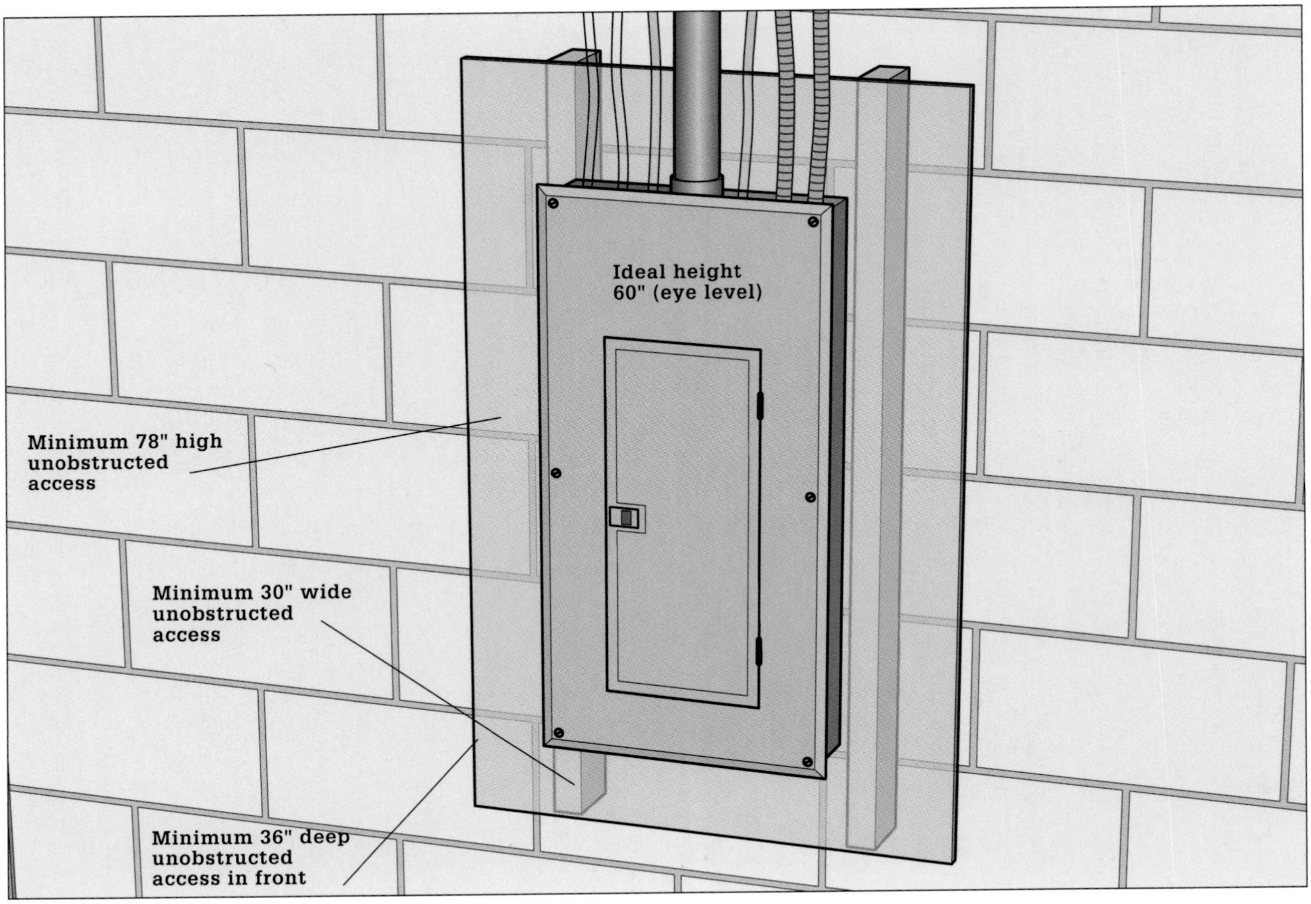
Ideal height
60" (eye level)
Minimum 78" high
unobstructed
access
Minimum 30" wide
unobstructed
access
Minimum 36" deep
unobstructed
access in front

Your equipment should include a safe space above, in front of, and below all electrical panels and similar electrical equipment. If your panel does not meet these standards, have it relocated by a professional.

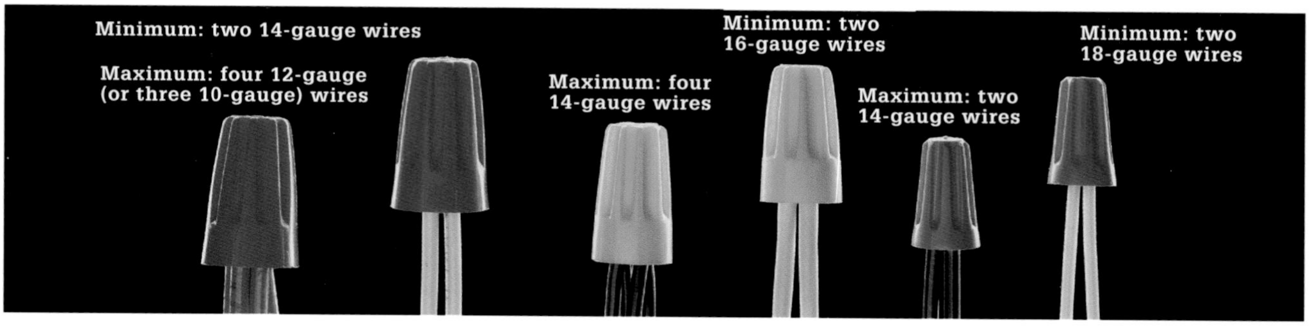

Use wire connectors rated for the wires you are connecting. Wire connectors are color-coded by size, but the coding scheme varies according to manufacturer. The wire connectors shown above come from one major manufacturer. To ensure safe connections, each connector is rated for both minimum and maximum wire capacity. These connectors can be used to connect both conducting wires and grounding wires. Green wire connectors are used only for grounding wires.

SPLICING WIRES

1. Splice (join) wires using only listed devices such as appropriate sized wire connectors. Use wire connector according to manufacturer's recommendations regarding the minimum and maximum number and size of wires that the connector can accommodate.
2. Cover spliced wires with material equal to the original insulation. This does not include electrical tape or similar materials.
3. For splice wires that will be buried in the ground, use only devices listed for direct burial and install them according to manufacturer's instructions.
4. Provide access to spliced wires, unless the splice and splicing device are specifically allowed to be concealed. Access is usually provided by an accessible, covered junction box.
5. Do not place wire splices in a raceway unless the raceway has a removable cover.

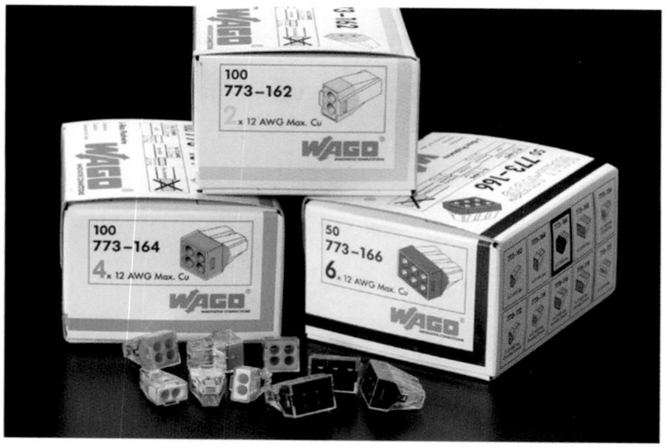

Push-in connectors are a relatively new product for joining wires. Instead of twisting the bare wire ends together, you strip off about ¾" of insulation and insert them into a hole in the connector. The connectors come with two to four holes sized for various gauge wires. These connectors are perfect for inexperienced DIYers because they do not pull apart like a sloppy twisted connection can.

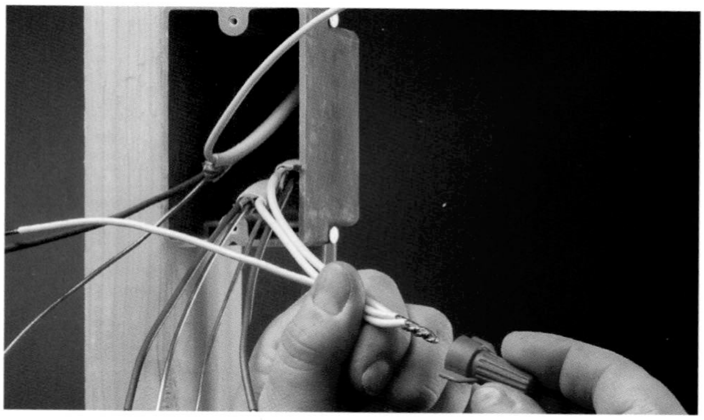

Twist wire connectors over the ends of individual conductors that have been stripped of insulation. Pre-twist wires together with pliers or linesmans' pliers (optional). Do not leave bare wire exposed beneath bottom of connector.

SPLICING ALUMINUM & COPPER WIRES

1. Splice (join) aluminum and copper wires together using devices listed for splicing aluminum and copper wires. Look for a mark or label such as AL/CU on the device or on the package for assurance that the device is listed for splicing aluminum and copper wires. Some wire nuts sold for residential use are not listed for splicing aluminum and copper wires.
2. Use only inhibitors and antioxidant compounds that are approved for splicing aluminum and copper wires. These materials should not degrade or damage the wires, wire insulation, or equipment. Read and follow manufacturer's instructions.

LENGTH OF WIRES EXTENDING FROM BOXES

1. Extend wires at least three inches beyond the opening of any electrical box, junction, or switch point, if the opening is less than eight inches in any direction. This applies to most switch, receptacle, and light fixture mounting boxes used in residential electrical systems.
2. Extend wires at least six inches beyond where the wires emerge from the raceway or cable sheathing. Example: NM cable enters a single residential switch box with one inch of intact sheathing (outer cover). Begin the six inches measurement where the sheathing ends. The cable should extend at least seven inches from the rear of the box. The NM cable should also extend at least three inches beyond the outside edge of the box.

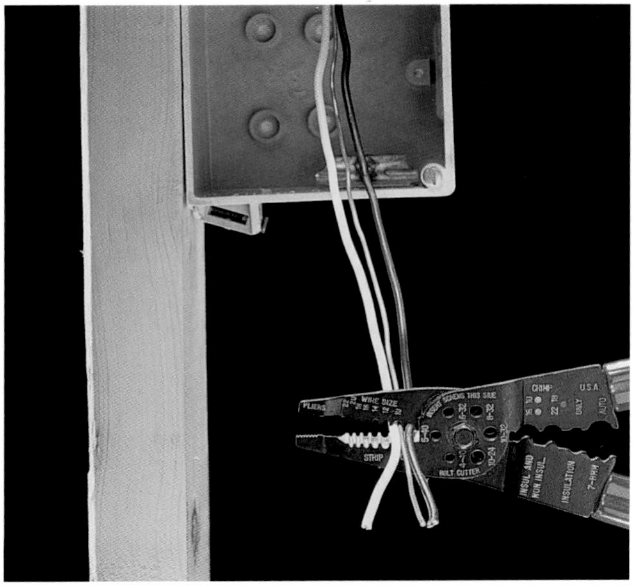

Extend wires past the box opening at least 3".

CONNECTING WIRES TO TERMINALS

1. Remove insulation from wires and connect wires to terminals without damaging the wire. Do not connect damaged wires to terminals. Example: if you nick, damage, or cut strands from a stranded wire, cut the wire back to where it is full size and use the full, undamaged wire.
2. Connect more than one wire to a terminal only if the terminal is identified to accept multiple wires. Example: many panelboards require one wire per terminal for the grounded (neutral) wires and allow two or more same gauge wires per terminal for the equipment grounding wires. Example: many circuit breakers allow only one hot (ungrounded) wire per circuit breaker terminal.
3. Connect aluminum wires to terminals only if the terminal is identified to accept aluminum wires.

VIOLATION! Do not connect multiple neutral or hot wires to a terminal unless specifically allowed (neutral bus bar seen here has two neutral conductors connected to single terminal).

VIOLATION! Never connect multiple hot wires to the same terminal on circuit breakers or other electrical devices unless specifically allowed by the manufacturer.

WIRE COLOR CODES

1. Use wires with white or gray colored insulation or wires with three white stripes on other than green insulation as neutral (grounded) wires. You may use wires with other than white or gray colored insulation as neutral (grounded) wires if they are larger than #6 AWG and if you mark them with a permanent white marking at all wire terminations.
2. Use wires with green colored insulation or wires with green colored insulation and at least one yellow stripe as equipment grounding wires. You may use uninsulated (bare) wires as equipment grounding wires in most circuits.
3. You may use any color other than white, gray, or green as hot (ungrounded) wires. The common colors are red and black. You may use a wire with white or gray insulation as a hot (ungrounded) wire if the wire is part of a cable (such as NM) and if you permanently mark it as a hot (ungrounded) conductor at all places where the wire is visible and accessible. This marking is usually done by wrapping the end of the wire with black or red electrical tape.

NEUTRAL & EQUIPMENT GROUNDING WIRE CONTINUITY

1. Connect neutral (grounded) wires together in device boxes if the neutral (grounded) wire is part of a multiwire branch circuit. Do not rely on any device, such as a receptacle or light fixture, to provide the connection for the neutral (grounded) wire in a multiwire branch circuit.
2. Connect equipment grounding wires together in all device boxes. Do not rely on any device, such as a receptacle or light fixture, to provide the connection for the equipment grounding wire in any circuit.
3. Install a wire (called a pigtail) between the connected wires and any device in the box.

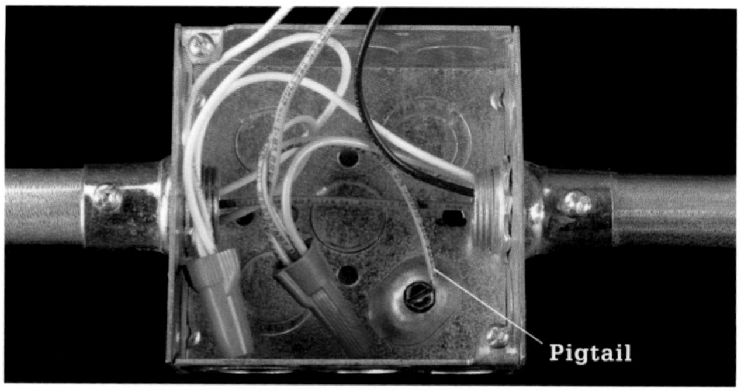

Use a pigtail when you need to connect multiple wires together and use one wire to connect to a terminal.

Wire Color Chart ▸

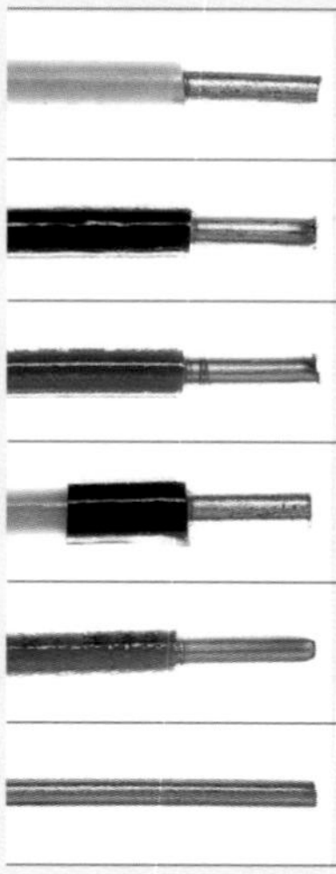

Wire color	Function
White	neutral wire: at zero voltage in many, but not all, circuits
Black	hot wire carrying current at full voltage
Red	hot wire carrying current at full voltage
White, Black markings	hot wire carrying current at full voltage
Green	serves as a grounding pathway
Bare copper	serves as a grounding pathway

Individual wires are color-coded to identify their function. In some circuit installations, the white wire serves as a hot wire that carries voltage. If so, this white wire may be labeled with black tape or paint to identify it as a hot wire.

Wire Size Chart ▸

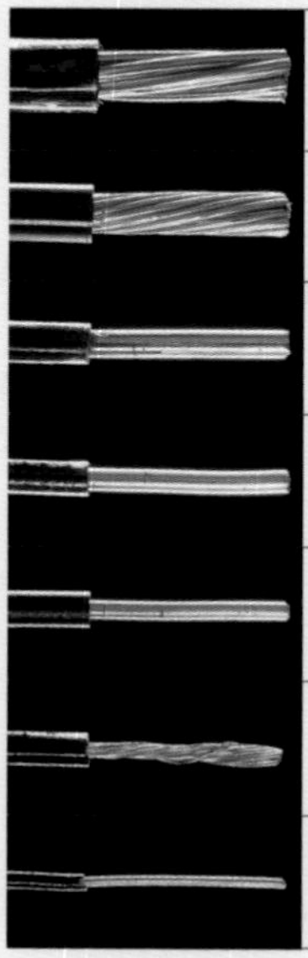

Wire gauge	Wire capacity & use
#6	55 amps; central air conditioner, electric furnace
#8	40 amps; electric range, central air conditioner
#10	30 amps; window air conditioner, clothes dryer
#12	20 amps; light fixtures, receptacles, microwave oven
#14	15 amps; light fixtures, receptacles
#16	light-duty extension cords
#18 to 22	thermostats, doorbells, security systems

Wire sizes (shown actual size) are categorized by the American Wire Gauge system. The larger the wire size, the smaller the AWG number.

Shut off power at the main electrical service panel before beginning any work. In some cases you may shut off individual circuits, but the safer precaution is always to throw the main breaker before starting work.

Service & Main Service Panel

DISCONNECTING ELECTRICAL SERVICE

1. Your system should include equipment to disconnect all electrical service to a building using not more than six switches or circuit breakers located in the same area. This means that a person must be able to turn off all electrical power to a building in not more than six hand motions without moving from one position.
2. The service disconnecting equipment as such. The label must be permanent and clearly marked.
3. Use only service disconnecting equipment listed and labeled for that purpose. The electric meter and meter enclosure are not service equipment. Do not rely on removing the electric meter to disconnect electrical service.
4. The service disconnecting equipment should be installed in a readily accessible place where every building occupant has access.
5. The service disconnecting equipment should be located outside the building or inside the building as close as possible to where the service entrance conductors enter the building. Check with the local building official for information concerning your area. Fifteen feet is one typical maximum, but the distance may be less in some jurisdictions.
6. Service disconnecting equipment should not be located in bathrooms.
7. Service disconnecting switches or circuit breakers should not be installed not more than 79 inches above the floor or ground.

A service disconnecting switch is required when the main service panel is located too far from the point where the service entrance conductors enter the house.

Identifying Your Service ▸

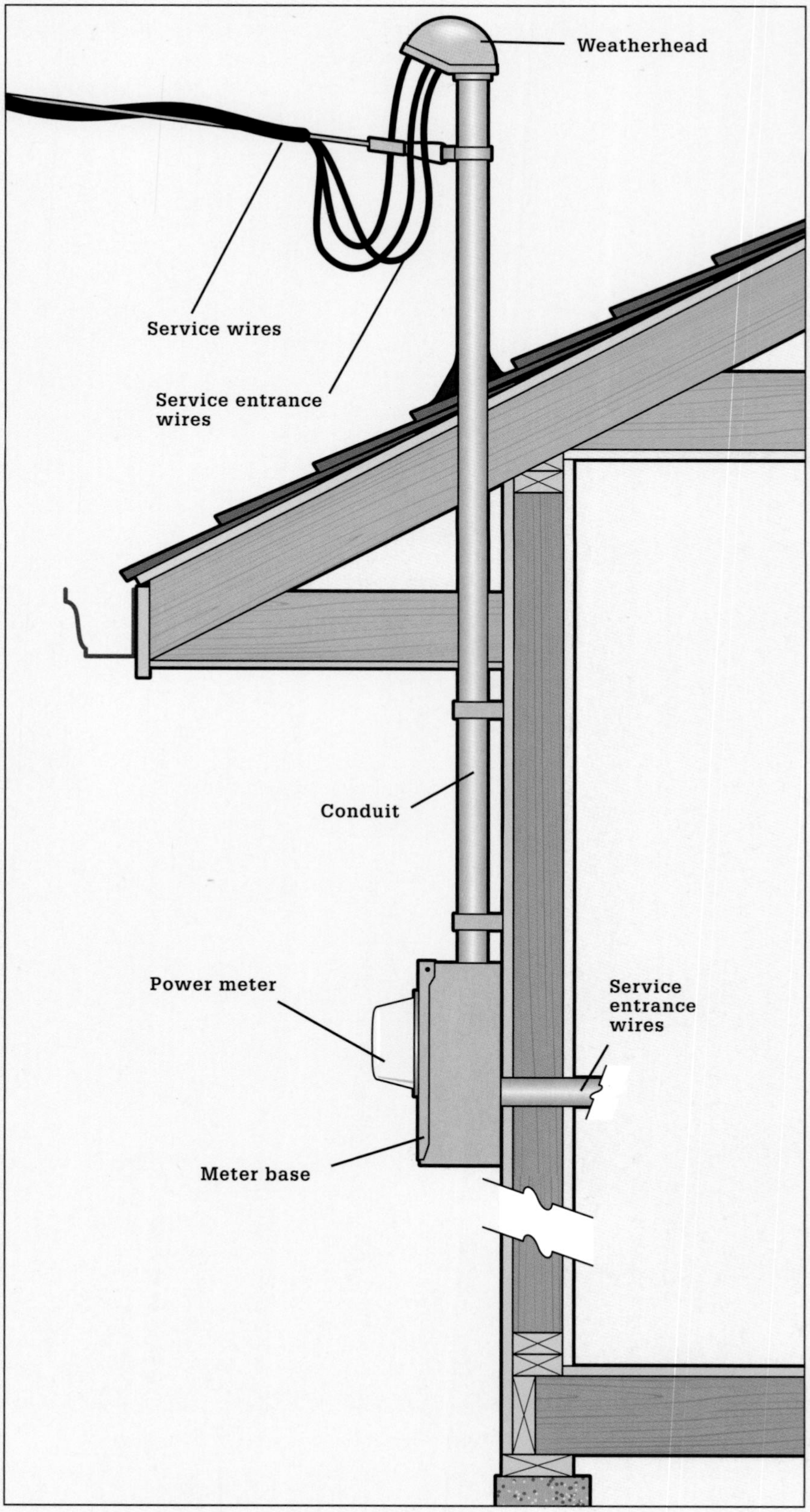
Weatherhead
Service wires
Service entrance wires
Conduit
Power meter
Service entrance wires
Meter base

Aboveground service. In this common configuration, the service wires from the closest transformer (called the service drop) are connected to the power distribution system in your house through a protective hood called a weatherhead. The service entrance wires are routed to a power meter that's owned by your utility company but housed in a base that may be your property. From the meter the entrance wires enter your house through the wall and are routed to the main service panel, where they are connected to the service equipment. Other above ground configurations are allowed.

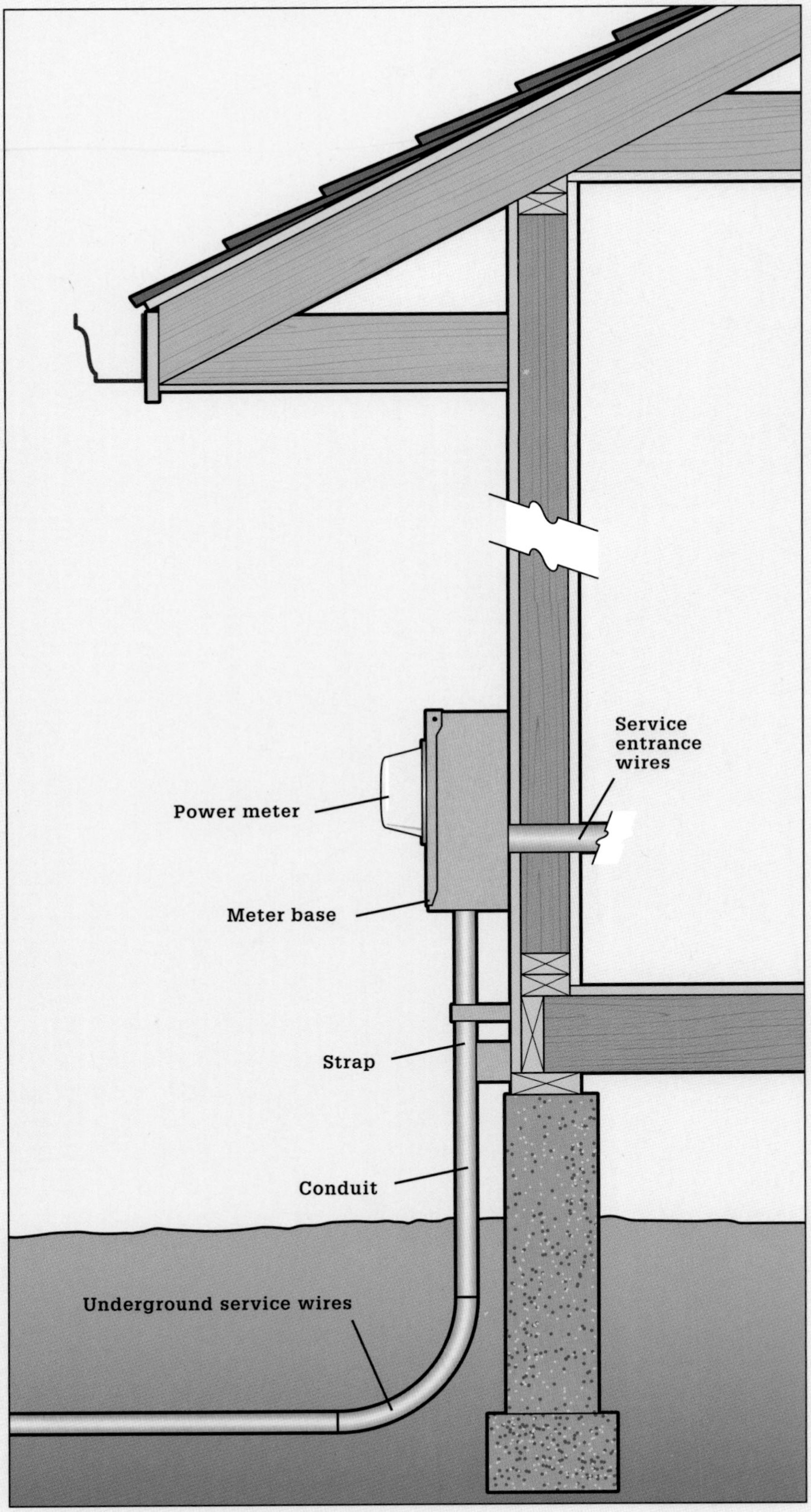
Service
entrance
wires
Power meter
Meter base
Strap
Conduit
Underground service wires

Underground service lateral
Increasingly, homebuilders are choosing to have power supplied to their new homes through underground service wires instead of an overhead service drop. Running the wires in the ground eliminates problems with power outages caused by ice accumulation or fallen trees, but it entails a completely different set of wire and conduit requirements. For the homeowner, however, the differences are minimal because the hookups are identical once the power service reaches the meter.

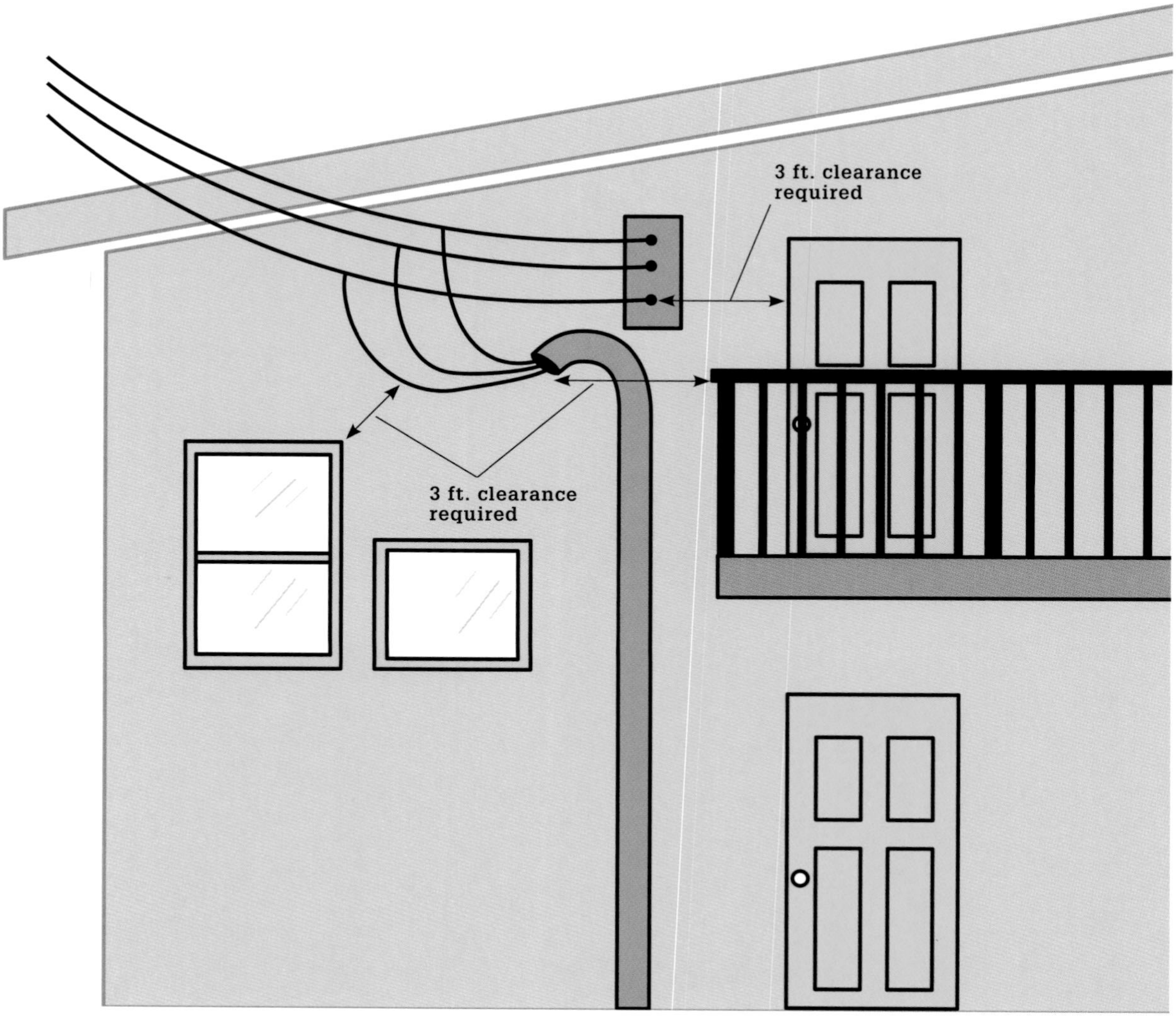
3 ft. clearance
required
3 ft. clearance
required

Inspect your service clearance to make sure individual service wires are within 3 ft. from doors, operable windows, and decks.

OVERHEAD SERVICE DROP WIRE CLEARANCES

1. Service should provide at least three feet clearance between service drop and service entrance wires and porches, decks, stairs, ladders, fire escapes, balconies, sides of doors, and sides and bottoms of operable windows (not the tops of windows). Clearance should be provided only to service drops and service entrance wires that consist of individual wires and wires that are not protected by a raceway or outer jacket. This means that clearances are usually required for utility service drop wires and are not required for SE type service entrance cable and for wires or cables installed in conduit or tubing.
2. Service should provide at least eight feet vertical clearance between service drop wires and a roof not designed for regular pedestrian traffic with a slope less than four inches in 12 inches.
3. Service should provide at least 10 feet vertical clearance between service drop wires and a roof designed for regular pedestrian traffic. Access to such a roof would usually be by stairs or by a door and the roof edges would be protected by a guard.
4. Service should provide at least three feet vertical clearance between service drop wires and roof with a slope at least four inches in 12 inches.
5. Service should provide at least 18 inches vertical clearance between service drop wires and a roof if:
   (a) the wires pass only over the overhang portion of the roof, and if
   (b) not more than six feet of wire pass over not more than four linear feet of roof surface measured horizontally, and if
   (c) the wires enter a through-the-roof mast or terminate at an approved support.

SERVICE DROP CLEARANCE ABOVE GROUND

1. Measure the vertical clearance between service drop wires and the ground, walkway, driveway, or street beginning at the lowest point of the service drop wires and ending at the surface under the wire's lowest point. The lowest point of the service drop wires is often at the drip loop, but it could be at the point of attachment to the house or it could be where the wires enter the house.
2. Provide at least 10 feet vertical clearance between service drop wires and areas or sidewalks accessed by pedestrians only.
3. Provide at least12 feet vertical clearance between service drop wires and residential property and driveways.
4. Provide at least 18 feet vertical clearance between service drop wires and public streets, alleys, roads, or parking areas subject to truck traffic.

Safety Tip ▸

If your electrical service entry does not conform to the codes, hire a professional to update it.

The service drop must occur at least 10 ft. above ground level, and as much as 18 ft. in some cases. Occasionally, this means that you must run the conduit for the service mast up through the eave of your roof and seal the roof penetration with a boot.

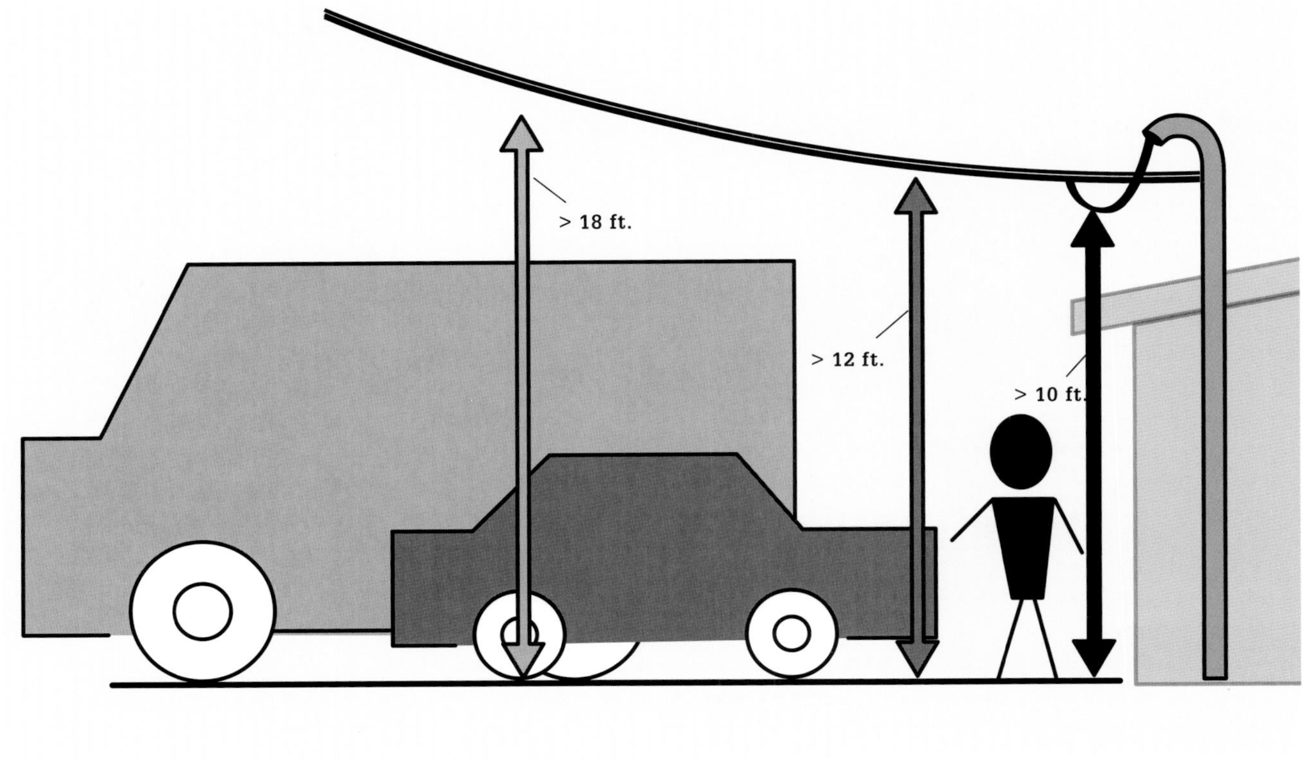

Safe clearance between service drop wires and the ground.

Electrical Grounding & Bonding

One of the important purposes of grounding and bonding can be summarized in this simple rule: Electricity wants to return to ground and will find the path of least resistance to get there. When the electrical system is working as intended, electricity enters through the hot (ungrounded) wire, does its work, and returns to ground through the neutral (ungrounded) wire. This is the path of least resistance.

When electricity finds its way out of the intended path, things get dangerous. Example: a rat sits on copper water pipe and chews through the insulation on electrical cable exposing the hot (ungrounded) wire. After electrocuting the unfortunate rat, the exposed wire lands on the water pipe. If the water pipe is connected without electrical interruption to ground (through bonding or because the water pipe is a grounding electrode), the electricity thinks that the water pipe is the neutral (grounded) wire and happily starts flowing through the water pipe. This is a ground fault. The electric current should quickly rise to the point where it trips a circuit breaker or blows a fuse, clearing the fault.

But what if the water pipe is not grounded or bonded to ground? Perhaps a water softener has been added to the system interrupting the electrical continuity of some or all of the water pipe. In our example, the water pipe is still energized but there is no way for the electricity to return to ground; that is, until someone grabs a metal water faucet handle and is standing on the ground or on some conducting surface. At that time, the electricity finds its path of least resistance to ground through the person. The person is injured or killed.

When trying to understand grounding and bonding, think like electricity. If metal can become energized, however unlikely that is, you must assume that it will become energized. Bonding metal together and connecting the metal to ground in an approved manner lets you, not the electricity, decide how electricity will flow in a fault condition.

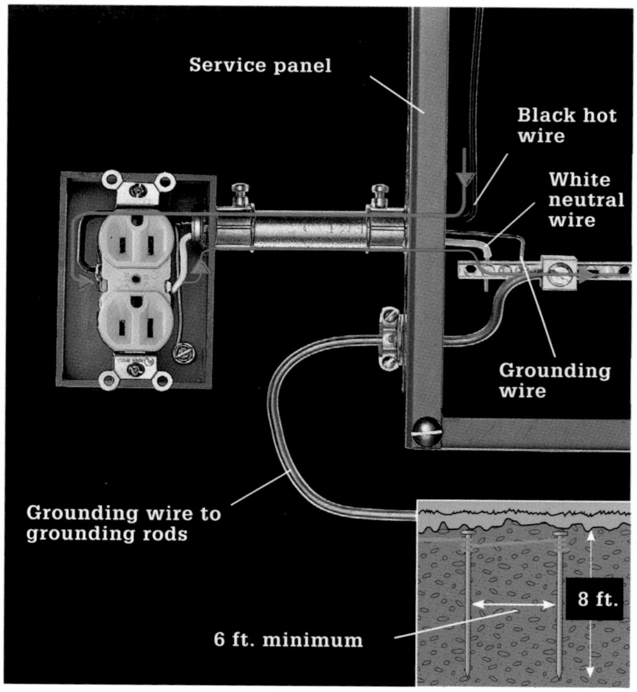

Normal current flow: Current enters the electrical box along a black hot wire, then returns to the service panel along a white neutral wire.

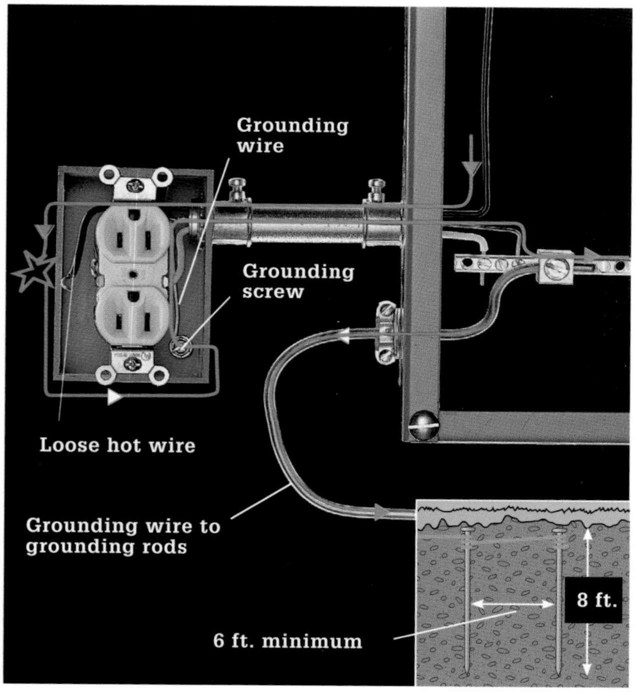

Ground fault: Current is detoured by a loose wire in contact with the metal box. The grounding wire picks it up and channels it safely back to the main service panel. There, it returns to its source along a neutral service cable or enters the earth via the grounding system.

Inspect Electrical Panels for Proper Grounding

GROUNDING & BONDING AT SERVICE PANELS AND SUBPANELS

1. The neutral (grounded) wire should be connected to the grounding electrode wire at the nearest accessible point at or before the service equipment (main disconnect). The service equipment is usually the most convenient accessible grounding point because the meter enclosure and points before it are usually locked or secured and not accessible. The grounding electrode wire connects the neutral (grounded) wire to a grounding electrode.
2. The neutral (grounded) wire should not be connected to ground at any other place downstream from the service equipment grounding point. An exception to this rule exists when two buildings are supplied by one electric service.
3. All metal parts of the electrical system should be connected to the neutral (grounded) wire. This includes service equipment and panelboard cases, any metal electrical conduit or tubing, and all metal pipes in the building (such as metal water and gas pipe).

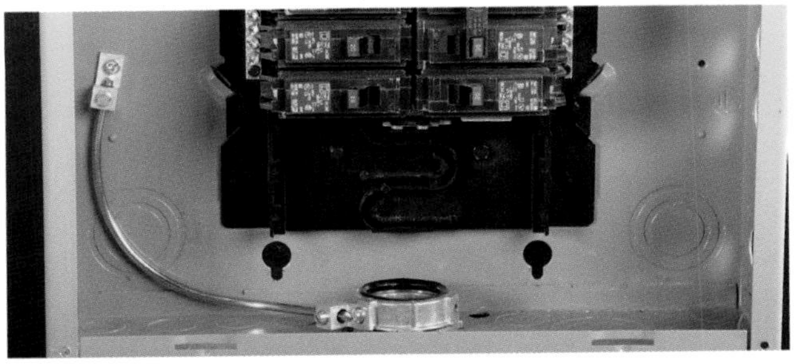

Metallic conduit must be physically and electrically connected to panel cabinets. A bonding bushing may be required, in some cases, where all of a knockout is not removed.

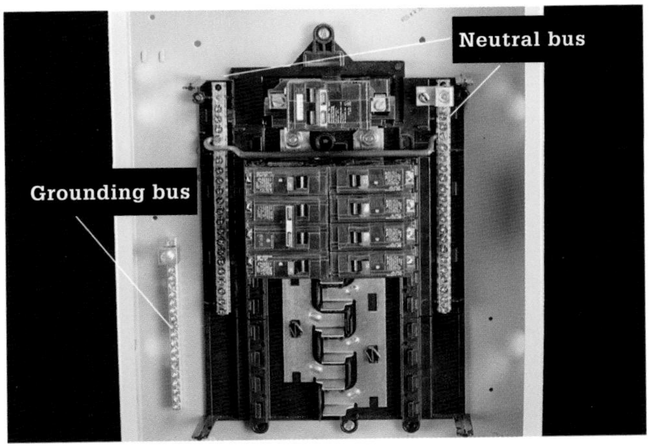

The neutral and grounding wires should not be connected to the same bus in most subpanels. The grounding bus should be bonded to the subpanel cabinet. The neutral bus should not be bonded to the subpanel cabinet.

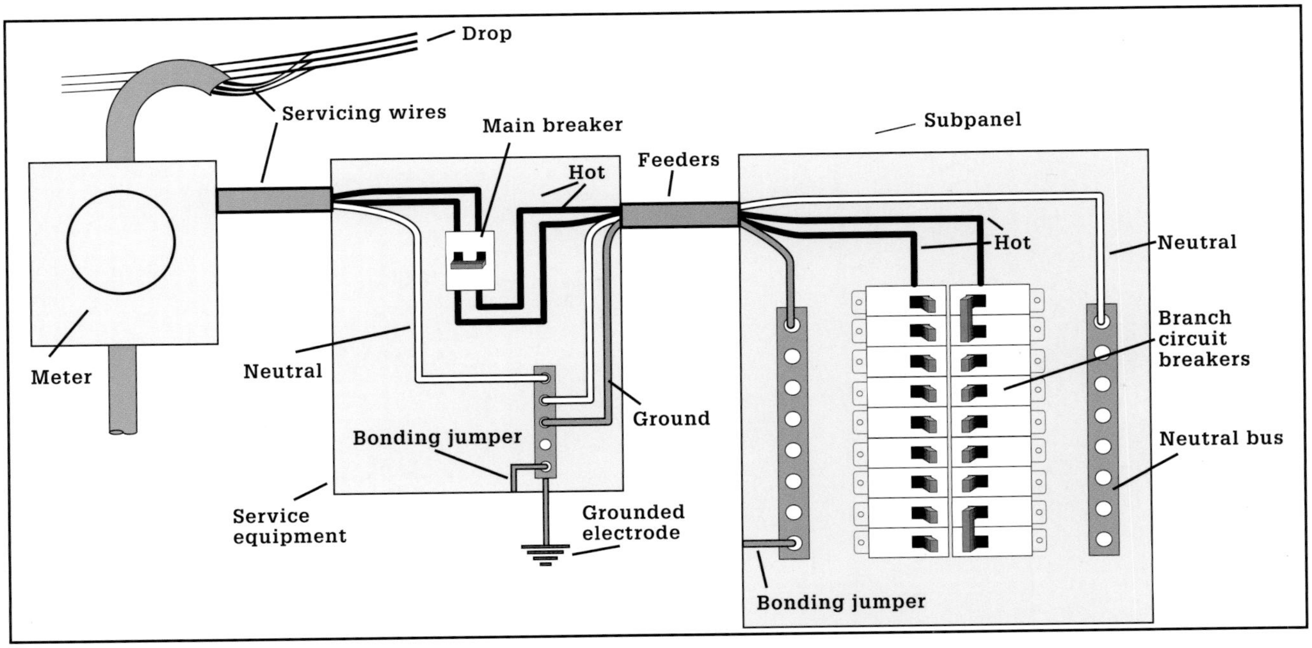

Parts of a common electrical service configuration.

SERVICE GROUNDING AT TWO BUILDINGS USING FOUR-WIRE FEEDER

1. This is the procedure that should be used when installing a new feeder cable to a second building from the building with the primary electric service. This procedure is not required if there is only one branch circuit in the second building and if the new feeder cable contains an equipment grounding wire.
(a) A feeder cable should be installed to the second building that contains an equipment grounding wire. The equipment grounding wire should have been sized as required by IRC Section E3908.
(b) A grounding electrode should be installed at both buildings.
(c) The feeder cable equipment grounding wire should be connected to the grounding electrode wire at the second building subpanel grounding bus. All second building branch circuit equipment grounding wires should be connected to the grounding bus.
(d) The subpanel case should be bonded to the grounding bus.
(e) The feeder cable neutral (grounded) wire should be connected to an isolated grounded bus at the second building subpanel. The grounded bus should not be connected to the subpanel case or to the grounding bus.

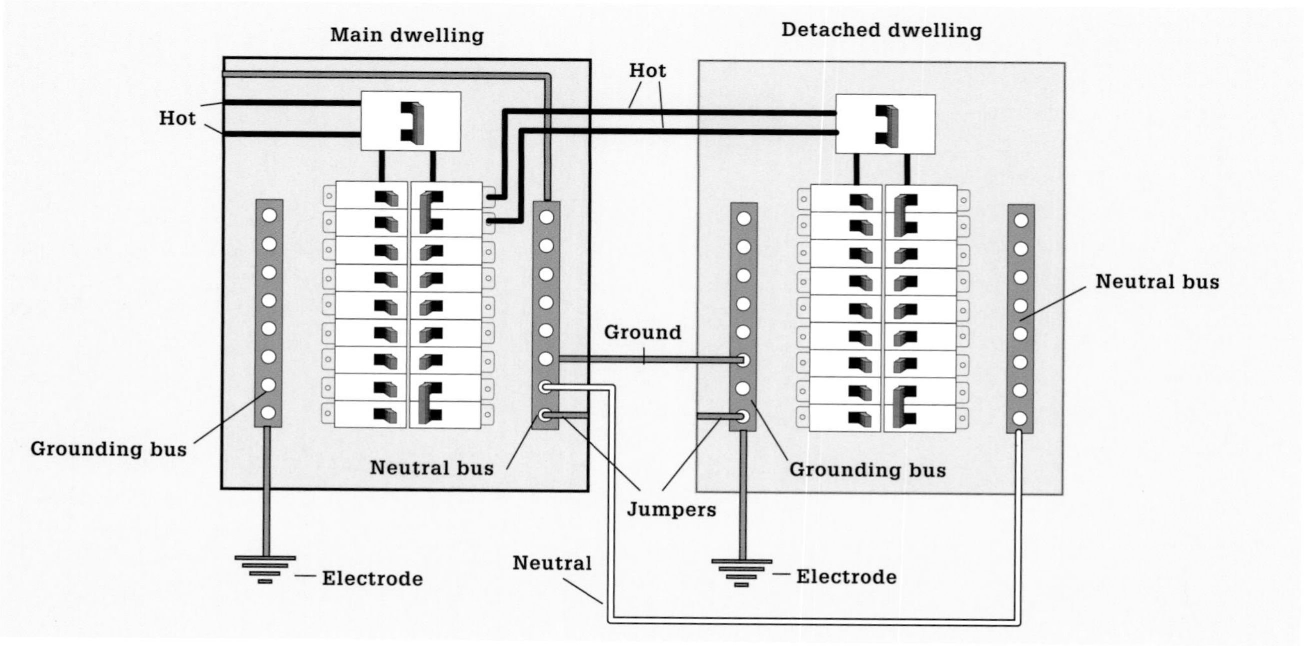

Wiring diagram for wiring a feeder from the main service panel to a subpanel in a separate building.

Grounding Electrodes & Electrode Wires

GENERAL REQUIREMENTS

1. Every electrical service should be provided at least one approved type of grounding electrode. The most common grounding electrodes are underground metal water pipe, driven rod and pipe, and concrete encased.
2. All grounding electrodes that may be available at a building should be bonded together. General codes do not require that all possible types of grounding electrodes be installed. They require that if a grounding electrode is installed, it must be connected (bonded) to all other grounding electrodes and to the neutral (grounded) wire.
3. A bonding jumper at least as large as the grounding electrode wire should be used to connect (bond) the grounding electrodes. Bonding jumpers may be connected between grounding electrodes at any convenient point.
4. The grounding electrode wire may be connected at any convenient grounding electrode.
5. Metal underground gas pipe should never be used as a grounding electrode.

UNDERGROUND WATER PIPE ELECTRODES

1. Metal underground water pipe that is in contact with the ground for at least 10 feet may be used as a grounding electrode. This includes all metal water pipe materials such as copper and steel. Underground water pipe includes metal well casing pipe that is electrically connected (bonded) to the electrical system. It also includes water pipes other than water service pipes such as metal irrigation system pipes.
2. All underground water pipe that satisfies the previous conditions must be considered as a grounding electrode and must be bonded to all other grounding electrodes.
3. A grounding electrode wire may not be connected to any interior metal water pipe at a point that is more than five feet from where the underground water pipe enters the building. Interior metal water pipe that is more than five feet from where the water pipe enters the building may not be used as a conductor for a grounding electrode.
4. Underground metal water pipe may not be used as the only grounding electrode. At least one other type of grounding electrode must be installed and bonded to the underground metal water pipe.
5. Bonding jumper wires must be installed around devices that might interrupt electrical continuity. Such devices include water meters, water pressure reducers, water softeners, and water filtration systems.

ROD & PIPE ELECTRODES

1. Rod and pipe grounding electrodes may be used only if one of the other types of grounding electrode is not available.
2. Metal pipe or conduit that is at least ¾-in. diameter and is at least eight feet long may be used as a grounding electrode. Iron and steel pipes should have corrosion resistant coating.
3. Iron or steel rod that is at least ⅝-in. diameter and is at least eight feet long may be used as a grounding electrode.
4. Listed stainless steel or nonferrous (such as copper) rod that is at least ½-in. diameter and is at least eight feet long may be used as a grounding electrode.
5. Aluminum may not be used as rod and pipe electrodes.

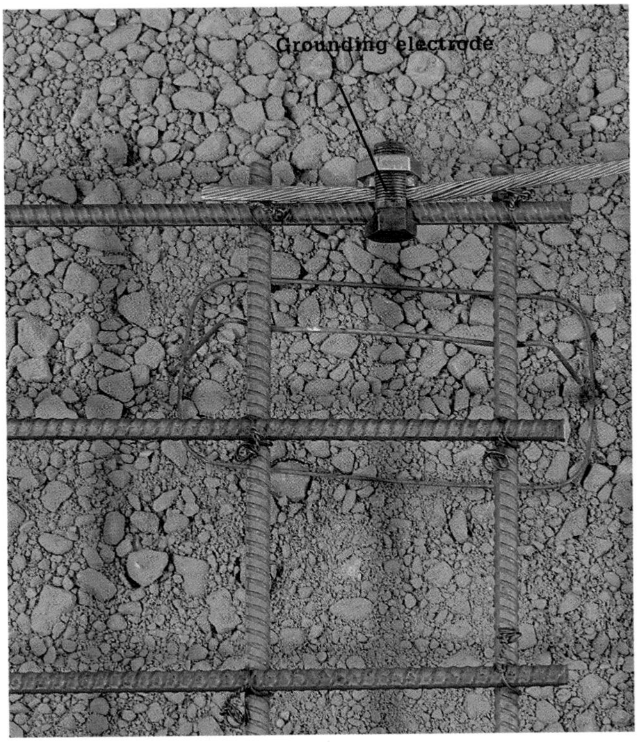

A piece of reinforcing bar encased in a concrete footing is a common grounding electrode in new construction. Called a ufer, the electrode must be No. 4 or larger rebar and at least 20 ft. long. (Shown prior to pouring concrete.)

CONCRETE ENCASED ELECTRODES

1. A ½-inch diameter (No. 4) reinforcing bar or at least #4 AWG bare copper wire may be used as a concrete encased grounding electrode. The electrode material must be at least 20 feet long.
2. The reinforcing bar or wire must be encased in at least two inches of concrete. The bar or wire should be placed near the bottom of the concrete. A moisture barrier should not be present between the concrete and the ground.
3. Wire ties or similar means may be used to connect (bond) reinforcing bars together to achieve the 20 ft. minimum length.
4. Concrete encased electrodes are also called "ufer" grounding electrodes after the man who designed this grounding electrode system.

GROUNDING ELECTRODE WIRE INSTALLATION: ALUMINUM

1. Aluminum or copper-clad aluminum grounding electrode wires should be used if the wire is in direct contact with masonry or with the ground or if the wire is in a corrosive environment.
2. Aluminum or copper-clad aluminum grounding electrode wires should not be installed within 18 inches of the ground when the wire is installed outside.

CONNECTING GROUNDING ELECTRODE WIRES TO THE ELECTRODE

1. One of the following methods should be used to connect grounding electrode wires to grounding electrodes: (a) a pipe fitting, pipe plug, or other approved device screwed into a pipe or pipe fitting, or (b) a listed bolted clamp made of cast bronze or brass, or plain or malleable iron.
2. A listed metal strap ground clamp may be used to connect indoor communications equipment grounding electrode wires to a grounding electrode.
3. The connection point for grounding electrode wires, join jumpers and electrodes should be accessible. The connection point need not be accessible for buried or concrete encased grounding electrodes.
4. Grounding electrode wire connection points and all clamps and fittings should be clean from nonconductive materials such as paint.
5. Use ground clamps or fittings that are either approved for installation without physical protection or that are enclosed in metal, wood, or an equivalent protective cover may be used.

A listed metal strap may be used to ground indoor communication wires such as telephone and cable TV.

CONNECTIONS AROUND EQUIPMENT & INSULATED FITTINGS

1. Bonding jumpers should be used around equipment such as water meters, pressure reducing valves, water softeners, water filtration equipment, dielectric fittings, and other equipment and fittings that interrupt the electrical continuity of metal piping used as a grounding electrode.
2. Bonding jumpers should be long enough to permit removal of the equipment and maintain electrical continuity.

METAL WATER PIPE BONDING

1. Interior metal water pipes should be bonded to the service equipment enclosure, or to the neutral (grounded) wire at the service equipment, or to the grounding electrode conductor, or to any grounding electrode.
2. A bonding jumper or wire that is at least as large as the grounding electrode wire should be used.
3. The bonding connection point should be accessible.

METAL GAS PIPE BONDING

1. Interior metal gas pipes and other metal pipes should be bonded to the service equipment enclosure, or to the neutral (grounded) wire at the service equipment, or to the grounding electrode conductor, or to any grounding electrode.
2. A bonding jumper that is at least as large as the equipment grounding wire should be used on the circuit that might energize the pipe. The equipment grounding wire that serves the equipment may be used as the bonding wire. Example: the equipment grounding wire that serves a furnace may be used as the bonding wire for the gas pipe connected to the furnace.
3. Make the bonding connection point accessible.

Electrical Branch Circuit Requirements

Every electrical circuit has its limits. Among the more basic tasks in evaluating your existing wiring system or planning a system expansion is to identify which loads will be drawing from which circuits so you can establish what each circuit capacity will need to be. In addition to letting you plan the circuits wisely, specific load knowledge lets you create a more balanced service panel, lessening the chances that you'll trip breakers.

Planning a code-compliant branch circuit starts with calculating the amount of load you expect the circuit to draw.

Branch Circuit Load Limits

15-AMP & 20-AMP CIRCUITS

1. Use only 15-amp and 20-amp, 120-volt circuits for multiple outlet branch circuits. A multiple outlet branch circuit has more than one light fixture and/or receptacle on the same circuit. One duplex receptacle (the common receptacle with two openings for plugs) counts as two receptacles. A circuit that serves one duplex receptacle is a multiple outlet branch circuit. This provision does not apply to a circuit that serves one single receptacle or one single light fixture.
2. Use only 120-volt branch circuits to supply residential light fixtures, and to supply receptacles for plug-and-cord connected loads not more than 1,440 watts, and to supply motor loads less than .25 horsepower.
3. You may use either 120- or 240-volt branch circuits to supply one plug-and-cord connected or one permanently wired appliance rated more than 1,440 watts. This means that branch circuits rated more than 120 volts are effectively limited to serving a single receptacle or permanently wired fixed equipment.
4. Do not connect one plug-and-cord device that exceeds 80 percent of a multiple outlet branch circuit's amperage rating. This means that one device (such as a vacuum cleaner or a toaster oven) may not exceed 12 amps (about 1,440 watts) on a 15-amp multiple outlet branch circuit and may not exceed 16 amps (about 1,920 watts) on a 20-amp multiple outlet branch circuit.
5. Do not connect one or more fixed devices that in total exceed 50 percent of a multiple outlet branch circuit's amperage rating. Fixed devices do not include light fixtures. This means that that all fixed devices (such as a permanently wired disposal or hot water circulating pump) on a multiple outlet branch circuit may not exceed 7.5 amps (about 900 watts) on a 15-amp multiple outlet branch circuit and may not exceed 10 amps (about 1,200 watts) on a 20-amp multiple outlet branch circuit.

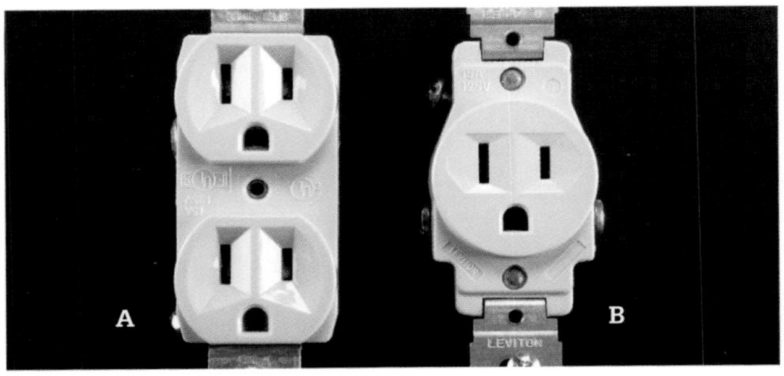

A duplex receptacle (A) contains two outlets. A single receptacle (B) contains one outlet.

30-AMP CIRCUITS

1. Do not connect one plug-and-cord device that exceeds 80 percent of a 30-amp branch circuit's amperage rating. This means that one device (such as a clothes dryer) may not exceed 24 amps (about 5,760 watts) on a 30-amp, 240-volt branch circuit.
2. Do not use a 30-amp branch circuit to serve loads other than a fixed device such as a water heater or a single plug-and-cord connected device such as a welder.

Safety Tip ▸

Always work with your local electrical inspector and an experienced wiring installer when adding electrical circuits.

ROOM AIR CONDITIONER CIRCUITS

1. Use wires that are rated at least 125 percent of a window or through-wall air conditioner's total rated current load if:
   (a) the air conditioner is connected to a receptacle by a plug-and-cord, and if
   (b) the air conditioner's total rated current load is shown on its nameplate (not just the individual motor load), and if
   (c) the air conditioner's total rated current load on the nameplate is not more than 40 amps and 250 volts, and if
   (d) the branch circuit overcurrent protection device does not exceed the branch circuit wire ampacity rating and the ampacity rating of the receptacle. Example: a plug-and-cord connected room air conditioner's total rated current load is 17 amps. Use wires rated for 1.25 times 17 amps equals 21.25 amps (#10 copper wire).
2. Do not install a window or through-wall air conditioner on a 15- or a 20-amp multiple outlet branch circuit if the air conditioner's total rated current load is more than 50 percent of the branch circuit's rating (80 percent for dedicated circuits).

KITCHEN SMALL APPLIANCE CIRCUITS

1. Provide at least two 20-amp, 120-volt branch circuits to serve only receptacles in the kitchen, pantry, breakfast and dining areas, and similar rooms. You may use the kitchen receptacle circuits to power a refrigerator, a wall clock, and the electrical requirements for gas cooking equipment. **You may not use the kitchen branch circuits to supply light fixtures or other outlets in these rooms, and you may not use the kitchen branch circuits to supply outlets in other rooms.**

Air-conditioner load ratings can be found on the nameplate.

An electric clothes dryer requires a separate, dedicated circuit (usually 240-volt, 30-amp).

BATHROOM RECEPTACLE CIRCUIT

1. Provide at least one 20-amp, 120-volt branch circuit to serve only receptacles located in the bathroom(s). You may not use the bathroom branch circuit to supply light fixtures or other outlets in the bathroom, and you may not use the bathroom branch circuit to supply outlets in other rooms.
2. You may provide each bathroom with its own dedicated 20-amp, 120-volt branch circuit. In this case, you may use the branch circuit to supply other bathroom outlets, such as light fixtures and exhaust fans.

LAUNDRY RECEPTACLE CIRCUIT

1. Provide at least one 20-amp, 120-volt branch circuit to serve only receptacles located in the laundry area. You may not use the laundry branch circuit to supply light fixtures or other outlets in the laundry, and you may not use the laundry branch circuit to supply outlets in other rooms. Electric clothes dryers require a dedicated 240-volt, 30-amp circuit.

MULTIWIRE BRANCH CIRCUITS

1. Run multiwire branch circuit wires from adjacent slots on the same panelboard. It is safer to originate a multiwire branch circuit from adjacent slots on the same side of the panelboard. This helps avoid overloading the shared neutral (grounded) wire.
2. Use a two-pole overcurrent device or two single pole devices that are connected by an approved handle tie to protect most multiwire branch circuits. Do not connect circuit breaker handles with nails, wires, or other unapproved handle tie substitutes.
3. Use wire ties or similar devices to group all ungrounded (hot) and grounded (neutral) wires of each multiwire brancch circuit in the cabinet where the circuit originates.

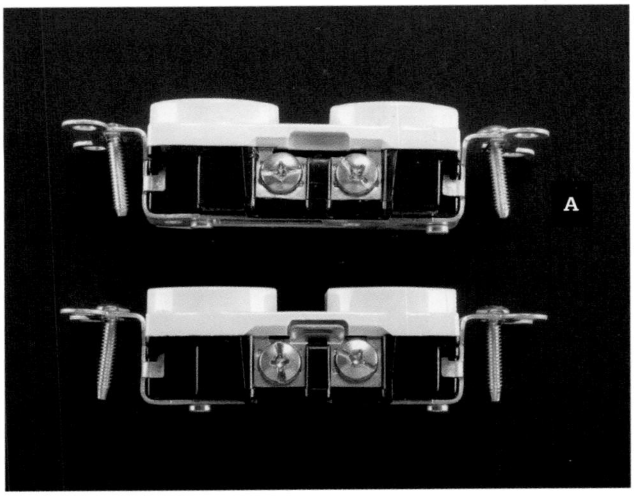

The receptacle yoke is removed (A) when it is split-wired using a multiwire branch circuit.

Connect both handles of circuit breakers protecting a multiwire branch circuit with an approved handle tie.

Quantity of Receptacles on a Branch Circuit ▸

A widely held belief exists that the IRC limits the number of receptacles on a residential branch circuit. This belief is incorrect. The IRC only requires that the number of branch circuits is sufficient to supply the connected load and that the load on any branch circuit does not exceed the IRC limits. This belief may come from restrictions on the number of outlets (both lights and receptacles) allowed for commercial electrical circuits. Commercial applications allow about 13 outlets on a 20-amp circuit and about 10 outlets on a 15-amp circuit. Wiring residential general lighting branch circuits based on these commercial outlet limits is often a good idea but is not required by the IRC.

Current Wiring Methods

Table 42 lists the wiring methods currently allowed in residential construction. **Note that certain wiring methods may not be used in certain applications.**

Table 42: Current Wiring Methods ▸

Wiring method	Abbreviation
Armored cable	AC
Electrical metallic tubing	EMT
Electrical nonmetallic tubing	ENT
Flexible metal conduit	FMC
Intermediate metal conduit	IMC
Liquidtight flexible conduit	LFC
Metal-clad cable	MC
Nonmetallic sheathed cable	NM
Rigid nonmetallic conduit	RNC
Rigid metallic conduit	RMC
Service entrance cable	SE
Surface raceways	SR
Underground feeder cable	UF
Underground service cable	USE

APPROVED USES FOR WIRING METHODS

1. Table 43 lists when a wiring method may be used in a specific application. Note that some wiring methods have restrictions or limitations shown by the following superscripts: (1) use less than six feet of LFC if the conduit walls are not reinforced, (2) insulate the neutral (grounded) wire unless the cable is used to supply other buildings on the same property, (3) insulate the neutral (grounded) wire, (4) use wires approved for wet locations and seal raceways to prevent water entry, (5) use materials listed as sunlight resistant, (6) protect metal raceways from corrosion, (7) use Schedule 80 RNC, (8) use materials listed as sunlight resistant if exposed to direct sunlight, (9) use less than six feet of conduit.

Table 43: Current Wiring Methods Allowed Uses ▸

Allowed application	AC	EMT	ENT	FMC	IMC RMC RNC	LFC[1]	MC	NM	SR	SE	UF	USE
Service entrance	NO	OK	OK[8]	OK[9]	OK	OK[9]	OK	NO	NO	OK	NO	OK
Feeder	OK	OK	OK	OK	OK	OK	OK	OK	NO	OK[2]	OK	OK[2]
Branch circuits	OK	OK	OK	OK	OK	OK	OK	OK	OK	OK[3]	OK	NO
Indoors (e.g., in stud walls)	OK	OK	OK	OK	OK	OK	OK	OK	OK	OK	OK	NO
Wet locations & exposed to sunlight	NO	OK	OK[8]	OK[4]	OK	OK	OK	NO	NO	OK	OK[5]	OK[5]
Damp locations	NO	OK	OK	OK[4]	OK	OK	OK	NO	NO	OK	OK	OK
Embedded in concrete in dry location	NO	OK	OK	NO	OK	NO	NO	NO	NO	NO	NO	NO
Embedded in concrete below grade	NO	OK[6]	OK	NO	OK[6]	NO	NO	NO	NO	NO	NO	NO
Embedded in plaster in dry location	OK	OK	OK	OK	OK	OK	OK	NO	NO	OK	OK	NO
Embedded in masonry	NO	OK	OK	NO	OK[6]	OK	OK	NO	NO	NO	NO	NO
In masonry voids & cells in damp location or below grade	NO	OK[6]	OK	OK[4]	OK[6]	OK	OK	NO	NO	OK	OK	NO
Fished in masonry voids	OK	NO	NO	OK	NO	OK	OK	OK	NO	OK	OK	NO
In masonry voids & cells in dry location	OK	OK	OK	OK	OK	OK	OK	OK	NO	OK	OK	NO
Exposed not subject to damage	OK	OK	OK	OK	OK	OK	OK	OK	OK	OK	OK	OK
Exposed subject to damage	NO	NO	NO	NO	OK[7]	NO	NO	NO	NO	NO	NO	NO
Direct burial	NO	OK[6]	NO	NO	OK[6]	OK	OK[6]	NO	NO	NO	OK	NO

RULES FOR NM CABLE

1. Use Table 44 to determine the maximum ampacity and overcurrent protection of NM cable. NM cable is often referred to by the trade name *Romex*. This table will apply to almost all branch circuit and feeder wiring in modern residential electrical systems. Example: the maximum rating for a circuit breaker protecting Number 12 copper wire is 20 amps.

Table 44: NM Cable Maximum Ampacity ▸

Wire size (AWG)	Copper wire (amps)	Aluminum wire (amps)
14	15	-
12	20	15
10	30	25
8	40	30
6	55	40
4	70	55
3	85	65
2	95	75
1	110	85

Rigid metal conduit has threaded ends for making watertight connections with female-threaded fittings and couplings.

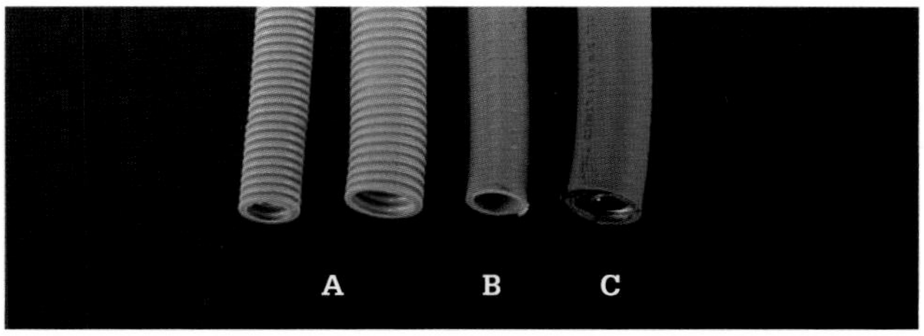

Electrical nonmetallic tubing (A) is an interior-rated material. Liquid-tight flexible conduit can be all nonmetallic (B) or it can be metallic conduit with a nonmetallic sheath (C).

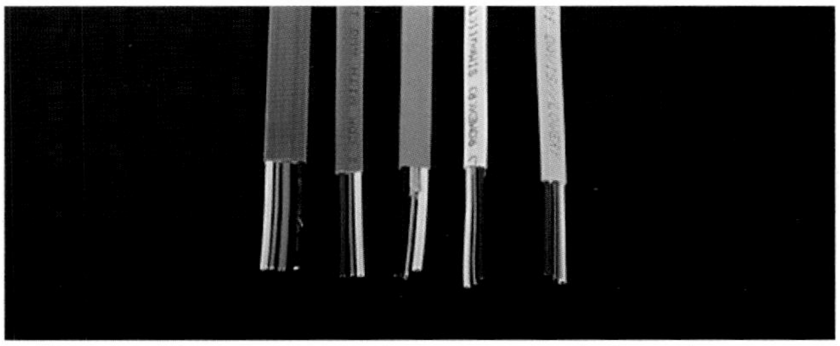

Nonmetallic sheathed cable is available in the most common gauges used in residential construction.

Table 45 ▸ Maximum hole or notch size in studs and joists

Framing member	Maximum hole size	Maximum notch size
2 × 4 load-bearing stud	1$\frac{7}{16}$" diameter	$\frac{7}{8}$" deep
2 × 4 nonload-bearing stud	2$\frac{1}{8}$" diameter	1$\frac{7}{16}$" deep
2 × 6 load-bearing stud	2$\frac{1}{4}$" diameter	1$\frac{3}{8}$" deep
2 × 6 nonload-bearing stud	3$\frac{5}{16}$" diameter	2$\frac{3}{16}$" deep
2 × 6 joists	1$\frac{7}{8}$" diameter	$\frac{7}{8}$" deep
2 × 8 joists	2$\frac{3}{8}$" diameter	1$\frac{1}{4}$" deep
2 × 10 joists	3$\frac{1}{16}$" diameter	1$\frac{1}{2}$" deep
2 × 12 joists	3$\frac{3}{4}$" diameter	1$\frac{7}{8}$" deep

This framing member chart shows the maximum sizes for holes and notches that can be cut into studs and joists when running cables. When boring holes, there must be at least $\frac{5}{8}$" of wood between the edge of a stud and the hole, and at least 2" between the edge of a joist and the hole. Joists can be notched only in the end $\frac{1}{3}$ of the overall span, never in the middle $\frac{1}{3}$ of the joist.

NM & UF CABLE INSTALLATION

1. Use NM and UF cable where the cable is not subject to physical damage. Physical damage can occur unless the cable is covered by drywall or other material or unless the cable is run in conduit or tubing. Physical damage includes damage by sunlight.
2. Protect NM and UF cable using RMC, IMC, EMT, or Schedule 80 RNC when the cable is subject to physical damage. Extend the protection at least six inches above the floor when the cable runs through the floor. This provision applies to exposed wall framing, such as unfinished basements and garages, and to cable that runs through framed and concrete slab floors. This provision does not apply to cable run in attics and in basement ceiling joists.
3. Protect NM and UF cable using nail guards or other approved physical protection when the cable is installed:
   (a) through holes, notches, or grooves that are closer than 1¼ inches to the edge of a stud or joist,
   (b) in notches and grooves in places such as drywall, plaster, and under carpet, unless the groove or notch is deeper than 1¼ inches,
   (c) through holes in metal framing (use grommets or bushings), and
   (d) parallel to the edge of a stud, joist, or furring strip when the cable is closer than 1¼ inches to the edge of the framing member.
4. Support NM and UF cable every 4½ feet. Use wire staples or other approved fasteners to secure vertical runs of NM and UF cable. Staple the cable only on the flat edge. NM and UF cable run across the tops of joists is usually considered supported.
5. Secure NM and UF cable not more than 8 inches from boxes and terminations that do not have cable clamps. This includes most plastic boxes. Secure NM and UF cable not more than 12 inches from boxes and terminations that have cable clamps. This includes most metal boxes. Measure the support distance from where the cable sheathing ends in the box, not from the box itself.
6. Use NM cable only in dry locations that are indoors and not within concrete or masonry that is exposed to the ground. Do not use NM cable in conduit that is buried in the ground. Buried conduit is considered a wet location. You may use UF cable in wet locations including outdoors and underground if it is not subject to damage.

VIOLATION! Do not install NM and UF cable on drywall.

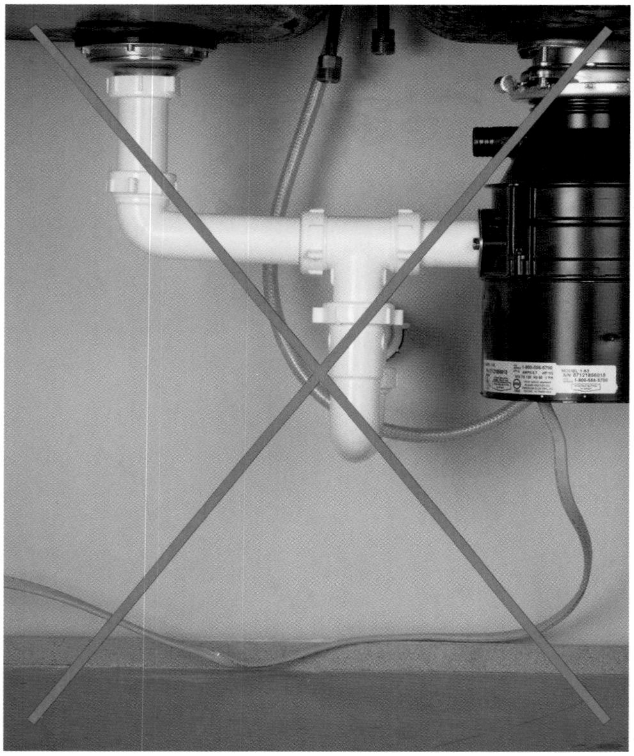

VIOLATION! Do not install NM and UF cable inside cabinets.

VIOLATION! Do not install NM and UF cable in exposed walls and ceilings. You may install NM and UF cable in exposed basement ceilings and attics under certain conditions.

VIOLATION! Do not install NM cable outdoors. Outdoors includes buried conduit. You may install UF cable outdoors if it is protected from physical damage.

Support NM and UF cable at least every 4½ ft. Cable on top of ceiling joists is considered supported.

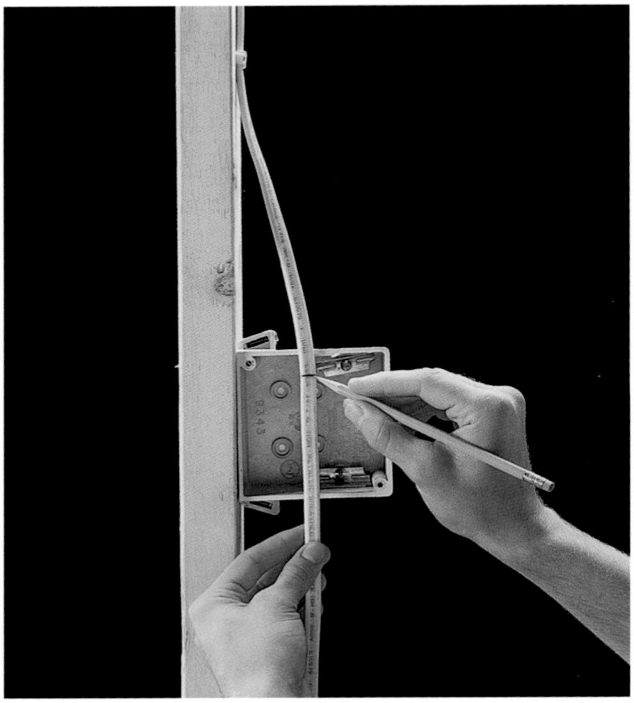

Secure NM and UF cable within 8" from where the cable enters or leaves a plastic box. Measure from where the cable sheathing ends in the box, not from the edge of the box.

CONDUIT & TUBING INSTALLATION

1. Apply the following installation requirements to EMT, IMC, RMC, ENT, FMC, LFC, and RNC:
(a) limit the number of 90-degree bends between junction boxes to not more than four,
(b) install bushings where conduit or tubing enters a box, fitting, or enclosure, unless the device provides equivalent protection against damage to any wires that may be pulled into the device,
(c) remove rough edges from the ends of all conduit and tubing that may damage wires,
(d) support EMT, IMC, and RMC not more than every 10 feet and within three feet of junction boxes or terminations,
(e) support ENT not more than every three feet, unless the ENT is in an accessible ceiling, such as a drop ceiling, and if the distance between light fixtures is not more than six feet, and
(f) support FMC and LFC not more than every 4½ feet and within 12 inches of junction boxes and terminations, unless the FMC and LFC is in an accessible ceiling, such as a drop ceiling, and if the distance between light fixtures is not more than six feet.
2. You may allow not more than 36 inches between the last support and a light fixture or other equipment that may need to be moved for service or replacement.

WIRING SUPPORT REQUIREMENTS

1. Table 46 lists the on center support requirements for wiring methods. Note that some wiring methods have special requirements shown by the following superscripts:
(1) support is not required in accessible ceilings, such as drop ceilings, if the distance between light fixtures is not more than six feet,
(2) you may allow not more than 24 inches between the last support and a light fixture or other equipment that may need to be moved for service or replacement,
(3) you may allow not more than 36 inches between the last support and a light fixture or other equipment that may need to be moved for service or replacement,
(4) support NM and UF cable not more than eight inches from boxes and terminations that do not have cable clamps. This includes most plastic boxes. Measure the support distance from where the cable sheathing ends in the box, not from the box itself,
(5) support NM and UF cable not more than 12 inches from boxes and terminations that have cable clamps. This includes most metal boxes.
(6) support RNC not more than five feet for conduit sizes more than one inch.

Table 46: Wiring Methods Support ▸

	AC	MC	EMT IMC RMC	ENT	FMC LFC	NM UF	RNC	SE USE (service)	SE USE (branch circuit or indoor feeder)
Maximum support spacing	4.5[1] ft.	6[1] ft.	10 ft.	3[1] ft.	4.5[1] ft.	4.5 ft.	3[6] ft.	2.5 ft.	4.5 ft.
Maximum support distance to box or termination (inches)	12[1,2] ft.	12[1,2] ft.	36 in.	36 in.	12[1,3] in.	8[4]-12[5] in.	36 in.	12 in.	12 in.

Use wood or other substantial guards to protect NM and UF cable installed perpendicular to rafters within the protection area.

Use wood or other substantial guards to protect NM and UF cable installed on top of ceiling joists within the protection area.

WIRING PROTECTION IN ATTICS

1. Protect electrical cables in accessible attics by using substantial guard strips that are at least as tall as the electrical cables when:
   (a) access to the attic is by permanent stairs or ladders (such as a pull-down attic ladder), and the cables are within seven feet vertically from the top of attic floor joists or truss bottom chords, or the cables run across the face (shortest dimension) of rafters, studs, or truss webs or chords, or
   (b) access to the attic is by scuttle hole or similar opening and the cables described in (a) are within six feet horizontally from the nearest point of the attic access opening.
2. You need not protect electrical cables in accessible attics when the cables are installed:
   (a) running parallel to the edge of the framing and at least 1¼ inches from the edge of the framing, or
   (b) in holes that are at least 1¼ inches from the edge of the framing.

Basement Ceilings: Running Boards ▸

A running board is a board, such as a 1 × 6, attached to the bottoms of the basement ceiling joists to create a mounting surface for NM and UF cables containing wires #10 AWG and smaller. You may not want to use this method if you intend to finish the basement.

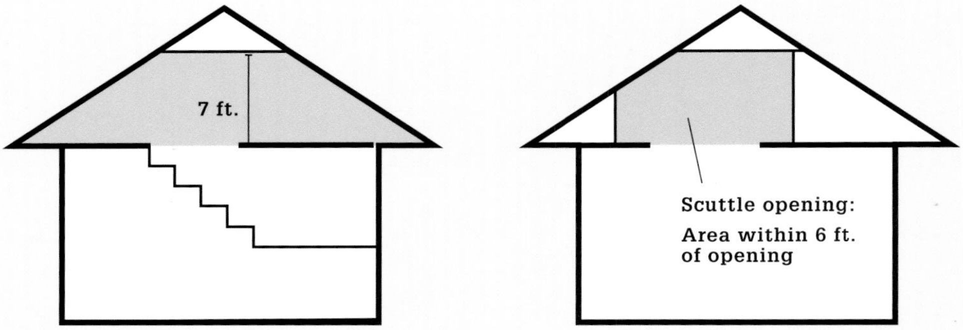
7 ft.
Scuttle opening:
Area within 6 ft.
of opening

Protect exposed NM and UF cable installed in accessible attics and within the shaded protection area.

Electrical Receptacle Installation

Whether you call them outlets, plug-ins, or receptacles, these important devices represent the point where the rubber meets the road in your home wiring system. From the basic 15-amp, 120-volt duplex receptacle to the burly 50-amp, 240-volt appliance receptacle, the many outlets in your home do pretty much the same thing: transmit power to a load.

Learning the essential differences between receptacles does not take long. Amperage is the main variable, as each receptacle must match the amperage and voltage of the circuit in which it is installed. A 15-amp circuit should be wired with 15-amp receptacles; a 20-amp circuit needs 20-amp receptacles (identified by the horizontal slot that Ts into each tall polarized slot). A 20-amp multi-receptacle circuit may use either 15- or 20-amp receptacles. Receptacles for 240-volt service have unique slot configurations so you can't accidentally plug in an appliance that's not rated for the amperage in the circuit. Some receptacles can be wired using the push-in wire holes, but this is not recommended. Some receptacles provide built-in, ground-fault circuit protection, tripping the circuit breaker if there is a short circuit or power surge. These are easy to identify by reset and test buttons.

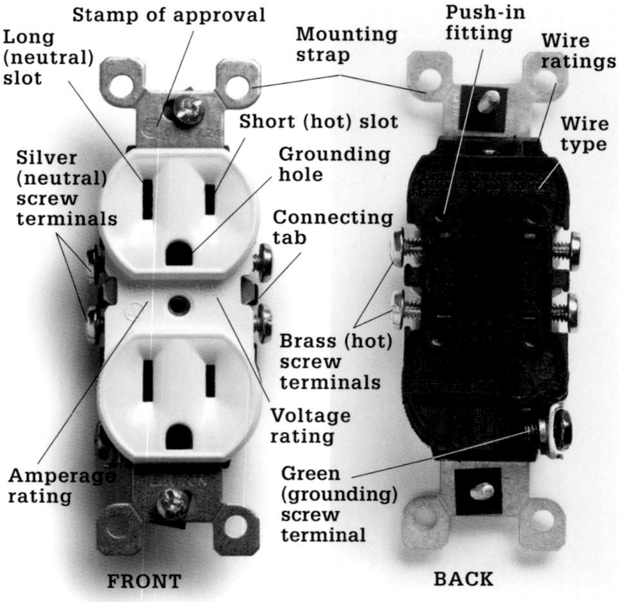

RECEPTACLE INSTALLATION IN ROOMS

1. Apply these provisions to receptacles in living rooms, family rooms, bedrooms, dens, sunrooms, recreation rooms, dining rooms, breakfast rooms, libraries, and similar living areas. Kitchens, bathrooms, hallways, garages, laundry rooms, and exterior receptacles have their own installation requirements.
2. Install the required interior receptacles so that any point along a wall is not more than six feet from a receptacle. Do not include operable doors, fireplaces, closet interiors, and similar openings when measuring a wall. A wall begins at the edge of an opening and continues around any corners to the next opening. Walls include fixed (not sliding) panels in doors that are at least two feet wide. Walls include partial height walls that serve functions such as room dividers and walls that form breakfast bars and similar bar-type counters. Walls include guards and railings at balconies, raised floors, and other areas where furniture could be placed.
3. Locate floor receptacles intended to serve as required interior receptacles not more than 18 inches from the wall. You may install interior floor receptacles at any safe place, but you may count only receptacles not more than 18 inches from the wall among the required receptacles.
4. Install receptacles not more than 66 inches above the finished floor. You may install receptacles at any height, but you may count only receptacles not more than 66 inches above the finished floor among the required receptacles.

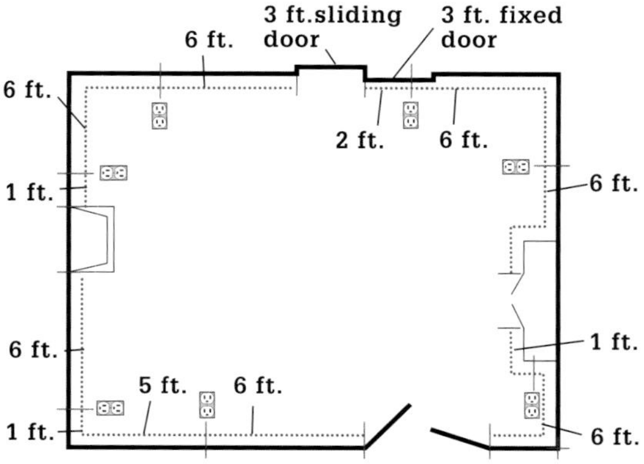

Example of receptacle spacing requirements in a typical room. Measure receptacle spacing distance along the wall line. Install receptacles along partial height walls and along balcony guards in lofts and similar areas.

KITCHEN COUNTERTOP RECEPTACLE INSTALLATION

1. Install a GFCI protected receptacle at every kitchen countertop that is at least 12 inches wide.
2. Install kitchen countertop receptacles so that all points along the countertop wall are not more than two feet from a receptacle. A wall begins at the edge of an opening or appliance and continues around any corners and ends at the next opening or appliance. Include windows when measuring the wall unless the window is above a sink or cooking appliance.
3. Install receptacles behind a sink or cooking appliance located along a straight wall if the countertop behind the sink or cooking appliance is at least 12 inches wide. Install receptacles behind a sink or cooking appliance located along a wall corner if the countertop behind the sink or cooking appliance is at least 18 inches wide.
4. Install receptacles not more than 20 inches above the countertop. You may install receptacles at any height, but you may include only receptacles not more than 20 inches above the countertop among the required kitchen countertop receptacles.
5. Do not include among the required kitchen countertop receptacles:
   (a) receptacles located in appliance garages, and
   (b) receptacles dedicated for a fixed-in-place appliance, and
   (c) receptacles not readily accessible for use by small appliances.
6. Do not install receptacles face up on work surfaces.

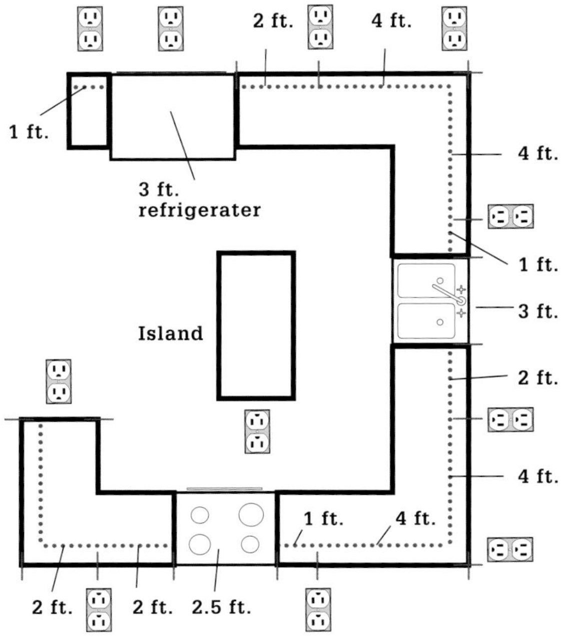

Example of countertop receptacle spacing in a typical kitchen.

You must install receptacles behind a short run of countertop if it is at least 12" wide along a straight wall.

You must install receptacles behind a sink or cooking appliance if the countertop behind the sink or cooking appliance is at least 18" wide in a corner cabinet.

Safety Tip ▸

Always shut off power at main service panel before inspection, repairing or installing receptacles.

KITCHEN ISLAND & PENINSULA RECEPTACLES WITHOUT A SINK OR COOKING APPLIANCE

1. Install at least one GFCI protected receptacle at every kitchen island and peninsula that measures at least 24 inches by at least 12 inches. Measure a peninsula from the interior connecting edge of the countertop.
2. Install kitchen countertop receptacles along any wall space above an island or peninsula countertop. Such wall space occurs when an island or peninsula is installed at a partial height wall.
3. You may install receptacles not more than 12 inches below an island or peninsula countertop if the countertop is flat and there is no wall space above the countertop. Do not install the required kitchen island or peninsula receptacle below a breakfast bar or other countertop that extends more than six inches beyond the supporting base.

KITCHEN ISLAND RECEPTACLES WITH A SINK OR COOKING APPLIANCE

1. Install at least one GFCI protected receptacle not more than 24 inches from each side of a sink or cooking appliance installed in a kitchen island.
2. Install receptacles behind a sink or cooking appliance if the countertop behind the sink or cooking appliance is at least 12 inches wide or at least 18 inches wide if the sink or cooking appliance is installed in a corner.
3. Install kitchen countertop receptacles along any wall space above an island countertop. Such wall space occurs when an island is installed at a partial height wall.
4. You may install receptacles not more than 12 inches below an island countertop if the countertop is flat and there is no wall space above the countertop. Do not install the required kitchen island receptacles below a breakfast bar or other countertop that extends more than six inches beyond the supporting base.
5. Do not install receptacles face up on work surfaces.

Install at least one GFCI-protected receptacle in a kitchen island.

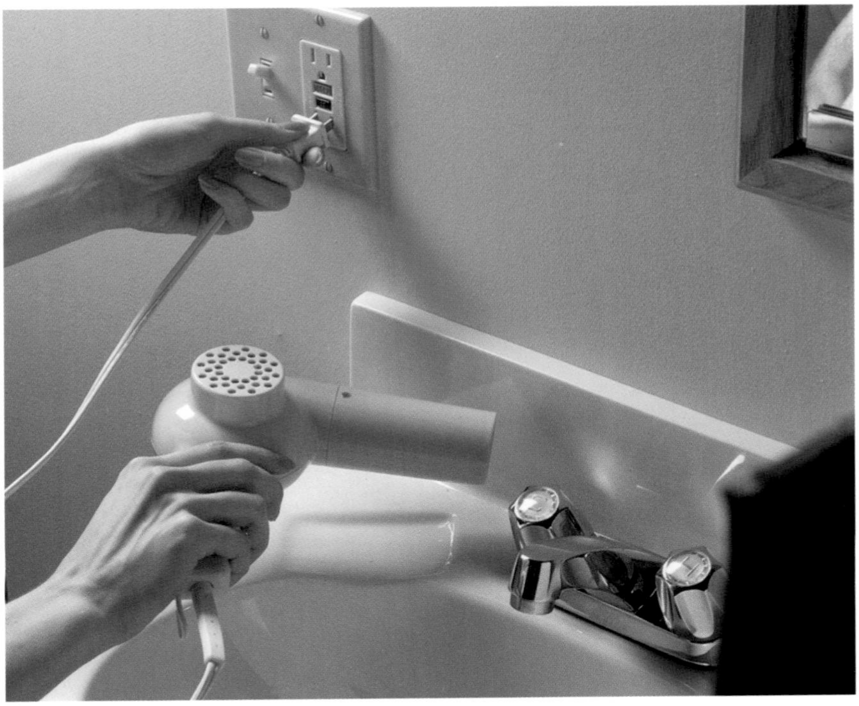

A GFCI protected receptacle must be installed within 36" of each bathroom sink basin.

BATHROOM SINK RECEPTACLES

1. Install at least one GFCI protected receptacle not more than 36 inches from the outside edge of each sink basin in a bathroom. You may install the receptacle along a wall adjacent to the sink. An adjacent wall usually means the wall on which the mirror is usually placed or on the wall perpendicular to the "mirror wall." You may also install the receptacle on the side or face of the basin cabinet if the receptacle is not more than 12 inches below the countertop. Receptacles in light fixtures do not count as the required sink receptacle.
2. Do not install receptacles face up on work surfaces.

An exterior-rated receptacle should be installed on both the front and back exterior walls of your house.

EXTERIOR RECEPTACLES

1. Install at least one GFCI protected, 15- or 20-amp, 120-volt receptacle on the front and back exterior wall of every home. Locate the receptacle so that it is accessible from grade level and is not more than 78 inches above finished grade level.

BASEMENT RECEPTACLES

1. Install at least one GFCI protected, 15- or 20-amp, 120-volt receptacle in an unfinished basement. Install at least one GFCI protected receptacle in the unfinished part of a basement that is partially finished.

GARAGE RECEPTACLES

1. Install at least one GFCI protected, 15- or 20-amp, 120-volt receptacle in an attached garage. Install at least one GFCI protected receptacle in a detached garage if the garage is supplied with electricity. You are not required to supply electricity to detached garages, but if you do you must install a receptacle.

Ground-fault (GFCI) & Arc-fault (AFCI) Protection

GROUND-FAULT LOCATION REQUIREMENTS

1. Kitchen. Install ground-fault circuit interrupt (GFCI) protection on all 120-volt receptacles that serve kitchen countertops. This does not include receptacles under the kitchen sink and receptacles located on kitchen walls that do not serve the countertop.
2. Bathroom. Install ground-fault circuit interrupt (GFCI) protection on all 120-volt receptacles located in bathrooms. This applies to all receptacles regardless of where they are located in the bathroom and includes receptacles located at countertops, inside cabinets, and along bathroom walls. Install ground-fault circuit interrupt (GFCI) protection on all circuits serving electrically heated floors in bathrooms.
3. Garage and Accessory Building Receptacles. Install ground-fault circuit interrupt (GFCI) protection on all 120-volt receptacles located in garages and grade-level areas of unfinished accessory buildings. You do not need to provide GFCI protection for receptacles that are not readily accessible such as receptacles in the garage ceiling. You do not need to provide GFCI protection for dedicated receptacles that serve an appliance that is not easily moved. Examples of dedicated receptacles include receptacles for water softeners, refrigerators, alarm systems, and central vacuums. The receptacle must be a single receptacle when serving a single appliance or a duplex receptacle if serving two appliances. A duplex receptacle serving one appliance is a violation.
4. Exterior receptacles. Install ground-fault circuit interrupt (GFCI) protection on all 120-volt receptacles located outdoors. This does not apply to receptacles that are dedicated for deicing equipment and are located under the eaves. This applies to holiday lighting receptacles located under the eaves.
5. Basement receptacles. Install ground-fault circuit interrupt (GFCI) protection on all 120-volt receptacles located in unfinished basements. An unfinished basement is not intended as habitable space and is limited to storage and work space.

Ground-fault receptacles and circuit breakers detect unwanted current running between an energized wire and a grounded wire.

A combination ARC-fault circuit breaker detects sparking (arcing) faults along damaged energized wires and detects these faults between wires. A branch ARC-fault circuit breaker only detects arcing faults between wires. Use only combination ARC-fault circuit breakers in new work and when replacing old ARC-fault breakers.

The exceptions for garage receptacles apply to unfinished basement receptacles.

6. Crawl space receptacles. Install ground-fault circuit interrupt (GFCI) protection on all 120-volt receptacles located in crawl spaces. Receptacles in crawl spaces are not required unless equipment requiring service is located there.
7. Laundry, utility, and bar sink receptacles. Install ground-fault circuit interrupt (GFCI) protection on all 120-volt receptacles that are located within six feet of the outside edge of a laundry, utility, or bar sink. This includes wall, floor, and countertop receptacles. This includes any appliance receptacles within the six feet distance, such as the washing machine receptacle.
8. Boathouse receptacles. Install ground-fault circuit interrupt (GFCI) protection on all 120-volt receptacles located in boathouses.
9. Spas, tubs, and other circuits requiring ground-fault protection. Install ground-fault circuit interrupt (GFCI) protection on all circuits serving spa tubs, whirlpool tubs, hot tubs, and similar equipment. Refer to the general codes for more information about receptacles serving these components.

ARC-FAULT LOCATION REQUIREMENTS

1. Install an arc-fault circuit interrupter (AFCI) on each 120-volt branch circuit serving bedrooms. This means that lighting, smoke alarm, receptacle, and any other bedroom outlets must be AFCI protected. Install the AFCI at the origination of the branch circuit.
2. Use only combination type AFCI after January 1, 2008.
3. You may install the AFCI not more than six feet from the origination of the branch circuit if you run the wires in metal conduit or a metallic sheath. Measure the six feet along the branch circuit wires.
4. Note that the 2008 National Electrical Code (NEC) requires AFCI protection for all 15- and 20-amp branch circuits. This requirement is controversial and may not be adopted in every jurisdiction. Verify local adoption of the 2008 NEC requirement with your local building official.

Receptacles for whirlpool tubs must be GFCI protected.

Junction Boxes, Device Boxes & Enclosures

All electrical boxes are available in different depths. A box must be deep enough so a switch or receptacle can be removed or installed easily without crimping and damaging the circuit wires. Replace an undersized box with a larger box using the Electrical Box Fill Chart (see page 202) as a guide. **The NEC also says that all electrical boxes must remain accessible. Never cover an electrical box with drywall, paneling, or wall coverings.**

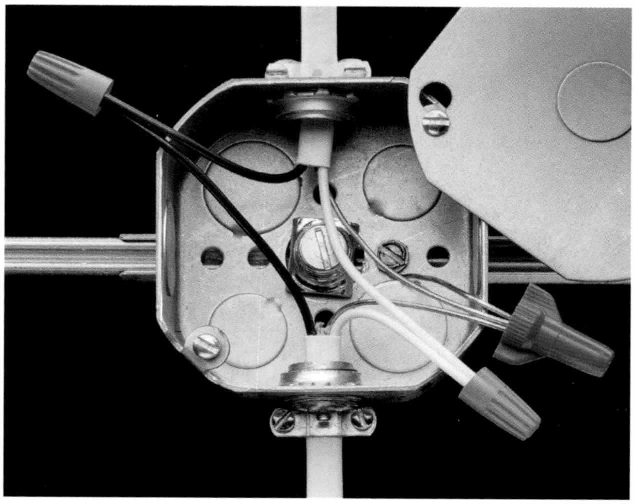

Box shape is directly related to function, as electrical fixtures are created to fit on boxes of a particular shape. Octagonal and round boxes generally are designed for ceiling mounting, while square and rectangular boxes are sized for single-pole, duplex, and other standard switch and receptacle sizes.

NONMETALLIC BOX INSTALLATION

1. Use nonmetallic boxes only with NM type cable or with nonmetallic conduit or tubing. You may use nonmetallic boxes with metallic conduit or tubing if you maintain the electrical continuity of the metallic conduit or tubing by installing a bonding jumper through the box. In many situations it is easier to use a metallic box with metallic conduit or tubing.
2. Extend NM cable sheathing at least 1/4 inch into a nonmetallic box knockout opening.
3. Secure NM cable, conduit, and tubing to each box. You may secure NM cable with cable clamps inside the box or with compression tabs provided where the cable enters the box. You do not need to secure NM cable to a standard single-gang box (2 1/4 by four inches) mounted in a wall or ceiling if you fasten the cable not more than eight inches from the box and if the sheathing enters the box at least 1/4 inch. Measure the eight inches along the length of the sheathing, not from the outside of the box.

Do not support heavy light fixtures using only the light fixture electrical box. The eye hook supporting this chandelier is driven into the same ceiling joist to which the electrical box is mounted.

LIGHT FIXTURE BOX INSTALLATION

1. Use boxes designed for mounting light fixtures if a light fixture is to be mounted to the box. These boxes are usually four-inch round or octagonal. You may use other boxes if the light fixture weighs not more than six pounds and is secured to the box using at least two #6 or larger screws.
2. Support light fixtures weighing at least 50 pounds independently from the light fixture box. You may use the light fixture box to support light fixtures weighing less than 50 pounds. Note that ceiling fans are not light fixtures.

BOX CONTENTS LIMITATIONS

1. Limit the number of wires, devices (such as switches and receptacles), and fittings in a box. This limitation is primarily based on the heat generated by the wires and devices in the box. The actual size of the box relative to its contents is a secondary consideration.
2. Use the cubic inch volume printed on the box or provided in the box manufacturer's instructions to determine box volume. Do not attempt to measure the box volume. Do not estimate box volume from the volume of similar size boxes. You will probably not get the same volume as provided by the manufacturer.
3. Use Table 47 to determine the volume units required by wires, devices, and fittings in a box.

BOX INSTALLATION TOLERANCES

1. Install boxes in non-combustible material, such as masonry, so that the front edge is not more than ¼ inch from the finished surface.
2. Install boxes in walls and ceilings made of wood or other combustible material so that the front edge is flush with the finished surface or projects from the finished surface.
3. Cut openings for boxes in drywall and plaster so that the opening is not more than ⅛ inch from the perimeter of the box.

Boxes must be installed so the front edges are flush with the finished wall surface, and the gap between the box and the wall covering is not more than ⅛".

Table 47: Wire Volume Unit ▸

Wire size (AWG)	Wire volume
18	1.50 $in.^3$
16	1.75 $in.^3$
14	2.00 $in.^3$
12	2.25 $in.^3$
10	2.50 $in.^3$
8	3.00 $in.^3$
6	5.00 $in.^3$

Volume Units ▸

Calculate the volume units required by wires, devices, and fittings based on the following definitions:

Volume units for current-carrying wires. Allow one volume unit for each individual hot (ungrounded) and neutral (grounded) wire in the box. Use Table 47 to determine the volume units of common wire sizes. Example: two pieces of #14/2 NM are in a box. Each piece of this cable contains one hot (ungrounded) and one neutral (grounded) wire and one grounding wire. From Table 47, each #14 wire uses 2.00 cubic inches in the box. The total volume units required by the hot (ungrounded) and neutral (grounded) wires is eight cubic inches.

Volume units for devices. Allow two volume units for each device (switch or receptacle) in the box. Base the volume units on the largest hot (ungrounded) or neutral (grounded) wire in the box. Example: NM cable size #14 and #12 are in a box. From Table 47, #14 wire uses 2.00 cubic inches and #12 wire uses 2.25 cubic inches. Allow 4.5 cubic inches volume units (2 × 2.25 cubic inches) for each switch or receptacle in the box based on the volume of the larger #12 NM cable.

Volume units for grounding wires. Allow one volume unit for all grounding wires in the box. Base the volume unit on the largest hot (ungrounded) or neutral (grounded) wire in the box.

Volume units for clamps. Allow one volume unit for all internal cable clamps in the box, if any. Base the volume unit on the largest hot (ungrounded) or neutral (grounded) wire in the box.

Volume units for fittings. Allow one volume unit for all fittings in the box, if any. Base the volume unit on the largest hot (ungrounded) or neutral (grounded) wire in the box.

Table 48: Electrical Box Fill Chart ▸

Box size and shape (If volume not labeled by manufacturer)	Maximum number of volume units permitted (see Notes below)			
	14 AWG	12 AWG	10 AWG	8 AWG
junction boxes				
4 × 1¼" R or O	6	5	5	4
4 × 1½" R or O	7	6	6	5
4 × 2⅛" R or O	10	9	8	7
4 × 1¼" S	9	8	7	6
4 × 1½" S	10	9	8	7
4 × 2⅛" S	15	13	12	10
411/16 × 1¼" S	12	11	10	8
4 11/16 × 1½" S	14	13	11	9
4 11/16 × 2⅛" S	21	18	16	14
device boxes				
3 × 2 × 1½"	3	3	3	2
3 × 2 × 2"	5	4	4	3
3 × 2 × 2¼"	5	4	4	3
3 × 2 × 2½"	6	5	5	4
3 × 2 × 2¾"	7	6	6	4
3 × 2 × 3½"	9	8	7	6
4 × 2⅛ × 1½"	5	4	4	3
4 × 2⅛ × 1⅞"	6	5	5	4
4 × 2⅛ × 2⅛"	7	6	5	4

Notes:
- R = Round; O = Octagonal; S = Square or rectangular
- Each hot or neutral wire entering the box is counted as one volume unit
- Grounding wires are counted as one volume unit in total—do not count each one individually.
- Raceway fittings and external cable clamps do not count. Internal cable connectors and straps count as one volume unit.
- Devices (switches and receptacles mainly) each count as two volume units.
- When calculating total volume units, any non-wire components should be assigned the gauge of the largest wire in the box.
- For wire gauges not shown here, contact your local electrical inspections office.

BOX SUPPORT IN WALLS, CEILINGS & FLOORS

1. Provide support for boxes that rigidly and securely fasten them in place. You may use nails or screws to support these boxes.
2. Protect screws inside boxes so that the threads will not damage the wires.
3. Wood braces used to support boxes must be at least one by two inches.
4. Use "cut-in" or "old work" retrofit boxes only if they have approved clamps or anchors that are identified for the location where they are installed.

DAMP LOCATIONS

1. Install a receptacle box cover that is weatherproof when the cover is closed and a plug is not inserted into a receptacle located in a damp location. This applies to 15-amp and 20-amp receptacles. A damp area is protected from direct contact with water. Refer to the definition of damp location. You may use a receptacle cover suitable for wet locations in a damp location.
2. Install a watertight seal between a flush-mounted receptacle and its faceplate. This will require a gasket or sealant between the finished surface (such as stucco, brick, or siding) and the faceplate.

WET LOCATIONS

1. Install a receptacle box cover that is weatherproof when the cover is closed on any receptacle located in a wet location. This applies to 15-amp and 20-amp receptacles in any indoor or outdoor wet location. This applies regardless of whether or not a plug is inserted into the receptacle. Refer to the definition of wet location (see page 167).
2. Install a watertight seal between a flush-mounted receptacle and its faceplate. This will require a gasket or sealant between the finished surface (such as stucco, brick, or siding) and the faceplate.

BOX SUPPORT BY RACEWAYS

1. Do not support any junction or device boxes using only conduit or tubing if the box volume is larger than 100 cubic inches.
2. Support boxes that do not contain switches, receptacles, or light fixtures by using at least two lengths of conduit threaded wrench-tight into the box. Secure the conduit not more than three feet from the box if the conduit enters from different sides of the box. Secure the conduit not more than 18 inches from the box if the conduit enters from the same side of the box. Example: if the conduit enters the box from the top and bottom of the box, then secure the conduit not more than three feet from the box. Example: if the conduit enters the box from only the top or only from the bottom, then secure the conduit not more than 18 inches from the box.
3. Support boxes that contain switches or receptacles or light fixtures by using at least two lengths of conduit threaded wrench-tight into the box. Secure the conduit not more than 18 inches from the box.
4. You may use RMC or IMC metal conduit to support light fixtures under certain conditions. Refer to the IRC for the exceptions.

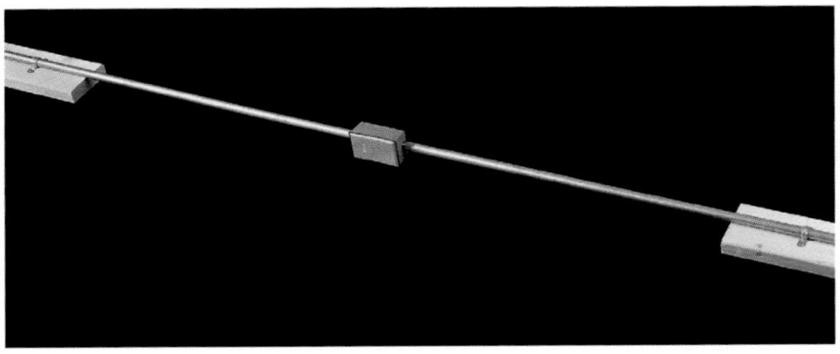

Secure conduit supporting a junction box within 3 ft. from the box if the conduit enters the box from opposite directions.

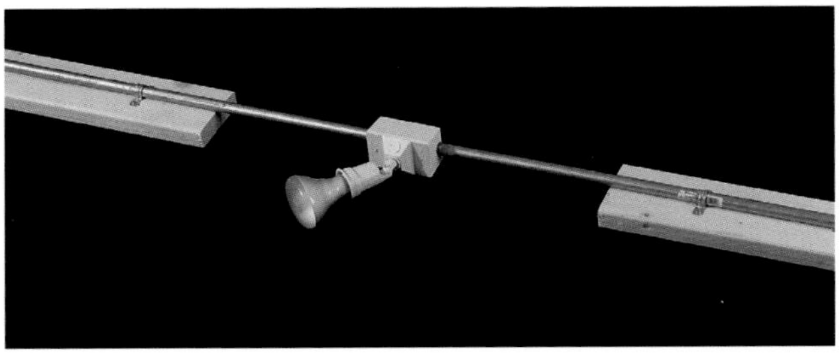

Secure conduit supporting a box containing a switch or receptacle within 18" from the box regardless of how the conduit enters the box.

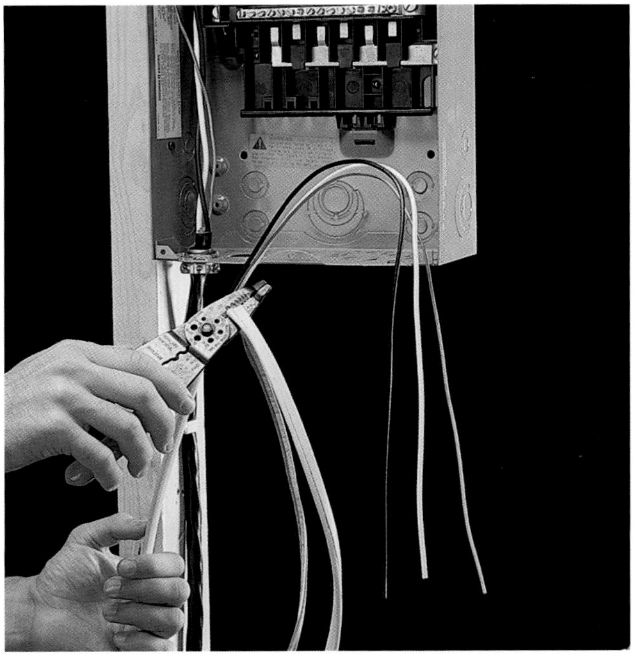

Secure each cable to a cabinet using an approved cable clamp.

Panel boxes, including the main service panel and subpanel boxes, also require the use of properly sized cable clamps wherever cables enter or exit the box.

CABLES SECURED TO A CABINET

1. Secure each individual cable to panelboard cabinets and to similar enclosures, unless the exception applies.
2. You may run NM cable into the top of a surface-mounted cabinet through an accessible rigid raceway under certain conditions. Refer to IRC Chapter 39 for the conditions.

Electrical Box Types

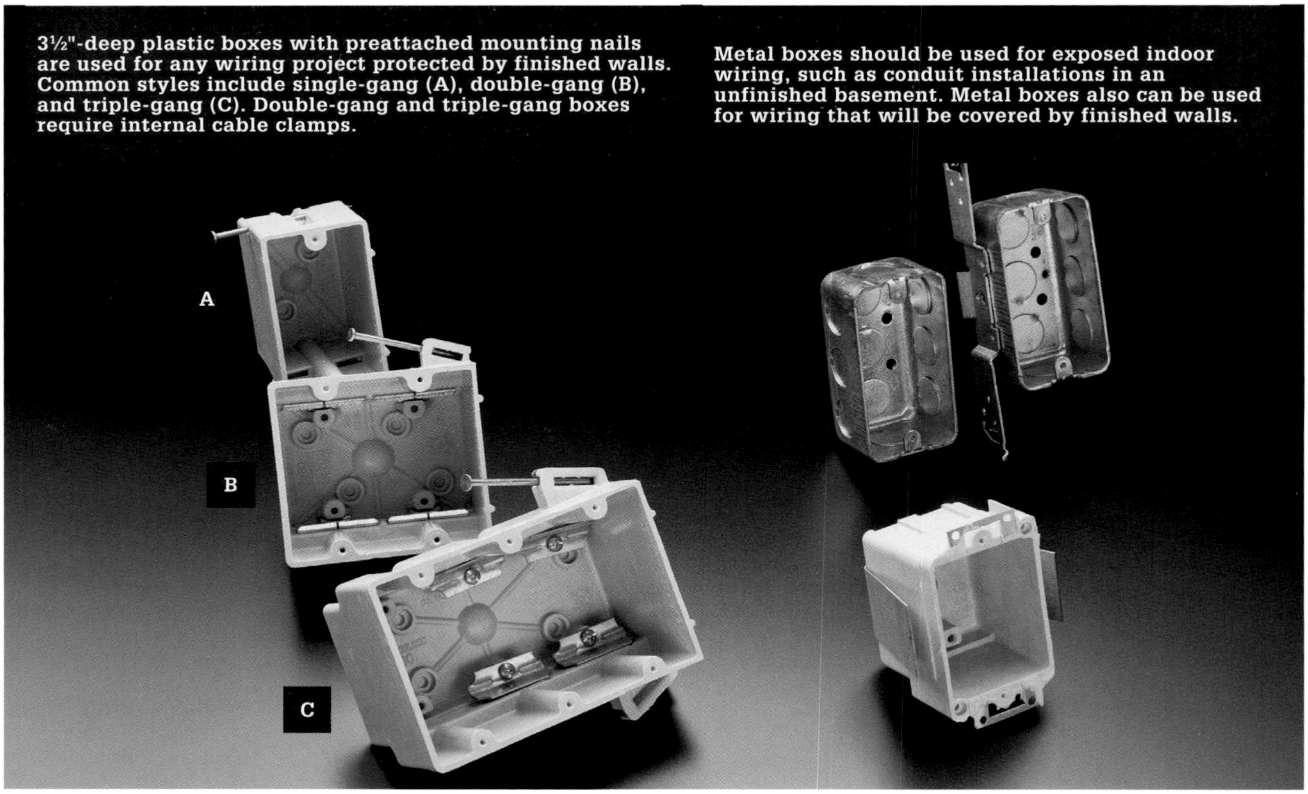

3½"-deep plastic boxes with preattached mounting nails are used for any wiring project protected by finished walls. Common styles include single-gang (A), double-gang (B), and triple-gang (C). Double-gang and triple-gang boxes require internal cable clamps.

Metal boxes should be used for exposed indoor wiring, such as conduit installations in an unfinished basement. Metal boxes also can be used for wiring that will be covered by finished walls.

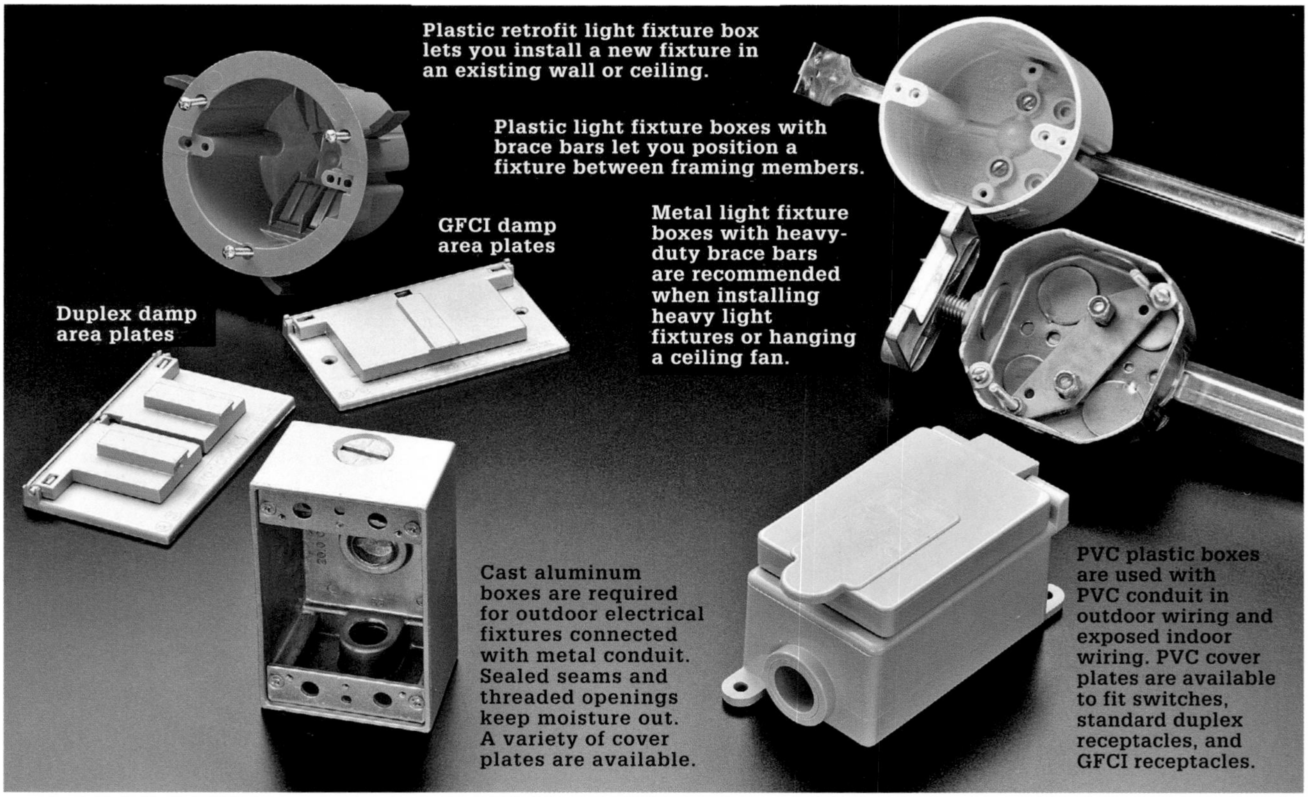

Plastic retrofit light fixture box lets you install a new fixture in an existing wall or ceiling.

Plastic light fixture boxes with brace bars let you position a fixture between framing members.

GFCI damp area plates

Metal light fixture boxes with heavy-duty brace bars are recommended when installing heavy light fixtures or hanging a ceiling fan.

Duplex damp area plates

Cast aluminum boxes are required for outdoor electrical fixtures connected with metal conduit. Sealed seams and threaded openings keep moisture out. A variety of cover plates are available.

PVC plastic boxes are used with PVC conduit in outdoor wiring and exposed indoor wiring. PVC cover plates are available to fit switches, standard duplex receptacles, and GFCI receptacles.

Box Installation Specifications

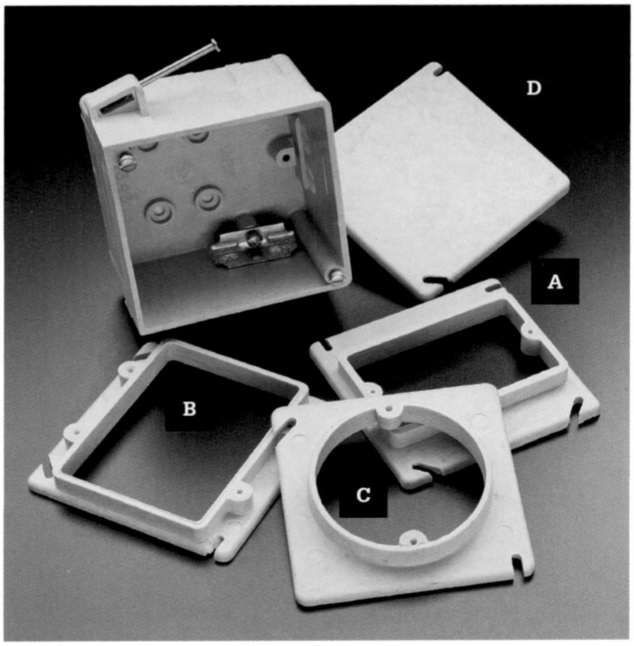

High-quality nonmetallic boxes are rigid and don't contort easily. A variety of adapter plates are available, including single-gang (A), double-gang (B), light fixture (C), and junction box cover plate (D). Adapter plates come in several thicknesses to match different wall constructions.

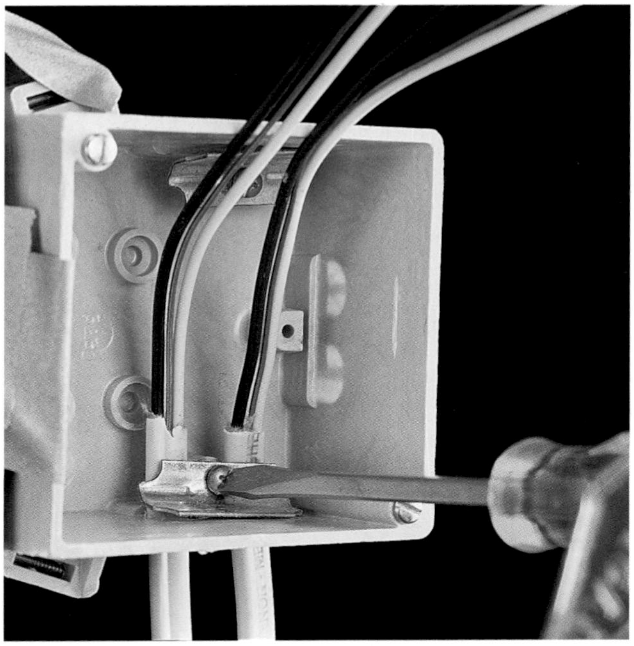

Boxes larger than 2 × 4" and all retrofit boxes must have either compression tabs or internal cable clamps. After installing cables in the box, tighten cable clamps over the cables so they are gripped firmly, but not so tightly that the cable sheathing is crushed.

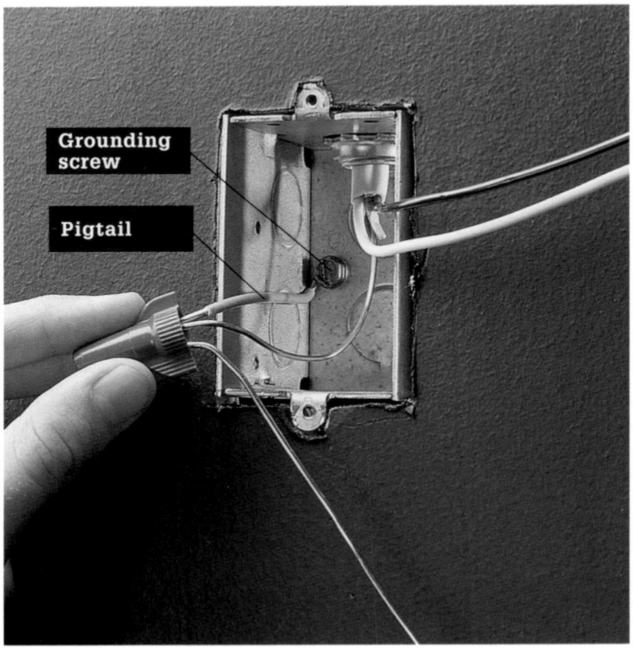

Metal boxes must be grounded to the circuit grounding system. Connect the circuit grounding wires to the box with a green insulated pigtail wire and wire connector (as shown) or with a grounding clip.

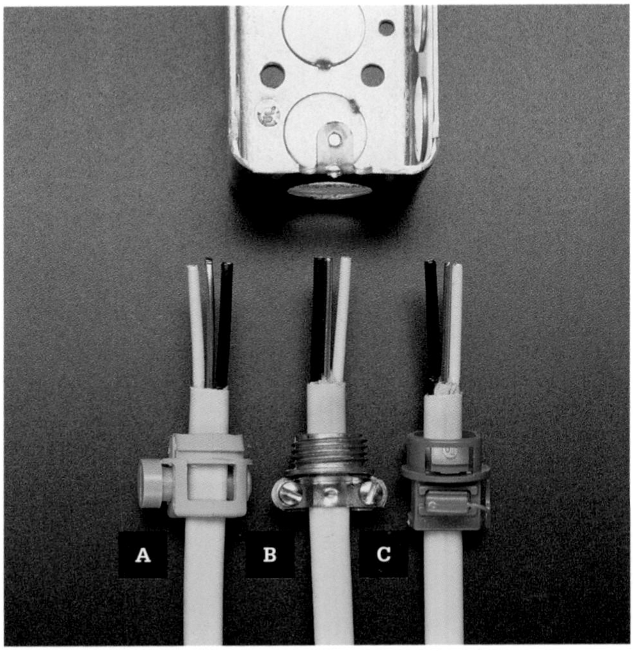

Cables entering a metal box must be clamped. A variety of clamps are available, including plastic clamps (A, C) and threaded metal clamps (B).

Guide to Your Service Panel ▸

The circuit breaker panel is the electrical distribution center for your home. It divides the current into branch circuits that run throughout the house. Each branch circuit is protected by a circuit breaker or fuse from dangerous current overloads. When installing new circuits, the last step is to connect the wires to new circuit breakers at the panel. Always shut off the main circuit breaker and test for power before touching any parts inside the panel, and never touch the service entrance wire lugs. If unsure of your skills, hire an electrician to make the final circuit connections. If you have an older electrical panel with fuses instead of circuit breakers, always have an electrician make these final hookups.

If the panel does not have enough open slots to hold new circuit breakers, one option is to hire a professional to install a subpanel.

Before installing any new wiring, evaluate your electrical service to make sure it provides enough current to support

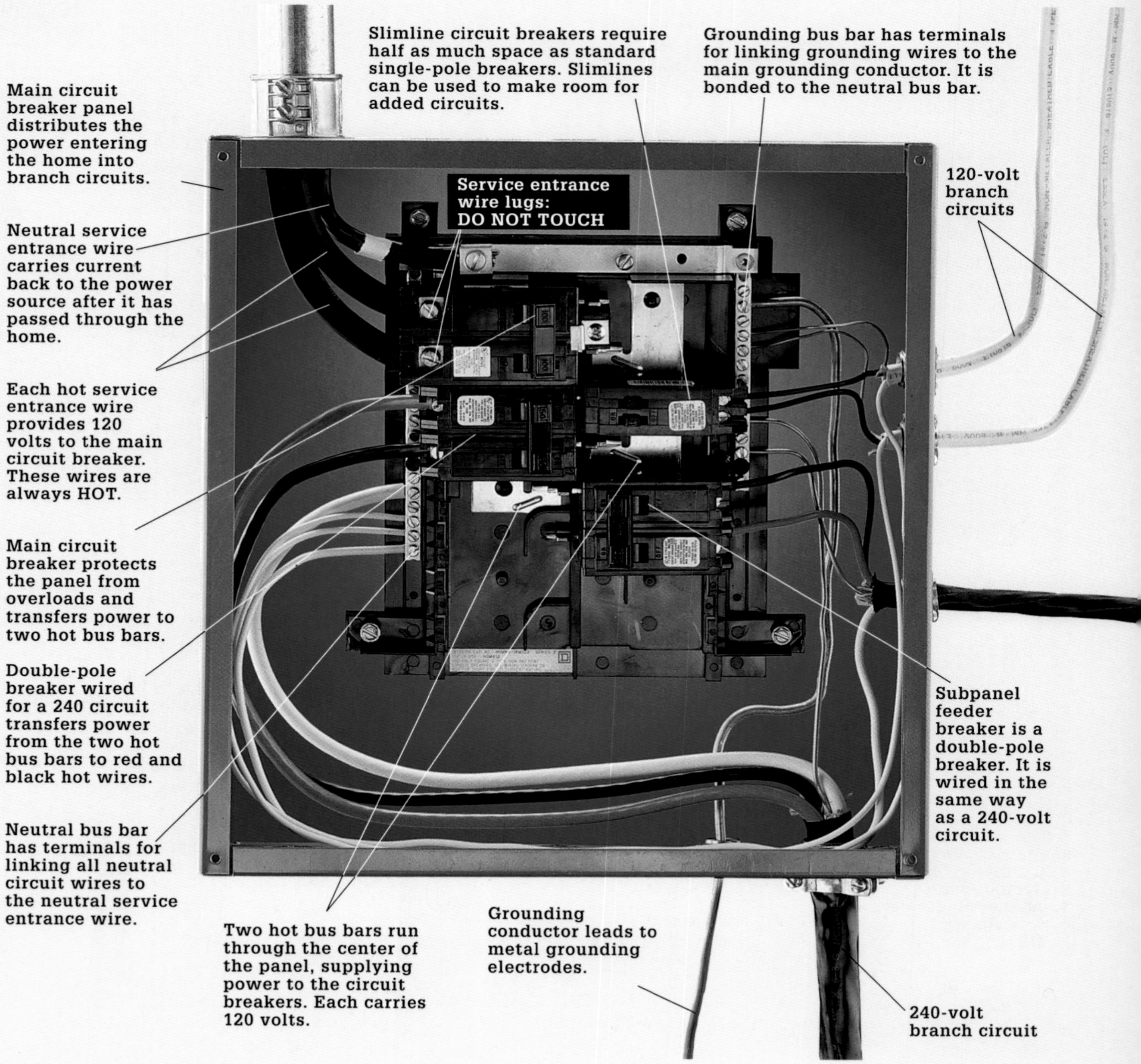

Main circuit breaker panel distributes the power entering the home into branch circuits.
Neutral service entrance wire carries current back to the power source after it has passed through the home.
Each hot service entrance wire provides 120 volts to the main circuit breaker. These wires are always HOT.
Main circuit breaker protects the panel from overloads and transfers power to two hot bus bars.
Double-pole breaker wired for a 240 circuit transfers power from the two hot bus bars to red and black hot wires.
Neutral bus bar has terminals for linking all neutral circuit wires to the neutral service entrance wire.
Two hot bus bars run through the center of the panel, supplying power to the circuit breakers. Each carries 120 volts.
Grounding conductor leads to metal grounding electrodes.
240-volt branch circuit
Subpanel feeder breaker is a double-pole breaker. It is wired in the same way as a 240-volt circuit.
120-volt branch circuits
Grounding bus bar has terminals for linking grounding wires to the main grounding conductor. It is bonded to the neutral bus bar.
Slimline circuit breakers require half as much space as standard single-pole breakers. Slimlines can be used to make room for added circuits.
Service entrance wire lugs: DO NOT TOUCH

both the existing circuits and any new circuits. If your service does not provide enough current, have an electrician upgrade it to a higher amp rating. During the upgrade, the electrician will install a new circuit breaker panel with enough extra breaker slots for the new circuits you want to install.

Safety Warning ▸

Never touch any parts inside a circuit breaker panel until you have checked for power (page 169). Circuit breaker panels differ in appearance, depending on the manufacturer. Never begin work in a circuit breaker panel until you understand its layout and can identify the parts.

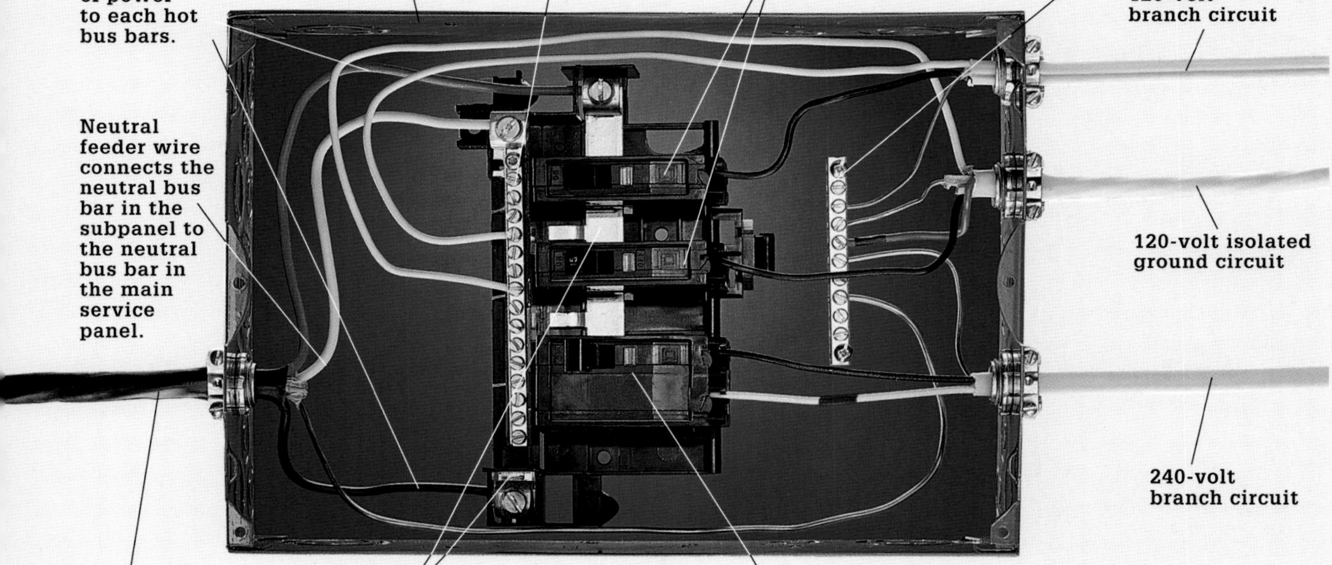

Circuit breaker subpanel can be installed when the main circuit breaker panel does not have enough space to hold circuit breakers for new circuits you want to install.
Neutral bus bar has terminals for linking neutral circuit wires to the neutral feeder wire.
Grounding bus bar has terminals for connecting circuit grounding wires. In a circuit breaker subpanel, the grounding bus bar is usually not bonded to the neutral bus bar.
Single-pole circuit breaker transfers 120 volts from one hot bus bar to the black hot wire in a two-wire cable.
Each hot feeder wire supplies 120 volts of power to each hot bus bars.
120-volt branch circuit
Neutral feeder wire connects the neutral bus bar in the subpanel to the neutral bus bar in the main service panel.
120-volt isolated ground circuit
240-volt branch circuit
Feeder cable brings power from the main circuit breaker panel. A 30-amp, 240-volt subpanel requires a 10/3 feeder cable protected by a 30-amp double-pole circuit breaker.
Two hot bus bars pass through the center of the subpanel, supplying power to the individual circuit breakers. Each carries 120 volts.
Double-pole breaker wired for 240 volts transfers power from both hot bus bars to white and black hot wires in a two-wire cable. A 240-volt circuit has no neutral wire connection; the white wire is tagged with black tape to identify it as a hot wire.

Switch Installation

SWITCH CURRENT LOAD LIMITATIONS

1. Do not use a switch in a circuit if the current load on the circuit exceeds the current rating of the switch. Example: a 15-amp snap switch may be overloaded if it switches ten 200-watt, 120-volt flood lights. Beware of overloads if the switch controls multiple high wattage flood lights or other high current draw equipment.
2. Use switches that are rated at least 80 percent of a motor's full load current rating.

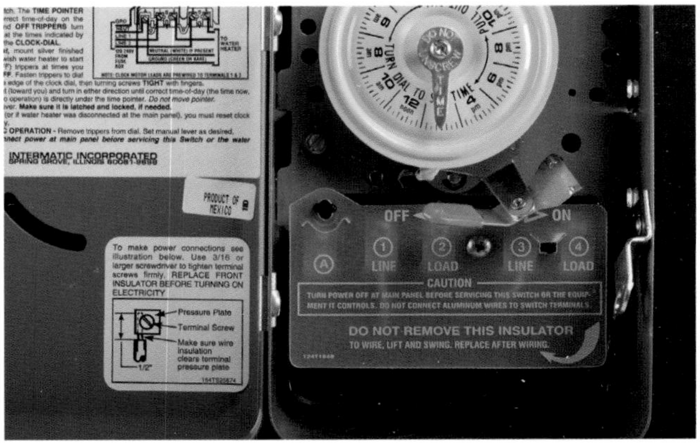

Cover exposed electrical connections in timer boxes using the manufacturer-supplied cover.

SWITCH ORIENTATION

1. Install single-throw switches so that ON is in the up position when the device is installed vertically. You may install single-throw switches horizontally.
2. Use switches that clearly indicate whether the switch is in the ON or OFF position. This does not apply to three-way and four-way switches. This requirement is frequently waived when rocker type switches are used.

TIMER SWITCHES

1. Use timer switches with energized parts that are enclosed in the switch's case or enclose the timer switch in a cabinet or box.
2. Install a barrier to guard against contact with energized parts.

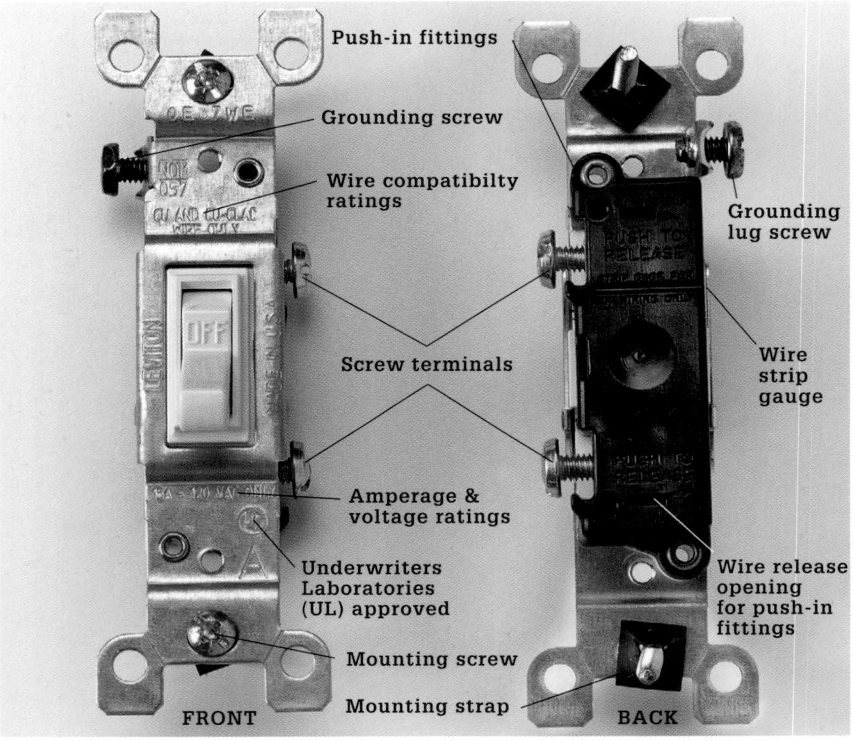
Push-in fittings
Grounding screw
Wire compatibilty ratings
Grounding lug screw
Screw terminals
Wire strip gauge
Amperage & voltage ratings
Underwriters Laboratories (UL) approved
Wire release opening for push-in fittings
Mounting screw
Mounting strap
FRONT
BACK

A typical 15-amp single pole switch seen front and back.

SWITCH HEIGHT

1. Locate switches not more than 79 inches above the finished floor or finished grade. Measure to the center of the handle when in the up position.
2. Locate switches in readily accessible places.

GROUNDING OF SWITCHES, BOXES & FACEPLATES

1. Ground metal boxes containing switches, the switches themselves, and metal faceplates covering switches. Ground the switch by mounting the switch to a grounded metal box using metal screws or by connecting an equipment grounding wire to the switch. Connect switches to the equipment grounding wire when using nonmetallic boxes.

SWITCHES IN WET LOCATIONS

1. Enclose switches and circuit breakers installed in wet locations in a weatherproof cabinet or enclosure.
2. Do not locate switches in shower or tub spaces unless the switch is part of a listed tub or shower assembly.

SWITCH MOUNTING IN BOXES

1. Mount switches in boxes that are recessed from the wall by seating the switch's extension ears at the top and bottom of the switch against the wall surface.
2. Mount switches in boxes that are flush with the wall by seating the switch's mounting yoke or strap against the box.
3. Do not allow the switch body to move when the switch is operated. This can, over time, cause wires to loosen, potentially causing arcing and a fire.

SWITCH FACEPLATE INSTALLATION

1. Install switch faceplates so that the plate completely covers the switch and so that the faceplate is flush against the wall. No gaps should exist between the switch handle and the faceplate, and between the faceplate and the wall.

Switch Only Hot Wires ▸

Switch only the hot (ungrounded) wire unless the switch simultaneously disconnects all wires in the circuit. Maintain required wire color-coding throughout three-way and four-way circuits.

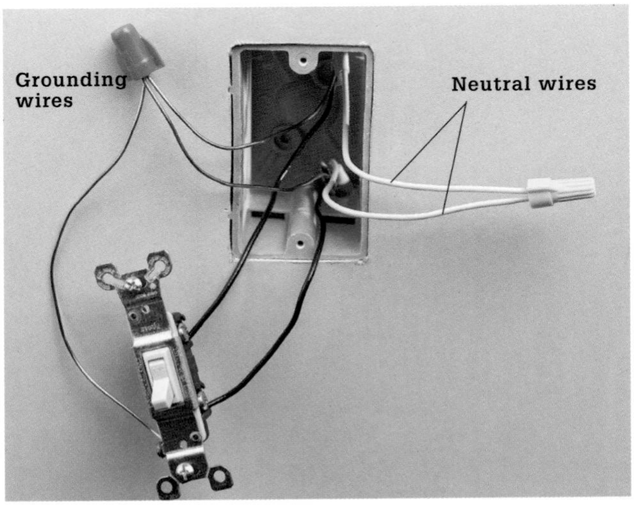

Connect the grounding wire to the switch grounding terminal when mounting the switch in a plastic box.

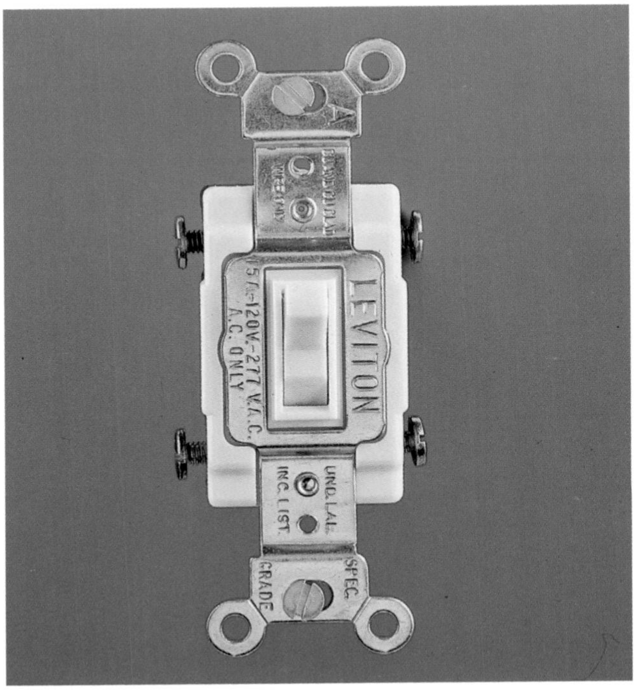

Three-way switches and four-way switches are required for circuits with fixtures controlled by multiple switches. A four-way switch is seen here. Note that ON and OFF are not indicated on the toggle because these settings can change based on which switch was used last.

Light Fixture Installation

LIGHTS REQUIRED IN HABITABLE ROOMS

1. Install at least one switch-controlled light in every habitable room and bathroom. This light may be a switched (half-hot) receptacle in habitable rooms other than kitchens and bathrooms. In kitchens and bathrooms, the outlet must be a switched wall or ceiling lighting outlet. You may use lights controlled by occupancy sensors if the sensors have a manual override that allows switch control of the light.

LIGHTS REQUIRED IN OTHER INTERIOR SPACES

1. Install at least one switch-controlled light outlet in every hallway, stairway, attached garage, and detached garage if the detached garage is provided with electricity. Note that a light outlet may be a switched receptacle instead of a light fixture. A light fixture is usually a better, but not required, choice.

LIGHTS REQUIRED AT EXTERIOR DOORS

1. Install at least one switch-controlled light outlet on the exterior side of every exterior door with grade level access. Exterior lights are not required at garage vehicle doors.

LIGHTS REQUIRED IN ATTICS, CRAWLSPACES & BASEMENTS

1. Install at least one light outlet in attics, crawlspaces, utility rooms, and basements if the area is used for storage or if it contains equipment that requires service. Locate the light outlet near any equipment that requires service.
2. Locate a switch for the light at the usual point of entry into the area. You may use a pull-chain controlled light if the light is located at the usual point of entry into the area. This means that if the light is not at the entrance to the area, the light must be switched at the entrance.

LIGHT FIXTURE SUPPORT

1. You may use a securely attached box to support light fixtures weighing less than 50 pounds. Note that ceiling fans are not considered light fixtures.
2. Do not use the screw shell of a light fixture to support anything that weighs more than six pounds or is more than 16 inches in any dimension.

RECESSED LIGHTS

1. Use recessed lights that are labeled as being thermally protected. Thermal protection shuts off power to the light at high temperatures. Thermal protection is not required if the recessed light is made, labeled, and installed so that it functions as if it were thermally protected.
2. Use insulation contact (IC) rated recessed lights when the recessed parts are installed in an insulated attic. IC rated recessed lights may not require clearance to insulation or to combustible materials

LIGHTS IN WET & DAMP LOCATIONS

1. Install lights in wet and damp locations so that water cannot enter or accumulate in the wiring or energized parts.
2. Use only lights labeled SUITABLE FOR WET LOCATIONS when installing lights that may be subject to direct contact with water. Refer to the definition of wet location (see page 167).

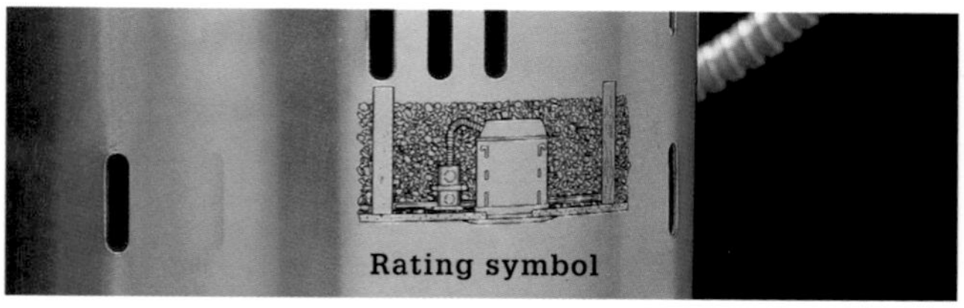

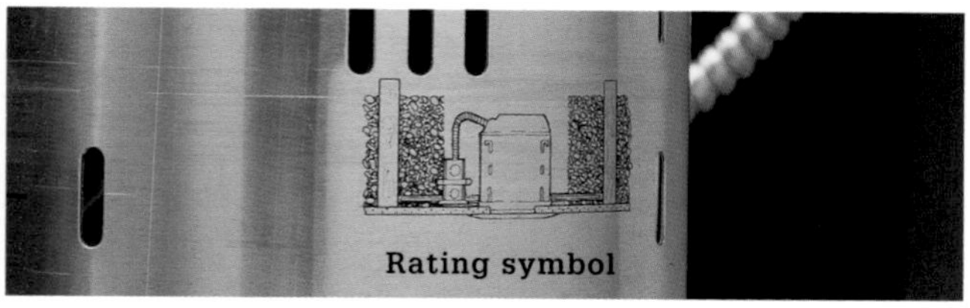

Choose the proper type of recessed light fixture for your project. There are two types of fixtures: those rated for installation within insulation (left), and those which must be kept at least 3" from insulation (right). Self-contained thermal switches shut off power if the unit gets too hot for its rating. A recessed light fixture must be installed at least ½" from combustible materials.

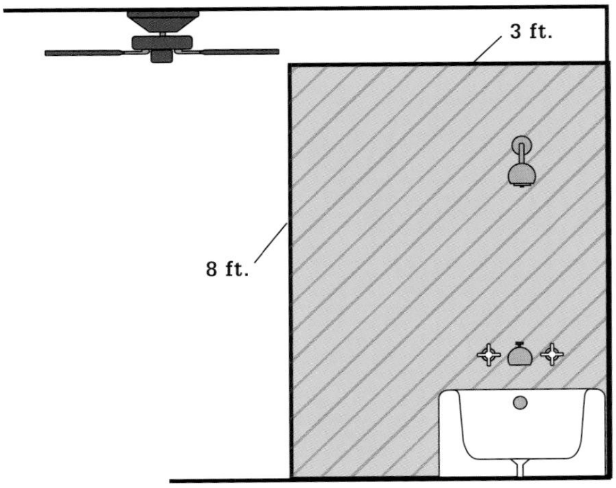

Keep all parts of lights and ceiling fans at least 3 ft. horizontally and 8 ft. vertically from bathtubs and showers.

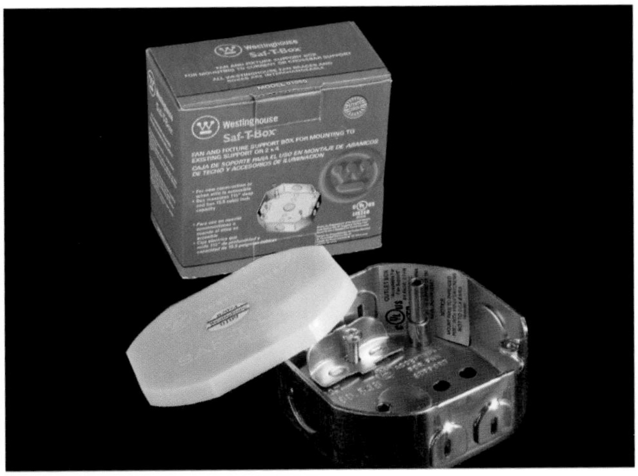

Look for heavy-duty ceiling boxes that are specifically rated for ceiling fans and heavy light fixtures.

3. Use lights labeled either SUITABLE FOR WET LOCATIONS or SUITABLE FOR DAMP LOCATIONS when installing lights in damp locations. Refer to the definition of damp location (see page 166). Light fixtures, including ceiling fans, intended for indoors may not be installed in either wet or damp locations.

CEILING FANS

1. Support ceiling fans weighing not more than 70 pounds using boxes listed and labeled to support the fan.
2. Support ceiling fans weighting more than 70 pounds independently from the box.

CEILING FANS & LIGHTS NEAR TUBS & SHOWERS

1. Install ceiling fans, cord-connected lights, lights suspended by cords, chains, or cables, and track lights so that no part of the light or fan falls within an exclusion zone measuring three feet horizontally from the base of the tub or shower stall threshold and eight feet vertically from the top of the tub rim or shower stall threshold. Parts include fan blades, bulb enclosures, hanging chains, and other parts connected to or hanging from the light or fan.
2. Use light fixtures that are listed for damp locations if the fixture is located in the exclusion zone.
3. Use light fixtures that are listed for wet locations if the fixture is: (a) located in the exclusion zone, and (b) subject to shower spray.

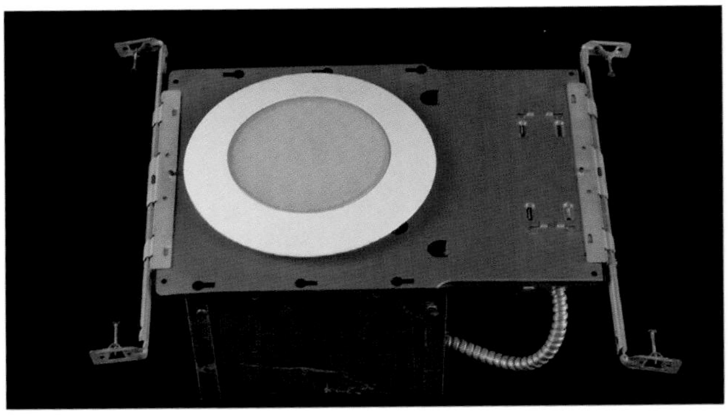

Light fixtures installed in damp areas should be rated for moisture exposure.

A sturdy metal brace with an integral box that is installed between ceiling joists can be used to support ceiling fans and heavy light fixtures.

Closet Lights

APPLICABLE CODE DEFINITIONS FOR CLOSETS:

Clothes closet: A space intended for storage of clothing. A clothes closet usually contains a horizontal rod for hanging clothing. As with all codes, application of this section depends on interpretation by the local code official.

Closet storage area: The closet storage area is a space consisting of a hanging rod storage area and a shelf storage area. The required clearance applies to both areas. The clearances to light fixtures apply whether or not shelves or hanging rods are currently installed in the closet.

Hanging rod storage area: This area begins at the closet floor and ends six feet above the closet floor or at the highest hanging rod, whichever is higher. The hanging rod storage area includes all of the space within 24 inches horizontally from the back and sides of the closet walls.

Shelf storage area: This begins six feet above the closet floor or at the highest hanging rod, whichever is higher, and ends at the closet ceiling. The shelf storage area includes all of the space within 12 inches horizontally from the back and sides of the closet walls or within the width of the shelf, whichever is wider.

LIGHT FIXTURE CLEARANCES IN CLOTHING CLOSETS

1. Do not install any incandescent light fixture in a clothes closet if any part of the lamp is exposed. This includes both surface mounted and recessed light fixtures. This includes incandescent light fixtures that have lamps such as compact fluorescent installed.
2. Provide at least 12 inches between surface mounted incandescent light fixtures and the closest point of the closet storage area.
3. Provide at least six inches between recessed incandescent light fixtures and the closest point of the closet storage area.
4. Provide at least six inches between fluorescent light fixtures and the closest point of the closet storage area.

USING FLEXIBLE CORDS WITH EQUIPMENT

1. Use flexible cords only to connect an appliance to a receptacle and only if the appliance manufacturer's instructions allow connection by a flexible cord.
2. Do not run or conceal flexible cords in walls, ceilings, floors, or raceways.
3. Do not splice or tap flexible cords.
4. Provide power to flexible cords through an attachment plug. Do not hard-wire flexible cords directly to a power source.
5. Do not use flexible cords as a substitute for permanent wiring.

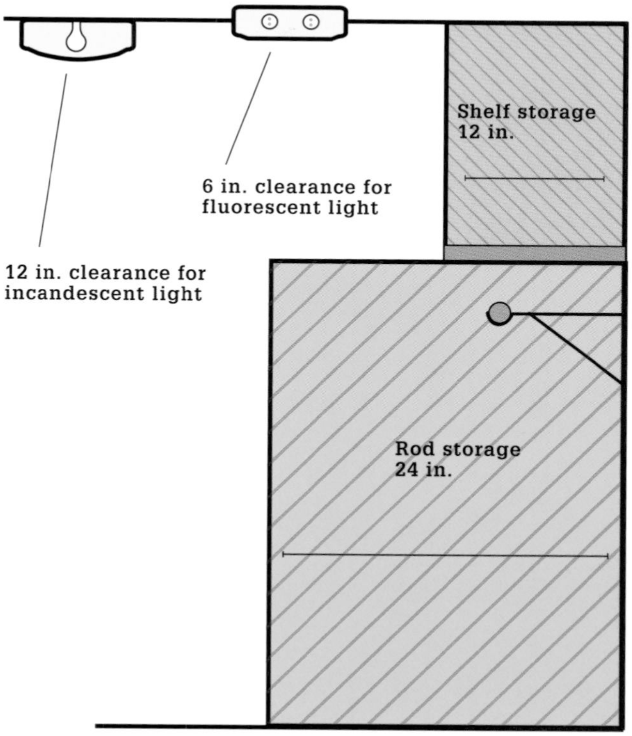

Closet hanging rod and shelf storage areas.

Electric Equipment Grounding ▸

1. Ground metal parts in an electrical system including equipment cases, cabinets, boxes, conduit, tubing, light fixtures, and water pumps. Equipment cases include furnaces, air conditioning condensers, water heaters, dishwashers, and similar equipment.
2. You may ground metal parts in an electrical system by using any currently accepted wiring method that provides a mechanically and electrically continuous path to the service grounding connection. These methods include:
   (a) grounding wires contained in NM cable, and
   (b) separate equipment grounding wires, and
   (c) metal conduit and tubing when the fittings at terminations are listed for grounding.
3. Do not use a separate earth ground as the only means of grounding equipment. Example: do not install a separate driven ground rod to ground an air conditioning condenser.
4. In older homes, the electrical wires do not have a separate grounding wire. Some people install a wire between the grounding screw of a grounded receptacle and the neutral terminal. This is not safe.

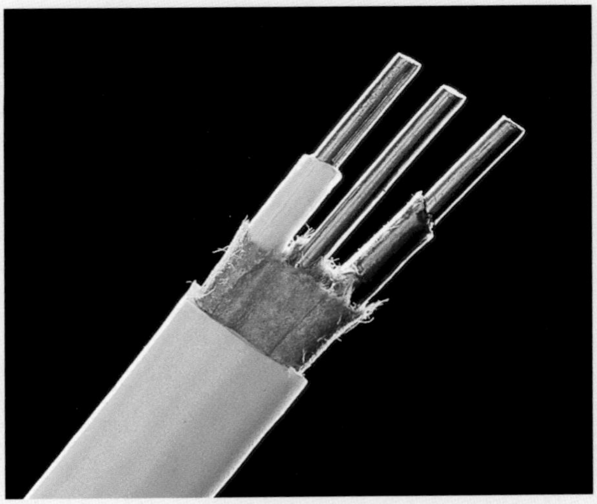

Modern NM (nonmetallic) cable, found in most wiring systems installed after 1965, contains a bare copper wire that provides grounding for receptacle and switch boxes.

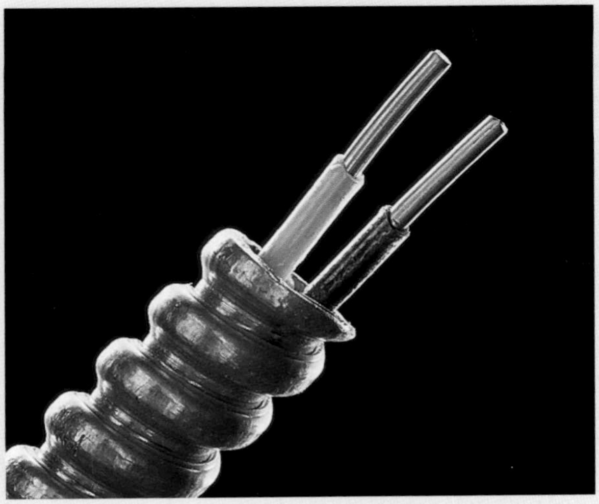

Armored cable has a metal sheath that serves as the grounding pathway. Many codes no longer allow armored cable jackets to function as the ground.

Polarized receptacles have a long slot and a short slot. Used with a polarized plug, the polarized receptacle keeps electrical current directed for safety.

Three-slot receptacles are required by code for all new installations. They are usually connected to a standard two-wire cable with ground.

Receptacle adapter allows three-prong plugs to be inserted into two-slot receptacles. The grounding loop or wire of the adapter must be attached to the cover plate mounting screw of the receptacle.

Satellite Dishes, Television & Radio Antennas

This material applies to receiving antennas such as satellite dishes, and traditional radio and television antennas. It does not apply to cable TV system wiring, and it does not apply to network powered broadband communication system wiring. This material also applies to radio transmission antennas and towers such as those used by amateur radio operators.

ANTENNA PROHIBITED INSTALLATION LOCATIONS

1. Do not attach or install antennas on electric service entrance masts, on poles that support electric power wires, on plumbing vent pipes, or on furnace vent pipes.
2. Provide clearance between antennas and masts and electric power wires so that if the antenna falls, it is unlikely to fall on the electric power wires.

Television aerials and satellite dishes must be located well away from power lines. They should be properly grounded and protected against lightning strikes.

ANTENNA WIRE & CABLE CLEARANCE TO ELECTRIC POWER LINES

1. Do not install outdoor, aboveground antenna wires and cables so that they cross over electric power wires. Avoid, if possible, installing outdoor, aboveground antenna wires that cross under electric power wires. Electric power wires include wires on overhead power poles, overhead service drop wires, and any electric power wires running between buildings.
2. Provide at least two feet clearance between outdoor, aboveground antenna wires and cables and electric power lines that can swing freely.
3. Provide at least four inches between outdoor antenna wires and cables and most residential electric power wires when both are secured so that they cannot move.
4. Provide at least 12 inches clearance between underground antenna wires and underground cables and electric power wires.
5. Provide at least a two-inch clearance between indoor antenna wires and cables and indoor electric power wires.

GROUNDING ANTENNAS, MASTS, WIRES & CABLES

1. Install a ground wire between metal antenna masts, towers, and support poles and an approved grounding point. Metal antenna masts include the short metal mast commonly found on satellite dishes.
2. Install a ground wire between the coaxial cable shield and an approved grounding point. You must ground both the coaxial cable shield and any metal antenna mast.
3. Use at least #10 AWG copper wire or #17 copper clad steel wire as the grounding wire. You may use a #8 AWG aluminum grounding wire if it is not in contact with masonry, is not installed in a corrosive environment, and is installed at least 18 inches above the ground at all points including at the connection to the grounding point. Insulation is not required on the grounding wire. You may use solid or stranded grounding wire.
4. Run the grounding wire in as straight a line as possible from where the antenna wire or cable enters the building to an approved grounding point near where the antenna wire or cable enters the building.
5. Connect the grounding wire(s) to one of the following approved grounding points:
   (a) the building electrical system grounding electrode, grounding electrode wire, or other metal part of the building electrical grounding electrode system such as a grounding electrode system metal enclosure,
   (b) a metal water service pipe not more than five feet from where the water service pipe enters the building,
   (c) the service equipment cabinet or metal service equipment raceway, or
   (d) the other system bonding connection described in the IRC.
6. Do not connect the antenna mast or coaxial cable to its own ground rod unless both of the following are true: (a) none of the approved grounding points exists (extremely rare), and (b) the separate ground rod is bonded to the building electrical system as described in the IRC Section.

GROUNDING WIRE CONNECTION TO THE GROUNDING POINT

1. Use a listed clamp, listed pressure connector, or other listed means to connect the grounding wire to the grounding point.
2. Install the listed connector so that it is both physically and electrically connected to the grounding point. This means removing paint, lacquer, rust, and other nonconductive material before attaching the listed connector to the grounding point.
3. Connect not more than one grounding wire to a listed connector unless the connector is listed to accept more than one wire.
4. Use a listed connector that is compatible with both the grounding point and the grounding wire material. Example: an iron or steel clamp is not compatible with a copper water pipe. Both materials will corrode over time.

Source for This Material ▸

The material in this section is based on the National Electrical Code (NEC) ®, 2005 Edition. Most local building officials use the NEC as a supplement to or in place of the IRC when dealing with residential electrical issues. The IRC does not address antennas, so the NEC is usually the appropriate source for rules regarding installation of antennas and the wires that connect them to the receiving equipment. Verify with the local building official which version, if any, of the NEC is adopted in your area.

Broadband Cable Wiring

This material applies to network powered broadband communication system wiring. These systems usually deliver television, telephone, Internet, and similar services. They operate at up to 150 volts and 100 watts. This material does not apply to standard cable TV system wiring, and it does not apply to satellite TV antenna wiring. Some new communication systems use fiber-optic cables. This article does not apply to fiber-optic cables.

OVERHEAD BROADBAND CABLE CLEARANCE

1. Install outdoor, aboveground broadband communication cables above electric power wires whenever possible.
2. Avoid installing outdoor, aboveground broadband communication cables near electric power wires that can swing freely. Electric power wires include wires on overhead power poles, overhead service drop wires, and any electric power wires running between buildings. Provide at least 12 inches clearance between outdoor, aboveground broadband communication cables and electric power lines that can swing freely. Increase clearance to at least 40 inches at the power pole.
3. Provide at least four inches between outdoor broadband communication cables and most residential electric power wires when both are secured so that they cannot move.
4. Measure the vertical clearance between overhead broadband cables and the ground, walkway, driveway, or street beginning at the lowest hanging point of the cables and ending at the surface under the lowest point.
5. Provide at least 9½ feet vertical clearance between broadband cables and finished grade, sidewalks, or platforms accessed by pedestrians only.
6. Provide at least 11½ feet vertical clearance between overhead broadband cables and residential property and driveways.
7. Provide at least 15½ feet vertical clearance between overhead broadband cables and public streets, alleys, roads, or parking areas subject to truck traffic.
8. Provide the same clearance between overhead broadband cables and swimming pools, spas, and hot tubs as for electrical wires.
9. Provide at least eight feet vertical clearance between broadband cables and most low-slope roofs.
10. Provide at least 18 inches vertical clearance between broadband cables and roof overhangs if not more than four feet of cable passes over the roof and if the cable terminates at a through-the-roof raceway or support. This is similar to clearances allowed for service drop wires.
11. Provide at least three feet vertical clearance between broadband cables and roofs with a slope of at least four inches in 12 inches.

BROADBAND CABLE BURIAL DEPTH

1. Bury broadband cables at least 18 inches deep when the cables are not covered by concrete or enclosed in conduit or other raceways. You may reduce the depth to at least 12 inches when the cables are under concrete residential driveways, patios, and similar concrete slabs. Refer to the NEC for burial depths when the cables are enclosed in conduit or raceways.

Low & Medium Power Broadband System Definition ▸

Low power broadband systems operate at not more than 100 volts, and medium power systems operate at not more than 150 volts. Verify voltage rating and system classification with the broadband service provider. The operating voltage of the system affects how the cables are installed.

GROUNDING BROADBAND CABLES

1. Install an insulated copper grounding wire at least #14 AWG between the coaxial cable shield and an approved grounding point.
2. Run the grounding wire in as straight a line as possible from where the broadband cable enters the building to an approved grounding point near where the broadband cable enters the building.
3. Limit the length of the grounding wire to not more than 20 feet. If where the broadband cable enters the building is more than 20 feet from an approved grounding point, you may install at least a five-foot long ground rod near where the broadband cable enters the building and bond the ground rod to the electrical service grounding system using at least #6 AWG copper wire.
4. Connect the copper grounding wire to one of the following approved grounding points:
   (a) the building electrical system grounding electrode, grounding electrode wire, or other metal part of the building electrical grounding electrode system such as a grounding electrode system metal enclosure,
   (b) a metal water service pipe not more than five feet from where the water service pipe enters the building,
   (c) the service equipment cabinet or metal service equipment raceway, or
   (d) the other system bonding connection described in the IRC.
5. Do not connect the broadband cable to its own ground rod unless both of the following are true: (a) no approved grounding point exists within 20 feet from where the coaxial cable enters the building (extremely rare), and (b) the separate ground rod is bonded to the building electrical system as described in the IRC.

BROADBAND CABLE & ELECTRIC POWER WIRE SEPARATION

1. Do not run low power or medium power broadband cables in the same conduit, tubing, raceway, junction and device box, or enclosure with electric power wires unless one of two exceptions exist. Example: do not run NM cable and any broadband cables in the same conduit.
2. You may have low power and medium power broadband cables and electric power wires in the same raceway, box, and enclosure if the wires are separated by a permanent physical barrier.
3. You may install low power and medium power broadband cables and electric power wires in the same cabinet or box when the electric power wires are intended to supply power to the broadband cable system.
4. Separate indoor broadband cables and electric power wires by at least two inches. You may run broadband cables and electric power wires near each other in a bundle and through the same bored holes in joists and studs if all the electric power wires are contained in metal or nonmetallic sheathing or raceways. Example: you may run sheathed NM cable and broadband cables near each other in a bundle and through the same bored holes in joists and studs if the sheathing of the NM cable remains intact over the entire length of the run.

APPENDIX: Common Mistakes

An electrical inspector visiting your home might identify a number of situations that are not up to code. These situations may not be immediate problems. In fact, it is possible that the wiring in your home has remained trouble free for many years.

Nevertheless, any wiring or device that is not up to code carries the potential for problems, often at risk to your home and your family. In addition, you may have trouble selling your home if it is not wired according to accepted methods.

Most local electrical codes are based on the National Electrical Code (NEC), a book updated and published every three years by the National Fire Protection Agency. This code book contains rules and regulations for the proper installation of electrical wiring and devices. Most public libraries carry reference copies of the NEC.

All electrical inspectors are required to be well versed in the NEC. Their job is to know the NEC regulations and to make sure these rules are followed in order to prevent fires and ensure safety. If you have questions regarding your home wiring system, your local inspector will be happy to answer them.

While a book cannot possibly identify all potential wiring problems in your house, we have identified some of the most common wiring defects here and will show you how to correct them. When working on home wiring repair or replacement projects, refer to this section to help identify any conditions that may be hazardous.

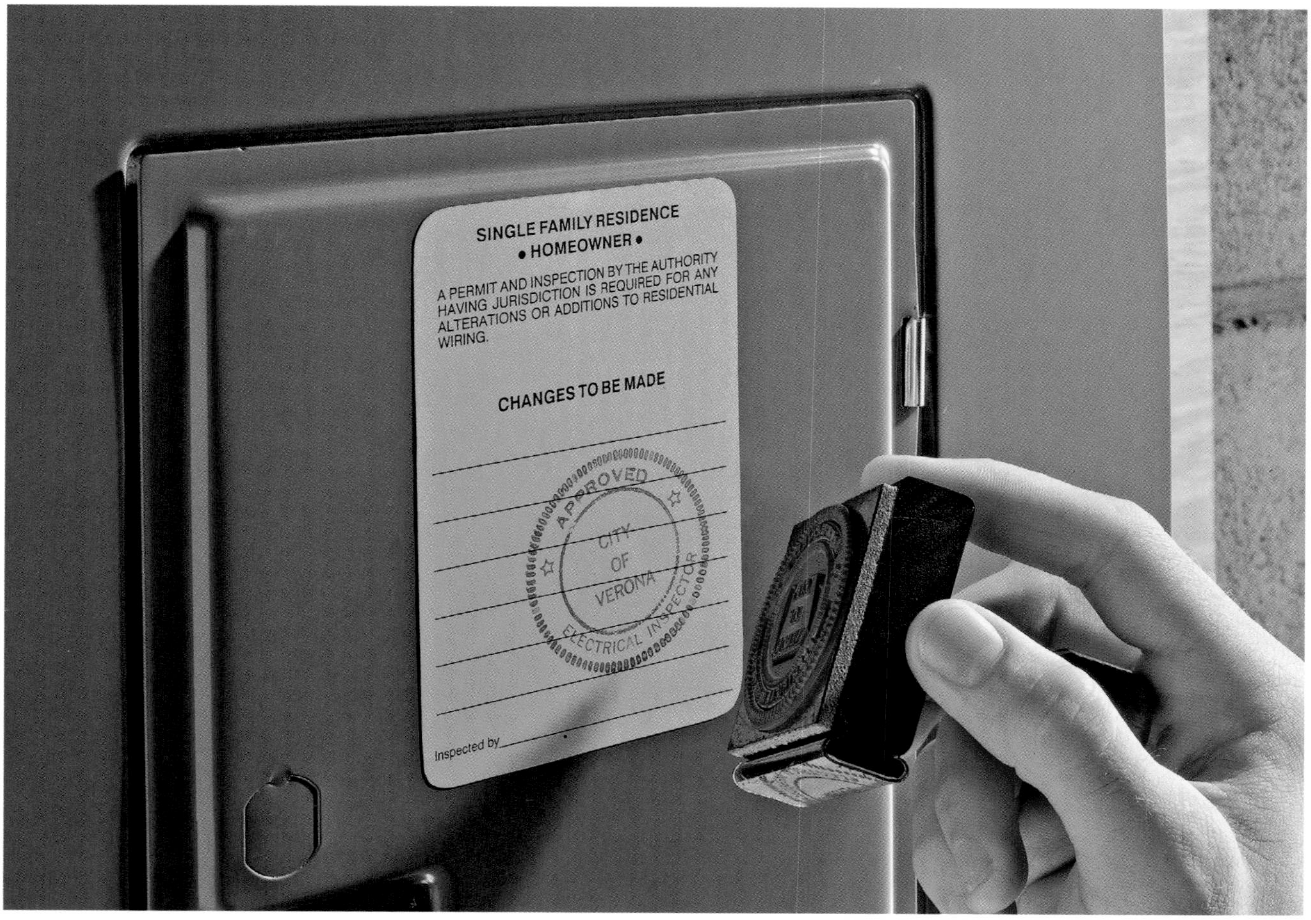

Electrical inspectors are on the lookout for common mistakes. The following pages detail problems to avoid so you will pass inspection on the first try.

Service Panel Inspection

Problem: Rust stains are found inside the main service panel. This problem occurs because water seeps into the service head outside the house and drips down into the service panel.

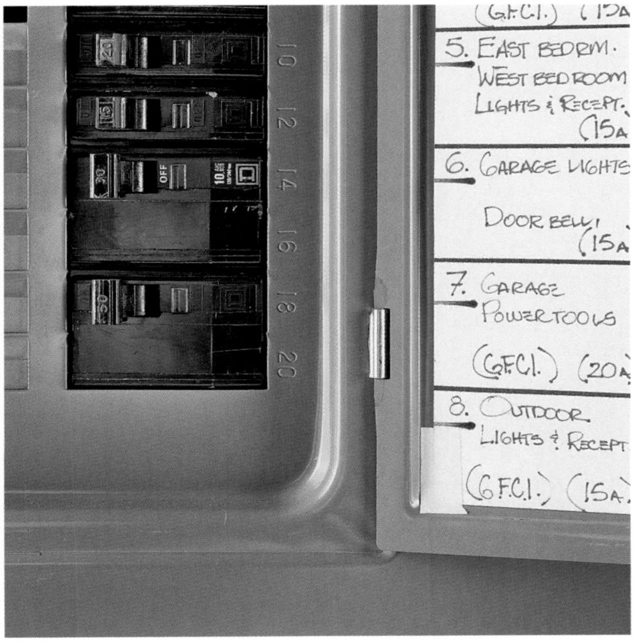

Solution: Have an electrician examine the service head and the main service panel. If the panel or service wires have been damaged, new components must be installed.

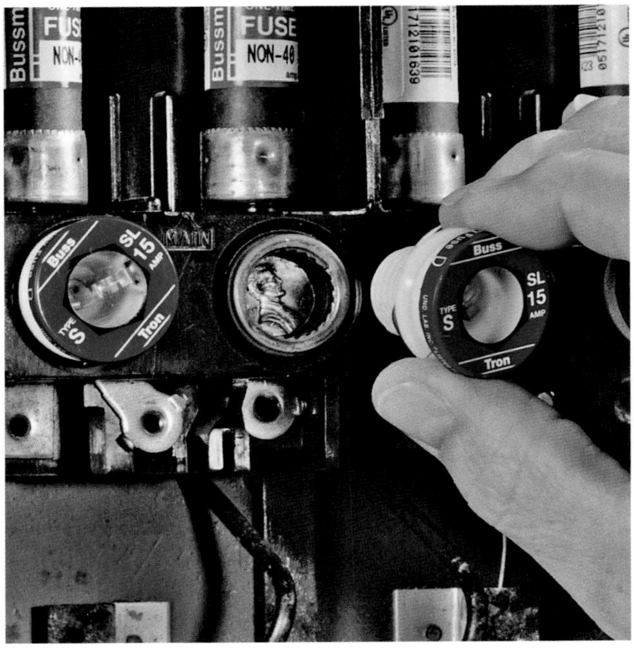

Problem: This problem is actually a very old and very dangerous solution. A penny or a knockout behind a fuse effectively bypasses the fuse, preventing an overloaded circuit from blowing the fuse. This is very dangerous and can lead to overheated wiring.

Solution: Remove the penny and replace the fuse. Have a licensed electrician examine the panel and circuit wiring. If the fuse has been bypassed for years, wiring may be dangerously compromised, and the circuit may need to be replaced.

Problem: Two wires connected to one single-pole breaker is a sign of an overcrowded panel and also a dangerous code violation unless the breaker is approved for such a connection.

Solution: If there is room in the panel, install a separate breaker for the extra wire. If the panel is overcrowded, have an electrician upgrade the panel or install a subpanel.

Recognizing Aluminum Wire ▸

Inexpensive aluminum wire was used in place of copper in many wiring systems installed during the late 1960s and early 1970s, when copper prices were high. Aluminum wire is identified by its silver color and by the AL stamp on the cable sheathing. A variation, copper-clad aluminum wire, has a thin coating of copper bonded to a solid aluminum core.

By the early 1970s, solid conductor-aluminum wire was found to pose a safety hazard if connected to a switch or receptacle with brass or copper screw terminals. Because aluminum expands and contracts at a different rate than copper or brass, the wire connections could become loose. In some instances, fires resulted.

Existing aluminum wiring in homes is considered safe if proper installation methods have been followed, and if the wires are connected to special switches and receptacles designed to be used with aluminum wire. If you have aluminum wire in your home, have a qualified electrical inspector review the system.

For a short while, switches and receptacles with an Underwriters Laboratories (UL) wire compatibility rating of AL-CU were used with both aluminum and copper wiring. However, these devices proved to be hazardous when connected to aluminum wire. AL-CU devices should not be used with aluminum wiring.

In 1971, switches and receptacles designed for use with aluminum wiring were introduced. They are marked CO/ALR. This mark is now the only approved rating for aluminum wires. If your home has aluminum wires connected to a switch or receptacle without a CO/ALR rating stamp, replace the device with a switch or receptacle rated CO/ALR.

A switch or receptacle that has no wire compatibility rating printed on the mounting strap or casing should not be used with aluminum wires. These devices are designed for use with copper wires only.

WITH GROUND TYPE NM 600V

CO/ALR
REPLACE ONLY WITH
CO/ALR DEVICE

Inspecting the Bonding Jumper Wire

Problem: Bonding system jumper wire is missing or is disconnected. In most homes the grounding jumper wire attaches to water pipes on either side of the water meter. Because the ground pathway is broken, this is a dangerous situation that should be fixed immediately.

Solution: Attach a jumper wire to the water pipes on either side of the water meter using pipe clamps. Use wire that is the same size and type as the grounding electrode wire. The typical sizes include #6 copper for services 150 amps or smaller and #4 copper for 200 amp services.

Common Cable Problems

Problem: Cable running across joists or studs is attached to the edge of framing members. Electrical codes forbid this type of installation in exposed areas like unfinished basements or walk-up attics.

Solution: Protect cable by drilling holes in framing members at least 2" from exposed edges and threading the cable through the holes.

Problem: Cable running along joists or studs hangs loosely. Loose cables can be pulled accidentally, causing damage to wires.

Solution: Anchor the cable to the side of the framing members at least 1¼" from the edge using plastic staples. NM (nonmetallic) cable should be stapled every 4½ ft. and within 8" of each electrical box.

Problem: Cable threaded through studs or joists lies close to the edge of the framing members. NM (nonmetallic) cable (shown cutaway) can be damaged easily if nails or screws are driven into the framing members during remodeling projects.

Solution: Install metal nail guards to protect cable from damage. Nail guards are available at hardware stores and home centers.

Problem: Unclamped cable enters a metal electrical box. Edges of the knockout can rub against the cable sheathing and damage the wires. *(Note: With plastic boxes, clamps are not required if cables are anchored to framing members within 8" of box.)*

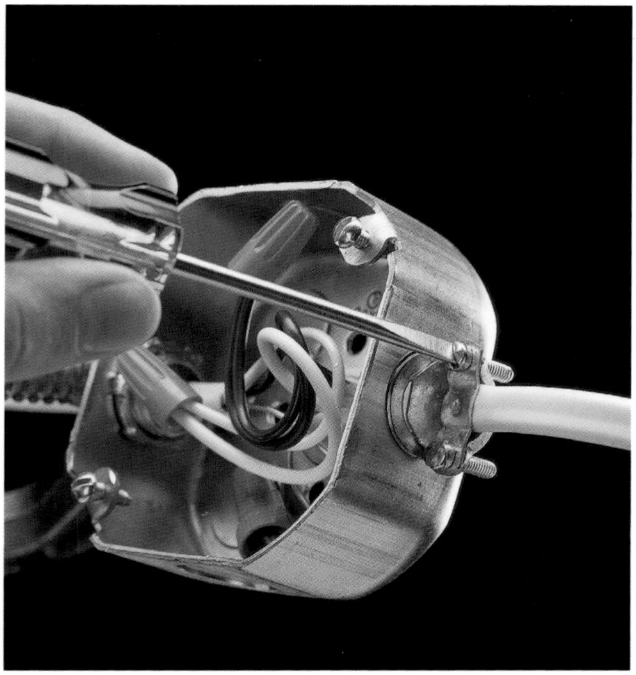

Solution: Anchor the cable to the electrical box with a cable clamp. Several types of cable clamps are available at hardware stores and home centers.

Problem: Cables are spliced outside an electrical box. Exposed splices can spark and create a risk of shock or fire.

Solution: Bring installation up to code by enclosing the splice inside a metal or plastic electrical box. Make sure the box is large enough to accommodate the number of wires it contains.

Checking Wire Connections

Problem: Two or more wires are attached to a single-screw terminal. This type of connection is seen in older wiring but is now prohibited by the National Electrical Code.

Solution: Disconnect the wires from the screw terminal, then join them to a short length of wire (called a pigtail) using a wire connector. Connect the other end of the pigtail to the screw terminal.

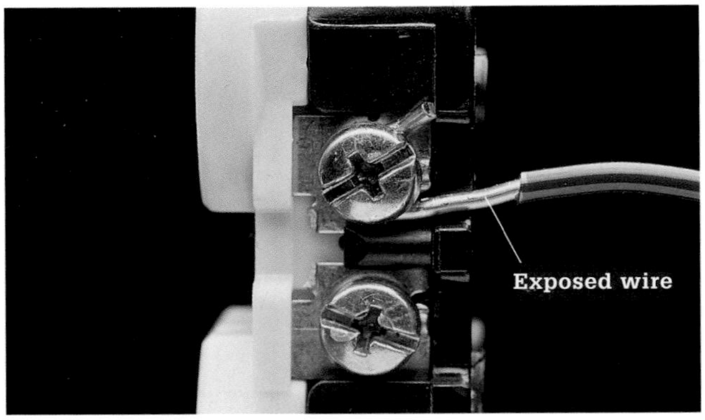

Problem: Bare wire extends past a screw terminal. Exposed wire can cause a short circuit if it touches the metal box or another circuit wire.

Solution: Clip the wire and reconnect it to the screw terminal. In a proper connection, the bare wire wraps completely around the screw terminal, and the plastic insulation just touches the screw head.

Problem: Wires are connected with electrical tape. Electrical tape was used frequently in older installations, but it can deteriorate over time, leaving bare wires exposed inside the electrical box.

Solution: Replace electrical tape with wire connectors. You may need to clip away a small portion of the wire so the bare end will be covered completely by the connector.

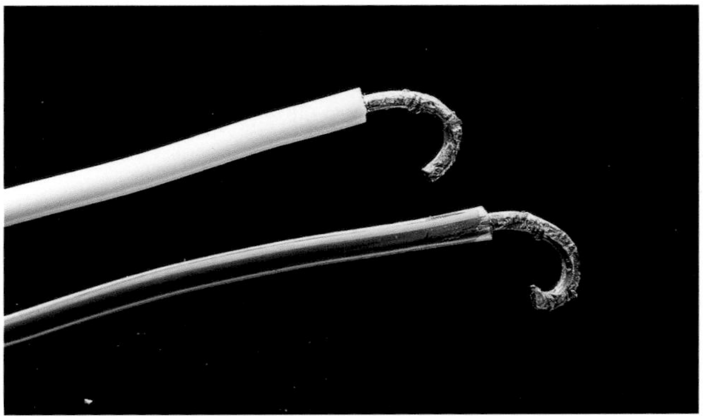

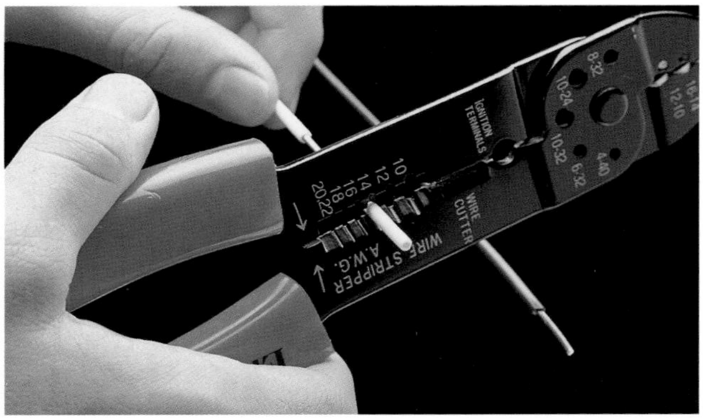

Problem: Nicks and scratches in bare wires interfere with the flow of current. This can cause the wires to overheat.

Solution: Clip away damaged portion of wire, then restrip about ¾" of insulation and reconnect the wire to the screw terminal.

Electrical Box Inspection

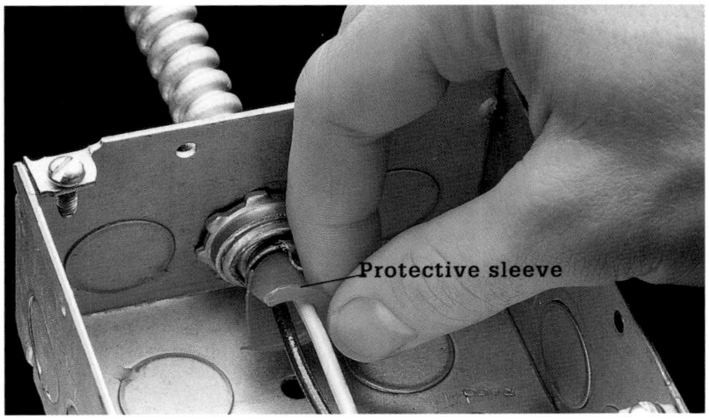

Problem: No protective sleeve on armored cable. Sharp edges of the cable can damage the wire insulation, creating a shock hazard and fire risk.

Solution: Protect the wire insulation by installing a plastic sleeve around the wires. Sleeves are available at hardware stores. Wires that are damaged must be replaced.

Problem: Insulation on wires is cracked or damaged. If damaged insulation exposes bare wire, a short circuit can occur, posing a shock hazard and fire risk.

Solution: Wrap damaged insulation temporarily with plastic electrical tape. Damaged circuit wires should be replaced by an electrician.

Problem: Open electrical boxes create a fire hazard if a short circuit causes sparks (arcing) inside the box.

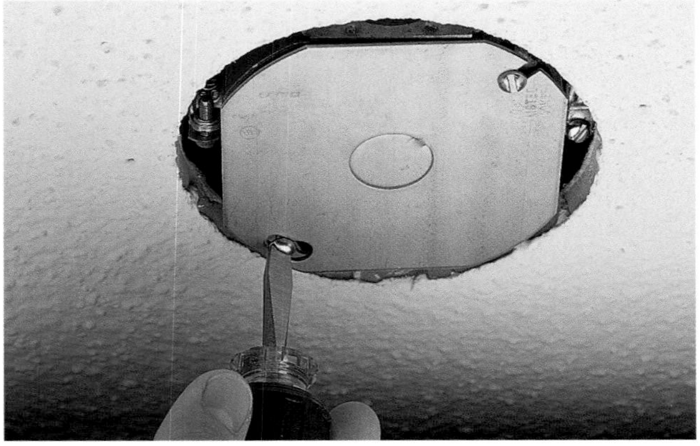

Solution: Cover the open box with a solid metal cover plate, available at any hardware store. Electrical boxes must remain accessible and cannot be sealed inside ceilings or walls.

Problem: Short wires are difficult to handle. The National Electrical Code (NEC) requires that each wire in an electrical box have at least 6" of workable length.

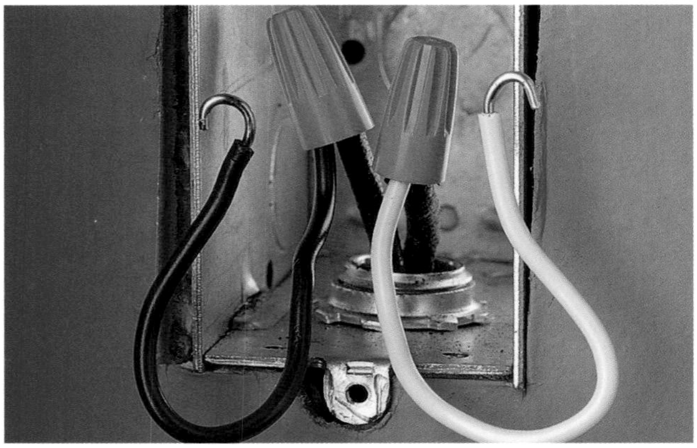

Solution: Lengthen circuit wires by connecting them to short pigtail wires using wire connectors. Pigtails can be cut from scrap wire but should be the same gauge and color as the circuit wires and at least 6" long.

Problem: A recessed electrical box is hazardous, especially if the wall or ceiling surface is made from a flammable material, like wood paneling. The National Electrical Code prohibits this type of installation.

Solution: Add an extension ring to bring the face of the electrical box flush with the surface. Extension rings come in several sizes and are available at hardware stores.

Problem: Open electrical boxes create a fire hazard if a short circuit causes sparks (dust and dirt in electrical box can cause hazardous high-resistance short circuits). When making routine electrical repairs, always check the electrical boxes for dust and dirt buildup.

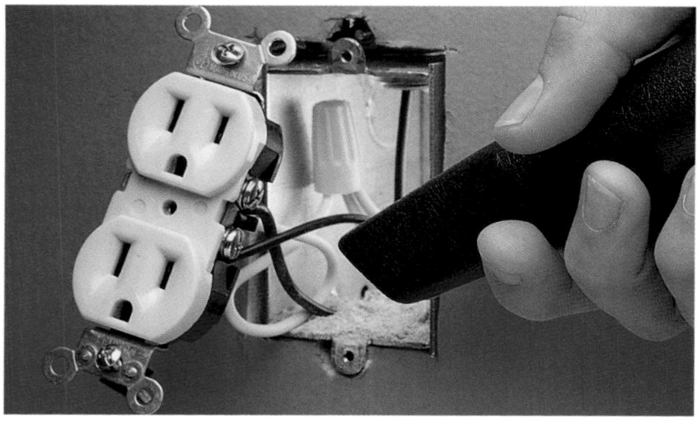

Solution: Vacuum the electrical box clean using a narrow nozzle attachment. Make sure power to the box is turned off at main service panel before vacuuming.

Problem: Crowded electrical box (shown cutaway) makes electrical repairs difficult. This type of installation is prohibited because heat in the box may cause a fire.

Solution: Replace the electrical box with a deeper electrical box.

Problem: Light fixture is installed without an electrical box. This installation exposes the wiring connections and provides no support for the light fixture.

Solution: Install an approved electrical box to enclose the wire connections and support the light fixture.

Common Electrical Cord Problems

Problem: Lamp or appliance cord runs underneath a rug. Foot traffic can wear off insulation, creating a short circuit that can cause fire or shock.

Solution: Reposition the lamp or appliance so that cord is visible. Replace worn cords.

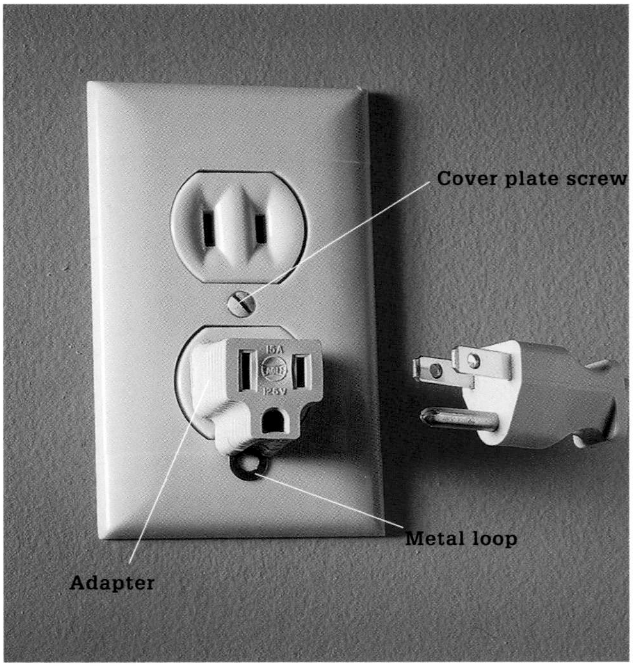

Problem: Three-prong appliance plugs do not fit two-slot receptacle. Do not use three-prong adapters unless the metal loop on the adapter is tightly connected to the cover plate screw on receptacle.

Solution: Install a three-prong grounded receptacle if a means of grounding exists at the box. Install a ground-fault circuit-interrupter (GFCI) receptacle in kitchens and bathrooms, or if the electrical box is not grounded.

Problem: Lamp or appliance plug is cracked, or electrical cord is frayed near plug. Worn cords and plugs create a fire and shock hazard.

Solution: Cut away damaged portion of wire and install a new plug. Replacement plugs are available at appliance stores and home centers.

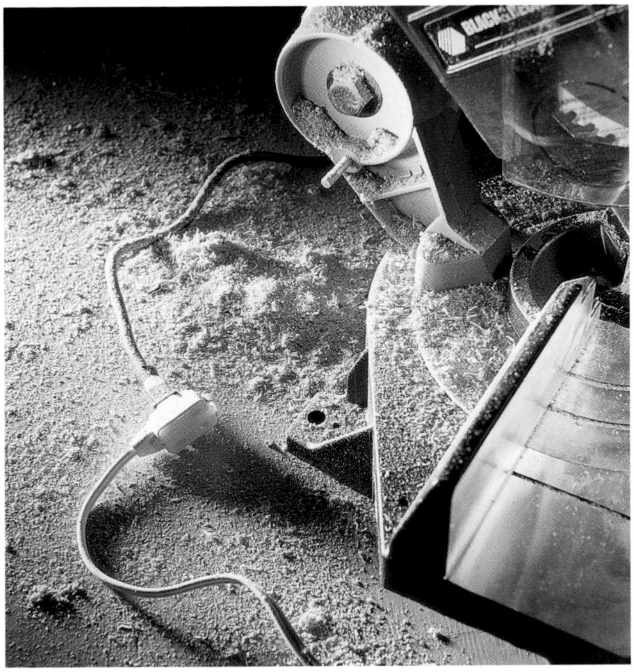

Problem: Extension cord is too small for the power load drawn by a tool or appliance. Undersized extension cords can overheat, melting the insulation and leaving bare wires exposed.

Solution: Use an extension cord with wattage and amperage ratings that meet or exceed the rating of the tool or appliance. Extension cords are for temporary use only. Never use an extension cord for a permanent installation.

Inspecting Receptacles & Switches

Problem: Octopus receptacle attachments used permanently can overload a circuit and cause overheating of the receptacle.

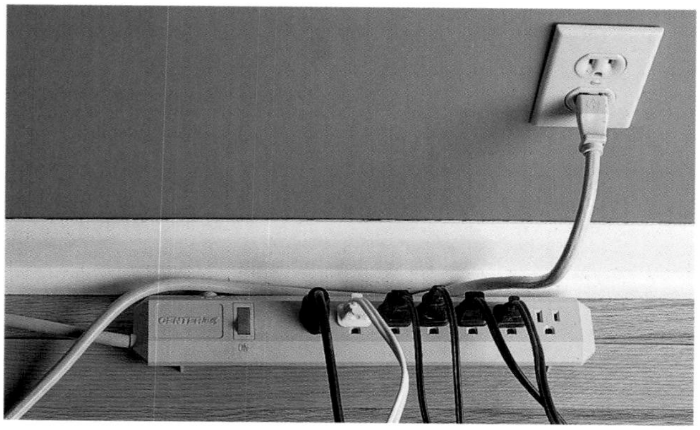

Solution: Use a multi-receptacle power strip with built-in overload protection. This is for temporary use only. If the need for extra receptacles is frequent, upgrade the wiring system.

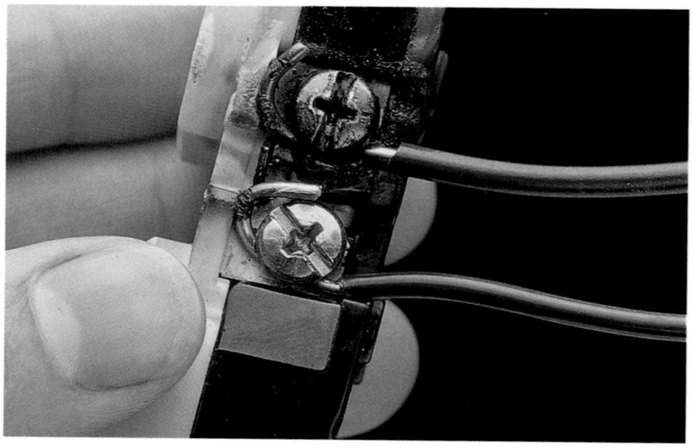

Problem: Scorch marks near screw terminals indicate that electrical arcing has occurred. Arcing usually is caused by loose wire connections.

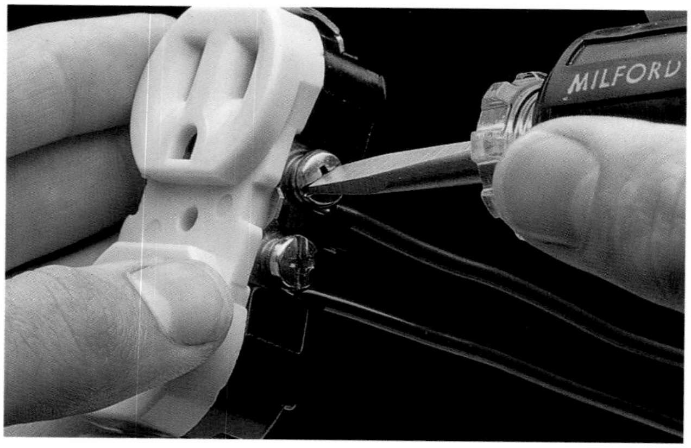

Solution: Replace the receptacle. Make sure wires are connected securely to screw terminals.

Problem: Exterior receptacle box allows water to enter box when receptacle slots are in use.

Solution: Replace the old receptacle box with an in-use box that has a bubble cover to protect plugs from water while they are in the slots.

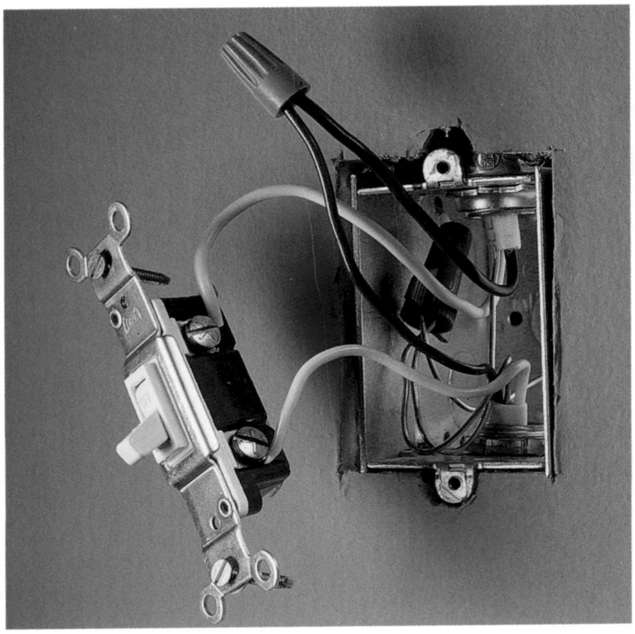

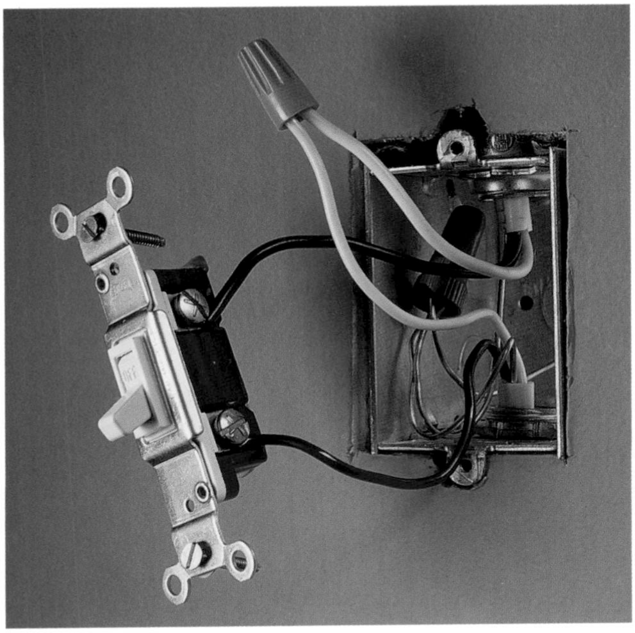

Problem: White neutral wires are connected to switch. Although the switch appears to work correctly in this installation, it is dangerous because the light fixture carries voltage when the switch is off.

Solution: Connect the black hot wires to the switch, and join the white wires together with a wire connector.

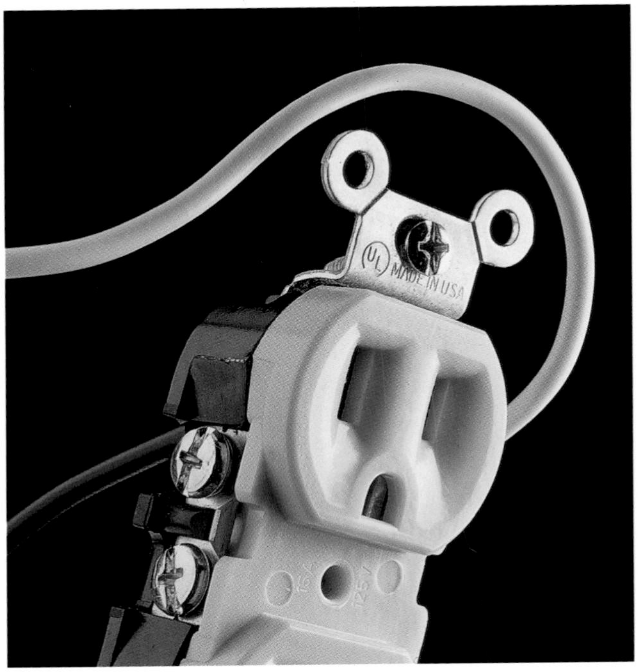

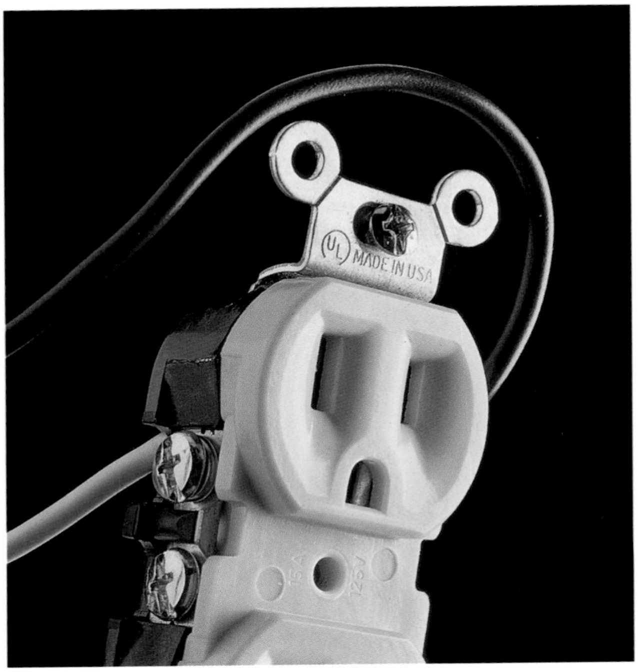

Problem: White neutral wires are connected to the brass screw terminals on the receptacle, and black hot wires are attached to silver screw terminals. This installation is hazardous because live voltage flows into the long neutral slot on the receptacle.

Solution: Reverse the wire connections so that the black hot wires are attached to brass screw terminals and white neutral wires are attached to silver screw terminals. Live voltage now flows into the short slot on the receptacle.

Conversion Chart

Metric Equivalent

Inches (in.)	1/64	1/32	1/25	1/16	1/8	1/4	3/8	2/5	1/2	5/8	3/4	7/8	1	2	3	4	5	6	7	8	9	10	11	12	36	39.4
Feet (ft.)																								1	3	3 1/12
Yards (yd.)																									1	1 1/12
Millimeters (mm)	0.40	0.79	1	1.59	3.18	6.35	9.53	10	12.7	15.9	19.1	22.2	25.4	50.8	76.2	101.6	127	152	178	203	229	254	279	305	914	1,000
Centimeters (cm)							0.95	1	1.27	1.59	1.91	2.22	2.54	5.08	7.62	10.16	12.7	15.2	17.8	20.3	22.9	25.4	27.9	30.5	91.4	100
Meters (m)																								.30	.91	1.00

Converting Measurements

To Convert:	To:	Multiply by:
Inches	Millimeters	25.4
Inches	Centimeters	2.54
Feet	Meters	0.305
Yards	Meters	0.914
Miles	Kilometers	1.609
Square inches	Square centimeters	6.45
Square feet	Square meters	0.093
Square yards	Square meters	0.836
Cubic inches	Cubic centimeters	16.4
Cubic feet	Cubic meters	0.0283
Cubic yards	Cubic meters	0.765
Pints (U.S.)	Liters	0.473 (Imp. 0.568)
Quarts (U.S.)	Liters	0.946 (Imp. 1.136)
Gallons (U.S.)	Liters	3.785 (Imp. 4.546)
Ounces	Grams	28.4
Pounds	Kilograms	0.454
Tons	Metric tons	0.907

To Convert:	To:	Multiply by:
Millimeters	Inches	0.039
Centimeters	Inches	0.394
Meters	Feet	3.28
Meters	Yards	1.09
Kilometers	Miles	0.621
Square centimeters	Square inches	0.155
Square meters	Square feet	10.8
Square meters	Square yards	1.2
Cubic centimeters	Cubic inches	0.061
Cubic meters	Cubic feet	35.3
Cubic meters	Cubic yards	1.31
Liters	Pints (U.S.)	2.114 (Imp. 1.76)
Liters	Quarts (U.S.)	1.057 (Imp. 0.88)
Liters	Gallons (U.S.)	0.264 (Imp. 0.22)
Grams	Ounces	0.035
Kilograms	Pounds	2.2
Metric tons	Tons	1.1

Converting Temperatures

Convert degrees Fahrenheit (F) to degrees Celsius (C) by following this simple formula: Subtract 32 from the Fahrenheit temperature reading. Then mulitply that number by 5/9. For example, 77°F - 32 = 45. 45 × 5/9 = 25°C.

To convert degrees Celsius to degrees Fahrenheit, multiply the Celsius temperature reading by 9/5, then add 32. For example, 25°C × 9/5 = 45. 45 + 32 = 77°F.

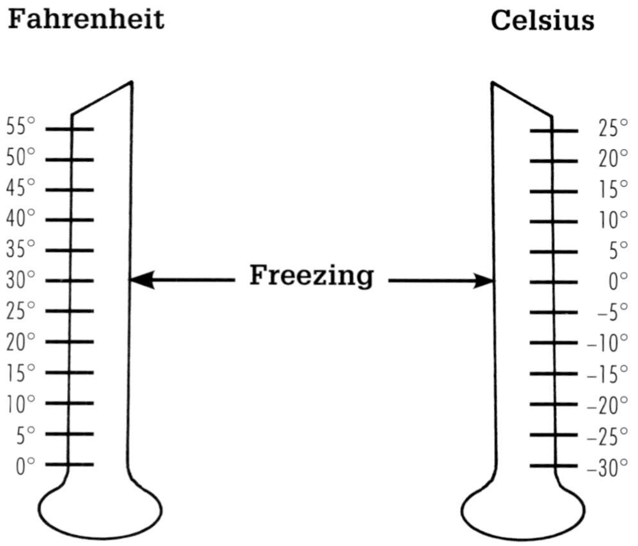

Resources & Credits

Air Diffusion Council (ADC)
Flexible air ducts
p. 110
847-706-6750
www.flexibleduct.org

American Concrete Institute
Document ACI 332
p. 47
248-848-3800
www.concrete.org/bookstorenet

American Society of Home Inspectors (ASHI)
Information and references
800-743-2744
www.ashi.org

American Wood Council
"Prescriptive Residential Deck Construction Guide"
p. 52
202-463-2766
www.awc.org

Black & Decker Corporation
Power tools & accessories
800-544-6986
www.blackanddecker.com

International Association of Plumbing and Mechanical Officials (IAPMO)
Publishes *Uniform Plumbing Code* ® and *Uniform Mechanical Code*®
909-472-4100
www.iapmo.org

International Code Council (ICC)
Develops residential and commercial building codes
Publishes *International Residential Code*®
888-422-7233
www.iccsafe.org

National Fire Protection Association (NFPA)
Publishes *National Electrical Code*® (NEC)
800-344-3555
www.nfpa.org

Red Wing Shoes Co.
Work boots and shoes
800-733-9464
www.redwingshoes.com

Photography Credits

iStock Photo / www.istockphoto.com
p. 9 (lower), 107, 214

City of Swainsboro
p. 9 (top)

Moberg Fireplaces / www.mobergfireplaces.com
p. 96

Index